Hands-On Machine Learning on Google Cloud Platform

Implementing smart and efficient analytics using Cloud ML Engine

Giuseppe Ciaburro
V Kishore Ayyadevara
Alexis Perrier

BIRMINGHAM - MUMBAI

Hands-On Machine Learning on Google Cloud Platform

Commissioning Editor: Sunith Shetty
Acquisition Editor: Tushar Gupta
Content Development Editor: Cheryl Dsa
Technical Editor: Dinesh Pawar
Copy Editor: Vikrant Phadkay
Project Coordinator: Nidhi Joshi
Proofreader: Safis Editing
Indexer: Mariammal Chettiyar
Graphics: Tania Dutta
Production Coordinator: Arvindkumar Gupta

First published: April 2018

Production reference: 1260418

Published by Packt Publishing Ltd.
Livery Place
35 Livery Street
Birmingham
B3 2PB, UK.

ISBN 978-1-78839-348-5

www.packtpub.com

`mapt.io`

Mapt is an online digital library that gives you full access to over 5,000 books and videos, as well as industry leading tools to help you plan your personal development and advance your career. For more information, please visit our website.

Why subscribe?

- Spend less time learning and more time coding with practical eBooks and Videos from over 4,000 industry professionals

- Improve your learning with Skill Plans built especially for you

- Get a free eBook or video every month

- Mapt is fully searchable

- Copy and paste, print, and bookmark content

PacktPub.com

Did you know that Packt offers eBook versions of every book published, with PDF and ePub files available? You can upgrade to the eBook version at `www.PacktPub.com` and as a print book customer, you are entitled to a discount on the eBook copy. Get in touch with us at `service@packtpub.com` for more details.

At `www.PacktPub.com`, you can also read a collection of free technical articles, sign up for a range of free newsletters, and receive exclusive discounts and offers on Packt books and eBooks.

Contributors

About the authors

Giuseppe Ciaburro holds a PhD in environmental technical physics and two master's degrees. His research is on machine learning applications in the study of urban sound environments. He works at Built Environment Control Laboratory, Università degli Studi della Campania Luigi Vanvitelli (Italy). He has over 15 years' experience in programming Python, R, and MATLAB, first in the field of combustion, and then in acoustics and noise control. He has several publications to his credit.

V Kishore Ayyadevara has over 9 years' experience of using analytics to solve business problems and setting up analytical work streams through his work at American Express, Amazon, and, more recently, a retail analytics consulting startup. He has an MBA from IIM Calcutta and is also an electronics and communications engineer. He has worked in credit risk analytics, supply chain analytics, and consulting for multiple FMCG companies to identify ways to improve their profitability.

Alexis Perrier is a data science consultant with experience in signal processing and stochastic algorithms. He holds a master's in mathematics from Université Pierre et Marie Curie Paris VI and a PhD in signal processing from Télécom ParisTech. He is actively involved in the DC data science community. He is also an avid book lover and proud owner of a real chalk blackboard, where he regularly shares his fascination of mathematical equations with his kids.

About the reviewers

Mikhail Berlyant is a data warehousing veteran. He has been a data developer since the late 1970s. Since 2000, he has led data systems, data mining, and data warehouse teams at Yahoo! and Myspace.

He is a Google Cloud expert and senior VP of Technology, at Viant Inc., a people-based advertising tech company that enables marketers to plan, execute, and measure their digital media investments through a cloud-based platform. At Viant, he led the migration of a petabyte-sized data warehouse to Google Cloud. He is currently focusing on self-serve/productivity tools for BigQuery/GCP.

> *I'd like to say thanks to my beautiful wife, Svetlana, for supporting me in all my endeavors.*

Sanket Thodge is an entrepreneur by profession in Pune, India. He is an author of *Cloud Analytics with Google Cloud Platform*. He founded Pi R Square Digital Solutions. With expertise as a Hadoop developer, he has explored the cloud, IoT, machine learning, and blockchain. He has also applied for a patent in IoT and has worked with numerous startups and MNCs, providing consultancy, architecture building, development, and corporate training across the globe.

Antonio Gulli is a transformational software executive and business leader with a passion for establishing and managing global technological talent for innovation and execution. He is an expert in search engines, online services, machine learning, and so on. Currently, he is a site lead and director of cloud at Google Warsaw, driving European efforts for serverless, Kubernetes, and Google Cloud UX. Antonio has filed for 20+ patents, published multiple academic papers, and served as a senior PC member in multiple international conferences.

Chirag Nayyar is helping organizations to migrate their workload from on-premise to the public cloud. He has experience in web app migration, SAP workload on the cloud, and EDW. He is currently working at Cloud Kinetics Technology Solutions. He holds a wide range of certifications from all major public cloud platforms. He also runs meetups and is a regular speaker at various cloud events.

Packt is searching for authors like you

If you're interested in becoming an author for Packt, please visit `authors.packtpub.com` and apply today. We have worked with thousands of developers and tech professionals, just like you, to help them share their insight with the global tech community. You can make a general application, apply for a specific hot topic that we are recruiting an author for, or submit your own idea.

Table of Contents

Preface

Google Cloud ML Engine combines the services of Google Cloud Platform with the power and flexibility of TensorFlow. With this book, you will not only learn how to build and train different complexities of machine learning models at scale, but also to host them in the cloud to make predictions.

This book is focused on making the most of the Google Machine Learning Platform for large datasets and complex problems. You will learn how to create powerful machine-learning-based applications from scratch for a wide variety of problems by leveraging different data services from the Google Cloud Platform. Applications include NLP, speech-to-text, reinforcement learning, time series, recommender systems, image classification, video content inference, and many others. We will implement a wide variety of deep learning use cases and will also make extensive use of data-related services comprising the Google Cloud Platform ecosystem, such as Firebase, Storage APIs, Datalab, and so forth. This will enable you to integrate machine learning and data processing features into your web and mobile applications.

By the end of this book, you will be aware of the main difficulties that you may encounter, and be familiar with appropriate strategies to overcome these difficulties and build efficient systems.

Who this book is for

This book is for data scientists, machine learning developers, and AI developers who want to learn Google Cloud Platform services to build machine learning applications. Since interaction with the Google ML platform is mostly done via the command line, the reader should have some familiarity with the bash shell and Python scripting. Some understanding of machine learning and data science concepts will also be handy.

What this book covers

Chapter 1, *Introducing the Google Cloud Platform*, explores different services that may be useful to build a machine learning pipeline based on GCP.

Chapter 2, *Google Compute Engine*, helps you to create and fully manage your VM via both the online console and command-line tools, as well as how to implement a data science workflow and a Jupyter Notebook workspace.

Chapter 3, *Google Cloud Storage*, shows how to upload data and manage it using the services provided by the Google Cloud Platform.

Chapter 4, *Querying Your Data with BigQuery*, shows you how to query data from Google Storage and visualize it with Google Data Studio.

Chapter 5, *Transforming Your Data*, presents Dataprep, a service useful for preprocessing data, extracting features, and cleaning up records. We also look at Dataflow, a service used to implement streaming and batch processing.

Chapter 6, *Essential Machine Learning*, starts our journey into machine learning and deep learning; we learn when to apply each one.

Chapter 7, *Google Machine Learning APIs*, teaches us how to use Google Cloud machine learning APIs for image analysis, text and speech processing, translation, and video inference.

Chapter 8, *Creating ML Applications with Firebase*, shows how to integrate different GCP services to build a seamless machine-learning-based application, mobile or web-based.

Chapter 9, *Neural Networks with TensorFlow and Keras*, gives a good understanding of the structure and key elements of a feedforward network, how to architecture one, and how to tinker and experiment with different parameters.

Chapter 10, *Evaluating Results with TensorBoard*, shows how the choice of different parameters and functions impacts the performance of the model.

Chapter 11, *Optimizing the Model through Hyperparameter Tuning*, teaches us how to use hypertuning in TensorFlow application code and interpret the results to select the best performing model.

Chapter 12, *Preventing Overfitting with Regularization*, shows how to identify overfitting and make our models more robust to previously unseen data by setting the right parameters and defining the proper architectures.

Chapter 13, *Beyond Feedforward Networks – CNN and RNNs*, teaches which type of neural network to apply to different problems, and how to define and implement them on GCP.

Chapter 14, *Time Series with LSTMs*, shows how to create LSTMs and apply them to time series predictions. We will also understand when LSTMs outperform more standard approaches.

Chapter 15, *Reinforcement Learning*, introduces the power of reinforcement learning and shows how to implement a simple use case on GCP.

Chapter 16, *Generative Neural Networks*, teaches us how to extract the content generated within the neural net with different types of content—text, images, and sounds.

Chapter 17, *Chatbots*, shows how to train a contextual chatbot while implementing it in a real mobile application.

To get the most out of this book

In this book, machine learning algorithms are implemented on the Google Cloud Platform. To reproduce the many examples in this book, you need to possess a working account on GCP. We have used Python 2.7 and above to build various applications. In that spirit, we have tried to keep all of the code as friendly and readable as possible. We feel that this will enable our readers to easily understand the code and readily use it in different scenarios.

Download the example code files

You can download the example code files for this book from your account at www.packtpub.com. If you purchased this book elsewhere, you can visit www.packtpub.com/support and register to have the files emailed directly to you.

You can download the code files by following these steps:

1. Log in or register at www.packtpub.com.
2. Select the **SUPPORT** tab.
3. Click on **Code Downloads & Errata**.
4. Enter the name of the book in the **Search** box and follow the onscreen instructions.

Once the file is downloaded, please make sure that you unzip or extract the folder using the latest version of:

- WinRAR/7-Zip for Windows
- Zipeg/iZip/UnRarX for Mac
- 7-Zip/PeaZip for Linux

The code bundle for the book is also hosted on GitHub at `https://github.com/PacktPublishing/Hands-On-Machine-Learning-on-Google-Cloud-Platform`. In case there's an update to the code, it will be updated on the existing GitHub repository.

We also have other code bundles from our rich catalog of books and videos available at `https://github.com/PacktPublishing/`. Check them out!

Download the color images

We also provide a PDF file that has color images of the screenshots/diagrams used in this book. You can download it here: `https://www.packtpub.com/sites/default/files/downloads/HandsOnMachineLearningonGoogleCloudPlatform_ColorImages.pdf`.

Conventions used

There are a number of text conventions used throughout this book.

`CodeInText`: Indicates code words in text, database table names, folder names, filenames, file extensions, pathnames, dummy URLs, user input, and Twitter handles. Here is an example: "Where GROUP is a service or an account element and COMMAND is the command to send to the GROUP."

A block of code is set as follows:

```
import matplotlib.patches as patches
import numpy as np
fig,ax = plt.subplots(1)
```

When we wish to draw your attention to a particular part of a code block, the relevant lines or items are set in bold:

```
text="this is a good text"
from google.cloud.language_v1 import types
document = types.Document(
        content=text,
        type='PLAIN_TEXT')
```

Any command-line input or output is written as follows:

```
$ gcloud compute instances list
```

Bold: Indicates a new term, an important word, or words that you see onscreen. For example, words in menus or dialog boxes appear in the text like this. Here is an example: "Click on **Create a new project.**"

Warnings or important notes appear like this.

Tips and tricks appear like this.

Get in touch

Feedback from our readers is always welcome.

General feedback: Email feedback@packtpub.com and mention the book title in the subject of your message. If you have questions about any aspect of this book, please email us at questions@packtpub.com.

Errata: Although we have taken every care to ensure the accuracy of our content, mistakes do happen. If you have found a mistake in this book, we would be grateful if you would report this to us. Please visit www.packtpub.com/submit-errata, selecting your book, clicking on the Errata Submission Form link, and entering the details.

Piracy: If you come across any illegal copies of our works in any form on the Internet, we would be grateful if you would provide us with the location address or website name. Please contact us at copyright@packtpub.com with a link to the material.

If you are interested in becoming an author: If there is a topic that you have expertise in and you are interested in either writing or contributing to a book, please visit authors.packtpub.com.

Reviews

Please leave a review. Once you have read and used this book, why not leave a review on the site that you purchased it from? Potential readers can then see and use your unbiased opinion to make purchase decisions, we at Packt can understand what you think about our products, and our authors can see your feedback on their book. Thank you!

For more information about Packt, please visit `packtpub.com`.

1
Introducing the Google Cloud Platform

The goal of this first introductory chapter is to give you an overview of the **Google Cloud Platform** (**GCP**). We start by explaining why **machine learning** (**ML**) and cloud computing go hand in hand as the demand for ever more hungry computing resources grows for today's ML applications. We then proceed with a 360° presentation of the platform's data-related services. Account and project creation as well as role allocation close the chapter.

A data science project follows a regular set of steps: in extracting the data, exploring, cleaning it, extracting information, training and assessing models, and finally building machine-learning-enabled applications. For each step of the data science flow, there are one or several services in the GCP that are adequate.

But, before we present the overall mapping of the GCP data-related services, it is important to understand why ML and cloud computing are truly made for each other.

In this chapter, we will cover the following topics:

- ML and the cloud
- Introducing the GCP
- Data services of the Google platform

ML and the cloud

In short, **artificial intelligence** (**AI**) requires a lot of computing resources. Cloud computing addresses those concerns.

ML is a new type of microscope and telescope, allowing each of to us to push the boundaries of human knowledge and human activities. With ever more powerful ML platforms and open tools, we are able to conquer new realms of knowledge and grow new types of businesses. From the comfort of our laptops, at home, or at the office, we can better understand and predict human behavior in a wide range of domains. Think health care, transportation, energy, financial markets, human communication, human-machine interaction, social network dynamics, economic behavior, and nature (astronomy, global warming, or seismic activity). The list of domains affected by the explosion of AI is truly unlimited. The impact on society? Astounding.

With so many resources available to anyone with an online connection, the barrier to joining the AI revolution has never been lower than it is now. Books, tutorials, MOOCs, and meet-ups, as well as open source libraries in a myriad of languages, are freely available to both the seasoned and the beginner data scientist.

As veteran data scientists know well, data science is always hungry for more computational resources. Classification on the Iris or the MINST image datasets or predictive modeling on Titanic passengers does not reflect real-world data. Real-world data is by essence dirty, incomplete, noisy, multi-sourced, and more often than not, in large volumes. Exploiting these large datasets requires computational power, storage, CPUs, GPUs, and fast I/O.

However, more powerful machines are not sufficient to build meaningful ML applications. Grounded in science, data science requires a scientific mindset with concepts such as reproducibility and reviewing. Both aspects are made easier by working with online accessible resources. Sharing datasets and models and exposing results is always more difficult when the data lives on one person's computer. Reproducing results and maintaining models with new data also requires easy accessibility to assets. And as we work on ever more personalized and critical data (for instance in healthcare), privacy and security concerns become all the more important to the project stakeholders.

This is where the cloud comes in, by offering scalability and accessibility while providing an adequate level of security.

Before diving into GCP, let's learn a bit more about the cloud.

The nature of the cloud

ML projects are resource intensive. From storage to computational power, training models sometimes require resources that cannot be found on a simple standalone computer. Physical limitations in terms of storage have shrunk in recent years. As we now enjoy reliable terabyte storage accessible at reduced prices, storage is no longer an issue for most data projects that are not in the realm of big data. Computing power has also increased so much that what required expensive workstations a few years ago can now run on laptops.

However, despite all this amazingly rapid evolution, the power of the standalone PC is finite. There is an upper limit to the volume of data you can store on your machine and to the time you're willing to wait to get your model trained. New frontiers in AI, with speech-to-text, video captioning in real time, self-driving cars, music generation, or chatbots that can fool a human being and pass the turing test, require ever larger resources. This is especially true of deep learning models, which are too slow on standard CPUs and require GPU-based machines to train in a reasonable amount of time.

ML in the cloud does not face these limitations. What you get with cloud computing is direct access to **high-performance computing** (**HPC**). Before the cloud (roughly before AWS launched its **Elastic Computing Cloud** (**EC2**) service in 2006), HPC was only available via supercomputers, such as the Cray computers. Cray is a US company that has built some of the most powerful supercomputers since the 1960s. China's Tianhe-2 is now the most powerful supercomputer in the world, with a capacity of 100,000 petaflops (that's $10^2 \times 10^{15}$, or 10 to the power of 17 floating-point operations per second!).

A supercomputer not only costs millions of US dollars but also requires its own physical infrastructure and has huge maintenance costs. It is also out of reach for individuals and for most companies. Engineers and researchers, hungry for HPC, now turn to on-demand cloud infrastructures. Cloud service offers are democratizing access to HPC.

Computing in the cloud is built on a distributed architecture. The processors are distributed across different servers instead of being aggregated in one single machine. With a few clicks or command lines, anyone can sign up massively complex banks of servers in a matter of minutes. The amount of power at your command can be mind-blowing.

Cloud computing can not only handle the most demanding optimization tasks but also carry out a simple regression on a tiny dataset. Cloud computing is extremely flexible.

To recap, cloud computing offers:

- **Instantaneity**: Resources can be made available in a matter of minutes.
- **On-demand**: Instances can be put on stand by or decommissioned when no longer needed.
- **Diversity**: The wide range of operating systems, storage, and database solutions, allow the architect to create project-focused architectures, from simple mobile applications to ML APIs.
- **Unlimited resources**: If not infinite yet, the volume of resources for storage computing and networks you can assemble is mind-blowing.
- **GPUs**: Most PCs are based on CPUs (with the exception of machines optimized for gaming). Deep learning requires GPUs to achieve human-compatible speeds for training models. Cloud computing makes GPUs available at a fraction of the cost needed to buy GPU machines.
- **Controlled accessibility and security**: With granular role definitions, service compartmentalization, encrypted connections, and user-based access control, cloud platforms greatly reduce the risk of intrusion and data loss.

Apart from these, there are several other types of cloud platforms and offers on the market.

Public cloud

There are two main types of cloud models depending on the needs of the customers: public versus private and multi-tenant versus single-tenant. These different cloud types offer different levels of management, security, and pricing.

A public cloud consists of resources that are located off-site over the internet. In a public cloud, the infrastructure is typically multi-tenant. Multiple customers can share the same underlying hardware or server. Resources such as networking, storage, power, cooling and computing are all shared. The customer usually has no visibility of where this infrastructure is hosted except for choosing a geographic region. The pricing mode of a public cloud service is based on the volume of data, the computing power that is used and other infrastructure-management-related services—or, more precisely, a mix of RAM, vCPUs, disk, and bandwidth.

In a private cloud, the resources are dedicated to a single customer; the architecture is single-tenant instead of multi-tenant. The servers are located on premise or in a remote data center. Customers own (or rent) the infrastructure and are responsible for maintaining it. Private cloud infrastructures are more expensive to operate as they require dedicated hardware to be secured for a single tenant. Customers of the private cloud have more control over their infrastructure, and therefore they can achieve their compliance and security requirements.

Hybrid clouds are composed of a mix of public clouds and private ones.

The GCP is a public multi-tenant cloud platform. You share the servers you use with other customers and let Google handle the support, the data centers, and the infrastructure.

Managed cloud versus unmanaged cloud

The cloud market has also diversified into two large segments—managed cloud versus unmanaged cloud.

In an unmanaged cloud platform, the infrastructure is self-served. In case of failure, it is the responsibility of the customer to have some mechanisms in place to restore the operations. Unmanaged cloud requires the customer to have the qualified expertise and resources to build, manage, and maintain cloud instances and infrastructures. Focused on self-serving applications, unmanaged cloud offers do not include support with their basic tiers.

In a managed cloud platform, the provider will support the underlying infrastructure by offering monitoring, troubleshooting, and around-the-clock customer service. Managed cloud brings along qualified expertise and resources to the team right away. For many companies, having a service provider to handle their public cloud can be easier and more cost-effective than hiring their own staff to operate their clouds.

The GCP is a public, multi-tenant, and unmanaged cloud service. So are AWS and Azure. Rackspace, on the other hand, is an example of a managed cloud service company. As an example, Rackspace just started offering managed services for GCP in March 2017.

IaaS versus PaaS versus SaaS

Another important distinction is to be made with respect to the amount of work done by the user or by the cloud platform provider. Let us take a look at this distinction with the help of the following service levels:

- **Infrastructure as a Service (IaaS)**: At the minimum level, IaaS, the cloud provider, handles the machines, their virtualization and the required networking. The user is responsible for everything else—OS, middleware, data, and application software. The provider is the host of the resources on which the user builds the infrastructure. Google compute Engine, SQL, DNS, or load balancing are examples of IaaS services within the GCP.
- **Platform as a service (PaaS)**: In a PaaS offering, the user is only responsible for the software and the data. Everything else is handled by the cloud provider. The provider builds the infrastructure while the user deploys the software. The main advantage of PaaS over IaaS, besides the reduced workload and need for sysadmin resources, is the automatic scaling for web applications. The appropriate number of resources are automatically allocated as demand fluctuates. Examples of PaaS services include Heroku or the Google App Engine.
- **Software as a service (SaaS)**: In SaaS, the provider is a software company offering services online while the user consumes the service that are provided. Think Uber, Facebook, or Gmail.

While being mostly an IaaS provider, the GCP also has some PaaS offerings such as the Google App Engine. And its ML APIs (text, speech, video, and image) can be considered as SaaS.

Costs and pricing

Pricing of cloud services is complicated and varies across vendors. Basic cost structure of a cloud service can be broken down into:

- **Computing costs**: The duration of running VMs per number of vCPUs, per GB of RAM
- **Storage costs**: Disks, files, and databases per GB
- **Networking costs**: internal and external, inbound and outbound traffic

Google's preemptible VMs (AWS Spot instances) are VMs that are built on leftover, unused capacity and priced three to four times lower than normal on-demand VMs. However, Compute Engine may terminate (preempt) these instances if it requires access to those resources for other tasks. Preemptible instances are adapted to batch processing jobs or workflows that can withstand sudden interruptions. They may also not always be available. In the next chapter, we learn how to launch preemptible instances from the command line.

Google cloud also recently introduced price reduction for committed use. You get a discount when you reserve instances for a long period of time, typically committing to a usage term of 1 year or 3 years.

The argument of cost cutting when moving to the cloud holds when your infrastructure is evolving quickly and requires scalability and rapid modifications. If your applications are very static with stable load, the cloud may not result in lower costs. In the end, as the cloud offers much more flexibility and opens the way to implementing new projects quickly, the overall cost is higher than with a fixed infrastructure. But this flexibility is the true benefit of cloud computing.

See `https://cloud.google.com/compute/pricing` for the current Google Compute Engine pricing.

Price war
The costs of cloud services have dwindled in the past several years. The three major public cloud actors have gone through successive phases of price reduction since 2012, when AWS drastically reduced its storage prices to undermine the competition. The four main cloud providers reduced their prices 22 times in 2012 and 26 times in 2013. Reductions ranged from 6% to 30% and touched all types of services: computing, storage, bandwidth, and databases. As of January 2014, Amazon had reduced the price of their offerings over 40 times. These reductions have been matched or exceeded by the other main cloud service providers. Recently, the three main actors have further reduced their prices on storage, possibly reigniting the price war. According to a recent study of cloud computing prices, there isn't much data suggesting that cloud is anywhere near a commodity yet. 451 research said so, further predicting that relational databases are likely to be the next price war battleground.

ML

So, near-instant availability, low cost, flexible architecture, and near-unlimited resources are the advantages of cloud computing, at the expense of extra overhead and recurring costs.

In the global landscape of cloud computing, the GCP is a public unmanaged IaaS cloud offering, with some PaaS and SaaS services. Although Azure and GCP are directly comparable for standard cloud services such as from computing (EC2, Cloud Compute, and so on), databases (BigQuery, Redshift, and so on), network, and so forth; the Google Cloud approach to ML is quite different than Amazon's or Azure's.

In short, AWS offers, either all-in-one services for very specific applications—face recognition and Alexa-related applications, or a predictive analytics platform based on classic (not deep learning) models called Amazon ML. Microsoft's offer is more PaaS centered, with its Cortana Intelligence Suite. Microsoft's ML service is quite similar to AWS's, with more available models.

The GCP ML offer is based on TensorFlow, Google's deep learning library. Google offers a wide range of ML APIs based on pre-trained TensorFlow models for NLP, speech-to-text, translation, image, and video processing. It also offers a platform where you can train your own TensorFlow models and evaluate them (TensorBoard).

Introducing the GCP

The first cloud computing service dates back to 15 years ago, when, in July 2002, Amazon launched the AWS platform to expose technology and product data from Amazon and its affiliates, enabling developers to build innovative and entrepreneurial applications on their own. In 2006, AWS was relaunched as the EC2.

The early start of AWS gave Amazon a lead in cloud computing, one that has never faltered since. Competitors were slow to counteract and launch their own offers. The first alternative to the AWS cloud services from a major company came with the Google App Engine launched in April 2008 as a PaaS service for developing and hosting web applications. The GCP was thus born. Microsoft and IBM followed, with the Windows Azure platform launched in February 2010 and LotusLive in January 2009.

Google didn't enter the IaaS market until much later. In 2013, Google released the Compute Engine to the general public with enterprise **service-level agreements (SLA)**.

Mapping the GCP

With over 40 different IaaS, PaaS, and SaaS services, the GCP ecosystem is rich and complex. These services can be grouped into six different categories:

- Hosting and computation
- Storage and databases
- Networking
- ML
- Identity and security
- Resource management and monitoring

In the following section, we learn how to set up and manage a single VM instance on Google Compute Engine. But, before that, we need to create our account.

Getting started with GCP

Getting started on the GCP is pretty much straightforward. All you really need is a Google account. Go to `https://cloud.google.com/`, log in with your Google account, and follow the instructions. Add your billing information as needed. This gives you access to the web-based UI of the GCP. We'll cover command line and shell accessibility and related SSH key creation in the next chapter.

Free trials

At the time of writing this, Google has a pretty generous free trial offer with a 12-month period and a credit of $300 for new accounts. There are, however, limitations on some services. For instance, you cannot launch the Google Compute Engine VM instances with more than eight CPUs and you are limited in the number of projects you create, though you can request more than your allocated quota. There is no SLA. Using Google Cloud services for activities such as bitcoin mining is not allowed. Once you upgrade your account, these limitations no longer apply and the money left out of the initial $300 is credited to your account. More information on the free trial offer is available at `https://cloud.google.com/free/docs/frequently-asked-questions`.

Project-based organization

One key aspect of the GCP is its project-centered organization. All billing, permissions, resources, and settings are grouped within a user-defined project, which basically acts as a global namespace. It is simply not possible to launch a resource without specifying the project it belongs to first.

Each one of these projects has:

- A project name, which you choose.
- A project ID, suggested by GCP but editable. The project ID is used by API calls and resources within the project.
- A project number, which is provided by the GCP.

Both the project ID and project numbers are unique across all GCP projects. The project organization has several straightforward benefits:

- As resources are dedicated to a single project, budget allocation and billing are simplified
- As the resources allocated to a project are subject to the same regions-and-zones rules and share the same metadata, operations and communications between them work seamlessly
- Similarly, access management is coherent across a single project, limiting the overall complexity of access control

Project-based organization greatly simplifies the management of your resources and is a key aspect of what makes the GCP quite easy to work with.

Creating your first project

To create a new project:

1. Go to the resource management page, `https://console.cloud.google.com/cloud-resource-manager`.
2. Click on **CREATE PROJECT.**
3. Write down your project title and notice how Google generates a project ID on the fly. Edit it as needed.
4. Click on **Create.**
5. You are redirected to the **Role** section of the IAM service.

Roles and permissions

By default, when you create a new project, your Google account is set as the owner of the project with full permissions and access across all the project's resources and billing. In the roles section of the IAM page, `https://console.cloud.google.com/iam-admin/roles/`, you can add people to your project and define the role for that person. You can also create new custom roles on a service-by-service basis or allocate predefined roles organized by the services.

1. Go to the IAM page and select the project you just created, if it's not already selected: `https://console.cloud.google.com/iam-admin/iam/project`. You should see your Google account email as the owner of the project.
2. To add a new person to the project:
    1. Click on **+ ADD**.
    2. Input the person's Google account email (it has to correspond to an active Google account).
    3. Select all the roles for that person, as shown in the following screenshot:

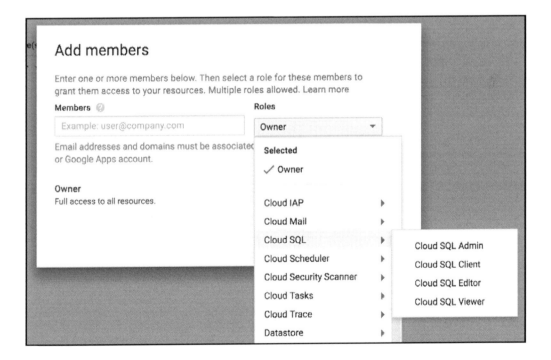

The role menu is organized by services and administrative domain (billing, logging, and monitoring), and for each service, by level of access. Although this differs depending on the service, you can roughly choose between four types of roles:

- **Admin**: Full control over the resources
- **Client**: Connectivity access
- **Editor/creator**: Full control except for user management, SSL certificates, and deleting instances
- **Viewer**: Read-only access

You can also create new custom made roles from the roles IAM page at `https://console.cloud.google.com/iam-admin/roles/project?project=packt-gcp`.

As you allocate new resources to your project, the platform creates the adequate and required roles and permissions between the services. You can view and manage these access permissions and associated roles from the info panel on the right of the manage resource page or the IAM page for the given project. Google does a great job of generating the right access levels, which makes the platform-user's life easier.

Our Google Cloud project
For this book I created the `packt-gcp` project. Since the name was unique across all other GCP projects, the project ID is also `packt-gcp`. And all the resources are created in the **us-central1** zone.

Further reading

Throughout the book, I will conclude the chapter with a list of online resources that recap or go beyond what was discussed in the chapter:

- Many excellent articles on the GCP use for big data can be found on the Google big data blog at `https://cloud.google.com/blog/big-data/`.
- What are the GCP services? Reto Meier, software engineer at Google, describes the different Google Cloud services in a simple way (for more information, see `https://hackernoon.com/what-are-the-google-cloud-platform-gcp-services-285f1988957a`). This is very useful for grasping the diversity of the GCP services.

- *An Annotated History of Google's Cloud Platform* is another post by Reto Meier on the history of the GCP. You can find it at: `https://medium.com/@retomeier/an-annotated-history-of-googles-cloud-platform-90b90f948920`. It starts with the bullet point: *Pre 2008 — Computers invented. Google Founded....* A much more detailed timeline of the GCP is available on Crunchbase at `https://www.crunchbase.com/organization/google-cloud-platform/timeline#/timeline/index`.

- The evolution of computing power, also known as Moore's law, is available at `http://www.cs.columbia.edu/~sedwards/classes/2012/3827-spring/advanced-arch-2011.pdf`, and a more recent version where the seven most recent data points are all NVIDIA GPUs is available at `https://en.wikipedia.org/wiki/Moore%27s_law#/media/File:Moore%27s_Law_over_120_Years.png`.

- For more on the pricing war of the three main cloud platforms, see this article: *Cloud Pricing Trends: Get the White Paper*, Rightscale, 2013, at `https://www.rightscale.com/lp/cloud-pricing-trends-white-paper`.

- A good article on *Supercomputing vs. Cloud Computing* by David Stepania can be found at `https://www.linkedin.com/pulse/supercomputing-vs-cloud-computing-david-stepania/`.

Summary

In this introductory chapter, we looked at the nature of the GCP and explored its services architecture. We created a new project and understood role creation and allocation. Although a new entrant on the cloud computing market, the GCP offers a complete set of services for a wide range of applications. We study these services in depth in the rest of this book.

We are now ready to get started with data science on the Google platform. In the next chapter, we'll create a VM instance on Google Compute Engine and install a data science Python stack with the Anaconda distribution. We'll explore the web UI and learn how to manage instances through the command line and the Google Shell.

2
Google Compute Engine

The core service of **Google Cloud Platform** (**GCP**) is **Google Compute Engine** (**GCE**). The GCE allows you to launch spin up **virtual machines** (**VMs**) with the right operating system, size, RAM, and appropriate number of CPUs or GPUs for your needs. It is an equivalent of AWS EC2. With GCE, we dive into the core of GCP.

In this chapter, you will learn how to:

- Create VM instances on GCE that are adapted to your projects.
- Use Google's command-line tools to manage your VMs.
- Set up a Python data science stack on a GCE VM with `conda` and `scikit-learn`.
- Access your VM via a password-protected Jupyter Notebook. And we'll cover more advanced topics related to images, snapshots, pre-emptibles VMs, startup script, and IPs.

By the end of this chapter, you will be able to create and fully manage your VM both via the online console and the command-line tools, as well as implement a data science workflow and a Jupyter Notebook workspace.

Google Compute Engine

Simply put, GCE is a service that lets you create and run VMs on Google infrastructure. The GCE allows you to launch spin up VMs with the right operating system, size, RAM, and the appropriate number of CPUs or GPUs for your needs. It is the equivalent of AWS EC2.

The GCE was announced on June 28, 2012, at Google I/O 2012 and made available to the general public on May 15, 2013. Compared to AWS EC2, an equivalent product, the GCE is a rather new service:

> **May 15th, 2013**
>
> - Google Compute Engine is available for open signups! We're excited to announce that Google Compute Engine is now available for open signups and anyone can sign up for the service. For signup instructions, see the signup page.

The following extracts from the release notes timeline illustrate the rapid evolution of the GCE service from a simple contender to a fully fledged player in the Cloud computing domain:

- May 15, 2013: GCE is available for everyone.
- August 6, 2013: GCE launches load balancing.
- December 3, 2013: GCE is announced as being production ready. *Users can now feel confident using Compute Engine to support mission-critical workloads with 24/7 support and a 99.95% monthly SLA.*
- June 25, 2014: **Solid-State Drives (SSD)** persistent disks are now available in general availability and open to all users and projects.
- September 08, 2015: Pre-emptible instances are now generally available to all users and projects.
- March 30, 2016: Persistent disks larger than 10 TB are generally available.
- July 1, 2016: Shutdown scripts are now generally available to use with compute engine instances.
- September 21, 2017: NVIDIA® Tesla® K80 GPUs are now generally available.
- September 26, 2017: Billing increments for GCE VM instances are reduced from per-minute increments to per-second increments.
- The most recent news at the time of writing this is the launch in beta of a staggering 96-vCPUs machine types.

In the past four years, Google has been steadily improving and developing its GCE offer at a rapid pace by:

- Expanding regions
- Adding more powerful machines and Intel CPU platforms
- Adding roles and features
- Steadily releasing new public images for Windows, Suse, CentOS, Debian, Ubuntu, RHEL, or CoreOS

As the timeline illustrates, the GCE service is a young and dynamic service that embraces the evolution of its customers needs and anticipates them with bold new offers. It reflects Google's drive to become a leader in the Cloud computing business and potentially offset Amazon's lead in Cloud computing.

Before we launch our first GCE VM, let's cover a few important concepts.

VMs, disks, images, and snapshots

A VM is an on-demand virtual server that you spin up for your needs. It is geographically located in one of Google's data centers, but you only choose the region and zone, not the precise location. Although you share some of the infrastructure resources with other users, this sharing is transparent to you.

A VM requires a persistent disk to run on and an operating system such as a Windows or Linux distribution to boot on. Although very much abstracted in a cloud computing context, a GCE disk would refer to a physical drive that the computer can boot on.

An image exists on top of a persistent disk, and includes the operating system necessary to launch the instance. A typical use of an image is to enable sharing a VM setup across many different VMs. An image consists of an operating system and boot loader and can be used to boot an instance.

A **snapshot** is a reflection of the content of a VM at a given time. A snapshot is mostly used for instant backups. Snapshots are stored as diffs, relative to the previous one, while images are not.

Images and snapshots are quite similar. It's possible to activate an instance using a snapshot or an image.

When you launch a new instance, GCE starts by attaching a persistent disk to your VM. This provides the disk space and gives the instance the root filesystem it needs to boot up. The disk uses the image you have chosen and installs the OS associated with that image. Public images are provided by Google with specific OS while private images are your own images.

By taking snapshots of an image, you can copy data from existing persistent disks to new persistent disks. Snapshots are meant for creating instant backups.

From the Google Shell, you can access and manage all your resources and files.

For example, let's list all our existing instances by typing:

```
$ gcloud compute instances list
```

We see our newly created sparrow instance.

Creating a VM

Let's now create our first VM instance using the web console.

Go to the GCE console, `https://console.cloud.google.com/`. Select the project we created in the previous chapter (or create one if you don't have one yet), and in the menu on the left, click on **Compute Engine**. Since you don't have a VM yet, you are greeted by the following message. Click on **Create** as shown in the following screenshot:

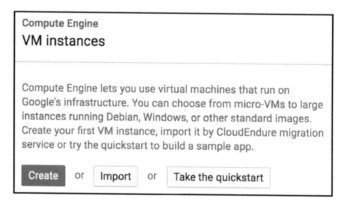

For this first VM, we will choose a small one and resize it as we go along.

There are several things you need to decide on at this point:

- The name of your instance. I will call mine **sparrow**. This name does not have to be unique across GCP. Feel free to name yours as you like.

- The region and the zone. It's often better to choose the zone closest to you to reduce latency. However, GCP services often open in the US first and become available only after a while in other parts of the world. Different zones may also have different rules and regulations. For instance, Europe offers stronger data related privacy laws than the US. Choose the zone as you see fit. It will always be possible to change the zone later.

- Selecting the right machine type is important. At time of writing this book, different machines are grouped in categories as small, standard, high CPU and high RAM:

  - **Small**: Shared CPUs and limited RAM

  - **Standard VMs**: 3.75 GB of RAM

  - **High-memory VMs**: 13 GB RAM

  - **High-CPU VMs**: 1.8 GB

The small category is perfect to get started with and build some hands-on experience with the platform. For more intense projects, you may want more more computational power or more memory.

 Note that free-trial accounts are limited to eight CPUs.

It is also possible to customize the machine you need by setting the number of CPUs or memory per CPU you want. This is also where you choose the number of GPUs to have on your machine, as shown in the following screenshot:

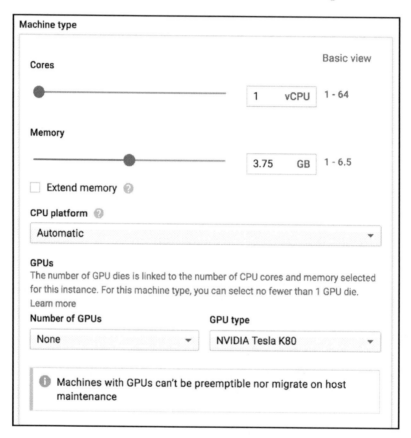

- Finally, you need to choose the OS for your VM. The Debian Linux distribution is offered by default. You have a choice among several OSes: Windows, CentOS, Suse, CoreOS, and Ubuntu. Although Ubuntu is often the most popular choice, there is actually little difference between Debian and Ubuntu and we will go with the default Debian distribution. If you're more familiar with the Ubuntu distribution, go for it. It should not cause any problems in this chapter.

Ubuntu or Debian? Debian is one of the first Linux distributions with a first stable release in 1996. Ubuntu started as a fork, a branched out version of Debian in 2004. The two distributions are very similar, with Ubuntu being more user friendly and having a better desktop/UI experience. Debian is usually preferred for servers, a massive package library, with a strong focus on stability and open-licensed software. A stable version of Debian is released approximately every two years. The Ubuntu release cycle is six months. Ubuntu takes the unstable branch of Debian, makes customization especially in terms of the UI, and releases it. For our work, there should be close to no difference between either distribution and we will use Debian for our VMs.

Leave all the rest of parameters to their default choices. We will come back to HTTPs traffic, disks, networking, and `ssh` keys in a few pages.

One very useful feature in the web console that lowers the learning curve to mastering the GCP is the two links at the bottom of the VM creation page, **Equivalent Rest or command line**, as shown in the following image:

Equivalent REST or command line

The **command line** link exists on multiple pages of the web console. It is a very useful feature to quickly learn the right syntax and parameters of the GCP command line tools.

Our VM is now created, up and running!

	Name ^	Zone	Recommendation	Internal IP	External IP	Connect	
☐ ✅	sparrow	us-east1-d		10.142.0.2	35.185.34.184	**SSH** ▾	⋮

Now that we have a brand new shiny VM, how do we access it? That nicely leads us to the Google Shell.

Google Shell

The Google Shell is Google's smart way of giving you a standalone terminal in your browser to access and manage your resources.

You activate the Google Shell by clicking on the >_ icon in the upper right part of the console page:

The browser window splits into half and the lower part is now a shell terminal:

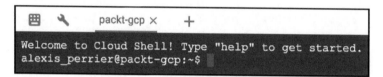

This terminal runs on an f1-micro GCE VM with a Debian operating system. It is created on a per user and per session basis. It persists when your Cloud Shell session is active and is deleted after 20 minutes of inactivity. The instance runs on a persistent disk with 5 GB storage. Both the disk and the image are available at no extra cost. Although the instance is not persistent across sessions, its associated disk is persistent across sessions. Everything you create via the Google Shell will be available as you've left it at the beginning of your next session. This includes all the files you store, the software you install and the configuration files you edit (.bashrc and .vimrc for instance). This disk is private and cannot be accessed by other users. And, finally, the Google Shell instance comes pre-installed with the Google Cloud SDK and other popular developer tools such as VIM.

Some of the commands you run via the web console will be memorized in your Google Shell VM. For instance, the SQL queries you run on a Google SQL instance, will show up in a .mysql_history file in your user's $HOME folder. More info on the Google Shell can be found in the README-cloudshell.txt in your $HOME folder.

From the Google Shell, you can access and manage all your resources and files. For example, let's list all our existing instances by typing:

```
$ gcloud compute instances list
```

We see our newly created sparrow instance:

```
alexis_perrier@packt-gcp:~$ gcloud compute instances list
NAME      ZONE        MACHINE_TYPE  PREEMPTIBLE  INTERNAL_IP   EXTERNAL_IP     STATUS
sparrow   us-east1-d  f1-micro                   10.142.0.2    35.196.158.218  RUNNING
```

To access the VM you just created, type in:

```
$ gcloud compute ssh sparrow
```

This will run through the creation of the necessary `ssh` keys. And you are now no longer on the Google's Cloud Shell VM instance but on the sparrow VM. To check which OS and version we're running in our sparrow instance, we run:

```
$ lsb_release -d
```

On the sparrow machine, I have Debian GNU/Linux 9 (stretch), while on the Google Shell VM, it's Debian GNU/Linux 8 (jessie). Which tells me that the Google Shell is not yet on the most recent version of the Debian distribution. You may, of course, see different results.

Google Cloud Platform SDK

GCP offers several standalone **command-line interfaces** (**CLIs**) to manage and interact with your GCP resources, `gcloud` being the main one. All secondary command-line tools are installed via `gcloud`. At time of writing this, the command-line tools are:

- `gcloud`: The main CLI to manage your GCP resources and projects: authentication, local configuration, developer workflow, and interactions with the GCP APIs. The following services can be handled via the `gcloud` CLI: app engine, auth, compute engine, container, DataFlow, Dataproc, machine learning, SQL databases as well as deployment of Cloud resources, Iam setup, and logging with Stackdriver and web resources such as DNS, Domains, or Firebase.

Gcloud also takes care of other command-line tools:

- `gsutil`: This is the CLI for Google Storage. You use `gsutil` to create and delete buckets, upload, download and move files around, set permissions, and so forth.
- `bq`: This is the CLI for interacting with BigQuery.
- `datalab`: The Datalab CLI.

All these CLI tools are Python scripts and require Python 2.7 installed on your system.

To install `gcloud`, the best way is to follow the instructions on the Cloud DSK page at `https://cloud.google.com/sdk/downloads`. Download the right package and run the appropriate commands for your machine. The install will guide you through the creation of `ssh` keys. It will install three files in your `~/.ssh` folder. Your public and private `ssh` keys (that is, `google_compute_engine.pub` and `google_compute_engine`) and the list of know hosts (`google_compute_known_hosts`).

You can verify that `gcloud` is properly installed by running `gcloud version` in the terminal. Your output will be similar to:

```
Google Cloud SDK 173.0.0
core 2017.09.25
gsutil 4.27
```

As we can see, `gcloud` is not a one-size-fits-all tool. `gcloud` comes loaded with components. They can either be other standalone CLIs such as `gsutils`, `bq`, `datalab` or `gcloud` extensions (`app-engine-python`), as well as Alpha and Beta release levels. To see which components are installed in your `gcloud`, run:

```
$ gcloud components list
```

You will obtain the following result:

	Components		
Status	Name	ID	Size
Update Available	BigQuery Command Line Tool	bq	< 1 MiB
Update Available	Cloud SDK Core Libraries	core	7.2 MiB
Update Available	Cloud Storage Command Line Tool	gsutil	3.0 MiB
Update Available	gcloud app Python Extensions	app-engine-python	6.2 MiB
Not Installed	App Engine Go Extensions	app-engine-go	97.7 MiB
Not Installed	Cloud Bigtable Command Line Tool	cbt	4.0 MiB
Not Installed	Cloud Bigtable Emulator	bigtable	3.5 MiB
Not Installed	Cloud Datalab Command Line Tool	datalab	< 1 MiB
Not Installed	Cloud Datastore Emulator	cloud-datastore-emulator	15.4 MiB
Not Installed	Cloud Datastore Emulator (Legacy)	gcd-emulator	38.1 MiB
Not Installed	Cloud Pub/Sub Emulator	pubsub-emulator	33.2 MiB
Not Installed	Emulator Reverse Proxy	emulator-reverse-proxy	14.5 MiB
Not Installed	Google Container Local Builder	container-builder-local	3.7 MiB
Not Installed	Google Container Registry's Docker credential helper	docker-credential-gcr	2.2 MiB
Not Installed	gcloud Alpha Commands	alpha	< 1 MiB
Not Installed	gcloud Beta Commands	beta	< 1 MiB
Not Installed	gcloud app Java Extensions	app-engine-java	116.9 MiB
Not Installed	gcloud app PHP Extensions	app-engine-php	21.9 MiB
Not Installed	kubectl	kubectl	15.9 MiB

To install or remove components in your current SDK version (173.0.0), use this:

```
$ gcloud components install COMPONENT_ID
$ gcloud components remove COMPONENT_ID
```

To update your SDK installation to the latest version (175.0.0), run:

```
$ gcloud components update
```

Gcloud

Let's go through a few commands to get a feel for the syntax of the gcloud CLI:

- To list all your projects, use:

```
$ gcloud projects list
```

- To list all your instances in the packt-gcp project, use:

```
$ gcloud compute instances list --project packt-gcp
```

The global generic syntax of the gcloud that also applies the other CLI tools is:

```
$ gcloud GROUP | COMMAND parameters
```

Where GROUP is a service or an account element and COMMAND is the command to send to the GROUP. For instance in gcloud projects list, projects is the GROUP, an element of your account and list is the COMMAND. In gcloud compute instances list --project packt-gcp, the GROUP is compute, followed by a sub-group instances, and the COMMAND is list while --project packt-gcp are the required parameters.

gcloud parameters include account settings (keys and region for instance), CLI settings (verbosity, format, or specific configuration) as well as arguments required by the commands. For example, to start our instance, we need to specify two parameters—the region and the instance ID:

```
$ gcloud compute instances start sparrow  --project packt-gcp --zone us-
east1-d
```

Gcloud config

To avoid having to specify the zone or other parameters, you can set them in the `config` with:

```
$ gcloud config set compute/zone us-east1-d
```

And to unset them in the `config`, you can use the following:

```
$ gcloud config unset compute/zone
```

For a list of all the different settings available in the `config`, run `gcloud config set --help`.

The zone and region can be also stored in the environment variable `CLOUDSDK_COMPUTE_ZONE` and `CLOUDSDK_COMPUTE_REGION`. Environment variables override default properties that you set with the `gcloud config` commands, but do not override explicit flags like `--zone` or `--region`.

To set the environment variable `CLOUDSDK_COMPUTE_ZONE`, run or add this line to your `.bashrc`:

```
$ export CLOUDSDK_COMPUTE_ZONE=us-east1-c
```

For more details, see `https://cloud.google.com/compute/docs/gcloud-compute/#set_default_zone_and_region_in_your_local_client`.

Accessing your instance with gcloud

There are two important things you want to do from the start:

- Accessing the instance
- Moving files between your instance and another machine. To do `ssh` into your instance, run:

```
$ gcloud compute ssh <instance_name>
```

In our case:

```
$ gcloud compute ssh sparrow
```

The first time you access your instance from your local system, the platform will propagate your keys to the instance, which may take a few minutes. Once connected, you can verify that your local public key (`cat ~/.ssh/google_compute_engine.pub`) is included in the list of `authorized_keys` on your instance (`cat ~/.ssh/authorized_keys`).

Transferring files with gcloud

Transferring files back and forth from your machine (or any other location) and your instance is done via Gcloud's version of the `.csp` command:

- To send a local file to your instance `$HOME` folder:

  ```
  $ gcloud compute scp ~/LOCAL-FILE :~/
  ```

- For instance, to send a file titled `hello_world.txt` to sparrow, you would run this:

  ```
  $ gcloud compute scp ~/hello_world.txt  sparrow:~/
  ```

- Similarly, to download a file from the instance to your local machine `$HOME` folder:

  ```
  $ gcloud compute scp  <instance-name>:~/REMOTE-FILE ~/
  ```

We will explore the `gsutil` and `bq` command-line tools in the next chapter and the Datalab CLI in `Chapter 4`, *Querying Your data with BigQuery*.

Managing the VM

There are several operations that you will want to do as you start working with a VM on Google Compute, such as starting instances, stopping instances, resizing and modifying disks, and taking snapshots. We go over the most important ones:

1. Start and shut down the VM:

   ```
   $ gcloud compute instances start sparrow --project packt-gcp
   $ gcloud compute instances stop sparrow --project packt-gcp
   ```

2. Check the VM status:

   ```
   $ gcloud compute instances list --project packt-gcp
   ```

The instance we started with is an f1-micro with not-enough CPU, RAM, or disk space for a real-world data science project. We want to change the underlying machine and augment its disk space. But, before that, we should take a snapshot of our current machine as a backup. If anything goes wrong, we'll be able to restore the instance from the snapshot:

1. Taking a snapshot of a VM:

   ```
   $ gcloud compute disks snapshot [DISK_NAME]
   ```

2. In our case, let's call our disk `sparrow-backup` as we run:

   ```
   $ gcloud compute disks snapshot sparrow-backup --project packt-gcp
   ```

3. Changing the machine type, you first need to stop your instance with `$ gcloud compute instances stop sparrow --project packt-gcp`. Once that's done, changing the machine type is doable with the generic command:

   ```
   $ gcloud compute instances set-machine-type INSTANCE --machine-type MACHINE-TYPE
   ```

4. In our case, if we want to change the type to `n1-standard-1` (3.75 GB memory and 1 vCPU), we should run this:

   ```
   $ gcloud compute instances set-machine-type sparrow --machine-type n1-standard-1
   ```

5. While we're at it, we would also like to resize the underlying disk from 10 GB to 100 GB:

   ```
   $ gcloud compute disks resize sparrow --size 100
   ```

6. Another important setting is to make sure that the disk will not be deleted when the instance is deleted:

   ```
   $ gcloud compute instances set-disk-auto-delete
   ```

   This is an important parameter that can also be set in the compute engine console by unselecting **Delete boot disk when instance is deleted** when creating or editing an instance:

Firewall ⊘
Add tags and firewall rules to allow specific network traffic from the Internet

☐ Allow HTTP traffic
☐ Allow HTTPS traffic

Management   Disks   Networking   SSH Keys

Deletion rule
☐ Delete boot disk when instance is deleted

7. Instance configuration: The entire instance configuration is available via `$ gcloud` compute instances describe sparrow.

8. Creating the right VM from scratch: in this all these parameters are available when you create a VM from scratch. Running the following command will create a new `n1-standard-1` instance named `hummingbird` in the `europe-west1-c` zone, when running on Ubuntu 17.04, with a 100 GB disk also named `hummingbird`. Note that this instance is pre-emptible (`--preemptible`) and the disk will persist once the instance is deleted (`--no-boot-disk-auto-delete`):

```
$ gcloud compute --project packt-gcp instances create hummingbird \
--zone europe-west1-c --machine-type n1-standard-1 \
--image ubuntu-1704-zesty-v20171011 --image-project ubuntu-os-cloud \
\
--boot-disk-size 100  --boot-disk-type "pd-standard"  \
--boot-disk-device-name hummingbird \
--preemptible --no-boot-disk-auto-delete
```

We can verify that we now have two instances in our project:

To keep our resources under control, we should delete this new instance with:

```
$ gcloud compute instances stop hummingbird --zone europe-west1-c  --
project packt-gcp
```

Note that if you have set up a different zone as default either in the `config` setup or as an environment variable, you need to specify the zone of the instance before you can delete it; otherwise, a `resource not found` error message will be generated.

IPs

You must have noticed the presence of an internal and an external IP associated with our VMs. Each GCP project comes with a **Virtual Private Cloud** (**VPC**) network, which is automatically created with the project. A VPC is basically a private and isolated virtual network partition that enables your resources to talk to each other within a given project, while allowing control of external access to the VPC. Upon creation, each instance gets an internal IP address assigned to allow other resources within the project's VPC to communicate with the instance. To communicate with entities outside the VPC, including connections with the internet, the instance requires an external IP address.

IP addresses, both internal and external, can be ephemeral or static. Ephemeral IP addresses remain associated with the instance only as long as the instance is running. When the instance stops or is terminated, the IP address is released in the global GCP pool of IP addresses. For an instance to have a stable IP address, the IP address needs to become static. Static addresses generate extra costs.

Changing the nature of an IP address from ephemeral to static can be done via the console. Stop the VM and edit it. In the **Network interface** section, select the right type for the internal and external IPs of the VM:

The management of IPs and VPCs is accessible from the VPC network console at `https://console.cloud.google.com/networking/networks/list`.

You can create a new static IP address and then attach it to your instance directly from the **External IP addresses** page:

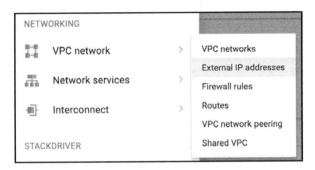

Click on **Reserve a static address**, select regional for region type, set the region to your instance's region, and attach it to your sparrow instance:

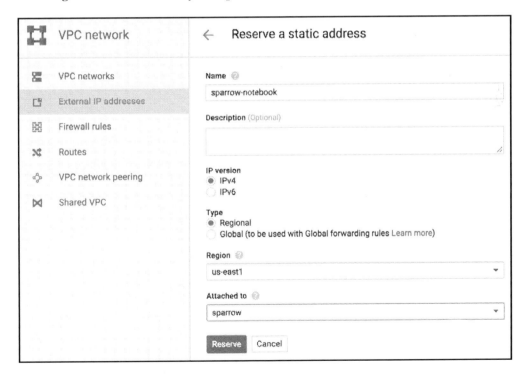

The command-line equivalent of creating a static IP and adding it to the instance is:

```
$ gcloud compute --project=packt-gcp addresses create sparrow-notebook --
region=us-east1
$ gcloud compute --project=packt-gcp instances add-access-config sparrow --
zone=us-east1-d --address=IP_OF_THE_NEWLY_CREATED_STATIC_ADDRESS
```

As static IPs are billed even when not used, it is important to release them when no longer needed.

Setting up a data science stack on the VM

So, now we have a VM running and we're able to send files to it, connect to it, and modify it. Everything is ready for us to set it up for data science!

We will install the Python Miniconda stack from continuum, much smaller than the full Conda distribution. Do SSH into your instance.

1. Install the mini `sudo apt-get update sudo apt-get install bzip2 wget` from `https://repo.continuum.io/miniconda/Miniconda2-latest-Linux-x86_64.sh` using the following command:

   ```
   bash Miniconda2-latest-Linux-x86_64.sh
   ```

2. And then install the Python stack with `conda`:

   ```
   $ conda install scikit-learn pandas jupyter ipython
   ```

   Don't forget to do this:

   ```
   $ source .bashrc
   ```

BOX the ipython console

To launch a Jupyter Notebook in your instance and access it over the Web, you need to promote the ephemeral external IP address provided by default to your VM to a static external IP.

You also need to make sure that your instance is accepting HTTP and HTTPS traffic. For that, go to your VM page, edit it, and check the following checkboxes:

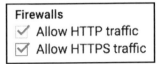

Since your Jupyter Notebook is open to all traffic on the web, you password-protect it:

1. Generate a configuration:

```
$ jupyter notebook --generate-config
```

2. And add a password with:

```
$ jupyter notebook password
```

More info on how to protect your public Notebook, including using ssh keys and adding encryption, is available at http://jupyter-notebook.readthedocs.io/en/latest/public_server.html.

3. Launch your Jupyter Notebook with:

```
$ jupyter notebook --ip=0.0.0.0 --port=8888 --no-browser &
```

This generates a token and the following message:

```
The Jupyter Notebook is running at:
http://0.0.0.0:8888/?token=7b1deb1b1467a3b3c9c23946e2f2efa12d9dc2c2
58353660
and access it in your browser via
http://104.196.129.173:8888/?token=7b1deb1b1467a3b3c9c23946e2f2efa1
2d9dc2c258353660
```

Troubleshooting

There is an alternative solution if you encounter problems in accessing your Notebook. The idea is to launch the Jupyter Notebook with IP 0.0.0.0, without having to set up a static IP first:

```
jupyter notebook --ip=0.0.0.0 --port=8888 --no-browser
```

This will generate a token. Do SSH into another terminal, adding the following flags `--ssh-flag="-L" --ssh-flag="2222:localhost:8888"`:

```
$ gcloud compute ssh sparrow --ssh-flag="-L" --ssh-
flag="2222:localhost:8888"
```

This is how it associates the URL `localhost:2222` with the Jupyter Notebook URL `localhost:8888`. You can then access your Notebook at `http://localhost:2222`. You also need to enter the token you were given a moment ago.

This alternative was given by the comments on this blog post by Jeff Delaney, *Running a Python Jupyter Notebook on Google Cloud Engine*: `https://jeffdelaney.me/blog/running-jupyter-notebook-google-cloud-platform/`.

Adding GPUs to instances

Check and request for an increase in your quotas for GPUs:

- Search for GPU. If you have 0 in your allocated quotas, select the type of GPU and region and click on edit the quotas. Fill in the request form (`https://console.cloud.google.com/iam-admin/quotas?project=packt-gcp`).

There are several restrictions when it comes to using GPUs on Google Compute. GPUs are not available in shared or pre-emptible machines. GPU instances are terminated for regular (weekly) maintenance events. See `https://cloud.google.com/compute/docs/gpus/` for up-to-date information on the restrictions. See also `https://cloud.google.com/compute/docs/gpus#introduction` to learn what machine types are available based on your desired GPU count.

To create a VM with GPU from the console:

1. Go to the VM console and click on **Create Instance**
2. Select a zone that is GPU compatible
3. Click on customize the machine type and again on the GPUs link
4. Select the **Number of GPUs** and the associated type you require:

Similarly you can create a GPU-enabled instance with `gcloud` with the following command:

```
$ gcloud compute instances create [INSTANCE_NAME] \
--machine-type [MACHINE_TYPE] --zone [ZONE] \
--accelerator type=[ACCELERATOR_TYPE],count=[ACCELERATOR_COUNT] \
--image-family [IMAGE_FAMILY] --image-project [IMAGE_PROJECT] \
--maintenance-policy TERMINATE --restart-on-failure \
--metadata startup-script='[STARTUP_SCRIPT]'
```

Where `--accelerator type=` specifies the type of GPU and `count=` specifies the number of GPUs.

For instance, this command will create an Ubuntu 1604 instance with one NVIDIA® Tesla® K80 GPU and two vCPUs in the `us-east1-d` zone. The startup-script metadata instructs the instance to install the CUDA toolkit with its recommended driver version:

```
$ gcloud compute instances create gpu-instance-1 \
--machine-type n1-standard-2 --zone us-east1-d \
--accelerator type=nvidia-tesla-k80,count=1 \
--image-family ubuntu-1604-lts --image-project ubuntu-os-cloud \
--maintenance-policy TERMINATE --restart-on-failure \
--metadata startup-script='#!/bin/bash
echo "Checking for CUDA and installing."
# Check for CUDA and try to install.if ! dpkg-query -W cud
a-8-0; then
  curl -O
http://developer.download.nvidia.com/compute/cuda/repos/ubuntu1604/x86_64/c
uda-repo-ubuntu1604_8.0.61-1_amd64.deb
  dpkg -i ./cuda-repo-ubuntu1604_8.0.61-1_amd64.deb
  apt-get update
  apt-get install cuda-8-0 -y
fi'
```

The startup script installs the right CUDA driver for the Ubuntu. For other drivers and operating systems, follow the instructions at `https://developer.nvidia.com/cuda-downloads`.

Once the driver has finished installing, you can verify that it is properly installed:

1. Do `ssh` into your instance
2. Type `nvidia-smi` to see your driver version and how much GPU memory you have

The command `nvcc --version` shows the current CUDA version.

Startup scripts and stop scripts

Startup scripts allow you to run a script when starting up or creating an instance. For instance, to always install `miniconda` and related data science packages when creating a new instance, simply write the following script in a file on your local machine:

```
#! /bin/bash
apt-get install bzip2
wget https://repo.continuum.io/miniconda/Miniconda2-latest-Linux-x86_64.sh
sudo bash Miniconda2-latest-Linux-x86_64.sh
conda install scikit-learn
```

```
conda install pandas
conda install jupyter
conda install ipython
```

Then as you start the new instance, supply the `--metadata-from-file` flag, followed by `startup-script=PATH/TO/FILE`, where `PATH/TO/FILE` is a relative path to the startup script:

```
$ gcloud compute instances create example-instance --metadata-from-file
startup-script=examples/scripts/install.sh
```

You can also use a startup script in extension in the command line or from a file stored in Google Storage. For more on startup scripts, visit `https://cloud.google.com/compute/docs/startupscript`.

Stop scripts are scripts that are automatically run when an instance is terminated or restarted. Similar to startup scripts, you can associate a stop script with an instance at creation by adding the `--metadata-from-file flag`, followed by `shutdown-script=PATH/TO/FILE`:

```
$ gcloud compute instances create example-instance --metadata-from-file
shutdown-script=examples/scripts/shutdown.sh
```

Resources and further reading

The following are a few interesting articles on setting TensorFlow on GCE:

- **Running distributed TensorFlow on Compute Engine**: `https://cloud.google.com/solutions/running-distributed-tensorflow-on-compute-engine`
- **Jupyter + TensorFlow + Nvidia GPU + Docker + GCE**: `https://medium.com/google-cloud/jupyter-tensorflow-nvidia-gpu-docker-google-compute-engine-4a146f085f17`
- **Using a GPU and TensorFlow on GCP**: `https://medium.com/google-cloud/using-a-gpu-tensorflow-on-google-cloud-platform-1a2458f42b0`
- **Running Jupyter Notebooks on GPU on Google Cloud**: `https://medium.com/google-cloud/running-jupyter-notebooks-on-gpu-on-google-cloud-d44f57d22dbd`

Some docker-related resources:

- **Docker config to create machines on GCE**: `https://docs.docker.com/machine/drivers/gce/`
- **Logging with stackcriver**: `https://medium.com/google-cloud/how-to-log-your-application-on-google-compute-engine-6600d81e70e3`

Summary

The GCE is a GCP core service, offering a wide variety of scalable VMs based on different OSes. The multiplicity of available OSes, the range of machines with CPUs, GPUs, small to huge disk space, and RAM make the GCE a powerful Cloud environment adapted to a wide variety of projects and contexts.

In this chapter you learned:

- How to create, launch, back up, modify, and access multiple VMs
- The different parameters and variables related to a VM
- How to access and use the Google Shell
- How to use the `gcloud` CLI to carry out the same operations in the GCP
- How to install a data science Python stack
- How to launch a Jupyter Notebook

There are many more possibilities offered by the power and flexibility of the GCE that we haven't covered. Hopefully, by the end of this chapter, you should feel comfortable working with instances that are appropriate for your projects in a data-focused context.

In the next chapter, we will learn how to store data on the GCP with Google Storage and Google SQL.

3
Google Cloud Storage

In this chapter, we will explore two data storage services from the Google Cloud platform, Google Storage, for files, and Google SQL, for structured data. Google Storage is a file-hosting service that allows you to store files in the cloud. Quite simple and straightforward, it is very similar to the Amazon S3 service. To go beyond basic usage, we will look into some advanced subjects, such as signed-URLs, collaboration bucket settings, optimizing upload speeds, and transferring big datasets

Google SQL is Google's simple SQL database service. Less developed at the moment than Amazon SQL services in terms of types of SQLs, it comes with MySQL as the main database. A beta version of Postgre is also available. We will look at the differences between the two in terms of respective functionalities.

Making services talk to one another, or more precisely, allowing data transfers between different data stores and data consumers, is usually where the difficulty lies when using cloud-based solutions for data science projects.

Issues such as volume, latency, and throughput can affect the speed of your scripts and the efficiency of your work. Setting the right level of permissions so that your data can be accessed within your project environment while still being protected from outside access is also key.

In this chapter, you will learn:

- How to store files on Google Storage with gsutil
- How to create databases and seed them with data on Google SQL
- How to access your Google Storage files and your Google SQL database

At the end of the chapter, you will be able to upload data and manage it using the services provided by the Google Cloud platform and understand the potential of Google Cloud SQL for the creation of relational database management systems.

Google Cloud Storage

Cloud storage is a model for storing data on computers available on the network, where the data is stored on multiple servers, real and/or virtual, generally hosted at third-party facilities or on dedicated servers. Through this model, it is possible to access personal or business information, whether it be videos, music, photographs, databases, or files, without knowing the physical location of the data, from any part of the world with any suitable device. The advantages of this methodology are numerous: infinite capacity of memory space, payment only of the actual amount of memory used, files accessible from anywhere in the world, highly reduced maintenance, and greater security, as the files are protected from theft, fire, or damage that may occur on local computers.

Google Cloud Storage is the Google proposal for Cloud storage: it's a developer service provided by Google that allows you to save and manipulate data directly on Google's infrastructure. In more detail, Google Cloud Storage provides a programming interface that makes use of simple HTTP requests to perform operations on its infrastructure. With Google Cloud Storage you can perform the following operations: uploading a file, downloading a file, deleting a file, obtaining a list of files, or obtaining the size of a given file. Each of these HTTP requests contains information about the method used and the resource to request. It follows that it becomes possible to create an application that, using these HTTP requests, provides a service in which applications save data remotely, generally via third-party servers.

The Google Storage platform is an enterprise storage solution that offers three levels of storage with different accessibility needs and associated pricing:

- Standard storage is for fast access to large amounts of data. At $0.026/GB, it offers a high speed of response to requests.
- **Durable Reduced Availability (DRA)** is for long-term data storage and infrequent access. It is priced lower, at $0.02/GB.
- Finally, nearline storage is for even-less-frequent access. It is the cheapest version of the service, with much longer response time. It is the cheapest option, currently priced at $0.01/ GB.

Box–storage versus drive

Google Drive is used for storing personal files. It is free up to 15 GB across all your different personal services (email, photo, and so on). It offers further data storage volume for a monthly fee (for instance $9.99/month for 1 TB). But, compared to Google Storage, there is no data compression or data encryption. It is not offered by Google as an enterprise platform with associated features, support, and reliability. There are no advanced management features, such as metadata, and no data organization management through buckets. There are also no advanced storage tiers (cold versus hot data).

The main features of the Google Drive service are as follows:

- There is no data storage based on tiers
- It is not a commercial solution
- It does not support advanced data management features
- The storage plan is limited to 30 TB

To understand the potential offered by Google Cloud Storage, see the following:

- It provides unlimited space
- It has more security than Google Drive thanks to the use of OAuth
- It offers advanced storage levels
- It provides REST API support for advanced integration of enterprise services and applications
- It has the possibility to resume data transfer after an error

By analyzing only some of the features offered by Google Cloud Storage, it appears evident its superiority justifies the cost.

Accessing control lists

The documentation says it best, **Access Control Lists** (**ACLs**) allow you to control who can read and write your data, and who can read and write the ACLs themselves.

If not specified at the time an object is uploaded (e.g., via the `gsutil cp -a` option), objects will be created with a default object ACL set on the bucket (see `gsutil help defacl` https://cloud.Google.com/storage/docs/gsutil/commands/defacl). You can replace the ACL on an object or bucket using the gsutil acl set command, or modify the existing ACL using the `gsutil acl ch` command (see `gsutil help acl:` https://cloud.Google.com/storage/docs/gsutil/commands/acl).

ACL are assigned to objects (files) or buckets. By default all files in a bucket have the same ACL as the bucket they're in.
A couple of points to remember are:

- There is no write access for objects; attempting to set an ACL with write permission for an object will result in an error
- The object ACL is what determines read access independently of the bucket ACL read settings. (the folder permissions does not override the file access.)

Several presets are available. The available canned ACLs are:

- **Project-private:** Gives permission to the project team based on their roles. Anyone who is part of the team has read permission, and project owners and project editors have owner permission. This is the default ACL for newly created buckets. This is also the default ACL for newly created objects unless the default object ACL for that bucket has been changed. For more details see gsutil help projects.
- **Private:** Gives the requester (and only the requester) owner permission for a bucket or object.
- **Public-read:** Gives all users (whether logged in or anonymous) read permission. When you apply this to an object, anyone on the internet can read the object without authenticating.
- **Public-read-write:** Gives all users read and write permission. This ACL applies only to buckets. Setting a bucket to public-read-write will allow anyone on the internet to upload anything to your bucket. You will be responsible for this content. There are other settings, check the doc.

Access and management through the web console

In the previous sections, we introduced the service provided by the GCP. Now it's time to see how to access the service and how to manage it. To do this, Google has created a web-based interface for completely online service management and gsutil, a command-line tool that allows you to perform all the operations you need on the service.

gsutil

gsutil is the command-line tool, a subset of `gcloud` shell scripts, that allows you to manage buckets and objects (files) on Google Storage. The operations available via gsutil go from simple straightforward commands for creating buckets and moving files around, to management commands to manage settings, storage class, and permissions. More advanced commands include setting access control via ACLs, defining life cycle rules (delete all files after 1 year), logging, creating notifications, and troubleshooting with perfdiag.

Let's start with the simple commands. We will create a bucket named `packt-gcp`, upload some files, get info on these files, move them around, and change the storage class.

gsutil cheatsheet

The following is a list of the most-used commands that we can issue via gsutil:

- Creating a bucket named `packt-gcp`:
    - `gsutil mb gs://packt-gcp`
- Uploading a file to the bucket:

    - `gsutil cp gs://packt-gcp/`
- Creating a subfolder in the bucket:
    - `gsutil cp your-file gs://packt-gcp/`
- Listing the folder:
    - `gsutil ls gs://packt-gcp/`
- Getting help on gsutil commands:
    - `gsutil help`

- How much storage are we using (the –h makes it readable):
    - `gsutil du -h gs://packt-gcp/`
- Copying a whole folder to a bucket:
    - `gsutil cp -r gs://packt-gcp/`

For instance, I have a local `./img` directory with some images. I can copy the whole directory and create the bucket subdirectory at the same time with the following command:

`gsutil cp -r ./img gs://packt-gcp/`

Let's analyze an option that is particularly useful: I refer to the –m flag. If you are performing a sequence of `gsutil` operations it may run significantly faster if you instead use `gsutil -m -o`, this means to run in parallel. This can significantly improve performance if you are performing operations on a large number of files over a reasonably fast network connection but may make performance worse if you are using a slower network.

The –m flag is particularly suited to the following commands: `ls`, `mb`, `mv`, `rb`, and `du`.

Advanced gsutil

Previously, we have seen some simple basic commands that we can import using `gsutil`. But with this tool we can do something else:

- `gsutil` supports wildcards (and ?) and limits a wildcard to files. To include folders in the wildcard target double the sign: `gsutil ll gs:///**.txt` will list all the text files in subdirectories.

- `gsutil` requires use of UTF-8 character encoding. For Windows: to use Unicode characters you need to run this command in the command shell before the first time you use `gsutil` in that shell: `chcp 65001`.

- The `.boto` file in your local machine user path is the configuration file for the gsutil CLI. You can edit it directly or via the `gsutilconfig` command. Some interesting parameters in the `.boto` file are as follows:

    - `parallel_composite_upload_threshold`: This is used to specify the maximum size of a file to be uploaded in a single stream. Files larger than this threshold will be uploaded in parallel. The `parallel_composite_upload_threshold` parameter is for the moment disabled by default.

- `check_hashes`: This is used to enforce integrity checks when downloading data, always, never, or conditionally.
- `prefer_api`: This parameter value is JSON or XML.
- `aws_access_key_id`: This is used for interoperability with S3.
- `aws_secret_access_key`: This is used for interoperability with S3.

Signed URLs

Signed URLs is a mechanism for query string authentication for buckets and objects. Signed URLs provide a way to give time-limited read or write access to anyone in possession of the URL, regardless of whether they have a Google account.

Why use a signed URL? Sometimes, it is necessary to control the access of users who do not have a Google account. To grant these users access to Google Cloud Storage we can provide them with a signed URL, which allows the user to read, write, or delete access to that resource for a limited period of time. Access to the resource is allowed to the owner of the URL until the URL expires.

There are two ways to create a signed URL:

- Creating signed URLs with `gsutil`
- Creating signed URLs with a program.

The easiest way to create a signed URL is to use the `gsutil signurl` command. To do this, you first need to generate a private key or use an existing private key. To create a private key you first have to create an OAuth client ID for a service account.

To create a new private key visit: `https://console.cloud.Google.com/apis/credentials?project=packt-gcp`

Follow the instructions and download the file. Two formats are available:

- **JSON**: Required if you are using application default credentials in a production environment outside of Google Cloud platform
- **PKCS12**: Supported by many different programming languages and libraries

To restrict the role that can access GCP: Get JSON file downloaded to your computer.

You can now create a signed URL for one of your files with `gsutil` via the following command:

```
gsutil signurl -d 10m -m GET Desktop/privatekey1.json gs://packt-gcp/file1.csv
```

Remember, signed URLs do not work on directories. If you want to give access to multiple files you can use wildcards as follows:

```
gsutil signurl -d 10m -m GET Desktop/privatekey1.json gs://packt-gcp/img/.png
```

But that will generate one signed URL per `.png` file in the `img/` folder.

Signed URLs can also be used to upload files (`-m` PUT and POST) and specify the content type with `-c text/plain` or `-c image/jpg`.

Creating a bucket in Google Cloud Storage

As we said previously, a bucket is a container that holds your data. Everything saved in Google Storage must be contained within a bucket, corresponding to the folders. You can use them to organize and control access to data, but, unlike folders, you can not create sub-buckets. In Google Storage, individual data is saved in the form of objects. Such objects can be files of any type, extension, and size; tables created with BigQuery are also considered objects, as we will see in Chapter 4, *Querying Your Data with BigQuery*. All objects related to a single job must be contained in a bucket.

Objects are immutable, so an object cannot be edited directly in Google Storage. It is important to specify that it is not possible to make any kind of changes to the content of an object; if you want to modify an object stored in Google Storage it can only be replaced. In case you do not want to delete it and reload it, you can do the same thing with just one operation, by overwriting it.

Google Storage namespace

Google Storage uses a hierarchical structure to store buckets and objects. All buckets are in this one environment, and all objects are also inside a hierarchy within a certain bucket. Based on this hierarchical structure, a bucket name has to be unique across all the existing Google Storage buckets. Each bucket name must be unique across the entire Cloud storage namespace.

To name a bucket, we cannot use a name that has already been chosen by another user. While objects must have a unique name only within a given bucket, we can therefore have multiple buckets that always contain an object with the same name.

Naming a bucket

To name a bucket, we have to follow some rules imposed by the fact; as we anticipated, all the buckets reside in the only Google Storage namespace. Bucket names must comply with the following rules:

- They must be 3 to 63 characters long
- They must start and end with a number or a letter
- They must contain only lowercase letters, numbers, dots, and dashes
- They cannot be represented as an IP address in dotted decimal notation
- They cannot start with the prefix GOOG
- They cannot contain two adjacent points or a dash before or after a point

Finally, it should be noted that once you have created the name of a bucket, you cannot change it. To change it, you should create a new bucket with the desired name and move the contents from the old bucket to the new bucket.

Naming an object

In Google Storage, individual data is saved in the form of objects. Object names must comply with the following rules:

- They can contain any sequence of valid Unicode characters, of length 1-1,024 bytes when UTF-8 encoded
- They cannot contain carriage return or line feed characters
- They cannot start with well-known/acme-challenge

To eliminate the limitations given by the flat hierarchy, we can use the slash (/) character in the object names. For example, if we have to use the same name for two different objects we could name an object `/NewYork/Stadium.jpg` and another `/Boston/Stadium.jpg`. In this way it is possible to organize the objects as if they were inside directories and manage them as such. In fact, Google Storage sees objects as independent objects that have no hierarchical relationship.

Creating a bucket

To operate in Google Cloud Storage we can use two tools: console and gsutil. The first tool makes use of typical graphic interfaces, while the second uses command-line windows.

Google Cloud Storage console

To start with, we will see how to create a bucket using the Google Cloud Storage console. First, when we access it, we can get to that console starting from the main Google Cloud Platform by clicking on the left in the Resources section on the entry Cloud Storage. The following window will be open:

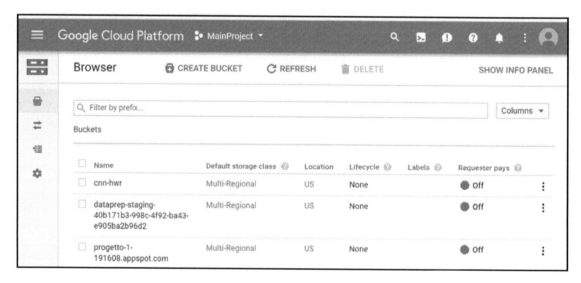

In the window that opens, all the buckets related to the account are present. For each of them, there are the following features:

- **Name**: Bucket name.
- **Default storage class**: Storage class assigned by default to the objects added to a bucket.
- **Location**: Place where data is stored.
- **Lifecycle**: Allows you to set rules for automatically deleting objects or downgrading their storage class.
- **Labels**: Help organize your buckets. Labels are also included in your bill, so you can see the distribution of costs across your labels.
- **Requester pays**: If On, requests for the bucket's data will be billed to the requester's project.

To create a new bucket, simply click on the **CREATE BUCKET** button at the top of the Google Cloud Storage browser. The following page is opened:

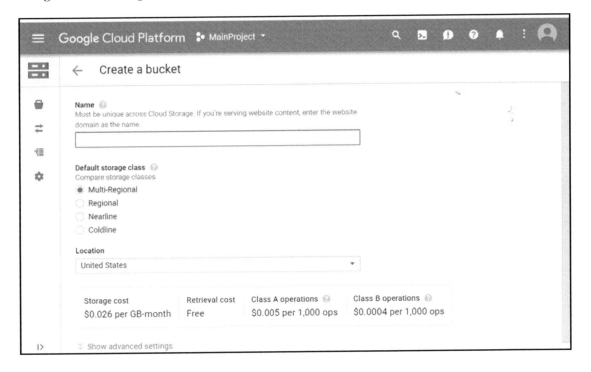

On the page that opens, you need to specify the following information:

- **Name**: Remember, it must be unique across Cloud Storage
- **Default storage class**: Four options are available: Multi-Regional, Regional, Nearline, and Coldline
- **Location**: This drop-down menu allows us to choose the location

After making these choices, just click on the **CREATE** button and a new bucket will be added to the Google Cloud Storage browser.

Now we have the container, it is time to enrich it with contents. To do this, we must first access the simple bucket by clicking on its name. The following page is opened:

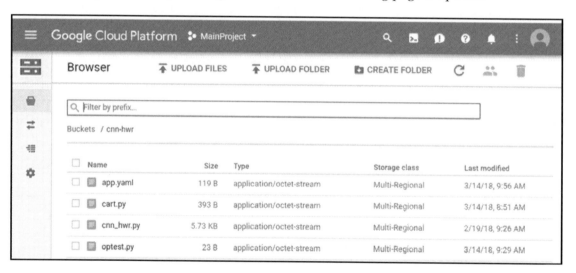

On the page that opens, all the contents of the buckets is listed. For each object, a series of information is proposed:

- **Name**: Object name
- **Size**: Object dimension
- **Type**: Object type
- **Storage class**: Storage class assigned to the objects added to a bucket
- **Last modified**: Date of last modification of the object

To add another object to the bucket:

1. Simply click on the **UPLOAD FILES** button at the top of the Google Cloud Storage browser. A dialog window is opened.
2. In the dialog window, select the file or folder you want to upload to your bucket.
3. Click **Open**.

If we use Chrome as a browser it is possible to perform folder uploads. This way, we can load the entire contents of a folder into a bucket. Otherwise, we can first create a folder, using the **CREATE FOLDER** button and then upload all the objects individually.

To rename, copy, and move objects simply click the more options button (three vertical dots) associated with the object. A context menu is opened. In it we will be able to carry out the following operations:

- Edit permissions
- Edit metadata
- Copy
- Move
- Rename

For each option, a relative window will be opened that will guide us in the operation.

Google Cloud Storage gsutil

We have seen that using the Google Cloud Storage browser is simple and intuitive. But in some cases it is necessary to operate through a command window. In such cases, as we have seen in previous sections, we can use gsutil. Previously, we had already seen a series of commands via gsutil.

To create a bucket using gsutil, use the mb command. For example, use the following command:

```
gsutil mb gs://NameBucket1
```

This creates a bucket named NameBucket1. It is important to remember that bucket names must be unique within the entire Google Storage namespace. If another user has already created a bucket with the name we want to use, we must choose another name.

Once the buckets are created, we can import the objects within them. With the `cp` command, we can copy files from our computer to Google Storage:

```
gsutil cp figure.jpg gs://NameBucket1/fig.jpg
```

This copies the image `figure.jpg` from the folder in which we are positioned with the shell in the bucket `NameBucket1` renaming the object in `fig.jpg`.

To list our buckets or the objects contained in them you must use the `ls` command.

 The `ls` command is used in Unix-like operating systems to display information about files and directories. If we open a terminal and type `ls`, we get the list of files and directories of the current directory.

The following command lists all the buckets we have created:

```
gsutil ls
```

While this command lists the objects contained in `NameBucket1`:

```
gsutil ls gs: // NameBucket1
```

You can also use the `-L` option of the `ls` command to get more information about objects and buckets. The following command provides information about the size of objects, the date of the last modification, the data type, and the **Access Control Lists** (ACL) of all objects contained in the `NameBucket1` bucket:

```
gsutil ls -L gs: // NameBucket1
```

While the following command provides information on our buckets, such as the number of objects contained, the total size, and the ACL of all our buckets:

```
gsutil ls -L
```

Finally, to transfer an object from one bucket to another, use the `mv` command, this command can also be used to rename an object. For example, the following command transfers the image `figure.png` from the `NameBucket1` bucket to the `NameBucket2` bucket:

```
gsutil mv gs://NameBucket1/figure.png gs:// NameBucket2/
```

While this command renames the image `figure.png` to `fig.png`:

```
gsutil mv gs://NameBucket1/figure.png gs://NameBucket1/fig.png
```

Life cycle management

With Google Cloud Storage, the life cycle management of objects becomes simple and immediate. The life cycle of an object is the time between the creation of an object and its destruction. The rules for the duration of the object vary significantly between the programming platforms. In the case of archived objects we refer to the time in which the object remains stored in the space assigned to it.

The life cycle of a bucket can be managed through its configuration. The configuration contains a set of rules that apply to all objects in the bucket. The action specified on the object is performed when the object meets the criteria of one of the rules.

To enable life cycle for a bucket using the Google Cloud Console:

1. Go to Open the Google Cloud Platform Console and click on the Cloud Storage browser; the following window is opened:

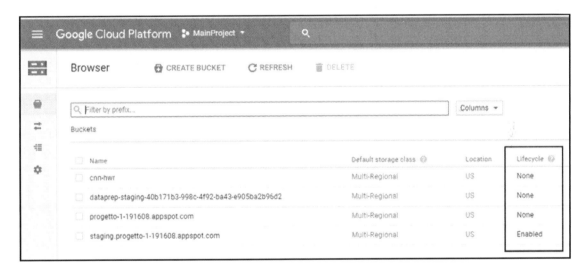

2. In this window, examine the **Lifecycle** column, choose the bucket, and click on the entry **None**; a new page is opened.
3. In this window, click on **Add Rule**.
4. In the page that opens, we can specify the configuration by selecting the conditions and the actions.
5. Finally, click on the **Save** button.

A similar procedure can be performed to check the life cycle configuration set on a bucket, and to disable life cycle management for a bucket.

Google Cloud SQL

Google Cloud SQL is a database service of the Google Cloud Platform that allows the creation, management, and administration of relational databases in the cloud for their applications. The service guarantees excellent performance and scalability thanks to the Google infrastructure on which the databases will be hosted. Like every service on the platform, the simplicity of use is fundamental: there is no need to install any software, make updates manually, or take care of backups and replications of their databases. The Google platform will take care of all of it and ensure an availability of 99.95%. The data is encrypted before being saved in the databases and in the backups, to guarantee the security of the infrastructure.

You can also set up a network firewall for each database instance to directly regulate access to the instances. The service can be used with any type of Cloud-based application or website that is compatible with MySQL or PostgreSQL, and the instances are easily accessible through the app engine, compute engine, and platform workstation.

The cost of the service does not require any initial payment, but is calculated minute by minute for the entire duration of use and only the resources actually allocated will be charged. In the case of MySQL databases, the standard price range for a Cloud SQL instance is $0.0150 – $4.0240 per hour (up to 208 GB of RAM), while for storage space it goes from $ 0.08 per GB/month for backups, $ 0.09 per GB/month for HDD storage, and $ 0.17 GB/month for SSD storage. To these must be added the costs for the management of the network through the compute engine.

Databases supported

With Google Cloud SQL, it is possible to create two types of relational databases:

- MySQL
- PostgreSQL

MySQL is an open source **relational database management system** (**RDMB**) available for free using **Structured Query Language** (**SQL**). SQL is the most popular language for adding, accessing, and managing content in a database. It is known for its rapid processing, proven reliability, ease, and flexibility of use. MySQL is an essential part of almost all open source PHP applications.

PostgreSQL is an advanced database system with a long history behind it. It is available for a wide range of platforms and is used in microscopic embedded systems as well as in huge multi-terabyte systems. PostgreSQL has earned an excellent reputation over the years for its innovative features, data integrity, security, and reliability.

PostgreSQL support is still in beta, so features such as replication or high availability are not available. The instances of the platform they support MySQL 5.7 or PostgreSQL 9.6 databases in the cloud and allow for up to 208 GB of RAM, 32 CPUs, and 10 TB of storage. The data, encrypted on Google networks and within tables and backups, are accessible from their applications created through the app engine (written in Java, Python, PHP, Node.js, Go, or Ruby), through clients MySQL/PostgreSQL using standard protocols, or even through external applications, with the possibility of using secure connection protocols, such as SSL.

In general, there are no noticeable differences between the functionality provided by the standard MySQL/PostgreSQL instances locally and those provided by the Cloud SQL instances. In particular, we remind you that it is impossible to create new functions in MySQL using the CREATE FUNCTION statement and the lack SUPER (MySQL) and SUPERUSER (PostgreSQL) privileges.

Google Cloud SQL performance and scalability

Cloud SQL offers excellent performance and scalability. As mentioned previously, the maximum storage capacity is 10 TB (to be distributed between HDD and SSD), while the maximum RAM that can be selected is 208 GB, and the maximum number of CPUs is 32. Google also guarantees a maximum of 25,000 IOPS, that is, input/output operations per second. The possibility to choose such resources allows us therefore to use Cloud SQL for every type of application, from those with lower workloads to applications that require intense performance. There are no limits of **query per second** (**QPS**), but there are some limits regarding the connections. In fact, up to a maximum of 4,000 concurrent connections are possible in the case of second-generation MySQL instances, while for the other cases the limits are more stringent.

For first-generation MySQL databases only, where incoming requests are briefly queuing before establishing a connection, there is a limit of 100 queued connections at the same time. The databases are also easily scalable both vertically, increasing or reducing the available resources (storage space, CPU, and RAM), and horizontally increasing the number of servers and instances that work simultaneously. Once you have created your instance, you can change the resources allocated for it directly from the console. In general, the changes are applied immediately, but the restart of the instance will close the existing connections and will need a few moments (in the case of first-generation MySQL) or a few minutes (second generation) to get back online.

Google Cloud SQL security and architecture

Regarding security, the data available on Cloud SQL is encrypted within the tables, in temporary files, in backup copies, and during the movements within the Google infrastructure from one server to another using secure network protocols. The platform infrastructure is therefore designed to ensure the security of its data at every stage of information management. No action is required by the user: the data is automatically encrypted by the platform through the compute engine, so all the services provided by it will comply with these requirements.

From a design point of view, the security of the infrastructure on a global scale is organized according to a layered architecture. This architecture allows the safe use of services, data, and communications between services, users, and administrators.

Starting from the lowest level, that is, hardware, we have data centers that Google designs and builds autonomously, accessible only to a small number of employees and monitored by equipment such as metal detectors, video cameras, or biometric identification technologies. Individual data centers are made up of multiple servers connected to a single local network: it is always up to Google to verify that the components, designed by themselves, and their suppliers meet the company's security standards. The individual server machines, individually identified to be easily traceable, are controlled by digital signatures on each individual low-level component and validated at each start-up.

Moving to the software level, every application written and made to run on the platform is run in multiple copies on multiple machines to use the necessary amount of resources for each workload. The software architecture is multi-tenant, in which a single instance of a software runs on a server and serves more tenants (that is, users who share access to the instance). It will be the task of the application to provide to each tenant a dedicated part of the instance. The concept is diametrically opposed to that of the multi-instance architecture, where there are several instances of software each dedicated to the single client.

Creating Google Cloud SQL instances

A Google Cloud SQL instance is a set of memory structures that manage database files. The instance manages its associated data and serves the users of the database. Every running Google Cloud SQL database is associated with at least one database instance.

Cloud SQL instances are fully managed, relational MySQL and PostgreSQL databases. Google handles replication, patch management, and database management to ensure availability and performance. When you create an instance, choose a size and billing plan to fit your application.

To create a Google Cloud SQL instance:

1. Go to the Google Cloud SQL instances page at the following URL: `https://console.cloud.google.com/sql/instances`.

2. Click on the **create instance** button at the middle of the page. A guided sequence will lead us to create the instance.

3. Choose the database type; two options are available: MySQL and PostgreSQL (MySQL is the default choice). After making your choice, click on the next button.

4. Choose a MySQL instance type; two options are available: MySQL Second Generation (recommended) and MySQL First Generation. MySQL Second Generation offers high performance, high storage capacity, and low cost. MySQL First Generation is the older version of Cloud SQL, providing basic performance and storage capacity. To make your choice, click on the Choose Second/First Generation button.

5. A new page is opened. In this page, a set of choices must be made, as shown in the following screenshot:

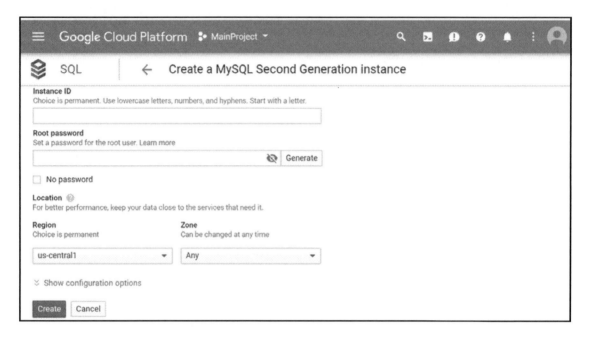

The first choice concerns the name of the instance. This is a name visible from the outside so it is advisable not to include sensitive or personally identifiable information in that name. Furthermore, it is not necessary to include the project ID in the instance name; if necessary, it is added automatically.

6. Set the password for the `'root'@'%'` user.
7. Set the region.
8. Set configuration options.
9. Finally, click on the `Create` button.

In this way, a new instance will have been created.

Summary

In this chapter, we have discovered two additional services offered by Google Cloud Platform: Google Cloud Storage, and Google Cloud SQL. Google Cloud Storage is a file hosting service that lets you store files in the cloud. We have seen how to store videos, music, photographs, databases or files, without knowing the physical location of data, from anywhere in the world, with any suitable device. We have performed the file uploading operations either using the browser or using the command line.

Afterward, we understood the potential of Google Cloud SQL for the creation of a relational database management system. Using Google Cloud SQL you can create, manage and administer relational databases. At first we discovered the characteristics of the service and later we learned to create a new database instance through a practical example.

4
Querying Your Data with BigQuery

Technological evolution has, over the last few years, led to a considerable increase in electronic devices able to automate numerous operations, both in the business world and in families. These devices generate a huge amount of data every day, the volume of which has seen an exponential growth in recent years.

This data represents a great resource that, in the past, has not been expressed for too long. Today, large companies are aware that the success of their activities depends at least, if not largely, on the information derived from the processing of such data. But dealing with a large amount of data requires a great deal of effort on the part of companies—both technological and human effort. Google was one of the first companies that understood the importance of data management, and over time it created a technological background that is available to companies and individuals today.

In this chapter, we will get an introduction to the BigQuery and Data Studio platform to manage and view data. To start, we will take a look at big data and the problems associated with managing large amounts of data. We will then analyze how to organize data and the tools used to correctly query databases. With this in mind, an introduction to the SQL language will be proposed. We will then analyze Google BigQuery, a web service that enables interactive analysis of massively large datasets. Finally, we will analyze how to create reports from our data using Google Data Studio.

The topics covered are:

- Big data
- Querying databases
- SQL language
- Google BigQuery
- Google Data Studio

At the end of the chapter, the reader will be able to apply these tools to analyze their data without the need for technological support. Several examples will be dealt with to make the use of such tools as realistic as possible in real cases.

Approaching big data

The explosion of social networks, combined with the unstoppable spread of smartphones, justifies the fact that one of the recurring terms in the world of innovation, marketing, and information technology in recent years is big data. This term indicates data produced in large quantities, with considerable speed, and in the most diverse formats, the processing of which requires technologies and resources that go well beyond the conventional systems of management and storage of data. But what is enclosed in this term?

In a widely quoted article, *The Age of Big Data*, Steve Lohr (a technology reporter for *The New York Times*) explained big data in this way:

> *"What is Big Data? A meme and a marketing term, for sure, but also shorthand for advancing trends in technology that open the door to a new approach to understanding the world and making decisions."*

 For a detailed reading of the entire article, refer to the following URL: http://www.nytimes.com/2012/02/12/sunday-review/big-datas-impact-in-the-world.html.

The term big data should not mislead us; in fact, at first sight, we may think that this phenomenon concerns only the data size. Although the dimensions certainly represent an element of the problem, there are other aspects or other properties of big data that are not necessarily associated with them.

"Big data has three dimensions—volume, variety, and velocity," says Michael Minelli. *"And within each of those three dimensions is a wide range of variables."*

Let's take a closer look at the three dimensions associated with big data:

- **Volume**: Big data implies huge volumes of data. Earlier, it was men who created data. Now that data is generated by machines, networks, and social media, the volume of data to be analyzed is enormous. Yet volume is not the only problem that needs to be addressed.
- **Variety**: The variety in data is due to the many sources and types of both structured and unstructured data in which such data is stored. In the past, data was stored in spreadsheets and databases. Now it is available in the form of photos, videos, audio, emails, and so on. This variety of unstructured data creates problems for storing, extracting, and analyzing data.
- **Velocity**: Finally, velocity refers to the sequence in which data arrives from sources such as industrial processes, machines, networks, social media, mobile devices, and so on. The flow of data is therefore massive and continuous. This real-time data can help researchers and companies make important decisions that offer strategic competitive advantages if they are able to manage the speed.

Companies are generating ever-increasing amounts of data, capturing trillions of information bytes on their customers, suppliers, and operations. This large amount of information is due to the fact that the data arrives massively from sources such as:

- Sensors that collect different types of data
- GPRS packages of mobile phones that map the position of potential customers
- Contents on social media
- Images—digital and video
- Online recordings of purchase transactions
- Any other source that can produce information of our interest

These are shown in the following diagram:

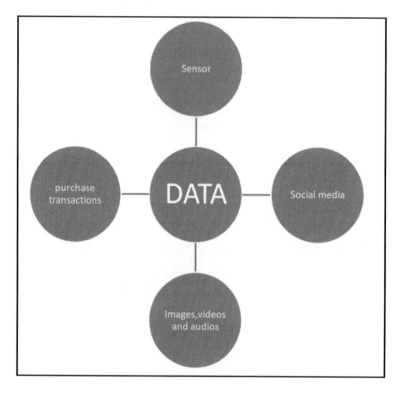

Functionally, gathering this large amount of structured and unstructured data can help organizations to:

- Reduce costs
- Improve operational efficiency and production performance
- Improve customer relationships
- Develop new products in a more informed way
- Accelerate and synchronize deliveries
- Formulate and respond to more in-depth requests
- Improve and simplify decision-making

All this is already the reality for many large companies. The challenge for the future is to make sure that even small companies as well as individuals can have access to resources that allow them to process data in a simple and functional way.

Thanks to data storage and cloud computing, the ability to memorize, aggregate, and combine data (and therefore to use the results to perform deep analysis) is gradually becoming more accessible. In other words, these services continue to reduce their costs and other technological barriers in the face of an increasingly performant and efficient service. For example, with cloud computing, highly scalable computing resources can be accessed through the internet, often at lower prices than those needed to install on their computers, as resources are shared among many users.

Data structuring

Every day, everywhere in the world, large volumes of data are generated by the different activities of man. Originally, these pieces of data are not structured as they come from sources of different natures. They therefore require an organization to be ready for use. Thus, the unstructured information collected must be processed according to specific requirements and subsequently stored as structured data. There are many forms of data structures, ranging from basic to advanced and complex, and their use is essential in the process of structuring data.

Data structuring consists of a set of linear or nonlinear operations performed on apparently random and unstructured data taken as input. These operations are intended to analyze the nature of the data and its importance. The system then divides the data into broad categories of information, as measured by the results of the analysis, and stores them or sends them for further analysis. This additional analysis can be used to subdivide the data into additional subcategories of nested categories. During the analysis, some data can also be considered useless and eventually discarded.

The result of this process is represented by structured data, which can be further analyzed or used directly to extract information not known until now. The shift from unstructured data to useful information is what the cycle of structuring and processing data is based on, and their success often determines the importance of data in a given field of application.

Data structuring is a methodology for organizing and archiving data so that it can be accessed and modified efficiently. In particular, a data structure consists of a collection of data values, in the relationships between them and in the functions or operations that can be applied to the data, as shown in the following diagram:

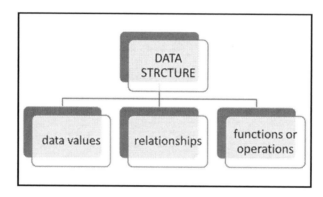

Over time, data has been organized in different ways, starting from very basic structures like arrays that are commonly used in programming languages, all the way to modern data structures that can take complex forms. Modern data structures are databases of different types that support a wide range of elaborations and extended operations, which allow easy manipulation, categorization, and sorting of data in many different ways.

Relational databases are the preferred data structure for many people because they have been widely used for many years. The term **database** indicates the set of data used in a specific information system, of a business, scientific, administrative, or some other type. A database consists of two different types of information, belonging to distinct levels of abstraction:

- Data, which represents the entities of the system to be modeled. The properties of these entities are described in terms of values (numeric, alphanumeric, and so on). The pieces of data are also grouped or classified into categories based on their common structure (for example, books, authors, and so on).
- Structures (metadata), which describe the common characteristics of various categories of data, such as names and types of property values.

A database must represent the different aspects of reality, and, in particular, in addition to the actual data, also the relationships between the data, that is, the logical connections among the various categories. For example, the association that binds each author to their books and vice versa must be represented. The database must also meet the following requirements:

- Data must be organized with minimal redundancy, that is, not be unnecessarily duplicated. This condition derives from the need to avoid not only the unnecessary use of storage resources, but also and above all the burden of managing multiple copies; furthermore, if the information relating to a category of data is duplicated, there is a risk that an update carried out on one of the copies and not shown on the others has negative consequences on the consistency and reliability of all data.
- Data must be usable at the same time by multiple users. This requirement derives from the previous point; the situation in which each user (or category of users) works on his own copy of the data is to be avoided, and there must be a single version of the data, to which all users can access; this implies the need for each type of user to have a specific view of the data and specific access rights to the data. Furthermore, techniques are necessary to prevent the activity of the various users from creating conflicts for the simultaneous use of the same data.
- Data must be permanent. This implies not only the use of mass memories, but also the application of techniques that preserve the set of data in case of malfunction of any component of the system.

The table is the fundamental data structure of a relational database. The tables represent the entities and relationships of the conceptual schema. It consists of records (rows or tuples) and fields (columns or attributes):

- Each record represents an instance (or occurrence or tuple) of the entity/relationship
- Each field represents an attribute of the entity/relationship

For each field a domain is identified (datatype): alphanumeric, numeric, date, Boolean, and so on.

The set of fields whose values uniquely identify a record within a table is called a **primary key**. When the primary key consists of only one field, it is called a **key field**. The following diagram shows an example of a primary key in a database:

PRIMARY KEY

ID	Surname	Name	Gender	City
1	Red	John	M	Boston
2	Black	Asia	F	Chicago
3	Blue	Mark	M	San Francisco

When a key field cannot be found between the attributes of an entity, a numeric ID field is defined that auto-increments (counter).

Referential integrity is a set of rules of the relational model that guarantees data integrity when relationships are associated with one another through the foreign key: these rules are used to validate associations between tables and to eliminate errors in inserting, deleting, or modifying linked data.

The index is relevant in a database. An index is a data structure designed to improve data search times. Fields in a table for which searches or join operations are required can be indexed. In the absence of an index, the search for the value of a field takes place sequentially on the records in the table. Indexes are automatically generated from the database for fields defined as keys.

Querying the database

So far we have seen how to move from unstructured information to structured information. In particular, we have learned that this operation requires a lot of resources. The need for properly structured data derives from the need to search for information in a database to extract knowledge.

Any **Database management system (DBMS)** provides a very powerful tool for consulting the contents of database tables: queries.

 A DBMS, is a software system designed to allow the creation, manipulation (by a DBA administrator) and the efficient query (by one or more client users) of databases, so also called a **database manager** or an **engine**, and hosted on a dedicated hardware architecture (server) or on a simple computer.

A query is a method for querying the database, that is, to display information extracted from the tables. For this purpose it is possible to perform several operations:

- Filter the data contained in a table according to various criteria
- Reassociate data contained in different tables
- Choose which fields to view
- Sort the result based on the values of some fields
- Group (aggregate) records that have the same values in a certain field

Queries can be executed to display the result only once, or they can be saved in the database to be executed several times. If you use a query again after changing the table, the query result returns the new table contents.

Suppose, for example, that you have a library database containing two tables:

- The Books table, represents the books in the catalog and contains the fields ID_Book (primary key), Title, Author, Year, Price, Publisher
- The Publisher table, represents the publishing houses with which the library has contacts and includes the fields Publishing House (primary key), City, Telephone

Think of wanting to define a query that shows the title and price of all books. This query will need to access the Books table and present the user with only the two fields chosen (Title and Price). In case the Books table contains 80 volumes, the query will display 80 Title and Price pairs in the result. If one of the records were deleted from the Books table, rerunning the already-defined query would result in only 79 Title and Price pairs, without having to intervene on the definition of the query.

SQL basics

At this point it is legitimate to ask the following question: *which language to use to formulate queries to a database?* We need a query language that is a language used to create queries on databases and information systems by users. It is used to make it possible to extract information from the database, through the relevant DBMS, querying the database, and then interfacing with the user and their service requests. The universally used query language is SQL.

SQL is a language for defining and manipulating data. As a manipulation language, SQL allows to select data of interest from the base and to update its content. The queries are used both in the SQL constructs of data definition and in those of updating the database.

SQL is a declarative language: it allows you to specify what to look for without saying how. When a query is executed by the query processor, it is translated into a procedural language inside the system which allows specifying how to access the data. There are generally several translations of a SQL query into the procedural language. The task of the query optimizer is to choose the most efficient execution plan.

A SQL query is performed on a database, then on a set of tables connected to one another by the mechanism of foreign keys. The result of a query is a table. We will introduce SQL by example, that is, showing increasingly rich and complex examples of interrogation.

To understand how SQL works, we analyze the table containing the number of visitors to Italian museums in the two years, as shown in the following screenshot:

	A	B	C	D	E
1	N	Museum	City	Visitors2016	Visitors2015
2	1	Colosseo e Foro Romano	ROMA	6408852	6551046
3	2	Scavi di Pompei	POMPEI	3283740	2934010
4	3	Galleria degli Uffizi	FIRENZE	2010631	1971758
5	4	Galleria dell'Accademia di Firenze	FIRENZE	1461185	1415397
6	5	Castel Sant'Angelo	ROMA	1234443	1047326
7	6	Venaria Reale	VENARIA R.	1012033	580786
8	7	Museo Egizio di Torino	TORINO	881463	863535
9	8	Circuito Museale Boboli …	FIRENZE	852095	772934
10	9	Reggia di Caserta	CASERTA	683070	497197
11	10	Galleria Borghese	ROMA	527937	506442
12					

This table in named **Museum**; the simplest interrogation that can be written is the following:

```
select *
from museum
```

The result is the entire museum table. The first line of the query is called `select` statement and is used to retrieves data from a database. The * operator allows us to select all columns. The second line of the query is called `from` statement and serves to indicate which tables to use. The `select` statement and that from are mandatory in a query. Pay close attention to the case, spacing, and logical separation of the components of each query by SQL keywords.

If we are interested only in the name and in the city of museums, we can select them in this way:

```
select Museum, City
from museum
```

The result is the following table:

Museum	City
Colosseo e Foro Romano	ROMA
Scavi di Pompei	POMPEI
Galleria degli Uffizi	FIRENZE
Galleria dell'Accademia di Firenze	FIRENZE
Castel Sant'Angelo	ROMA
Venaria Reale	VENARIA R.

Museo Egizio di Torino	TORINO
Circuito Museale Boboli…	FIRENZE
Reggia di Caserta	CASERTA
Galleria Borghese	ROMA

To clarify the difference between database tables and SQL tables, we see a simple query that generates a table with two columns with the same name:

```
select Museum, Museum
from museum
```

The result is the following table:

Museum	Museum
Colosseo e Foro Romano	Colosseo e Foro Romano
Scavi di Pompei	Scavi di Pompei
Galleria degli Uffizi	Galleria degli Uffizi
Galleria dell'Accademia di Firenze	Galleria dell'Accademia di Firenze
Castel Sant'Angelo	Castel Sant'Angelo
Venaria Reale	Venaria Reale
Museo Egizio di Torino	Museo Egizio di Torino
Circuito Museale Boboli …	Circuito Museale Boboli …
Reggia di Caserta	Reggia di Caserta
Galleria Borghese	Galleria Borghese

A SQL table can contain duplicate rows and columns of the same name. The columns are uniquely identified by their position. This is true for the tables resulting from the queries. The database tables, that is, those that are part of the database, cannot have columns of the same name.

Furthermore, we show a simple query that generates a table with equal rows:

```
select city
from museum
```

The result is the following table:

City
ROMA
POMPEI
FIRENZE
FIRENZE
ROMA
VENARIA R.
TORINO
FIRENZE
CASERTA
ROMA

Also, you can specify the `distinct` keyword after the `select` keyword to eliminate duplicates:

```
select distinct city
from museum
```

The result is the following table:

City
ROMA
POMPEI
FIRENZE
VENARIA R.
TORINO
CASERTA

Now let's introduce the `where` clause:

```
select Museum,City
from museum
where City = 'Rome'
```

The result is the following table:

Museum	City
Colosseo e Foro Romano	ROMA
Castel Sant'Angelo	ROMA
Galleria Borghese	ROMA

If you ever want to find a particular item or group of items in your database, you need one or more conditions. Conditions are contained in the `where` clause. For example, to find museums that in 2016 registered a number of visitors over one million, we will have to write:

```
select Museum, City, Visitors_2016
from museum
where Visitors_2016 >= 1000000
```

The result is the following table:

Museum	City	Visitors_2016
Colosseo e Foro Romano	ROMA	6408852
Scavi di Pompei	POMPEI	3283740
Galleria degli Uffizi	FIRENZE	2010631
Galleria dell'Accademia di Firenze	FIRENZE	1461185
Castel Sant'Angelo	ROMA	1234443
Venaria Reale	VENARIA R.	1012033

In this series of examples we have learned to correctly formulate queries to a database using the SQL language. As we have seen, using SQL is extremely simple. In the following table the some of the most important SQL commands are listed:

Command	Brief description
SELECT	Extracts data from a database
UPDATE	Updates data in a database
DELETE	Deletes data from a database
INSERT INTO	Inserts new data into a database
CREATE DATABASE	Creates a new database
ALTER DATABASE	Modifies a database
CREATE TABLE	Creates a new table
ALTER TABLE	Modifies a table
DROP TABLE	Deletes a table
CREATE INDEX	Creates an index (search key)
DROP INDEX	Deletes an index

We will now address other SQL queries so we can acquire further skills.

Google BigQuery

Data represents a fundamental factor for the management and growth of companies. Ensuring that data is protected, available and easily accessible is a fundamental requirement of any IT department. More importantly, another requirement is to ensure that data is used in the correct way: to manage processes, to inform decision makers, and to intervene intelligently in changing circumstances.

The way companies ensure data availability is rapidly changing. Cloud computing has seen impressive growth in recent years, both as a concept and as a practical component of the IT infrastructure.

Cloud computing is a technology that allows the use, via remote server, of software and hardware resources (such as mass storage for data storage), whose use is offered as a service by a provider, specifically by subscription.

A particularly interesting Cloud computing solution is Google BigQuery. BigQuery, is a web service designed to allow you to perform queries on large datasets; for example, it is able to perform selection and aggregation queries on tables with billions of records in a few seconds, so it would be a good step forward to obtain in an interactive way information that previously took days to be calculated.

BigQuery enables companies and developers around the world to manage large amounts of data in real time, without the support of any hardware or software investment. The service provided by Google is useful if, for example, a large multinational company has to optimize its daily spending based on sales and advertising data, but even if a small online retailer has to change the presentation of a product based on the user clicks. The system, as stated by the producers themselves, also aims to help many companies fight the prevailing world economic crisis.

By making BigQuery a public service, Google claims to have reached an important milestone in the effort to make Big data analytics accessible to all businesses through the Cloud service. BigQuery is accessible through a simple user interface that allows you to take advantage of the power of calculation offered by Google. The collected data is protected on multiple levels of security, replicated in multiple servers and can be easily exported. Developers and businesses can subscribe online to the service and take advantage of 100 GB of data per month for free.

The main features of BigQuery are:

- **Scalability**: One of the inherent advantages of Cloud computing is the ability to expand the infrastructure on demand, ensuring a dynamic scalability of application capacity based on the increase in needs. This is particularly useful when the peak usage level of hosted applications changes consistently with the passage of time.
- **Interactivity**: Manages to perform selection or group queries on billions of records in a matter of seconds.
- **Familiarity**: Uses an SQL dialect for writing queries.

It also allows a good sharing of data, the use of Google Storage allows you to create a collaboration hub. Whenever the need arises to share their data with other users it is possible to give access to the information available to those who want to appropriately by setting up the **access control list** (**ACL**).

An ACL is a mechanism used to express complex rules that determine whether some of the IT system's resources are accessed by its users.

BigQuery contains methods that allow both to create, populate, and delete tables, and to query above them. Writing queries in BigQuery is possible using a SQL dialect; in this dialect, some SQL methods have been modified to speed up the execution of some queries; in those cases, where the precision of the results is not essential, they are based on statistical estimates and return an indicative value.

BigQuery basics

BigQuery is the data warehouse of Google Analytics. It is basically a fully managed, petabyte and low-cost tool. BigQuery is NoOps: the term **NoOps** (short for **no operation**) identifies an IT environment so automated and abstracted from the underlying infrastructure that does not require a dedicated team to manage the software internally. In fact, in BigQuery there is no infrastructure to manage and a database administrator is not required. The time saved can be used to analyze data in order to find meaningful information. To form queries in BigQuery we can use a familiar SQL syntax, very simple to learn, and extremely effective. But the real convenience in using this technology comes from the actual savings due to the pay-as-you-go model that allows us to pay only for the actual use of the resources needed to perform a specific analysis.

To access BigQuery we can essentially use three modes:

- Using a graphical web UI
- Using a command-line tool
- Using API or client libraries

In this chapter, we will only analyze the operation of BigQuery through a graphical interface.

Using a graphical web UI

BigQuery can be accessed through a web graphical user interface that can be used to load and export data, perform queries, and perform other user and management tasks in the browser. The web user interface can be run in any browser, even if Google recommends using Chrome web browser as it produces maximum performance.

To access BigQuery via web UI, go to the following link:
`https://bigquery.cloud.google.com`

Once you have logged in, you will see the BigQuery console as shown in the following screenshot:

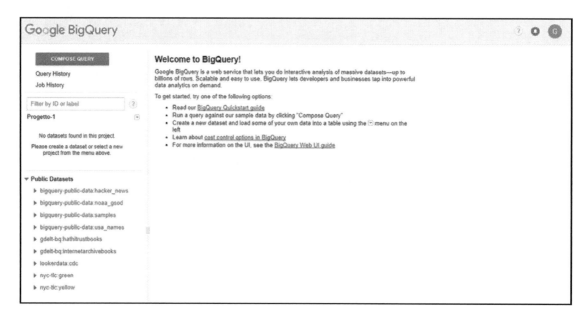

In the BigQuery console a welcome message is displayed. In it, various activities are proposed to us:

- Read the **BigQuery Quickstart guide**
- Run a query—on sample data already available to practice—by clicking **"Compose Query"**
- Create a new dataset and load data into a table using the menu on the left
- Discover the **cost control options in BigQuery**
- Finally, refer to the BigQuery web user interface guide for more information about the user interface

To analyze in detail the BigQuery console, we will choose the second option, then click on the **COMPOSE QUERY** button at the top left. In this way, the window shown in the following screenshot is displayed:

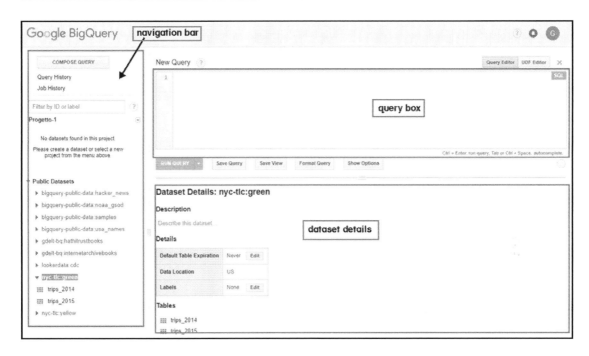

In the previous screenshot two main sections are highlighted:

- **Navigation bar**: Starting from the top, it contains a list of elements that describes what action you want to perform: compose a query, consult the query history, or consult the job history. Continuing down, we can identify a list of datasets in the current project that has read access, plus a public dataset called **public data**. This list shows a series of public databases made available to us for practicing. To be able to use this data, just click on the icon of the dataset expansion next to any dataset or the name of the dataset, so the link will be extended and we will be able to view the tables within that dataset.

- **Query box**: Represents a box where you can type a query in the SQL syntax. This is the main part of the window as it represents the place where we formulate our queries. As anticipated in order to formulate a query it is necessary to use the SQL syntax that we have at least partly seen in the previous sections. Of course, in the examples that we will propose we will have the opportunity to deepen the topic. After correctly formulating the query to execute it, just click on the **Run Query** button at the bottom of the query box.

- **Dataset details**: Represents the section that contains a summary of the data we have selected in the navigation bar. The name of the dataset, a brief description of its content, a series of details, and finally the tables contained in the dataset are proposed. To get a preview of the contents of a single table, simply click on the table name.

Let's take an example to understand the ease of use of the BigQuery console. We use one of the public datasets available:

`bigquery-public-data.new_york.tlc_yellow_trips_2015.`

This dataset is collected by the NYC **Taxi and Limousine Commission** (**TLC**) and includes trip records from all trips completed by yellow and green taxis in New York City from 2009 to present, and all trips in **for-hire vehicles** (**FHV**) from 2015 to present. Records include fields capturing pick-up and drop-off dates/times, pick-up and drop-off locations, trip distances, itemized fares, rate types, payment types, and driver-reported passenger counts.

In the following table are listed the several fields contained in the dataset with a brief description of the content:

Field name	Brief description
vendor_id	A code indicating the TPEP provider that provided the record. *1=Creative Mobile Technologies, LLC; 2=VeriFone Inc.*
pickup_datetime	The date and time when the meter was engaged.
dropoff_datetime	The date and time when the meter was disengaged.
passenger_count	The number of passengers in the vehicle. This is a driver-entered value.
trip_distance	The elapsed trip distance in miles reported by the taximeter.
pickup_longitude	Longitude where the meter was engaged.
pickup_latitude	Latitude where the meter was engaged.
rate_code	The final rate code in effect at the end of the trip. *1=Standard rate, 2=JFK, 3=Newark, 4=Nassau* or *Westchester, 5=Negotiated fare, 6=Group ride.*

store_and_fwd_flag	This flag indicates whether the trip record was held in the vehicle's memory before sending to the vendor, also known as **store and forward**, because the vehicle did not have a connection to the server. *Y=store and forward trip; N=not a store and forward trip.*
dropoff_longitude	Longitude where the meter was disengaged.
dropoff_latitude	Latitude where the meter was disengaged.
payment_type	A numeric code signifying how the passenger paid for the trip. *1=Credit card, 2=Cash, 3=No charge, 4=Dispute, 5=Unknown, 6=Voided trip.*
fare_amount	The time-and-distance fare calculated by the meter.
extra	Miscellaneous extras and surcharges. Currently, this only includes the $0.50 and $1 rush hour and overnight charges.
mta_tax	$0.50 MTA tax that is automatically triggered based on the metered rate in use.
tip_amount	Tip amount—this field is automatically populated for credit card tips. Cash tips are not included.
tolls_amount	Total amount of all tolls paid in trip.
imp_surcharge	$0.30 improvement surcharge assessed trips at the flag drop. The improvement surcharge began being levied in 2015.
total_amount	The total amount charged to passengers. Does not include cash tips.

To start, let's formulate a simple query to the database. *How many trips did Yellow taxis take each month in 2015?* This query must return monthly trip totals for all Yellow taxis in 2015. Someone may think that we are starting with operations that are too simple; in fact, it seems trivial to count the taxi calls made each month. This is true for most small cities but not for a metropolis like New York. In fact, we are talking about a database of dimensions equal to 18.1 GB and with a number of observations equal to 146,112,989.

Let's see then the SQL code to insert into the query box:

```
#standardSQL
SELECT
  TIMESTAMP_TRUNC(pickup_datetime,
      MONTH) month,
   COUNT(*) trips
FROM
   `bigquery-public-data.new_york.tlc_yellow_trips_2015`
GROUP BY
   1
ORDER BY
   1
```

Let's explain it line by line to understand the meaning of each command used. Let's start from the first line:

```
#standardSQL
```

The first line is inserted to let BigQuery know you want to use SQL standard. We can enable standard SQL for a query, so you do not have to insert this tag into your SQL. To do so, just click on the **Show Options** button located immediately below the query box. In the section that opens uncheck the **Use Legacy SQL** checkbox. Let's move forward in the analysis of the query:

```
SELECT
  TIMESTAMP_TRUNC(pickup_datetime, MONTH) month,
   COUNT(*) trips
```

In this piece of code we use the SELECT statement, which as already anticipated in the previous sections, retrieves data from a database. In the first part of the statement, you specify which data to retrieve. We have said that the number of trips for each month is in us. To do this we will count the number of lines for each month. Recall that each line in the database corresponds to a trip. The field containing this information is pickup_datetime. To return the data in an easily readable format, we used the TIMESTAMP_TRUNC function which truncates to TIMESTAMP value (the return value is of type TIMESTAMP). Then, we use the count () function that returns the number of rows that match a specified criteria. Let's move forward:

```
FROM
   `bigquery-public-data.new_york.tlc_yellow_trips_2015`
```

With the FROM clause, we select the table in which to search. Finally the last two lines:

```
GROUP BY
  1
ORDER BY
  1
```

These lines have been inserted to group and sort the data. The results are shown in the following table:

Row	month	trips
1	2015-01-01 00:00:00.000 UTC	12748986
2	2015-02-01 00:00:00.000 UTC	12450521
3	2015-03-01 00:00:00.000 UTC	13351609
4	2015-04-01 00:00:00.000 UTC	13071789
5	2015-05-01 00:00:00.000 UTC	13158262
6	2015-06-01 00:00:00.000 UTC	12324935
7	2015-07-01 00:00:00.000 UTC	11562783
8	2015-08-01 00:00:00.000 UTC	11130304
9	2015-09-01 00:00:00.000 UTC	11225063
10	2015-10-01 00:00:00.000 UTC	12315488
11	2015-11-01 00:00:00.000 UTC	11312676
12	2015-12-01 00:00:00.000 UTC	11460573

As you can see, the number of trips in each month ranges from a minimum of 11,130,304 to a maximum of 13,351,609. The following screenshot shows the results in the BigQuery console:

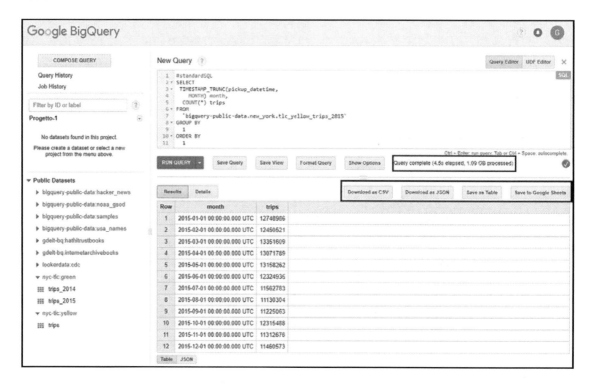

In the previous screenshot two details are highlighted:

- A report on calculation times and data processed
- A series of results storage options

In the first case, BigQuery tells us that to complete the operation, the Google resources have been committed to 4.5 s, and that 1.09 GB of data was processed during this time. This information will be useful for calculating the cost of the transaction.

In the previous image we highlighted the available storage options. Four options are offered to us:

- Download as CSV
- Download as JSON
- Save as table
- Save to Google Sheets

If you recall, the JSON syntax is a subset of the JavaScript syntax, while Google Sheets is an online spreadsheet app that lets users create and format spreadsheets and simultaneously work with other people.

In the previous screenshot, it is possible to notice that at the top of the results there are two tabs: **Results** and **Details**. So far, we have seen what is returned in the **Results** tab; let's see what we see if we click on the **Details** tab instead. A series of statistics on the operation performed are returned to us, as shown in the following:

```
Job ID    progetto-1-191608:bquijob_1d181029_1614bc7198f
Creation Time  Jan 31, 2018, 11:33:14 AM
Start Time     Jan 31, 2018, 11:33:15 AM
End Time Jan 31, 2018, 11:33:18 AM
User      xxxxxx@gmail.com
Bytes Processed     1.09 GB
Bytes Billed   1.09 GB
Slot Time (ms) 153 K
Destination Table
progetto-1-191608:_b6e2bd761c7590ee099d343a7b87889c01400431.anond9ac14f20bd
65f3658af2aa65b7b8847b7d677be
Use Legacy SQL false
```

This information refers once again to the query we performed and to the results obtained.

Visualizing data with Google Data Studio

Google Data Studio is a **FREE** tool that allows us to create captivating reports quickly and easily. We can finally say goodbye to redundant and confusing data sheets. With Data Studio, in fact, besides being able to insert simple tables, it is possible to attach customizable graphics with various colors and fonts that will be easily understandable. With Google Data Studio, sharing reports is even easier as it is a Google Drive application and works similarly.

The most important news for companies (but also, if not above all, for customers) lies in the extremely intuitive interface. To keep everything under control, moreover, Google gives the possibility to change the date range (at the report or chart level).

In a few clicks, in fact, you can realize the progress of the site almost in real time. Data Studio is useful for two types of users:

- **Who creates the reports**: Analysis and marketing employees
- **Who will read the reports**: Customers and CEOs of companies

Google Data Studio, currently available in beta, allows you to create dynamic reports and dashboards with a strong visual impact. With Data Studio it is possible to:

- Easily connect to different data sources
- View your data with dynamic, interactive, and eye-catching reports and dashboards
- Share and collaborate with others, following the logic in use on Google Drive

To view a report with Data Studio, the following requirements must be met:

- All you need is a web browser (the ones tested are: Chrome, Firefox, and Safari).
- You do not need a Google account.

While to create reports and data sources, the following requirements must be met:

- You need to be logged in to a Google account
- You need to be in one of the supported countries (in other words, all countries bar these: the People's Republic of China, Russia, Svalbard Islands and Jan Mayen, Iran, Iraq, Crimea, North Korea, Syria, Cuba)
- You need to be able to use Google Drive

Data sources use pipelines to secure datasets called **connectors**. When Data Studio first connects to a specific type of dataset, such as Google Analytics or AdWords, you are asked for permission to connect, which can be removed at any time. At this point, to connect to a certain type of dataset, for example, for Google Analytics, you can connect to only one account, one property and one view; for AdWords, you connect to an administrator or standard account; for BigQuery, you provide a project and a table or a custom query, and so on.

Creating reports in Data Studio

To start, let's see what are the first steps to be done to immediately create a report in Data Studio. To be able to use Data Studio, it is not necessary to fill in any registration form; you just need to have an active Google account. If you've already signed into your Google Account, just type the following URL in a browser: `https://datastudio.google.com/`.

This will take you directly to the Data Studio home page, as shown in the following screenshot:

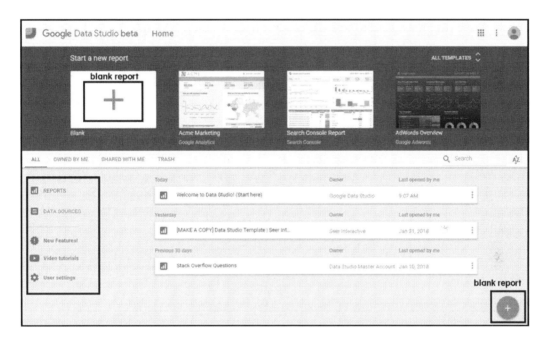

Once you have viewed the main page of Data Studio we can identify some sections that will help us to create our reports (in the previous screenshot they are highlighted). To start getting comfortable with the Data Studio interface we can consult some built-in templates to start already available. You can choose an existing model and modify it or simply start with a new blank report.

Clicking on the **All models** drop-down menu displays all the built-in templates. In this way we can choose any model that matches our needs and modify it using the available editor, in order to adapt it to our needs. Predefined templates are useful to get started or for those who have little time to spend on formatting settings. In fact, in these models the functionalities are already ready for use, thus saving a lot of time.

To understand effectively how to use Data Studio we will start from an empty report, in order to explain all the steps necessary to create a report. There are two ways to start with a new report:

- Click on the empty plus (+) page on the horizontal header (blank)
- Click on the (+) icon in the lower right corner

Both options are clearly highlighted in the previous figure, and in both cases the window that shows in the following screen is displayed:

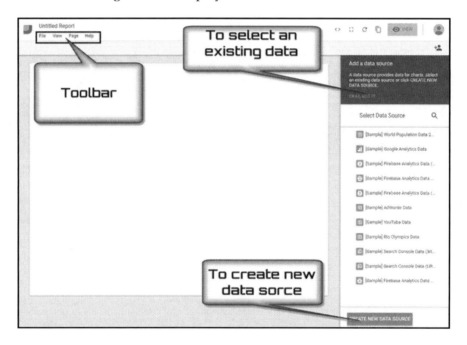

This displays the report editor with all the controls and elements needed to add charts and data, and to choose the style of your report. Initially, the new report has a default name (Untitled Report) at the top left of the screen, so just click on it and we will enter a new name for the report (First Report).

The first thing to do is to add a data source to the report. To do this we have two options again:

- An existing data source
- Create new data source

In the previous screenshot, the two areas in which the options can be activated are highlighted. It is possible to notice that data sources proposed by exercise are already available at the bottom of the data source selector. On this occasion, we will refer to these resources. For example, to select the first item that refers to `[Sample] World Population Data 2005-2014`, just click on it. This dataset contains the world population data from 2005 to 2014. In this case the window shown in the following screenshot will be displayed:

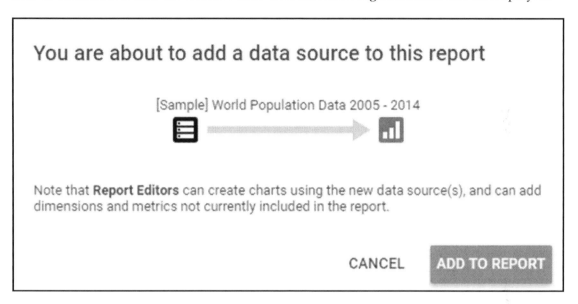

After clicking on the **ADD TO REPORT** button, the main window of Data Studio is enriched with new components:

- **Menu Bar**: This allows you to access many other menu functions by right-clicking on a component.
- **Toolbar**: This allows you to choose among various tools, pages, and control options. This toolbar is divided into five sections.
- **Layout and Theme properties panel**: We can control the way your report appears on the viewer's screen using the options in this panel. This is the default properties panel; it appears when no other component is selected.

In the following screenshot, you can see the new aspect of the Report Figure:

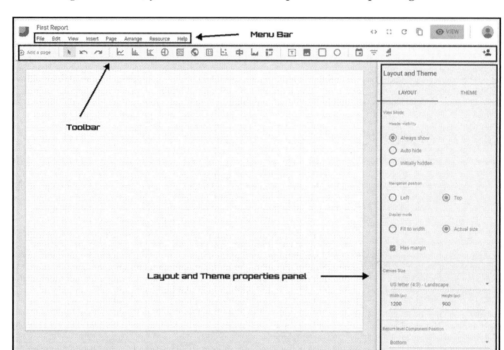

To add a chart to the page in our empty report, just click on one of the icons in the toolbar. For example, to add a bar chart of the world population from 2005 until 2014 will suffice:

1. Click on the second icon in the third area of the toolbar (Bar chart)
2. Position the viewfinder at the point on the page where you want the graph to be shown
3. Draw the graph under the title, to move it just click and drag it, or select it, and use the arrow keys on the keyboard

Once this is done, the bar chart of our data will appear in the main area and the **Layout** and **Theme** properties panel on the right will give way to the bar chart properties panel, as shown in the following screenshot:

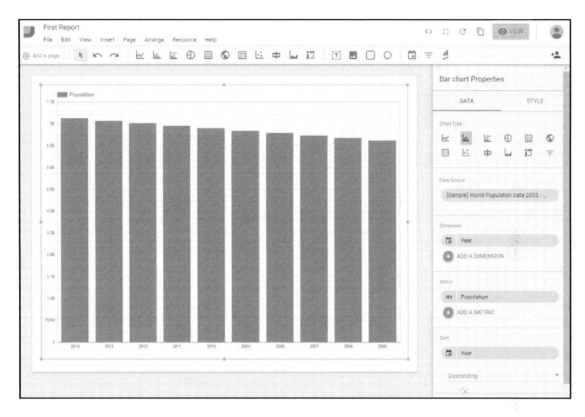

The bar chart properties panel becomes essential to make changes to the chart just added to our report. We can in fact change the type of chart, change the data source, add another dimension, add a new metric, and change the sorting of the data.

Data Studio does not allow the entire dashboard or multiple reports in a `.pdf` or other format. Although it is possible to export a single table or chart in a CSV format. To export a chart or a table:

- Click on the **View** tab at the top right to view the reports in view mode
- Hover over the graph or report you want to export
- Right click and select **Export CSV**

To export a whole dashboard as a PDF, there is not any internal functionality added yet that will help you export reports as `.pdf`. But by using a chrome extension you can do this very easily (Google Data Studio PDF Export). An alternative way of exporting a report to PDF is to print to PDF via your browser. You would have to do that for each report page.

Summary

In this chapter, an introduction of the BigQuery and Data Studio platform to manage and view data are proposed. To start, we explored the big data and the problems associated with managing large amounts of data. Then we analyzed how to organize data in a structured format to correctly query databases.

After this, you were introduced to SQL. SQL is a language for defining and manipulating data. As a manipulation language, SQL allows to select data of interest from the base and to update its content. The queries are used both in the SQL constructs of data definition and in those of updating the database.

Then a Google BigQuery introduction was performed. BigQuery is a web service that enables interactive analysis of massively large datasets. BigQuery enables companies and developers around the world to manage large amounts of data in real time, without the support of any hardware or software investment.

Finally, we have analyzed how to create reports from our data using Google Data Studio. Google Data Studio is a FREE tool that allows us to create captivating reports quickly and easily. With Data Studio, besides being able to insert simple tables, it is possible to attach customizable graphics with various colors and fonts that will be easily understandable.

In the next chapter, we will we present Dataprep a services useful to pre-process the data, extract features and clean up the records, and Dataflow a service to implement streaming and batch processing.

Transforming Your Data 5

Real-world datasets are very varied: variables can be textual, numerical, or categorical, and observations can be missing, false, or wrong (outliers). To perform a proper data analysis, we will understand how to correctly parse data, clean it, and create an output matrix optimally built for machine learning analysis. To extract knowledge, it is essential that the reader is able to create an observation matrix using different techniques of data analysis and cleaning.

In this chapter, we'll present Cloud Dataprep, a service useful to preprocess the data, extract features, and clean up the records. We'll also cover Cloud Dataflow, a service to implement streaming and batch processing. We'll go into some practical details with real-life examples. We'll start from discovering different ways to transform data and the degree of cleaning data. We will analyze the techniques available for preparing the most suitable data for analysis and modeling, which includes imputation of missing data, detecting and eliminating outliers, and adding derived variables. Then we will learn how to normalize the data, in which data units are eliminated, allowing us to easily compare data from different locations.

In this chapter, we will be covering the following topics:

- Different ways to transform data
- How to organize data
- Dealing with missing data
- Detecting outliers
- Data normalization

At the end of the chapter, we will be able to perform data preparation so that its information content is best exposed to the regression tools. We'll learn how to apply transforming methods to our own data and how these techniques work. We'll discover how to clean the data, identify missing data, and work with outliers and missing entries. We'll also learn how to use normalization techniques to compare data from different locations.

How to clean and prepare the data

A novice may think that once we complete collecting data and it is imported into Google Cloud, it is finally time to start the analysis process. Conversely, we must first proceed with the preparation of data (data wrangling).

 Data wrangling is the process of the transformation and mapping of data, turning raw data into formatted data, with the intent of making it more appropriate for subsequent analysis operations.

This process can take a long time and it is very cumbersome, in some cases taking up about 80 percent of the entire data analysis process.

However, it is a fundamental prerequisite for the rest of the data analysis workflow; so it is essential to acquire the best practices in such techniques. Before submitting our data to any machine learning algorithm, we must be able to evaluate the quality and accuracy of our observations. If we do not know how to switch from raw data to something that can be analyzed, we cannot go ahead.

Google Cloud Dataprep

For proper preparation of our data, it is necessary to perform a series of operations involving the use of different algorithms. As we have anticipated, this work can take a long time and uses many resources. Google, within the Cloud service, offers the ability to do this job in a simple and immediate way: Google Cloud Dataprep.

It is an intelligent data service that allows you to visually explore, clean up, and prepare for structured and unstructured data analysis. Google Cloud Dataprep is serverless and works on any scale. It is not necessary to distribute or manage any infrastructure.

Google Cloud Dataprep helps to quickly prepare data for immediate analysis or for training machine learning models. Normally, the data has to be manually cleaned up; however, Google Cloud Dataprep makes the process extremely simple by automatically detecting schemas, types, joins, and anomalies such as missing values. With regard to machine learning, different ways of data cleaning are suggested that can make the process of data preparation quicker and less prone to errors.

In Google Cloud Dataprep, it is possible to define data preparation rules by interacting with a sample of the data. Use of the application is free. Once a data preparation flow has been defined, you can export the sample for free or run the stream as a Cloud Dataprep job, which will be subject to additional costs.

With the use of Google Cloud Dataprep, you can perform the following operations:

- Import data from different sources
- Identify and remove or modify missing data
- Identify anomalous values (outliers)
- Perform searches from a dataset
- Normalize the values in the fields in the dataset
- Merge datasets with joins
- Add one dataset to another through merge operations

These operations can be performed without the need for technological infrastructure in a very short time.

Exploring Dataprep console

The first time you log into the Google Cloud Dataprep console, you will be asked to accept the terms of service, log into your Google account, and choose a cloud storage bucket to use with Cloud Dataprep. You will also be asked to allow Trifacta, the third-party application host, to access project data. After completing these steps, you will be offered the Cloud Dataprep home page with the **Flows** screen opened, as shown in the following screenshot:

For now, the console appears empty because we have not yet performed any operation; it will later be populated by our operations. At the top of the Google Cloud Dataprep console, you can find three links that open the following pages:

- **FLOWS**: This page shows the flows you have access to and allows you to create, review, and manage them. A flow is an object that allows us to gather and organize datasets to generate results.
- **DATASETS**: In this page, we can review the import and reference datasets to which we have access.
- **JOBS**: In this page, we can track the status of all of our running, complete, or failed jobs.

By default, a **Flows** page is open. To create a new flow, click on the **Create Flow** button. The following window opens, where we can set a name and description for the new flow:

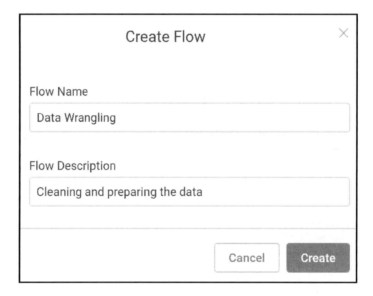

After we have done this, on the flows page, the new flow just created appears with suggestions of datasets that can be added to this flow to start wrangling. To analyze how a Google Cloud Dataprep example works, we will use a specially designed file that contains the data for a small sample of observation; it lists the results of a test. We'll grab `CleaningData.csv`, a spreadsheet that contains some of the issues we just listed. After correctly identifying this file on our computer and having it uploaded, the following window will be displayed (transformer page):

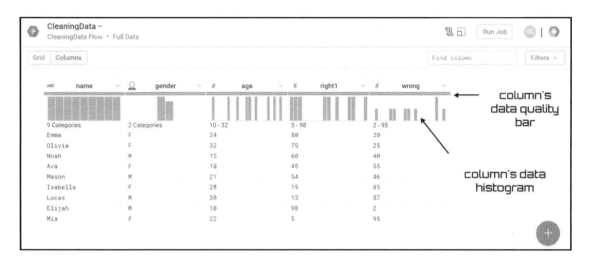

In this page, we can easily identify the data we have imported. At this point, we can program the transformations that we want to apply to this data. Once we have established what we want to do, we can immediately preview the results before making changes to the entire final dataset.

In the Transformer page, two panels are available: **Grid** and **Columns**. By default, the Transformer page displays the grid panel, in which the previews of the columns in a columnar grid are displayed. In the columns panel, additional statistical information on individual columns is returned. This panel is particularly useful for managing anomalous values, to review average, minimum, and maximum values.

From a first glance at the transformer page, you can get an idea of the data we have imported. In fact, we can view all fields and all observations.

Here, we have uploaded a file with just a few fields and observations. More generally, in the lower left part, we are given a summary of the number of rows, columns, and data types.

From the analysis of the returned window, we can extract useful information. Start from the name of each column, to the left of which appears a symbol that identifies the type of data automatically attributed to it. In this way we can verify that Dataprep has cataloged the variables as follows:

- name: Name (String)
- gender: Sex (Gender)
- age: Age (Integer)

- `right1`: Percentage of right answers (Integer)
- `wrong`: Percentage of wrong answers (Integer)

It seems that the attribution of the data type is correct. This information is returned to us using the cursor. In fact, as you move the cursor around the page, the cursor changes when it is over a selected data element. Immediately down the column header, there are useful summary graphs. In the column's data quality bar, the categories of values are shown. The following three types of values are available:

- Valid
- Mismatched
- Missing

Then, histograms are shown to provide us with statistics about the data contained in each column. Further information is returned to us by passing the cursor over it.

Since the values are few, we can also have a preview of all the data. Let's take a look to visually identify anomalies. Already, we can see that the age variable has one missing value. Missing values of any type of variable are indicated by the NA code, which means not available. The **Not a Number (NaN)** code, on the other hand, indicates invalid numeric values, such as a numeric value divided by zero. If a variable contains missing values, GCP cannot apply some functions to it. For this reason, it is necessary to process the missing values in advance.

On the transformation page, you can see that when you hover your mouse over the areas and related panels, a light bulb icon appears next to the cursor to indicate that suggestions are available.

On the left of each column header, you can see a drop-down column menu. With the help of this menu, we can perform several actions on the column data such as changing its data type, depending on the column data type. The following actions are available:

- **Rename**: Rename the column
- **Change type**: Change the data type of the column
- **Move**: Move the column to the beginning or end, or to a specified location in the dataset
- **Edit column**: Perform a series of edits to the column
- **Column Details**: Explore the interactive profile of the column details

- **Show related steps**: Highlight steps in the **Recipe** panel where the selected column is referenced
- **Find**: Find and replace specific values or extract patterned values from the column
- **Filter**: Filter the rows of the dataset based on literal or computed values from the column
- **Clean**: Clean the mismatched or missing values in the column, replacing values with fixed or computed values or removing the rows altogether
- **Formula**: Generate a new column containing the values computed from the source column based on the selected function
- **Aggregate**: Generate a summary table based on computations aggregated across groups, or add summary data as a new column in the current table
- **Restructure**: Change the structure of the dataset based on the values of the column
- **Lookup**: Perform a lookup of the column values against a set of values in another column of another dataset
- **Delete**: Remove the column from the dataset

The following screenshot shows the **Column** menu for the gender column:

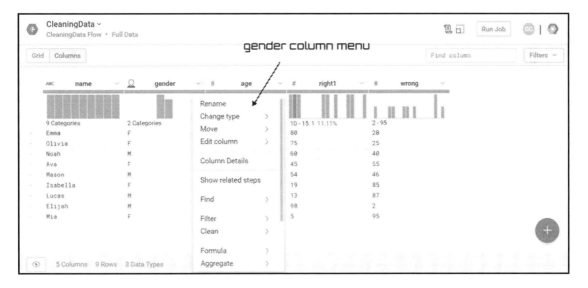

When selecting a column, a new suggestion panel opens to the right of the Transformer page. This panel shows a series of suggestions relevant to the type of data contained in the specific column. Suggestions vary depending on the selected data. By hovering over any of the suggestions, you can preview the results in the data grid to ensure that the proposed transformation works for the dataset. In the next section, we will be able to expand the use of the suggestion panel.

Removing empty cells

From a visual analysis of the imported data, we detect an empty cell at the third row and second column; this indicates the presence of a missing value. It is necessary to eliminate this anomaly before you can analyze the dataset.

In this case, identifying the empty cell was particularly easy given the small amount of data; in the case of large datasets, visual analysis does not work. Therefore, to identify missing values, we can analyze the data quality bar. Here, the missing values are identified in black.

To get a preview on the number of missing data, we can move our cursor over the black part of the data quality bar; the number of missing data is returned, as shown in the following screenshot:

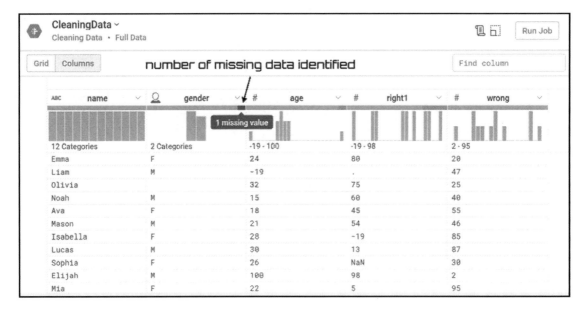

We have confirmed the presence of a missing value in the gender field. Recall that a missing value is a value that contains no content or is non-existent. These missing values may be due to a series of occurrences:

- Errors in the creation of the dataset; the values have been entered incorrectly, leaving empty cells
- The dataset contains fields created automatically with cells that do not contain values
- The result of an impossible calculation

Now, if we select the **gender** column, a new suggestion panel opens to the right of the Transformer page. As stated in the previous section, this panel shows a series of suggestions relevant to the type of data contained in the specific column. Several suggestions are proposed:

- Delete columns
- Rename
- Aggregate and group data
- Create a new column
- Set
- Values to columns

When we hover over different suggestions, a mini-preview appears to the left of each suggestion, as shown in the following screenshot:

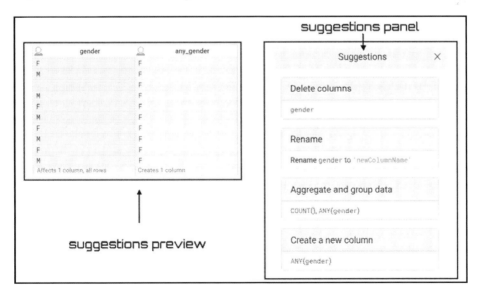

In the suggestion panel, a specific text called **missing value to** appears, meaning that the missing values identified in the column can be replaced with something else. By clicking on the Set item, two buttons appear: **Edit** and **Add**. By clicking on the **Edit** button a new box is opened; a new formula is proposed in this box as follows:

```
ifmissing($col, '')
```

The missing function writes out a specified value if the source value is a null or missing value. Upon inserting the NA string between the quotation marks, every time a missing value is identified in the column, it will be replaced by the NA value. After having modified the formula, we will be able to see a preview of the column in real time as modified by the formula applied; this is shown in the following screenshot:

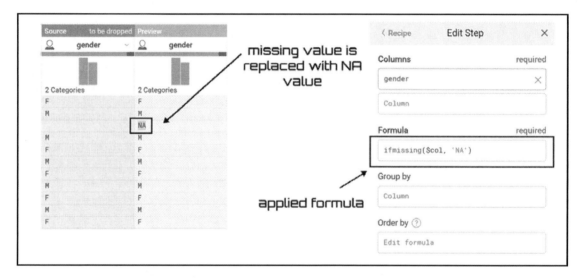

Now, to apply this suggestion, just click on the **Add** button in the suggestions panel. In this way, a new step will be added to the **Recipe** panel.

Note that the **Recipe** panel allows us to review and modify the steps of the recipe we have created so far, but, at the same time, it allows us to add new ones. If the panel is not displayed, to make it appear, just click on the icon (**Recipe**) at the top left of the **Run Job** button.

To generate a new set of suggestions on different columns, click on **Cancel**. Then, select a different set of columns or values within a column; in this way, a new suggestions panel will be opened.

Replacing incorrect values

The next step will allow us to replace the incorrect value indicators. If we take a look at the data again, we will see that in the age column, the value -19 is displayed. That's obviously an incorrect value since for that variable, permissible values are greater than zero (this is an age):

```
24 -19 32 15 18 21 28 30 26 100 22 NA
```

We can replace this value with the missing value indicator, NA. To do this, we will write the following formula in the set suggestions:

```
IF($col<0, 'NA',$col)
```

A new step will be added to the **Recipe** panel immediately after the one created in the previous section. At the same time, we can see a preview of the changes made on the dataset. The incorrect value is no longer present; in its place, there is a further NA value.

The same result can be obtained by operating directly in the **Recipe** panel:

1. Remember that to open the **Recipe** panel, you can just click on the icon (**Recipe**) at the top left of the **Run Job** button
2. Click on the **New Step** button; the Transform Builder is opened
3. In the **Transformation** drop-down menu, select **Apply formula** in the list of available transforms
4. Specify the **Columns** (**age**)
5. Edit the formula required in the **Formula** box
6. Click on the **Add** button
7. A new step is added to the **Recipe** panel

In the following screenshot, we can see the Transform Builder:

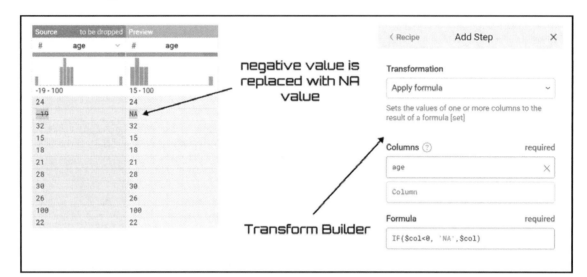

The result obtained is identical to the result we obtained by writing the formula in the set suggestions; even in this case, a negative value will no longer be present in the age column.

Mismatched values

A mismatched value is any value that seems to be of a different data type than the type specified for the column. In the database we are analyzing at this point, there are several values that seem to deviate from the type attributed to the column. For example, in the right column is a cell that contains a dot; it is clear that this is an error in the phase of populating the database. It is equally clear that such a value can cause many problems during the analysis phase, which is why it must be appropriately dealt with.

As seen for missing values, mismatched values are also represented in the data quality bar at the top of each column. In the data quality bar, mismatched values are identified in red, as shown in the following screenshot:

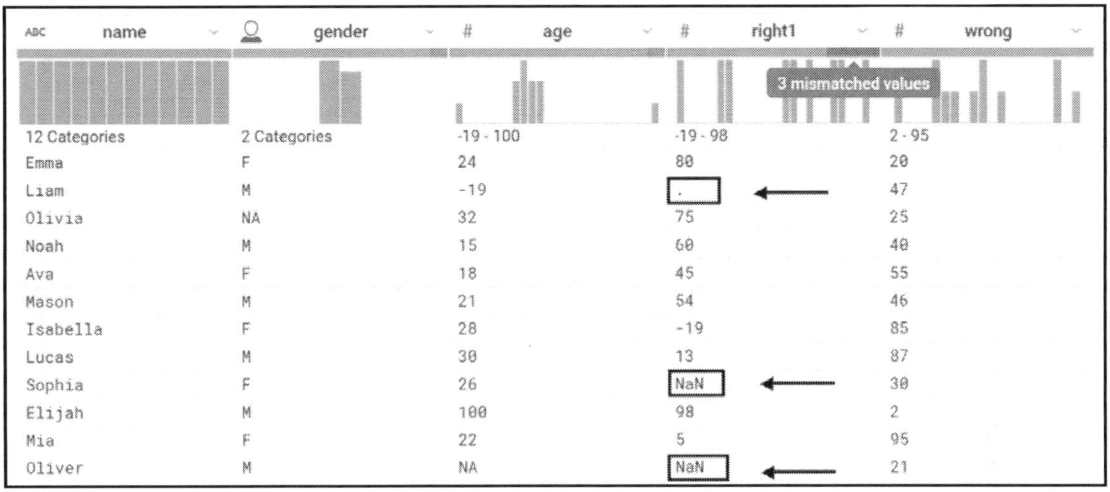

ABC name	⊖ gender	# age	# right1	# wrong
12 Categories	2 Categories	-19 - 100	-19 - 98	2 - 95
Emma	F	24	80	20
Liam	M	-19	.	47
Olivia	NA	32	75	25
Noah	M	15	60	40
Ava	F	18	45	55
Mason	M	21	54	46
Isabella	F	28	-19	85
Lucas	M	30	13	87
Sophia	F	26	NaN	30
Elijah	M	100	98	2
Mia	F	22	5	95
Oliver	M	NA	NaN	21

(note in right1 column: 3 mismatched values)

To fix mismatched data, there are several options available:

- Change the data type
- Replace the values with constant values
- Set the values with other columns' values
- Transform the data with functions
- Delete rows
- Hide the column for now
- Drop the column

In this case, since two of the selected lines contain mismatched data in other columns too, we will eliminate all three columns. To do this, simply click on the **Add** button in the **Delete rows** area of the suggestions panel.

Analyzing the dataset, we can see that mismatched data is still present. In fact, the data quality bar in the age column has an area in red. We try to fix this problem too. This time it is not appropriate to delete the entire row. In fact, by analyzing the first column, we can see that the NA value refers to a line whose name is clearly referring to a female (Olivia). So the most appropriate solution is to replace this value with a known value, in this case with 'F'.

To do this, we will write the following formula in the set item of the suggestions panel:

```
ifmismatched($col, ['Gender'], 'F')
```

A new step will be added to the **Recipe** panel. Once again, we can see a preview of the changes made to the dataset. In fact, we can see that the wrong value is no longer present; in its place, there is an `'F'`.

We have so far adjusted several things, but at first glance, there is still something to be done. If we pay attention to the **right1** column, which represents the percentage of correct answers provided, we notice that the range of values is as follows: -19 to 98. But -19 is obviously an incorrect value since for that variable, the permissible values are between 0 and 100 (this is a percentage). We can assume that a minus sign was added by mistake when creating the dataset. We can then modify this value, leaving only the value 19.

To do this, we perform the following steps:

1. Open the **Recipe** panel. Just click on the icon **(Recipe)** at the top left of the **Run Job** button.
2. Click on the **New Step** button. The Transform Builder is opened.
3. In the Transformation drop-down menu, select **Apply formula** in the list of available transforms.
4. Specify the **Columns (right)**.
5. Edit the following formula in the formula box:
6. `IF($col==-19,19,$col)`
7. Click on the **Add** button.
8. A new step is added to the **Recipe** panel.

The operations we have added to the **Recipe** panel are five, as shown in this screenshot:

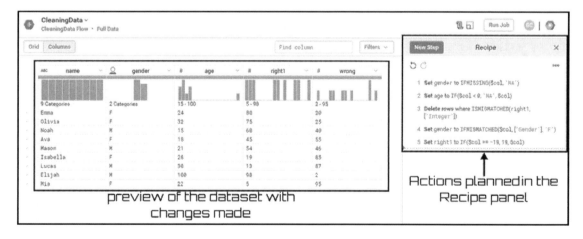

preview of the dataset with changes made

Actions planned in the Recipe panel

By analyzing the **Recipe** panel, we then have a summary of the actions we have planned on the dataset. Moreover, a visual analysis of the dataset preview with the changes made does not show any anomalies to be fixed. In the data quality bar at the top of each column, no red/black zones are highlighted, although it's too early to party yet! The data preparation work is far from done.

Finding outliers in the data

Outliers are the values that, compared to others, are particularly extreme (a value clearly distant from the other available observations). The presence of outliers causes a hindrance because they tend to distort the results of data analysis, in particular in descriptive statistics and correlations. It is ideal to identify these outliers in the data cleaning phase itself; however, they can also be dealt with in the next step of the data analysis. Outliers can be univariate when they have an extreme value for a single variable, or multivariate when they have an unusual combination of values for a number of variables.

Outliers are the extreme values of a distribution that are characterized by being extremely high or extremely low compared to the rest of the distribution, thus representing isolated cases in respect to the rest of the distribution.

There are different methods to detect outliers. Google Cloud Dataprep uses Tukey's method, which uses the **interquartile range (IQR)** approach. This method is not dependent on the distribution of the data and ignores the mean and the standard deviation, which are influenced by outliers.

As said before, to determine the outlier values, refer to the IQR given by the difference between the 25th percentile and the 75th percentile, that is, the amplitude of the range within which it falls. These 50 percent of observations occupy the central positions in the ordered series of data. An outlier is a value with positive deviation from the 75th percentile greater than two times the IQR or, symmetrically, a value with a negative deviation from the 25th percentile (in absolute value) greater than two times the IQR.

Practically, an outlier value is either of these two:

```
< (25th percentile) - (2 * IQR)
> (75th percentile) + (2 * IQR)
```

To identify outliers in individual columns, Google Cloud Dataprep has visual functionality and statistical information.

Visual functionality

Previously, we have talked about the histogram at the top of each column. This graph displays the count of each value detected in the column (for string data) or the count of values within a numeric range (for numerical data).

The visual functionality offered by Google Cloud Dataprep refers precisely to the use of these histograms to identify unusual values or outliers, which should be removed or corrected before performing any analysis on the entire dataset.

The type of histogram returned depends on the type of data contained in the column. In fact, for numeric data, each bar refers to a range of values and the bars are sorted in numerical order. For categorical types, each vertical bar covers a single value, ordered by the values that occur most frequently.

By moving the mouse over a bar of the histogram, a series of information is returned. In this way, we can highlight specific values, obtaining the count of a value and the percentage that that value represents in the total count of values in the column. We can also select a specific bar; in this case, the rows containing them are highlighted and the suggestion panel is displayed for the management of these values.

To select different bars at the same time:

- Use *Ctrl* + click to select multiple bars
- Click and drag over a range of bars

To better understand the usefulness of this visual functionality, let us refer to an example. In particular, we will analyze the dataset already used in the previous sections, which we have already had the opportunity to modify. Let's take a look at the age column, as it is currently presented in the preview offer with the changes already made effective. We can see that the histogram has four bars grouped on the left and only one bar isolated on the right. This particular form of the histogram is identifying the presence of an outlier, as shown in the following screenshot:

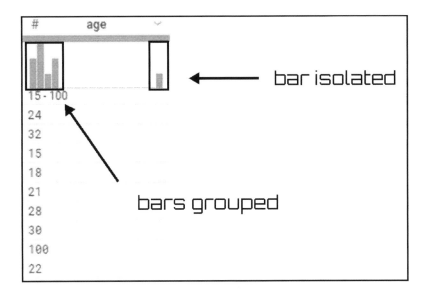

In this case, the presence of the anomalous value is evident; more generally, the presence of bars isolated at the ends of the graph must alert us.

If a dataset contains multiple instances of outliers, it is necessary to further investigate. Generally, if the dataset contains a large number of outliers, it is necessary to review these values and their data in other columns before performing operations to modify or remove these rows, since the removal of these values can become statistically significant.

Statistical information

The visual analysis we have done so far does not allow us to easily identify the presence of outliers in some cases. To obtain more information, we can examine detailed statistics of the values in the currently selected column, including data on outliers, available in the **Column Details** panel. To open the **Column Details** panel, just select **Column Details** from the drop-down menu of a column; the following panel is opened:

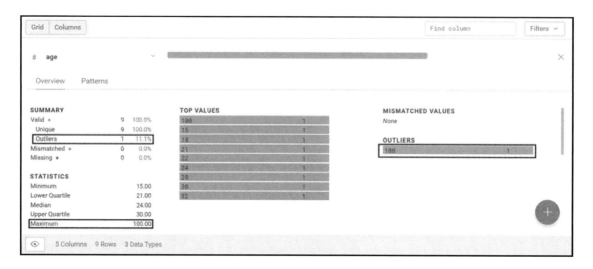

In this panel, a lot of information is available, some of which is as follows:

- Summary stats the count of valid (unique and outliers), mismatched, and missing values
- Statistics means you get many options such as, min, max, average, lowest and highest quartiles, median, and standard deviation
- Value histogram
- Top values
- Outliers

In this case, any outliers are clearly identified and indicated. Furthermore, the histogram is now much more precise, clearly indicating the arrangement of the bars.

Removing outliers

So far we have seen different techniques for identifying possible outliers. What should we do after identifying them? After identifying the values that are outliers in the column, you need to determine whether these values are valid or invalid for the dataset.

If these are invalid values due to an error in the population phase of the dataset, then we must correct them. This operation may involve the replacement of this value with a presumably valid one or the removal of the entire row. In this latter case, we must pay attention to the weight that this action can have on the whole dataset.

To replace the value `100`, which seems to us an invalid value in all respects (maybe it was `10` and an extra zero was added), we can insert the following formula:

```
IF(($col == 100),10, $col)
```

Instead, if the removal of this record does not assume statistically significant importance, we can adopt a simple erasing instruction, as shown here:

```
DELETE row: age == 100
```

If the data seems valid (in reality, a 100-year age is possible for human beings), we can leave it as it is. Or we can convert it into a value that seems to us to be statistically more significant. For example, we can decide to replace this value with the average value of the entire column so as to preserve at least the information of this observation derived from the other columns. To replace 100 with the average value of the column, use the following formula:

```
if($col > 80, average($col), $col)
```

Ultimately we choose the first option, so `100` will be replaced with `10` in the age column. To do this, we insert (as always) the formula just proposed in a new step, as shown in the following screenshot:

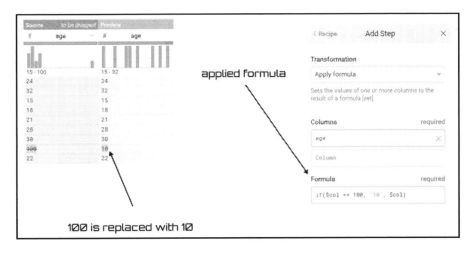

To view a preview of the change made, click on the **Add** button and a new step will be added to our **Recipe** panel. In the screenshot, we can also verify that now the range of values has been significantly reduced: 10 to 32 instead of 15 to 100. Not only that, but also the histogram no longer has bars isolated at the end.

Run Job

We have planned several operations on our database: it is time to make these changes. To do this, just click on **Run Job** on the Transformer page. In this way, the **Run Job** page will be open, where we can specify transformation and profiling jobs for the currently loaded dataset. Available options include output formats and output destinations.

The **Profile Results** option allows us to generate a visual result profile. The visual profile is very useful for examining the problems of our recipe and iterating, even if it is a process that requires a lot of resources. If the dataset we are processing is large, disabling the profiling of the results can improve the overall execution speed of the job.

After setting the available options correctly, we can queue the specified job for execution by simply clicking **Run Job**. Once this is done, the job is queued for processing. At the end of the process, you can view the results of successful runs using the **Dataset Details** page.

Flow processing times depend on the availability of the server and the size of the dataset. In our case, the dataset is really small, so we just have to wait for the service to become available. Click on **View Results** to open the job on the **Job Results** page, as shown in the following screenshot:

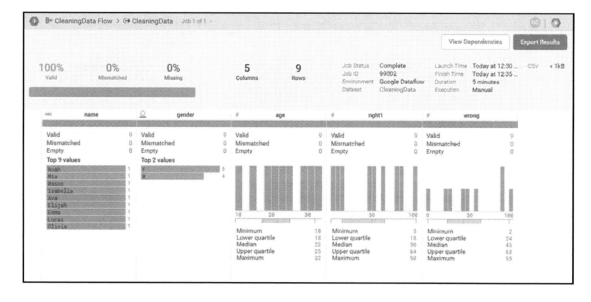

In the previous screenshot (**Job Results** page), it is possible to review the effects of the transformation recipe on the entire dataset. Statistics and data histograms are available that provide general visibility on the quality of our transformation recipe.

At the top of the screenshot on the left, you can find a series of summary information on the data contained in the generated dataset. In particular, the counts of valid values, non-corresponding values, and missing values are shown. These values are shown in full for the entire dataset.

A series of summary information on the work performed always appears in the upper part of the screenshot, but this time you can find it on the right.

In the lower part of the screenshot, we can visualize the details of the transformations made on the single columns. Depending on the data type of the column, the information about the variables is displayed.

Finally, in the upper part of the screenshot, on the right, there are two buttons:

- **View Dependencies**: To see the recipes and datasets on which the job depends
- **Export Results**: To export the results

Scale of features

Data scaling is a preprocessing technique usually employed before feature selection and classification. Many artificial intelligence-based systems use features that are generated by many different feature extraction algorithms, with different kinds of sources. These features may have different dynamic ranges. Popular distance measures, such as Euclidean distance, implicitly assign more weighting to features with large ranges than those with small ranges. Feature scaling is thus required to approximately equalize ranges of the features and make them have approximately the same effect in the computation of similarity.

In addition, in several data mining applications with huge numbers of features with large dynamic ranges, feature scaling may improve the performance of the fitting model. However, the appropriate choice of these techniques is an important issue. This is because applying scaling on the input could change the structure of data and thereby affect the outcome of multivariate analysis used in data mining.

So far, we have worked on the data to correct any errors or omissions. We can say that at this point all variables contained in the dataset are complete with consistent data. What about different variables characterized by different ranges and units? There can be variables in a data frame where values for one feature could range from 1 to 10 and values for another feature could range from 1 to 1,000.

In data frames such as these, owing to mere greater numeric range, the impact on response variables by the feature having greater numeric range could be more than the one having less numeric range, and this could, in turn, impact prediction accuracy. Our goal is to improve predictive accuracy and not allow a particular feature to impact the prediction due to a large numeric value range. Thus, we may need to scale values under different features such that they fall under a common range. Through this statistical procedure, it is possible to compare identical variables belonging to different distributions, but also different variables, or variables expressed in different units. Two methods are usually well known for rescaling data: normalization and standardization.

Remember, it is good practice to rescale the data before training a machine learning algorithm. With rescaling, data units are eliminated, allowing you to easily compare data from different locations.

Min–max normalization

Min-max normalization (usually called **feature scaling**) performs a linear transformation on the original data. This technique gets all the scaled data in the range (0, 1). The formula to achieve this is the following:

$$x_{scaled} = \frac{x - x_{min}}{x_{max} - x_{min}}$$

Min-max normalization preserves the relationships among the original data values. The cost of having this bounded range is that we will end up with smaller standard deviations, which can suppress the effect of outliers.

To better understand how to perform a min-max normalization, just analyze an example. We will use a dataset contained in the `Airquality.csv` file.

This dataset is available at the UCI machine learning repository, a large collection of data, at the following link: `https://archive.ics.uci.edu/ml/index.php`.

S. De Vito, E. Massera, M. Piga, L. Martinotto, G. Di Francia, *On field calibration of an electronic nose for benzene estimation in an urban pollution monitoring scenario*, Sensors and Actuators B: Chemical, Volume 129, Issue 2, 22 February 2008, Pages 750-757, ISSN 0925-4005 at: `https://www.sciencedirect.com/science/article/pii/S0925400507007691`.

These are the daily readings of the following air quality values for May 1, 1973 (a Tuesday) to September 30, 1973:

- **Ozone**: Mean ozone in parts per billion from 1300 to 1500 hours at Roosevelt island
- **Solar.R**: Solar radiation in Langleys in the frequency band 4000–7700 Angstroms from 0800 to 1200 hours at central park
- **Wind**: Average wind speed in miles per hour at 0700 and 1000 hours at LaGuardia airport
- **Temp**: Maximum daily temperature in degrees Fahrenheit at LaGuardia airport

The data was obtained from the New York State Department of Conservation (ozone data) and the **National Weather Service** or **NWS** (meteorological data).

A data frame consists of 154 observations on 6 variables:

Name	Type	Units
Ozone	numeric	ppb
Solar	numeric	lang
Wind	numeric	mph
Temp	numeric	degrees F
Month	numeric	1 to 12
Day	numeric	1 to 31

As can be seen, the six variables are characterized by different units of measurement. As we did in the previous sections, even in this case, we start preparing the data by creating a new flow from the flows screen, and then we import the .csv file into Google Cloud Dataprep. The following window opens:

ABC column	# Ozone	# Solar_R	# Wind	# Temp	# Month	# Day
153 Categories	1 - 168	7 - 334	2 - 21	56 - 97	5 - 9	1 - 31
"1"	41	190	7.4	67	5	1
"2"	36	118	8	72	5	2
"3"	12	149	12.6	74	5	3
"4"	18	313	11.5	62	5	4
"5"	NA	NA	14.3	56	5	5
"6"	28	NA	14.9	66	5	6
"7"	23	299	8.6	65	5	7
"8"	19	99	13.8	59	5	8
"9"	8	19	20.1	61	5	9
"10"	NA	194	8.6	69	5	10
"11"	7	NA	6.9	74	5	11
"12"	16	256	9.7	69	5	12
"13"	11	290	9.2	66	5	13
"14"	14	274	10.9	68	5	14
"15"	18	65	13.2	58	5	15
"16"	14	334	11.5	64	5	16
"17"	34	307	12	66	5	17

As we have anticipated, the four variables have different units of measure this implies that the ranges of values are very different. In fact, by analyzing the upper part of each column in the previous screenshot, we can obtain the following ranges:

- **Ozone**: 1 to 168
- **Solar.R**: 7 to 334
- **Wind**: 2 to 21
- **Temp**: 56 to 97

Before proceeding with standardization, we eliminate some problems highlighted in the data quality bar. Mismatched values have been identified. To be precise:

- **Ozone**: 37 mismatched values
- **Solar.R**: 7 mismatched values

First of all, we will try to fix these problems as we have learned to do in the previous section.

We start with the Ozone column; we proceed to click on the red area of the data quality bar. In this way, all 37 mismatched values are highlighted. At the same time, the suggestions panel is opened on the right of the window. In particular, the first suggestion advises us to delete the lines with mismatched values in Ozone. We simply click on the **Add** button. The following line will be added to the **Recipe** panel:

```
Delete rows where ISMISMATCHED(Ozone, ['Integer'])
```

We perform the same operation for the Solar_R column; the following line will be added to the **Recipe** panel:

```
Delete rows where ISMISMATCHED(Solar_R, ['Integer'])
```

In both cases, the preview window shows us that no mismatched value is now present in the data. At this point, we can take care of the normalization. As we have specified earlier, the variables ranges are very varied. We want to eliminate this feature through min-max normalization. As stated earlier, to apply this procedure we have to calculate the minimum and maximum for each variable. To do this, we can apply two functions available in Google Cloud Dataprep: MIN and MAX.

Google Cloud Dataprep support functions typically found in most desktop spreadsheet packages. Functions can be used to create formulas that manipulate data in the columns.

Previously, we have proposed the formula for normalization; to apply it to a column, we perform the following steps:

1. In the **Recipe** panel, click on the **NEW STEP** button. Remember? To open the **Recipe** panel, just click on the icon (**Recipe**) at the top left of the **Run Job** button.
2. From the Transformation drop-down menu, select **Apply formula** item (this item sets the values of one or more columns to the result of a formula).
3. From the column box, select the **Ozone** column, for example (the same procedure can be applied to all the dataset variables).
4. In the **Formula** box, edit the following formula: (Ozone− MIN(Ozone))/(MAX(Ozone)−MIN(Ozone))
5. Just click on the **Add** button.

The following statement is added to the **Recipe** panel:

```
Set Ozone to (Ozone-MIN(Ozone))/(MAX(Ozone)-MIN(Ozone))
```

We follow the same procedure for the other three variables: `Solar_R`, `Wind`, and `Temp`. At the end, we will have added the following lines to the **Recipe** panel:

```
Set Solar_R to (Solar_R -MIN(Solar_R))/(MAX(Solar_R)-MIN(Solar_R))
Set Wind to (Wind -MIN(Wind))/(MAX(Wind)-MIN(Wind))
Set Temp to (Temp -MIN(Temp))/(MAX(Temp)-MIN(Temp))
```

The Transformer page has been changed as follows:

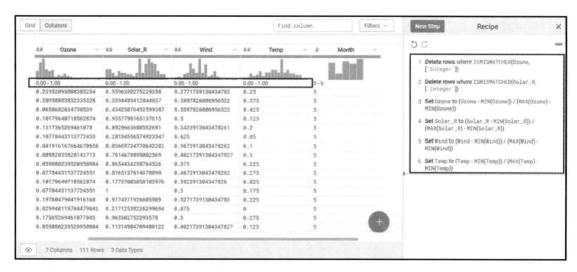

It is apparent that now the data is all between zero and one; this happens for each column of the dataset and then for each variable. The scale differences due to the different units of measurement have therefore been removed.

z score standardization

This technique consists of subtracting the mean of the column from each value in a column, and then dividing the result by the standard deviation of the column. The formula to achieve this is the following:

$$x_{scaled} = \frac{x - mean}{sd}$$

The result of standardization is that the features will be rescaled so that they'll have the properties of a standard normal distribution, as follows:

- $\mu=0$
- $\sigma=1$

μ is the mean and σ is the standard deviation from the mean.

In summary, the z score (also called the **standard score**) represents the number of standard deviations with which the value of an observation point or data differ than the mean value of what is observed or measured. Values more than the mean have positive z scores, while values less than the mean have negative z scores. The z score is a quantity without dimension, obtained by subtracting the population mean from a single rough score and then dividing the difference for the standard deviation of the population.

Once again, to standardize the data, we will use the same procedure used to min-max normalization. This time the two functions are changed as follows:

- AVERAGE: Calculates the average for each column
- STDEV: Calculates the standard deviation for each column

To perform a z score standardization, just analyze the same dataset used for min-max normalization. I refer to dataset called Airquality.csv, which contains daily readings of the following air quality values for May 1, 1973 (a Tuesday) to September 30, 1973.

To apply z score standardization to a dataset column, perform the following steps:

1. In the **Recipe** panel, click on the **NEW STEP** button. Again, to open the **Recipe** panel, just click on the icon (**Recipe**) at the top left of the **Run Job** button.
2. From the Transformation drop-down menu, select **Apply formula** (this item sets the values of one or more columns to the result of a formula).
3. From the column box, select the **Ozone** column (the same procedure can be applied to all the dataset variables).
4. In the **Formula** box, edit the following formula:
5. (Ozone- AVERAGE(Ozone))/STDEV(Ozone)
6. Just click on the **ADD** button.

The following statement is added to the **Recipe** panel:

```
Set Ozone to (Ozone- AVERAGE(Ozone))/STDEV(Ozone)
```

We follow the same procedure for the other three variables: `Solar_R`, `Wind`, and `Temp`. At the end, we will have added the following lines to the **Recipe** panel:

```
Set Solar_R to (Solar_R - AVERAGE(Solar_R))/STDEV(Solar_R)
Set Wind to (Wind - AVERAGE(Wind))/STDEV(Wind)
Set Temp to (Temp - AVERAGE(Temp))/STDEV(Temp)
```

The transformer page has been changed, as follows:

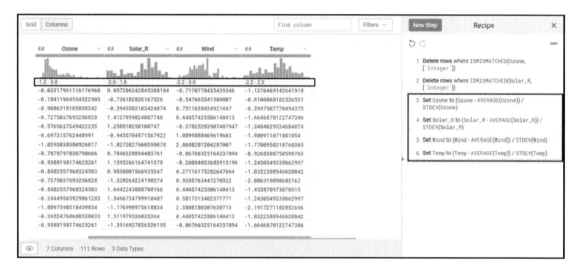

The modification made by the z score standardization is evident: the data ranges are quite similar. This happens for each column of the dataset, and then for each variable. The differences in scale due to the different units of measurement have therefore been removed.

According to the assumptions, all variables must have `average= 0` and `stdev =1`. Let's verify that. To do so, just use the statistical information available in the **Column Details** panel, already used in the previous sections. To open the **Column Details** panel, select **Column Details** from the drop-down menu of a column; the following panel is opened:

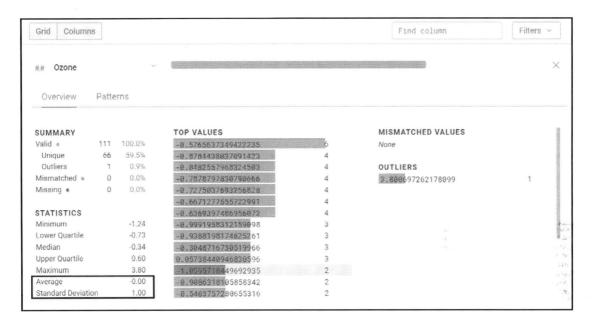

So, we have verified that the **Ozone** variable has an average of zero and a standard deviation of one. The same check can be executed for the other variables.

Google Cloud Dataflow

Google Cloud Dataflow is a fully managed service for creating data pipelines that transform, enrich, and analyze data in batch and streaming modes. Google Cloud Dataflow extracts useful information from data, reducing operating costs without the hassle of implementing, maintaining, or resizing the data infrastructure.

A pipeline is a set of data processing elements connected in series, in which the output of one element is the input of the next. The data pipeline is implemented to increase throughput, which is the number of instructions executed in a given amount of time, parallelizing the processing flows of multiple instructions.

By appropriately defining a process management flow, significant resources can be saved in extracting knowledge from the data. Thanks to a serverless approach to provisioning and managing resources, Dataflow offers virtually unlimited capacity to solve the most serious data processing problems, but you only pay for what you use.

Google Cloud Dataflow automates the provisioning and management of processing resources to reduce latency times and optimize utilization. It is no longer necessary to activate the instances manually or to reserve them. Automatic and optimized partitioning allows the pending job to be dynamically redistributed. You do not need to go for keyboard shortcuts or preprocess your input data. Cloud Dataflow supports rapid and simplified pipeline development using expressive Java and Python APIs in the Apache Beam SDK.

Cloud Dataflow jobs are billed per minute, based on the actual use of workers in batch mode or streaming of Cloud Dataflow. Jobs that use other GCP resources, such as Cloud Storage or Cloud Pub/Sub, are billed based on the price of the corresponding service.

Summary

In this chapter, we explored Google Cloud Dataprep, a service useful to preprocess the data, extract features, and clean up records. We got into practical details with real-life examples. We started by taking a look at the Cloud application interface to discover some preliminary information needed to access the platform. We then analyzed the techniques available for the preparation of the most suitable data for analysis and modeling, which includes the imputation of missing data, detecting and eliminating outliers, and mismatched values treatment. We discovered different ways to transform data and the degree of cleaning data. Then we learned how to normalize our data, in which data units are eliminated, allowing us to easily compare data from different locations.

Essential Machine Learning

6

So far, in previous chapters, we went through the various ETL processes available in GCP. In this chapter, we will start our journey of machine learning and deep learning through the following topics:

- Applications of machine learning
- Supervised and unsupervised machine learning
- Overview of major machine learning techniques
- Data splitting
- Measuring the accuracy of a model
- The difference between machine learning and deep learning
- Applications of deep learning

Applications of machine learning

Machine learning encompasses a set of techniques that learn from historical data. Based on the patterns learned from historical data, the machine learning technique predicts the probability of an event happening on a future dataset. Given the way in which machine learning works, there are multiple applications of the set of techniques. Let's explore some of them in the following sections.

Financial services

Some applications in the field of finance are as follows:

- Identifying the riskiness of a loan/credit card applicant
- Estimating the credit limit of a given customer
- Predicting whether a card transaction is a fraudulent transaction

- Identifying the customer segments that need to be targeted for a campaign
- Predicting whether a customer is likely to default in the next few months
- Recommending the right financial product that a customer should buy

Retail industry

The following are some applications of the different techniques of machine learning in the retail industry:

- Predicting the next product that a customer is likely to buy
- Estimating the optimal price point for a given product
- Forecasting the number of units a product will sell over time
- Targeting customers by bundling products for promotion
- Estimating a customer lifetime value

Telecom industry

Here are a few applications of machine learning in the telecom industry:

- Predicting the likelihood of a call drop before the start of a call
- Predicting if a customer is likely to churn in the next few months
- Identifying add-ons to monthly usage that could be sold to a customer
- Identifying the customers who are less likely to pay for postpaid services
- Workforce optimization for field force effectiveness

Supervised and unsupervised machine learning

Supervised machine learning constitutes the set of techniques that work towards building a model that approximate a function. The function takes a set of input variables, which are alternatively called independent variables, and tries to map the input variables to the output variable, alternatively called the dependent variable or the label.

Given that we know the label (or the value) we are trying to predict, for a set of input variables, the technique becomes a supervised learning problem.

In a similar manner, in an unsupervised learning problem, we do not have the output variable that we have to predict. However, in unsupervised learning, we try to group the data points so that they form logical groups.

A distinction between supervised and unsupervised learning at a high level can be obtained as shown in the following diagram:

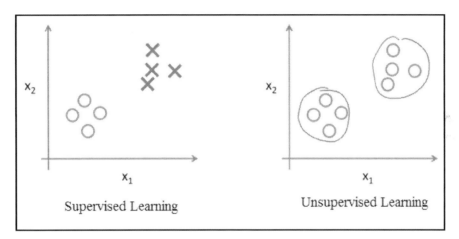

In the preceding diagram, the supervised learning approach can distinguish between the two classes, as follows:

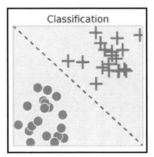

In supervised learning, there are two major objectives that can be achieved:

- Predict the probability of an event happening—classification
- Estimate the value of the continuous dependent variable—regression

The major methods that can help in classification are as follows:

- Logistic regression
- Decision tree
- Random forest
- Gradient boosting
- Neural network

Along with these (except logistic regression), linear regression also helps in estimating a continuous variable (regression).

While these techniques help in estimating a continuous variable or in predicting the probability of an event happening (discrete variable prediction), unsupervised learning helps in grouping. Grouping can be either of rows (which is a typical clustering technique) or of columns (a dimensionality reduction technique). The major methods of row groupings are:

- K-means clustering
- Hierarchical clustering
- Density-based clustering

The major methods of column groupings are:

- Principal component analysis
- **t-Distributed Stochastic Neighbor Embedding (t-SNE)**

Row groupings result in identifying the segments of customers (observations) that are there in our dataset.

Column groupings result in reducing the number of columns. This comes in handy when the number of independent variables is high. Typically when this is the case, there could be an issue in building the model, as the number of weights that need to be estimated could be high. Also, there could be an issue in interpreting the model, as some of the independent variables could be highly correlated with each other. Principal component analysis or t-SNE comes in handy in such a scenario, where we reduce the number of independent variables without losing too much of the information that is present in the dataset.

In the next section, we will go through an overview of all the major machine learning algorithms.

Overview of machine learning techniques

Before going through an overview of the major machine learning techniques, let's go through the function that we would want to optimize in a regression technique or a classification technique.

Objective function in regression

In a regression exercise, we estimate the continuous variable value. In such a scenario, our predictions can be lower than the actual value or higher; that is, the error value could be either positive or negative. In such a scenario, the objective function translates to minimizing the sum of squared values of the difference between the actual and predicted values of each of the observations in the dataset.

In mathematical terms, the preceding is written as follows:

$$SSE = \sum_{i=1}^{n}(y - y')^2$$

In the given equation:

- SSE stands for the *sum of squared errors*
- y refers to the actual value of the dependent variable
- y' refers to the estimated value of the dependent variable
- Σ refers to the summation of the squared errors across all the observations in the dataset

Given the objective function, let's understand how linear regression works at a high level.

Linear regression

In linear regression, we assume a linear relationship between the independent variables and the dependent variable. Linear regression is represented as follows:

$$Y = W \times X + b$$

In the given equation:

- Y is the dependent variable
- W is the weight associated with the independent variable X
- b is the intercept value

If there are multiple independent variables (let's say two independent variables, $x1$ and $x2$), the equation is as follows:

$$Y = w1 \times x1 + x2 \times x2 + b$$

In the given equation:

- $w1$ is the weight associated with variable $x1$
- $w2$ is the weight associated with variable $x2$

A typical linear regression looks as follows, where the x axis is the independent variable and the y axis is the dependent variable:

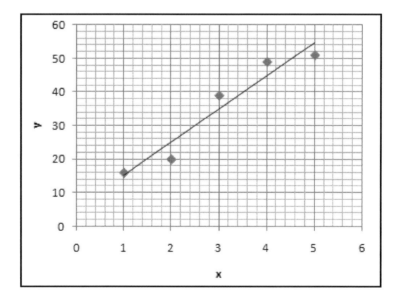

The straight line (with a certain slope and intercept) is the equation of linear regression.

Note that the line in the graph is the one that minimizes the overall squared error.

Decision tree

Decision tree is a technique that helps us in deriving rules from data. A rule-based technique is very helpful in explaining how the model is supposed to work in estimating a dependent variable value.

A typical decision tree looks like this:

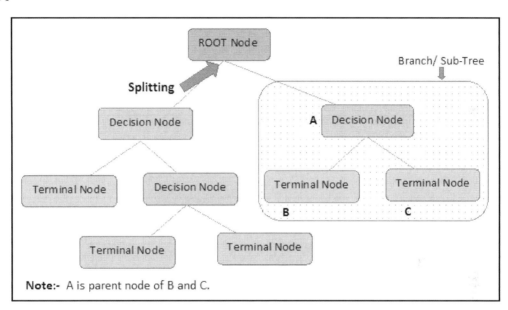

The preceding diagram is explained as follows:

- **ROOT Node:** This represents the entire population or a sample, and it is further divided into two or more further nodes.
- **Splitting**: A process of dividing a node into two or more subnodes based on a certain rule.
- **Decision Node:** When a subnode splits into further subnodes, it is called **decision node.**
- **Leaf/Terminal Node:** The final node in a decision tree is a leaf or terminal node.
- **Pruning:** When we remove the subnodes of a decision node, this process is called **pruning**. You can say it is the opposite process of splitting.
- **Branch/Sub-Tree:** A subsection of the entire tree is called a **branch** or a **sub-tree.**
- **Parent and child node:** A node that is divided into subnodes is called the **parent node** of subnodes, whereas the subnodes are the children of the parent node.

Given a dependent variable and an independent variable value, we will go through how a decision tree works using the following dataset:

var2	response
0.1	1996
0.3	839
0.44	2229
0.51	2309
0.75	815
0.78	2295
0.84	1590

In the preceding dataset, the variable `var2` is the input variable and the `response` variable is the dependent variable.

In the first step of the decision tree, we sort the input variable from lowest to highest and test multiple rules, one at a time.

In the first instance, all the observations of the dataset that have a `var2` value of less than `0.3` belong to the left node of a decision tree, and the other observations belong to the right node of the decision tree.

In a regression exercise, the predicted value of the left node is the average of the `response` variable for all the observations that belong to the left node. Similarly, the predicted value of the right node is the average of `response` for all the observations that belong to the right node.

Given a predicted value for the left node and a different predicted value for the observations that belong to the right node, the squared error can be calculated for each of the left and right nodes. The overall error for a probable rule is the sum of squared error in both left and right nodes.

The decision rule that is implemented is the rule that has the minimum squared error among all the possible rules.

Random forest

Random forest is an extension of decision trees. It is a forest as it is a combination of multiple trees, and is random as we randomly sample different observations for each of the decision trees.

A random forest works by averaging the prediction of each of the decision trees (which work on a sample of the original dataset).

Typically, a random forest works better than a single decision tree, as the influence of outliers is reduced in it (because in some samples, outliers might not have occurred), whereas, in a decision tree, an outlier would have definitely occurred (if the original dataset contained an outlier).

Gradient boosting

While a random forest works in a framework where multiple parallel trees are built, gradient boosting takes a different approach—building a deep framework.

The gradient in gradient boosting refers to the difference between actual and predicted values, and boosting refers to improvement, that is, improving the error over different iterations.

Gradient boosting also leverages the way in which decision trees work in the following way:

- Build a decision tree to estimate the dependent variable
- Calculate the error, that is, the difference between actual and predicted value
- Build another decision tree that predicts the error
- Update the prediction by taking the prediction of error of the previous decision tree into account

This way, gradient boosting continuously builds a decision tree that predicts the error of the previous decision tree and thus a depth-based framework in gradient boosting.

Neural network

A neural network provides a way to approximate nonlinear functions. Nonlinearity is achieved by applying activation functions on top of the summation of weighted input variables.

A neural network looks like this:

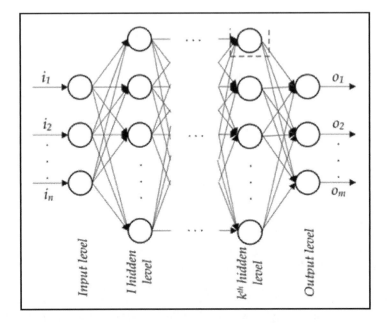

The input level contains the inputs and the hidden layer contains the summation of the weighted input values, where each connection is associated with a weight.

The nonlinearity is applied to the hidden layer. Typical non-linear activation functions could be sigmoid, tanh, or rectified linear unit.

The output level is associated with the summation of weights associated with each hidden unit. The optimal value of weights associated with each connection is obtained by adjusting the weights in such a way that the overall squared error value is minimized. More details of how a neural network works are provided in a later chapter.

Logistic regression

As discussed before, logistic regression is used to classify a prediction to one class or another depending on the input dataset. Logistic regression uses the sigmoid function to attain the probability of an event happening.

The sigmoid curve looks like this:

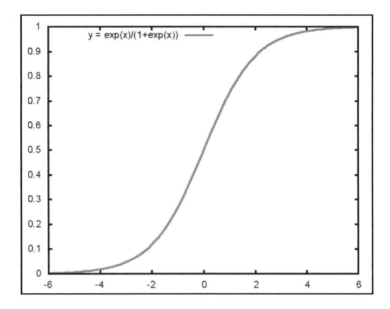

Note that the output is a high probability when the *x* axis value is greater than 3 and the output is a very low probability when the *x* axis value is less than 3.

Logistic regression differs from linear regression in the usage of the activation function. While a linear regression equation would be $Y = a + b * X$, a logistic regression equation would be:

$$Y = 1/(1 + exp(-(a + b * X)))$$

Objective function in classification

In a regression technique, we minimize the overall squared error. However, in a classification technique, we minimize the overall cross-entropy error.

A binary cross-entropy error is as follows:

$$-(y * logp + (1 - y) * log(1 - p))$$

In the given equation:

- y is the actual dependent variable
- p is the probability of an event happening

For a classification exercise, all the preceding algorithms work; it's just that the objective function changes to cross-entropy error minimization instead of squared error.

In the case of a decision tree, the variable that belongs to the root node is the variable that provides the highest information gain when compared to all the rest of the independent variables. Information gain is defined as the improvement in overall entropy when the tree is split by a given variable when compared to no splitting.

Data splitting

One of the key problems that need to be addressed while working on any machine learning model is: *how accurate can this model be once it is implemented in production on a future dataset?*

It is not possible to answer this question straight away. However, it is really important to obtain the buy-in from commercial teams that ultimately get benefited from the model build. Dividing the dataset into training and testing datasets comes in handy in such a scenario.

The training dataset is the data that is used to build the model. The testing dataset is the dataset that is not seen by the model; that is, the data points are not used in building the model. Essentially, one can think of the testing dataset as the dataset that is likely to come in future. Hence, the accuracy that we see on the testing dataset is likely to be the accuracy of the model on the future dataset.

Typically, in regression, we deal with the problem of generalization/overfitting. The overfitting problem arises when the model is so complex that it perfectly fits all the data points—thus resulting in a minimal possible error rate. A typical example of an overfitted dataset looks like this:

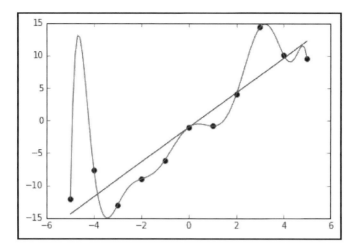

From the graph dataset, one can observe that the line (colored in black) does not fit all the data points perfectly, while the curve (colored in blue) fits the points perfectly and hence has minimal error on the data points on which it is trained.

However, the line has a better chance of being more generalizable when compared to the curve on a new dataset. Thus, in practice, regression/classification is a trade-off between generalizability and complexity of the model.

The lower the generalizability of the model, the higher the error rate on unseen data points.

This phenomenon can be observed in the following graph. As the complexity of the model increases, the error rate of unseen data points keeps reducing till a point, after which it starts increasing again:

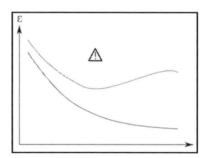

The curve colored in blue is the error rate on the training dataset, and the curve colored in red is the testing dataset error rate.

The validation dataset is used to obtain the optimal hyperparameters of the model. For example, in techniques such as random forest or GBM, the number of trees needed to build or the depth of a tree is a hyper parameter. As we keep changing the hyperparameter, the accuracy on unseen datasets changes.

However, we cannot go on varying the hyperparameter until the test dataset accuracy is the highest, as we would have seen the practically future dataset (testing dataset) in such a scenario.

The validation dataset comes in handy in such scenarios, where we keep varying the hyperparameters on the training dataset until we see that the accuracy on the validation dataset is the highest. That would thus form the optimal hyperparameter combination for the model.

Measuring the accuracy of a model

The methods of evaluating the accuracy of a model differ between supervised learning and unsupervised learning.

In a typical linear regression (where continuous values are predicted), there are a couple of ways of measuring the error of the model. Typically, error is measured on the validation and testing datasets, as measuring error on a training dataset (the dataset using which a model is built) is misleading. Hence, error is always measured on the dataset that is not used to build a model.

Absolute error

Absolute error is defined as the absolute value of the difference between the forecast value and actual value. Let's imagine a scenario as follows:

	Actual value	Predicted value	Error	Absolute error
Data point 1	100	120	20	20
Data point 2	100	80	-20	20
Overall	200	200	0	40

In the preceding scenario, we see that the overall error is 0 (as one error is +20 and the other is -20). If we assume that the overall error of the model is 0, we are missing out the fact that the model is not working well on individual data points.

Hence, in order to avoid the issue of a positive error and negative error canceling each other out and thus resulting in minimal error, we consider the absolute error of a model, which in this case is 40; and the absolute error rate is 40/200 = 20%.

Root mean square error

Another approach of solving the problem of inconsistent signs of error is to square the error (the square of a negative number is a positive number). The scenario discussed previously can be translated as follows:

	Actual value	Predicted value	Error	Squared error
Data point 1	100	120	20	400
Data point 2	100	80	-20	400
Overall	200	200	0	800

In this case, the overall squared error is 800 and root mean squared error is the square root of (800/2), which is 20.

The accuracy in the case of a classification exercise is measured as follows: absolute error and RMSE are applicable when predicting continuous variables. However, predicting an event with discrete outcomes is a different process. Discrete event prediction happens in terms of probabilities; that is, the result of the model is a probability that certain event happens. In such cases, even though absolute error and RMSE can be theoretically used, there are other metrics of relevance.

A confusion matrix counts the number of instances when the model predicted the outcome of an event and measures it against the actual values, as follows:

	Predicted fraud	Predicted non-fraud
Actual fraud	True positive (TP)	False negative (FN)
Actual non-fraud	False positive (FP)	True negative (TN)

$$Sensitivity\ or\ TP\ rate\ or\ recall = TP/\ (total\ positives) = TP/\ (TP+FN)$$

$$Specificity\ or\ TN\ rate = TN/\ (total\ negative) = TP/(FP + TN)$$

$$Precision\ or\ positive\ predicted\ value = TP/(TP + FP)$$

$$Accuracy = (TP + TN)/(TP + FN + FP + TN)$$

$$F1\ score = 2TP/\ (2TP + FP + FN)$$

A **receiver operating characteristic** (**ROC**) curve gives the relation between the true positive rate and false positive rate of various cutoffs. Let's say the model prediction is >0.8. We assume that we should classify the prediction as positive. The 0.8 here is the cutoff point. Cutoffs come into the picture here as a model's prediction will always be a probability number—a value between 0 and 1. Hence, an analyst needs to bring his/her judgment in ascertaining the optimal cutoff.

An ROC curve is a curve where (1-specificity) is on the *x* axis and sensitivity is on the *y* axis. The curve is generated by plotting the various combinations of sensitivity and (1-specificity) by changing the cutoff, which decides whether the predicted value should be a 1 or a 0.

In an ideal scenario, where data can be clearly segregated and accuracy is 100%, there lies a cutoff of the probability, after which the predicted value is of one class; it belongs to the other class for values below the cutoff. In such a scenario, for certain values of cutoffs, the ROC curve would be on the *y* axis only, that is, specificity=1. For the rest of its length, the curve is going to be parallel to the *x* axis.

A typical example of an ROC curve looks like this:

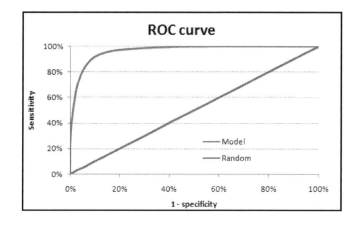

An ROC curve is a measure of how much better the model's performance is over a random guess. A random guess is where in case of a churn of 5% customers, the random guesser guesses that for every twenty customers, one among them will be labeled as a potential churner. In such a scenario, the random guess is going to capture 20% of all churners after randomly labeling 20% of all the customers.

A model's predictive power is in being able to move as close to 100% accuracy as possible, that is, moving away from random guesses as much as possible.

Area under the curve (**AUC**) is a measure of the area between the model curve and the random guess curve. The higher the AUC, the higher the predictive accuracy of the model.

The difference between machine learning and deep learning

So far, we have looked at how various machine learning algorithms work at a high level. In this section, we will understand how deep learning differs from machine learning.

One of the key attributes of a machine learning task is that the inputs are given by the analyst or data scientist. Quite often, feature engineering plays a key role in improving the accuracy of the model. Moreover, if the input dataset is an unstructured one, feature engineering gets a lot more tricky. More often than not, it boils down to the knowledge of individual in deriving relevant features to build a more accurate model.

For example, let's imagine a scenario where, given a set of words in a sentence, we are trying to predict the next word. In such a scenario, traditional machine learning algorithms work as follows:

- One-hot encode each word in a sentence
- Represent the input sequence of words using the one-hot encoded vector
- Represent the output word, also using a one-hot encoded vector
- Build a model to predict the output word vector given the set of input words by optimizing for the relevant loss function

While the preceding method works, we face three major challenges in building the model:

- Dimension of the one-hot encoded vector:
    - A piece of text is likely to have hundreds or thousands of unique words

- High-dimensional data is likely to result in multiple issues—such as multicollinearity and the time taken to build a model
- Order of words is missing in the input dataset
- Distance between two words is the same, irrespective of whether the words are similar to each other or not:
    - For example, in a one-hot encoded vector scenario, the distance between king and prince would be the same as the distance between king and cheese

Deep learning comes in handy in such a scenario. Using some of the techniques in deep learning (for example, Word2vec), we would be able to solve the following among the issues listed just now:

- Represent each word in a lower-dimensional space in such a way that words that are similar to each other have similar word vectors and words that are not similar to each other do not have similar vectors
- Moreover, by representing a word in a lower-dimensional space (let's say 100), we would have solved the problem of high dimensionality of data

There are multiple variants of the Word2vec technique, such as the continuous bag-of-words model and the continuous skip-gram model.

The architecture of a CBOW model is as follows:

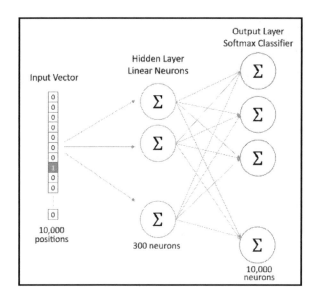

Note that the input vector is the one-hot encoded version (as we would have used in a typical machine learning model). The hidden layer neurons ensure that we represent the 10,000-dimensional input vector in a 300-dimensional word vector.

The actual values in the output layer represent the one-hot encoded versions of the surrounding words (which form the context).

Another technique in deep learning that comes in handy to solve the preceding problem is the **recurrent neural network** (**RNN**). An RNN works towards solving the sequence-of-words problem that traditional machine learning faced in the scenario laid out previously.

RNN provides each word vector in order to predict the next word in the sequence. More details of how RNN works will be provided in a different chapter. The popular variants of the RNN technique are **long short-term memory** (**LSTM**) and **gated recurrent unit** (**GRU**):

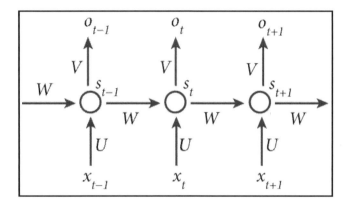

The preceding diagram represents a typical RNN, where $x_{(t-1)}$, $x_{(t)}$ and $x_{(t+1)}$ represent the words in each time period, W is the weightage associated with a previous word in predicting the next word, and $O_{(t)}$ is the output in time t.

LSTM comes in handy when the weightage that needs to be associated with a word that occurred much earlier in sequence would have be high in predicting the next word.

A combination of Word2vec and RNN, which are variants of neural networks, helps in avoiding the challenge of feature engineering with the given text data.

In order to solidify our understanding of the difference between machine learning and deep learning, let's go through another example: predicting the label of an image.

We will use a classic example—the MNIST dataset (we will be using MNIST a lot more in future chapters).

The MNIST dataset contains images of various digits, from zero to nine. Each image is 28 x 28 pixels in size. The task is to predict the label of the image by analyzing the various pixel values. A sample image in the MNIST dataset looks like this:

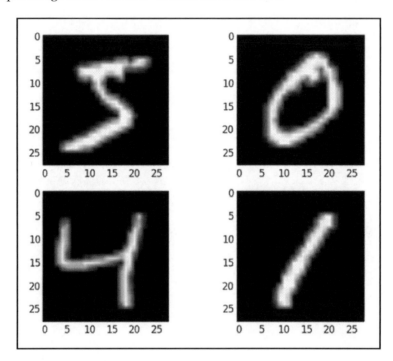

Traditional machine learning solves the preceding problem as follows:

- Treat each pixel as a separate variable; that is, we have a total of 784 variables
- One-hot encode the label column
- Predict the probability of a label occurring

The challenge with the way in which we solve the preceding problem is as follows:

- The model will not take pixel adjacencies into account
- The model will not account for translation or rotation of the image

For example, when the image is shifted appropriately, a zero could look like a six or vice versa. Similarly, if all the images are trained using a dataset that had all the numbers centered in the image but the test dataset has an image that is shifted slightly to the right or left, the prediction is likely to be inaccurate. This is because the model would have placed a weightage for each pixel.

In order to solve the preceding problem, a deep learning technique named **convolutional neural network** (**CNN**) comes in handy. A CNN works in such a way that it assigns weightages at a region level rather than at a pixel level. Essentially, this forms the convolution part of convolutional neural networks. In this way, pixel adjacencies are taken into account by using deep learning.

Similarly, translation of an image is accounted for by a technique called **max pooling** that is used in CNN.

The typical architecture of a CNN looks as follows, and more details of it will be explained in a later chapter:

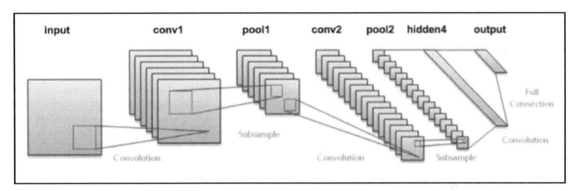

In the preceding diagram, the input is the image that we consider. **conv1** is the output when a convolution is applied between filters and input. Given that we apply multiple filters, we would have multiple convolutions, and **pool1** is the output of applying pooling on the convolution output. The process of convolution and pooling is applied repeatedly until we obtain the final fully connected unit, which is then linked to the output.

Applications of deep learning

In the previous section, we understood why deep learning shines over machine learning in some applications. Let's go through some of the applications of deep learning:

- Translation from one language to another
- Speech-to-text conversion
- Image analysis in multiple industries
- Identifying text present in images
- Image and audio synthesis
- Personalization to predict the next movie/product that a user is likely to watch/buy
- Time series analysis
- Detecting rare events

Summary

In this chapter, we understood the major difference between supervised and unsupervised learning and got an overview of the major machine learning algorithms. We also understood the areas where deep learning algorithms shine over traditional machine learning algorithms, through examples of text and image analysis.

Google Machine Learning APIs

7

As seen in the previous chapter, machine learning is used in a wide variety of applications. However, a few applications are easy to build, while a few are very hard to build, especially for a user who is less familiar with machine learning. Some of the applications that we are going to discuss in this chapter fall in the hard to build category, as the process of building a machine learning model for these applications is data intensive, resource intensive, and requires a lot of knowledge in the field.

In this chapter, we will go over five machine learning APIs provided by Google (as of March 2018). These APIs are meant to be used out of the box, as RESTful APIs. For each service mentioned in the following, we will show what type of application can benefit from it, and how to interpret the returned results:

- Vision has a label detection, OCR, face detection and emotions, logo,and landmark
- Speech means speech-to-text
- NLP has entities, sentiment, and POS
- Translation
- Video intelligence

Vision API

The Vision API lets us build quite a few applications related to vision:

- Detecting labels in an image
- Detecting the text in an image
- Face detection
- Emotion detection
- Logo detection
- Landmark detection

Before we dive into building applications using the preceding, let's get a quick understanding of how they might be built, using face emotion detection as an example.

The process of detecting emotions involves:

1. Collecting a huge set of images
2. Hand-labeling images with the emotion that is likely represented in the image
3. Training a **convolutional neural network** (**CNN**) (to be discussed in future chapters) to classify the emotion, based on an image as input

While the preceding steps are heavily resource intensive (as we would need a lot of humans to collect and hand-label images), there are multiple other ways to obtain face emotion detection. We are not sure how Google is collecting and labeling images, but we will now consider the API that Google has built for us, so that, if we want to classify images into the emotions they represent, we can make use of that API.

Enabling the API

Before we start building applications, we first have to enable the API, as follows:

1. Search for the **Google Cloud Vision API**:

2. Enable the **Google Cloud Vision API**:

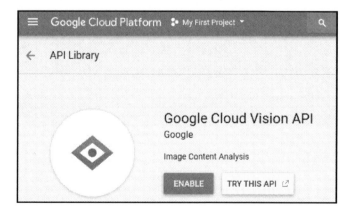

3. Once you click on **ENABLE,** the API will be enabled for the project (that is, **My First Project**), as seen in the preceding screenshot.
4. Fetch credentials for the API:

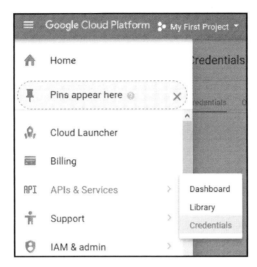

5. Click on **Service account key** after clicking on **Create credentials**:

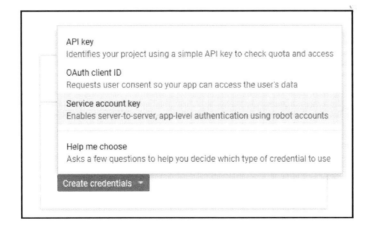

6. Click on **New service account**:

7. Enter a service account name (in my case, `kish-gcp`) and **Select a role** as the project **Owner**:

8. Click on **Create** to save the JSON file of keys.

Opening an instance

In order to open an instance, click on **VM instances,** as shown in the screenshot that follows, and then click on the **Activate google cloud shell** icon:

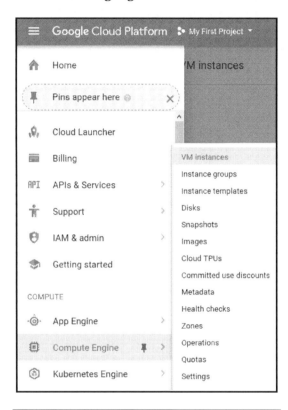

Creating an instance using Cloud Shell

Once we click on the cloud shell icon, we create an instance as follows:

1. An instance is created by specifying the following code:

```
datalab create --no-create-repository <instance name>
```

2. In the **Cloud Shell**, the preceding code looks as follows:

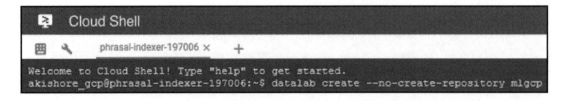

3. Once you have keyed in the responses for all of the prompts, you need to **Change port** to 8081 to access Datalab, which is done as follows:

4. Once you click on **Change port** you will get a window as follows. Enter 8081 and click on **CHANGE AND PREVIEW** to open Datalab:

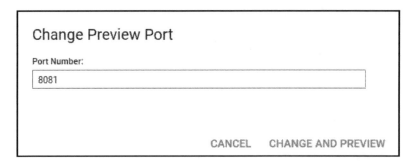

5. This will open up Datalab, which has functionalities that enable us to write all types of commands: bash, bigquery, python, and so on.

Now that the requirements are set up, let's fetch/install the requirements for the API:

1. Accessing the API keys in the previous section, we have downloaded the required keys. Now, let's upload the `.json` file to Datalab by clicking on the **Upload** button:

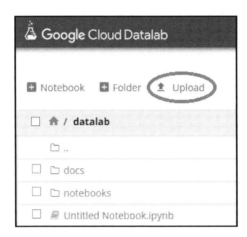

2. Once the `.json` file is uploaded, you should be able to access it through Datalab from here:

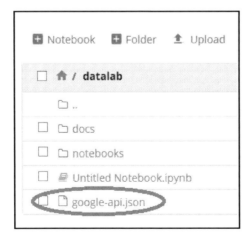

3. Open a notebook; you can open a notebook in Datalab by clicking on the **Notebook** tab, as follows:

4. To install `google-cloud`, once you open the **Notebook**, change the kernel from **python2** to **python3**:

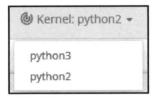

5. Install the `google-cloud` package, as follows:

```
%bash
pip install google-cloud
```

6. Once `google-cloud` is installed, make sure that the `.json` file uploaded earlier is accessible in the current Python environment, by specifying the following:

```
import os
os.environ["GOOGLE_APPLICATION_CREDENTIALS"] =
"/content/datalab/google-
api.json"
```

7. In order to upload an image of interest, we will look at transferring a file from the local machine into the **bucket,** and from the **bucket** to Datalab.

8. Search for `bucket` in the Google Cloud:

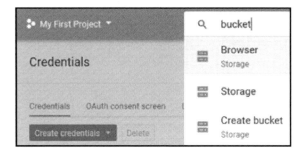

9. Now, name the bucket and create it:

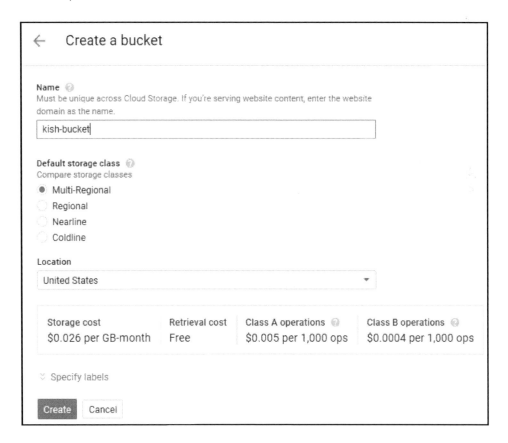

10. Click on **Upload files** to upload relevant files from the local machine to the bucket.

11. Once the file is uploaded to the bucket, fetch it from Datalab, as follows:

```
%bash
gsutil cp gs://kish-bucket/11.jpg /content/datalab/

Copying gs://kish-bucket/11.jpg...
/ [1 files][  3.4 MiB/  3.4 MiB]
Operation completed over 1 objects/3.4 MiB.
```

12. Now, you should notice that `11.jpg` is accessible in Datalab.

Now that the image to analyze is accessible in Datalab, let's understand the ways to leverage the Cloud Vision API to understand images better:

1. Import the relevant packages:

```
from google.cloud import vision
```

The preceding code snippet makes sure that the methods available in Vision are accessible in the current session.

2. Invoke the service that performs **Google Cloud Vision** API detection tasks (such as face, landmark, logo, label, and text detection) over client images—`ImageAnnotator`:

```
client = vision.ImageAnnotatorClient()
```

3. Verify that the image is uploaded per expectation:

```
import matplotlib.pyplot as plt
import matplotlib.image as mpimg
%matplotlib inline
img=mpimg.imread('/content/datalab/11.jpg')
plt.axis('off')
plt.imshow(img)
```

4. Invoke the `face_detection` method to fetch the relevant details of the image, as follows:

```
response = client.face_detection({'source' : {'image_uri':
"gs://kish-
bucket/11.jpg"},})
```

5. The responses to image annotations are as follows:

Fields	
face_annotations[]	FaceAnnotation If present, face detection has completed successfully.
landmark_annotations[]	EntityAnnotation If present, landmark detection has completed successfully.
logo_annotations[]	EntityAnnotation If present, logo detection has completed successfully.
label_annotations[]	EntityAnnotation If present, label detection has completed successfully.
text_annotations[]	EntityAnnotation If present, text (OCR) detection has completed successfully.

full_text_annotation	TextAnnotation If present, text (OCR) detection or document (OCR) text detection has completed successfully. This annotation provides the structural hierarchy for the OCR detected text.
safe_search_annotation	SafeSearchAnnotation If present, safe-search annotation has completed successfully.
image_properties_annotation	ImageProperties If present, image properties were extracted successfully.
crop_hints_annotation	CropHintsAnnotation If present, crop hints have completed successfully.
web_detection	WebDetection If present, web detection has completed successfully.
error	Status If set, represents the error message for the operation. Note that filled-in image annotations are guaranteed to be correct, even when error is set.

6. Now that we have run our method to detect faces in the image, let's look at the output - `response`. The output of `response` is a set of attributes, as described previously:

`response`

```
1  response

   face_annotations {
     bounding_poly {
       vertices {
         x: 1427
         y: 279
       }
       vertices {
         x: 2176
         y: 279
       }
       vertices {
         x: 2176
         y: 1149
       }
       vertices {
         x: 1427
         y: 1149
       }
     }
     fd_bounding_poly {
       vertices {
         x: 1494
         y: 461
       }
       vertices {
         x: 2098
         y: 461
       }
       vertices {
         x: 2098
```

The following are the few more points explained in detail:

- **Bounding polygon**: The bounding polygon is around the face. The coordinates of the bounding box are in the original image's scale, as returned in `ImageParams`. The bounding box is computed to frame the face in accordance with human expectations. It is based on the landmarker results. Note that one or more *x* and/or *y* coordinates may not be generated in the `BoundingPoly` (the polygon will be unbounded) if only a partial face appears in the image to be annotated.
- **Face detection bounding polygon**: The `fd_bounding_poly` bounding polygon is tighter than the `BoundingPoly`, and encloses only the skin part of the face. Typically, it is used to eliminate the face from any image analysis that detects the amount of skin visible in an image.
- **Landmarks**: Detected face landmarks.

There are few more terms explained in the following points:

- `roll_angle`: Roll angle, which indicates the amount of clockwise/anticlockwise rotation of the face, relative to the image . The range is [-180,180].
- `pan_angle`: Yaw angle, which indicates the leftward/rightward angle that the face is pointing, relative to the vertical plane perpendicular to the image. The range is [-180,180].
- `tilt_angle`: Pitch angle, which indicates the upwards/downwards angle that the face is pointing, relative to the image's horizontal plane. The range is [-180,180].
- `detection_confidence`: Confidence associated with the detection.
- `landmarking_confidence`: Confidence associated with the landmarking.
- `joy_likelihood`: Likelihood associated with the joy.
- `sorrow_likelihood`: Likelihood associated with the sorrow.
- `anger_likelihood`: Likelihood associated with the anger.
- `surprise_likelihood`: Likelihood associated with the surprise.
- `under_exposed_likelihood`: Likelihood associated with the exposed.
- `blurred_likelihood`: Likelihood associated with the blurred.
- `headwear_likelihood`: Likelihood associated with the headwear.

Face landmarks would further provide the locations of eyes, noses, lips, ears and so on.

We should be able to make a boundary box around the face identified.

The output of `face_annotations` is as follows:

```
response.face_annotations[0].bounding_poly.vertices

[x: 1427
y: 279
, x: 2176
y: 279
, x: 2176
y: 1149
, x: 1427
y: 1149
]
```

From the preceding code, we should be able to understand the coordinates of the bounding box. In the code that follows, we calculate the starting point of the bounding box, and the corresponding width and height of the bounding box. Once the calculation is done, we superimpose the rectangle over the original image:

```python
import matplotlib.patches as patches
import numpy as np
fig,ax = plt.subplots(1)

# Display the image
ax.imshow(img)

# Create a Rectangle patch
x_width = np.abs(response.face_annotations[0].bounding_poly.vertices[1].x-
    response.face_annotations[0].bounding_poly.vertices[0].x)
y_height = np.abs(response.face_annotations[0].bounding_poly.vertices[1].y-
    response.face_annotations[0].bounding_poly.vertices[3].y)

rect =
patches.Rectangle((response.face_annotations[0].bounding_poly.vertices[0].x
,
  response.face_annotations[0].bounding_poly.vertices[0].y),
x_width,y_height,linewidth=5,edgecolor='y',facecolor='none')

# Add the patch to the Axes
ax.add_patch(rect)
plt.axis('off')
plt.show()
```

The output of the preceding code is the image with a bounding box around the face, as follows:

Label detection

In the previous code snippet, we used the `face_detection` method to fetch the various coordinates.

In order to understand the label of the image, we will be using the `label_detection` method in place of `face_detection`, as follows:

```
response_label = client.label_detection({'source' : {'image_uri':
"gs://kish-
bucket/11.jpg"},})
```

```
response_label

label_annotations {
  mid: "/m/09g5pq"
  description: "people"
  score: 0.9678634405136108
  topicality: 0.9678634405136108
}
label_annotations {
  mid: "/m/0ytgt"
  description: "child"
  score: 0.954465389251709
  topicality: 0.954465389251709
}
label_annotations {
  mid: "/m/01k74n"
  description: "facial expression"
  score: 0.9380199909210205
  topicality: 0.9380199909210205
}
label_annotations {
  mid: "/m/06z04"
  description: "skin"
  score: 0.9294329881668091
  topicality: 0.9294329881668091
}
```

The output of label detection is a collection of labels, along with the scores associated with each label.

Text detection

The text in an image can be identified by using the `text_detection` method, as follows:

```
response_text = client.text_detection({'source' : {'image_uri': "gs://kish-bucket/11.jpg"},})
```

The output of `response_text` is as follows:

```
response

text_annotations {
  locale: "en"
  description: "LITTLE\nMISS\nMUCH\n"
  bounding_poly {
    vertices {
      x: 1374
      y: 1425
    }
    vertices {
      x: 2151
      y: 1425
    }
    vertices {
      x: 2151
      y: 2303
    }
    vertices {
      x: 1374
      y: 2303
```

Note that the output of the `text_detection` method is the bounding box of the various text that is present in the image.

Also, note that the description of `text_annotations` provides the text detected in the image.

Logo detection

Vision services also enable us to recognize the logo in an image by using the `logo_detection` method.

In the following code, you can see that we are able to detect the logo of `wikipedia` by passing the URL of the image's location, as follows:

```
response = client.logo_detection({'source' : {'image_uri':
"https://upload.wikimedia.org/wikipedia/commons/thumb/b/b3/Wikipedia-logo-v
2-
en.svg/135px-Wikipedia-logo-v2-en.svg.png"},})
```

The output of the `logo_detection` method is as follows:

```
response

logo_annotations {
  mid: "/m/0d07ph"
  description: "Wikipedia"
  score: 0.5256200432777405
  bounding_poly {
    vertices {
      x: 31
      y: 28
    }
    vertices {
      x: 113
      y: 28
    }
    vertices {
      x: 113
      y: 124
    }
    vertices {
      x: 31
      y: 124
    }
  }
}
```

Landmark detection

Note that, in the preceding lines of code, we have specified the URL of the image location in the `logo_detection` method, and it resulted in a description of the predicted logo, and also the confidence score associated with it.

Similarly, any landmark located in an image can be detected by using the `landmark_detection` method, as follows:

```
response = client.landmark_detection({'source' : {'image_uri':
  "https://upload.wikimedia.org/wikipedia/commons/thumb/1/1d/
  Taj_Mahal_%28Edited%29.jpeg/250px-Taj_Mahal_%28Edited%29.jpeg"},})
```

The output of the `landmark_detection` method is as follows:

```
response

landmark_annotations {
  mid: "/m/0l8cb"
  description: "Taj Mahal"
  score: 0.940950870513916
  bounding_poly {
    vertices {
      x: 6
      y: 9
    }
    vertices {
      x: 227
      y: 9
    }
    vertices {
      x: 227
      y: 155
    }
    vertices {
      x: 6
      y: 155
    }
  }
  locations {
    lat_lng {
      latitude: 27.174698469698683
      longitude: 78.042073
```

Cloud Translation API

The Cloud Translation API provides a simple, programmatic interface for translating an arbitrary string into any supported language, using state-of-the-art neural machine translation. The Translation API is highly responsive, so websites and applications can integrate with the Translation API for fast, dynamic translation of source text from the source language to a target language (for example, French to English). Language detection is also available for cases in which the source language is unknown.

Enabling the API

For us to be able to use Google cloud translation services, we need to enable, which is done as follows:

1. In order to enable the **Google Cloud Translation API**, search for the API in the console:

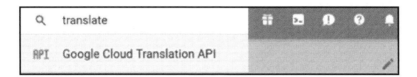

2. Enable the **Google Cloud Translation API**:

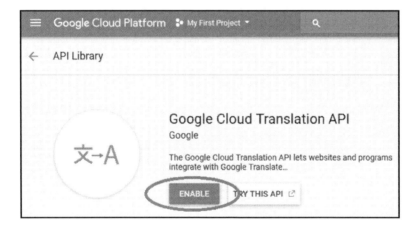

3. Once the Translation API is enabled, the next step is to create credentials to access the API. However, note that if you have already created credentials for one API, they can be used for any other API. Let's go ahead and initialize our instance using Cloud Shell:

```
Welcome to Cloud Shell! Type "help" to get started.
akishore_gcp@phrasal-indexer-197006:~$ datalab connect mlgcp
```

4. Once the instance starts, we will open Datalab on port 8081. We provide a path to the location of the `api-key` file as follows:

```
import os
os.environ["GOOGLE_APPLICATION_CREDENTIALS"] =
"/content/datalab/google-api.json"
```

5. The various methods to `translate` are imported by using the following statement:

```
from google.cloud import translate
```

6. Create a `client` object that creates a connection to the Cloud Translation service, as follows:

```
client = translate.Client()
```

The **Google Cloud Translation API** has three supported methods, and they are `get_languages()`, `detect_language()`, and `translate()`:

- The `client.get_languages()` method gives us a list of all of the available languages, and also their shorthand notations, as follows:

```
client.get_languages()

[{u'language': u'af', u'name': u'Afrikaans'},
 {u'language': u'sq', u'name': u'Albanian'},
 {u'language': u'am', u'name': u'Amharic'},
 {u'language': u'ar', u'name': u'Arabic'},
 {u'language': u'hy', u'name': u'Armenian'},
 {u'language': u'az', u'name': u'Azerbaijani'},
 {u'language': u'eu', u'name': u'Basque'},
 {u'language': u'be', u'name': u'Belarusian'},
 {u'language': u'bn', u'name': u'Bengali'},
 {u'language': u'bs', u'name': u'Bosnian'},
 {u'language': u'bg', u'name': u'Bulgarian'},
 {u'language': u'ca', u'name': u'Catalan'},
 {u'language': u'ceb', u'name': u'Cebuano'},
 {u'language': u'ny', u'name': u'Chichewa'},
 {u'language': u'zh', u'name': u'Chinese (Simplified)'},
 {u'language': u'zh-TW', u'name': u'Chinese (Traditional)'},
 {u'language': u'co', u'name': u'Corsican'},
 {u'language': u'hr', u'name': u'Croatian'},
 {u'language': u'cs', u'name': u'Czech'},
 {u'language': u'da', u'name': u'Danish'},
 {u'language': u'nl', u'name': u'Dutch'},
 {u'language': u'en', u'name': u'English'},
 {u'language': u'eo', u'name': u'Esperanto'},
 {u'language': u'et', u'name': u'Estonian'},
 {u'language': u'tl', u'name': u'Filipino'},
 {u'language': u'fi', u'name': u'Finnish'},
 {u'language': u'fr', u'name': u'French'},
 {u'language': u'fy', u'name': u'Frisian'},
```

- The `client.detect_language()` method detects the language that the text is written in:

```
client.detect_language(['Me llamo', 'I am'])

[{u'confidence': 1, 'input': 'Me llamo', u'language': u'es'},
 {u'confidence': 1, 'input': 'I am', u'language': u'en'}]
```

Note that in the preceding method, we have given two texts—one in Spanish, and the other in English. The preceding output represents the language of the text, along with the confidence associated with the detection of the language.

- The `client.translate()` method detects the source language and translates the text into English (by default), as follows:

```
client.translate('koszula')

{u'detectedSourceLanguage': u'pl',
 'input': 'koszula',
 u'translatedText': u'shirt'}
```

- The `client.translate()` method also gives us an option to specify the target language to which a text needs to be translated, as follows:

```
client.translate(['Me llamo Kishore', 'My name is Kishore'],target_language='de')

[{u'detectedSourceLanguage': u'es',
  'input': 'Me llamo Kishore',
  u'translatedText': u'Mein Name ist Kishore'},
 {u'detectedSourceLanguage': u'en',
  'input': 'My name is Kishore',
  u'translatedText': u'Mein Name ist Kishore'}]
```

Natural Language API

The Google Cloud Natural Language API reveals the structure and meaning of text by offering powerful machine learning models in an easy-to-use REST API. You can use it to extract information about people, places, events, and much more, that are mentioned in text documents, news articles, or blog posts. You can also use it to understand the sentiment about your product on social media, or to parse intent from customer conversations happening in a call center or a messaging app. You can analyze the text uploaded in your request, or integrate it with with your document storage on Google Cloud storage.

The **Cloud Natural Language API** can be found by searching for it in your console, as follows:

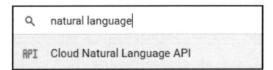

The **Cloud Natural Language API** is enabled in the resulting page:

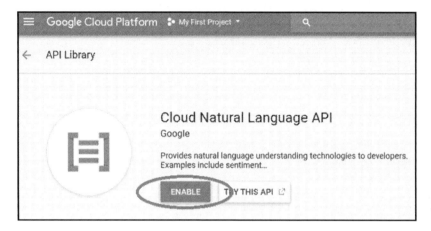

Similar to the Translation API, we do not have to create credentials for this API if at least one API is already enabled.

Natural language processing can be useful in extracting the sentiments associated with various text.

Sentiment analysis inspects the given text and identifies the prevailing emotional opinion within the text, to determine a writer's attitude as positive, negative, or neutral. Sentiment analysis is performed through the `analyzeSentiment` method.

In the following example, let's understand how to identify the sentiment of a statement:

1. Import the relevant packages:

    ```
    from google.cloud import language
    ```

2. Initialize the class corresponding to the language service:

    ```
    client = language.LanguageServiceClient()
    ```

The **Google Natural Language API** has the following supported methods:

*   `analyzeEntities`
*   `analyzeSentiment`
*   `analyzeEntitySentiment`
*   `annotateText`
*   `classifyText`

Each method uses a Document for representing text. Let's explore the analyzeSentiment method in the following example:

```
text="this is a good text"
from google.cloud.language_v1 import types
document = types.Document(
        content=text,
        type='PLAIN_TEXT')
sentiment = client.analyze_sentiment(document).document_sentiment
sentiment.score
```

Note that we have converted the input text into a Document type, and then analyzed the sentiment of the document.

The output of the sentiment score reflects the probability of a text being positive; the closer the score is to one, the more positive the statement is.

Similarly, one could pass on an HTML file, as follows:

```
document = language.types.Document(
        content=html_content,
        language='es',
        type='HTML',
)
```

Files that are stored in a Google Cloud bucket can also be referenced, by changing the content to gcs_content_uri, as follows:

```
document = language.types.Document(
        gcs_content_uri='gs://my-text-bucket/sentiment-me.txt'
        type=language.enums.HTML,
)
```

The analyze_entities() method finds named entities (that is, proper names) in the text. This method returns an AnalyzeEntitiesResponse:

```
document = language.types.Document(content='Michelangelo Caravaggio,
Italian    painter, is known for "The Calling of Saint Matthew".'
                            ,type='PLAIN_TEXT')
response = client.analyze_entities(document=document)

for entity in response.entities:
  print('name: {0}'.format(entity.name))
```

The output of the preceding loop is the named entities present in the document's content, as follows:

```
name: Michelangelo Caravaggio
name: Italian
name: The Calling of Saint Matthew
```

We can also extract the part of speech of each of the words in the given text by using the `analyze_syntax` method, as follows:

1. Tokenize the document into the corresponding words that constitute the text:

```
tokens = client.analyze_syntax(document).tokens
tokens[0].text.content
# The preceding output is u'Michelangelo'
```

2. The parts of speech of a `token` can then be extracted, as follows:

```
pos_tag = ('UNKNOWN', 'ADJ', 'ADP', 'ADV', 'CONJ', 'DET', 'NOUN',
'NUM','PRON', 'PRT', 'PUNCT', 'VERB', 'X', 'AFFIX')
for token in tokens:print(u'{}:
{}'.format(pos_tag[token.part_of_speech.tag],
                          token.text.content))
```

The output of the preceding code is:

```
NOUN: Michelangelo
NOUN: Caravaggio
PUNCT: ,
ADJ: Italian
NOUN: painter
PUNCT: ,
VERB: is
VERB: known
ADP: for
PUNCT: "
DET: The
NOUN: Calling
ADP: of
NOUN: Saint
NOUN: Matthew
PUNCT: "
PUNCT: .
```

Note that the majority of the words are classified into the right parts of speech.

Speech-to-text API

The Google Cloud Speech API enables developers to convert audio to text, by applying powerful neural network models in an easy-to-use API. The API recognizes over 110 languages and variants. One can transcribe the text of users dictating to an application's microphone, enable command-and-control through voice, or transcribe audio files, among many use cases.

In order to enable the speech to text API, search for it in the console, as follows:

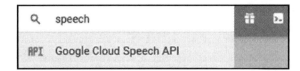

In the resulting web page, enable the API, as follows:

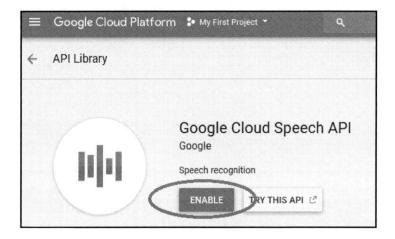

Similar to the APIs mentioned in the previous sections, credentials obtained for one API can be replicated for the other Google APIs. So, we don't have to create credentials separately for the speech to text API.

Once the API is enabled, let's start the Cloud Shell and Datalab, as we did in the previous sections.

In the following code, we transcribe a small audio file into text:

1. Import the relevant packages and the API key:

    ```
    from google.cloud import speech
    import os
    os.environ["GOOGLE_APPLICATION_CREDENTIALS"] =
    "/content/datalab/google-api.json"
    from google.cloud.speech import enums
    from google.cloud.speech import types
    ```

2. Invoke the speech service, as follows:

    ```
    client = speech.SpeechClient()
    ```

3. We can specify the audio that we want to convert, as follows:

    ```
    audio = types.RecognitionAudio(uri='gs://kish-
    bucket/how_are_you.flac')
    ```

 Note that **Free Lossless Audio Codec (FLAC)**.

An audio file (`.wav`) can be converted to a `.flac` file by using the converter located at `https://audio.online-convert.com/convert-to-flac`.

The file is located in the bucket we created earlier. We specify the audio configuration, as follows:

```
config = types.RecognitionConfig(
encoding=enums.RecognitionConfig.AudioEncoding.FLAC,
sample_rate_hertz=16000,
language_code='en-US')
```

A response is obtained by passing the `audio` content, as well as the configuration specified:

```
response = client.recognize(config, audio)
```

The results can now be accessed, as follows:

```
for result in response.results:
  print(result)
```

The output for this is:

```
alternatives {
  transcript: "how are you"
  confidence: 0.897314190865
}
```

The `recognize` method works when the input audio file is a short (<1 minute) duration audio.

If the `audio` file is longer in duration, the method to be used is `long_running_recognize`:

```
operation = client.long_running_recognize(config, audio)
```

The `result` can then be accessed by specifying the following:

```
response = operation.result(timeout=90)
```

Finally, the transcription and the confidence can be obtained by printing the response results, as was done previously.

Video Intelligence API

The Cloud Video Intelligence API makes videos searchable and discoverable, by extracting metadata with an easy-to-use REST API. You can now search every moment of every video file in your catalog. It quickly annotates videos stored in Google Cloud storage, and helps you to identify key entities (nouns) within your videos and when they occur.

The **Cloud Video Intelligence API** can be searched for and enabled as follows:

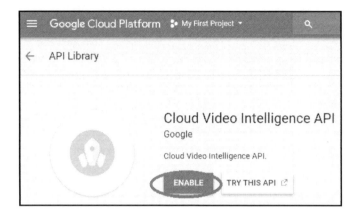

We import the required packages and add the path to the `api-key`, as follows:

```
from google.cloud import videointelligence
import os
os.environ["GOOGLE_APPLICATION_CREDENTIALS"] = "/content/datalab/google-
api.json"
from google.cloud.speech import enums
from google.cloud.speech import types
```

The method `features` enables us to specify the type of content that we want to detect in a video. The features available are as follows:

```
videointelligence.enums.Feature.
videointelligence.enums.Feature.EXPLICIT_CONTENT_DETECTION
videointelligence.enums.Feature.FACE_DETECTION
videointelligence.enums.Feature.FEATURE_UNSPECIFIED
videointelligence.enums.Feature.LABEL_DETECTION
videointelligence.enums.Feature.SHOT_CHANGE_DETECTION
```

Let's go ahead and detect labels in the video of interest to us:

```
features = [videointelligence.enums.Feature.LABEL_DETECTION]
```

We specify the `config` and context of the video, as follows:

```
mode = videointelligence.enums.LabelDetectionMode.SHOT_AND_FRAME_MODE
config = videointelligence.types.LabelDetectionConfig(
    label_detection_mode=mode)
context = videointelligence.types.VideoContext(
    label_detection_config=config)
```

The video then needs to be passed from Cloud storage, as follows:

```
path="gs://kish-bucket/Hemanvi_video.mp4"
operation = video_client.annotate_video(
        path, features=features, video_context=context)
```

The result of the `annotate_video` method is accessed as follows:

```
result = operation.result(timeout=90)
```

The annotation results for a video can be obtained at the:

- Video segment level
- Video shot level
- Frame level

Results at the segment level, after looping through each of the various segment label annotations, can be obtained as follows:

```
segment_labels = result.annotation_results[0].segment_label_annotations
for i, segment_label in enumerate(segment_labels):
    print('Video label description: {}'.format(
        segment_label.entity.description))
    for category_entity in segment_label.category_entities:
        print('\tLabel category description: {}'.format(
            category_entity.description))

    for i, segment in enumerate(segment_label.segments):
        start_time = (segment.segment.start_time_offset.seconds +
                        segment.segment.start_time_offset.nanos / 1e9)
        end_time = (segment.segment.end_time_offset.seconds +
                        segment.segment.end_time_offset.nanos / 1e9)
        positions = '{}s to {}s'.format(start_time, end_time)
        confidence = segment.confidence
        print('\tSegment {}: {}'.format(i, positions))
        print('\tConfidence: {}'.format(confidence))
    print('\n')
```

The output of the preceding code is:

```
Video label description: playground
        Label category description: city
        Segment 0: 0.0s to 15.6s
        Confidence: 1.0


Video label description: playground slide
        Segment 0: 0.0s to 15.6s
        Confidence: 0.790848553181


Video label description: outdoor play equipment
        Segment 0: 0.0s to 15.6s
        Confidence: 0.932455003262


Video label description: leisure
        Segment 0: 0.0s to 15.6s
        Confidence: 0.470728754997
```

Similarly, results at the shot level can be obtained as follows:

```
shot_labels = result.annotation_results[0].shot_label_annotations
for i, shot_label in enumerate(shot_labels):
    print('Shot label description: {}'.format(
        shot_label.entity.description))
    for category_entity in shot_label.category_entities:
        print('\tLabel category description: {}'.format(
            category_entity.description))

    for i, shot in enumerate(shot_label.segments):
        start_time = (shot.segment.start_time_offset.seconds +
                      shot.segment.start_time_offset.nanos / 1e9)
        end_time = (shot.segment.end_time_offset.seconds +
                    shot.segment.end_time_offset.nanos / 1e9)
        positions = '{}s to {}s'.format(start_time, end_time)
        confidence = shot.confidence
        print('\tSegment {}: {}'.format(i, positions))
        print('\tConfidence: {}'.format(confidence))
    print('\n')
```

The output of the preceding lines of code is:

```
Shot label description: fun
        Segment 0: 13.033333s to 14.0s
        Confidence: 0.58486521244
        Segment 1: 14.033333s to 15.6s
        Confidence: 0.686410725117


Shot label description: playground
        Label category description: city
        Segment 0: 0.0s to 13.0s
        Confidence: 1.0
        Segment 1: 13.033333s to 14.0s
        Confidence: 0.959590852261
        Segment 2: 14.033333s to 15.6s
        Confidence: 0.966488361359


Shot label description: playground slide
        Segment 0: 0.0s to 13.0s
        Confidence: 0.784813344479
        Segment 1: 13.033333s to 14.0s
        Confidence: 0.475744605064
        Segment 2: 14.033333s to 15.6s
        Confidence: 0.530465841293
```

Finally, the result at the frame level can be obtained as follows:

```
frame_labels = result.annotation_results[0].frame_label_annotations
for i, frame_label in enumerate(frame_labels):
    print('Frame label description: {}'.format(
        frame_label.entity.description))
    for category_entity in frame_label.category_entities:
        print('\tLabel category description: {}'.format(
            category_entity.description))

    # Each frame_label_annotation has many frames,
    # here we print information only about the first frame.
    frame = frame_label.frames[0]
    time_offset = (frame.time_offset.seconds +
                    frame.time_offset.nanos / 1e9)
    print('\tFirst frame time offset: {}s'.format(time_offset))
    print('\tFirst frame confidence: {}'.format(frame.confidence))
    print('\n')
```

The output of the preceding lines of code is:

```
Frame label description: play
        Label category description: person
        First frame time offset: 0.951819s
        First frame confidence: 0.886474370956


Frame label description: swing
        First frame time offset: 0.951819s
        First frame confidence: 0.453329116106


Frame label description: seesaw
        Label category description: playground
        First frame time offset: 0.951819s
        First frame confidence: 0.526799023151
```

Summary

In this chapter, we went through the major machine learning APIs that Google provides: vision, translate, NLP, speech, and video intelligence. We have learned how the various methods in each of the APIs enable us to replicate deep learning results, without having to code from scratch.

8
Creating ML Applications with Firebase

In the previous chapter, we learned about using some of the various Google machine learning APIs to predict/classify an event. However, we performed all our work in Datalab. In a real-world scenario, we could want to integrate machine learning APIs into a web application or a mobile application that we build. Firebase comes in handy in such a scenario. Firebase is a platform allows us to build web and mobile applications without server-side programming. Firebase provides multiple features that ensure that the developer focuses on building the application, while the backend is taken care of. Some of the features that Firebase provides are:

- Real-time database
- File storage
- Cloud functions
- Hosting
- Performance monitoring
- Analytics
- Authentication

In this chapter, we will understand more about the various features provided by Firebase. Also, to understand how Firebase helps in building applications with machine learning capabilities, we will build a web application and a mobile application that translates text in any given language into english using the Google Translate API and provides the most translated text.

Features of Firebase

Some of the features that Firebase provides are as follows:

- **Real-time database**: Enables us to store and sync app data in milliseconds
- **Cloud firestore**: Enables us to store and sync data on global scale
- **Cloud functions**: Enables us to run backend code without managing servers
- **Hosting**: Delivers web app assets with speed and security
- **Performance monitoring**: Helps gain insights into an app's performance
- **Crashlytics**: Enables us to prioritize and fix issues with powerful, real-time crash reporting
- **Authentication**: Helps us authenticate users simply and securely
- **Cloud storage**: Enables us to store and serve files at Google scale
- **Predictions**: Enables us to define dynamic user groups based on predicted behavior
- **Remote config**: Enables us to modify our app without deploying a new version
- **App indexing**: Enables us to drive search traffic to mobile app
- **Cloud messaging**: Enables us to send targeted messages and notifications
- **Dynamic links**: Enables us to drive growth by using deep links with attribution
- **Invites**: Enables us to drive growth by using deep links with attribution

In this chapter, we will build an application that takes an input text and translates it into English—first a web application and then a mobile application.

Building a web application

In order to build the web application, we make use of Node.js.

Download and install Node.js:

1. `node.js` can be downloaded from the link here: `https://nodejs.org/en/`. For the version that we are building now, we will use the 8.11.1 LTS version of Node.js on Windows 64-bit machine.
2. Once you download the executable file from `https://nodejs.org/dist/v8.11.1/node-v8.11.1-x64.msi`, make sure to install Node.js using the default parameters.

Create a Firebase project:

1. A Firebase project can be created by logging in to the Firebase console here: `https://console.firebase.google.com`
2. Within the console, click on **Add project**:

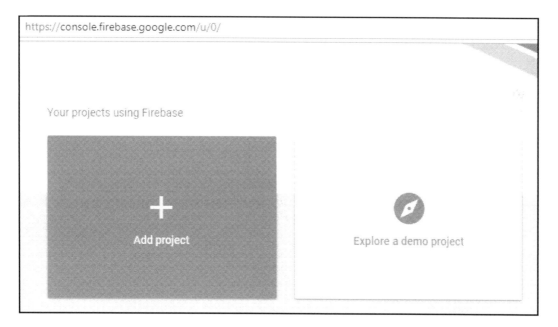

3. Enter project name (highlighted in red) and fetch project ID (highlighted in black), as follows:

4. Install Firebase tools using Node.js package manager, as follows:
   • Change directory to the folder where the `firebase` function files need to be stored. In the following screenshot, we are creating a folder named `firebase` in the E drive:

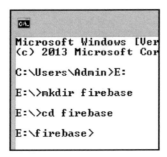

5. We install Firebase tools using the following code snippet:

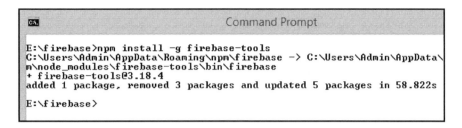

Log in and initialize Firebase:

1. We log into Firebase, by specifying:

   ```
   firebase login --reauth
   ```

2. The previous code snippet would allow us to log in using our credentials. Make sure to allow Firebase CLI to access your Google account.

3. Once we are logged into Firebase, we initialize firebase as follows:

   ```
   firebase init
   ```

4. You will get the following screen:

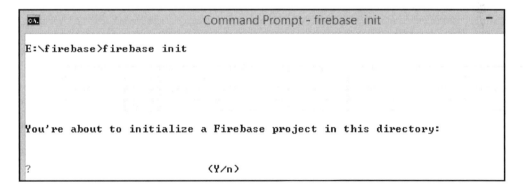

5. Press *Y* to initialize Firebase.

6. Select the features that are needed for the current application by pressing the space bar, and, once done with selection, press *Enter*:

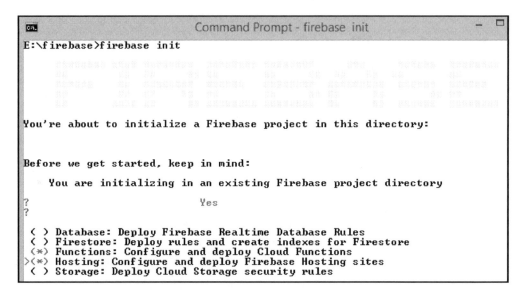

7. Once selected, for the version that we use here, let us specify that our functions are deployed with JavaScript, as follows:

```
=== Functions Setup

A            directory will be created in your project with a Node.js
package pre-configured. Functions can be deployed with            .

?                                                        (Use arrow keys
>
> JavaScript
  TypeScript
```

8. Once selected, we set the project with the project directory:

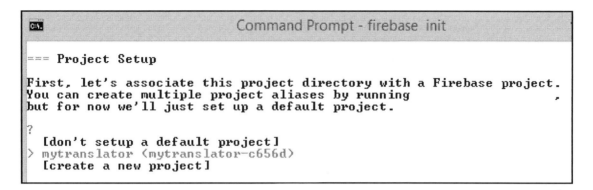

Note that mytranslator is the project that we created in *step 2*. Also note that once we've initialized Firebase, the folder structure looks like this:

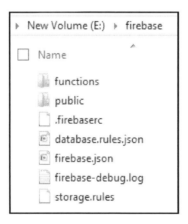

9. In Command Prompt, press *Enter* for the various prompts after initializing Firebase. At the end of initialization, you should get a confirmation upon completing initialization as follows:

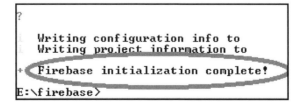

Install Google Translate using Node.js package manager after scrolling to the `functions` folder:

```
E:\firebase>cd functions

E:\firebase\functions>npm install @google-cloud/translate
+ @google-cloud/translate@1.1.0
added 12 packages in 6.67s
```

We specify all the functionalities (public API methods) that are required for our use case. These functions handle all the server programming:

1. In order to specify these, let us overwrite the `index.js` file present in the `functions` folder with the following code snippet.

```
const functions = require('firebase-functions');
const Translate = require('@google-cloud/translate');
const admin = require("firebase-admin")

//setting connection to db
admin.initializeApp();

const translate = new Translate({
    projectId: 'mytranslator-c656d'
});
//Extract the most searched term

exports.getMessageStats=functions.https.onRequest((req,res) =>
 {
 var output;
 var db = admin.database();
 var ref = db.ref("/translateMessageStats");

// Attach an asynchronous callback to read the data at our posts
reference
 ref.orderByChild("count").limitToLast(1).on("value",
function(snapshot) {

console.log(snapshot.forEach(element => {
 output=element.key+" : "+element.val().count + 'times'
 }))
 res.header("Access-Control-Allow-Origin", "*");
 return res.send(JSON.stringify(output));
 }, function (errorObject) {
 console.log("The read failed: " + errorObject.code);
 });
```

```
})

// create a public API method of name "translateMessage"

exports.translateMessage=functions.https.onRequest((req,res) =>
 {
 const input = req.query.text;

translate.translate(input,'en').then(results =>
 {
 const output = results[0];
 console.log(output);

const db = admin.database();
var ref = db.ref("/translateMessageStats");

//update database
 var dataRef= ref.child(input);

dataRef.once('value', function(snapshot) {
 if (snapshot.exists()) {
 dataRef.update({"count":snapshot.val().count+1});
 console.log("data exists")
 }
 else
 {
 console.log("data does not exist")
 dataRef.update({"count":1});
 }
 });

res.header("Access-Control-Allow-Origin", "*");
 return res.send(JSON.stringify(output));
 })
});
```

2. In this code, we import the required Node.js packages by using the following code:

```
const functions = require('firebase-functions');
const Translate = require('@google-cloud/translate');
const admin = require("firebase-admin")
```

3. We initialize the connection to the database by specifying the following:

```
admin.initializeApp();
```

4. We create `translate` object and pass the project ID as a parameter in it, as follows:

```
const translate = new Translate({
    projectId: 'mytranslator-c656d'
});
```

5. We then create a public facing API with name `translateMessage`, as follows:

```
exports.translateMessage=functions.https.onRequest((req,res) =>
```

6. The input given by user is fetched through the following line:

```
const input = req.query.text;
```

7. The translation of input text and the corresponding storage of translated text in the output is done by this code:

```
translate.translate(input,'en').then(results =>
{
    const output = results[0];
```

8. We create an instance of database, as follows:

```
const db = admin.database();
 var ref = db.ref("/translateMessageStats");
```

9. The input is updated in the database:

```
var dataRef= ref.child(input);
```

10. If a new input is given, `count` is initialized to 1; else, `count` is incremented by 1:

```
dataRef.once('value', function(snapshot) {
    if (snapshot.exists()) {
        dataRef.update({"count":snapshot.val().count+1});
        console.log("data exists")
    }
    else
    {
        console.log("data does not exist")
        dataRef.update({"count":1});
    }
});
```

Enable the **Google Cloud Translation API**, as follows:

Deploy the `firebase` function:

1. We can deploy the `firebase` function as shown in the following screenshot:

```
E:\firebase>firebase deploy --only functions

=== Deploying to 'mytranslator-c656d'...

  deploying
  functions: ensuring necessary APIs are enabled...
+ functions: all necessary APIs are enabled
  functions: preparing       directory for uploading...
  functions: packaged        (40.97 KB) for uploading
+ functions:       folder uploaded successfully
  functions: updating function        ...
+ functions[translateMessage]: Successful update operation.

+

        https://console.firebase.google.com/project/mytranslator-c656d/
overview
```

2. Once the function is deployed, check out **Functions** in the **DEVELOP** section of **Project Overview**:

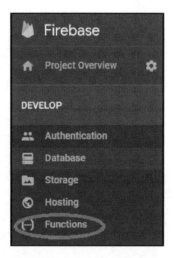

3. Once we click on **Functions**, we should be able to see a dashboard that contains the function that we just created—translateMessage:

Note that, the previous event provides us with a URL, using which we should be able to translate the input text, as follows:

Note the usage of `?text=` in the URL, which is the input.

In case there is an issue with the execution, we should be able to understand them in the **Logs** tab (of the **Functions** dashboard).

Additionally, all the inputs that we have searched for, are stored in database:

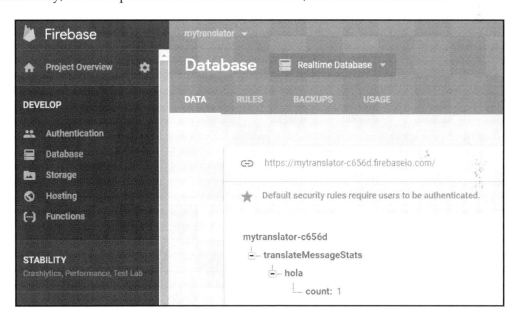

Note that the count value is initialized as searched for the term `hola`.

Replace the content of `index.html` file in the `public` folder with the following code snippet. The output of following code snippet would be to create a textbox that lets us give an input text, translate the text, and produce the translated output.

1. In your execution, replace the project ID `mytranslator-c656d` with your own project ID:

```html
<html>
  <script
src="https://ajax.googleapis.com/ajax/libs/jquery/3.1.0/jquery.min.
js"> </script>
  <script>

    $(document).ready(
      getMessageStats()
    );
<!-- The following code extracts the most searched term from the
database that we create in the next function -->

    function getMessageStats(){
      var xhr = new XMLHttpRequest();
      xhr.open('GET',
"https://us-central1-mytranslator-c656d.cloudfunctions.net/getMessa
geStats", true);
      xhr.send();
      xhr.onreadystatechange = processRequest;

      function processRequest(e) {
        if (xhr.readyState == 4) {
          var response = JSON.parse(xhr.responseText);
document.getElementById("mostSearched").innerHTML=response;
        }
      }
    }
<!-- the following function translates the input value into english
-->
    function translateText()
    {
      var textInput= document.getElementById("input").value;
      var xhr = new XMLHttpRequest();
      xhr.open('GET',
"https://us-central1-mytranslator-c656d.cloudfunctions.net/translat
eMessage?text="+textInput, true);
      xhr.send();

      xhr.onreadystatechange = processRequest;
      function processRequest(e) {
```

```
            if (xhr.readyState == 4) {
              var response = JSON.parse(xhr.responseText);
              document.getElementById("output").innerHTML=response;
              getMessageStats();
            }
          }
        }
      </script>
      <!-- the following code creates the layout of web application, with
      input text box and output-->
        <body>
          <label>Enter Input Text</label>
          <input id="input" type="text-area"></input>
          <button onclick="translateText()"
      id="btnTrans">Translate</button>
          <label id="output"></label>
          <br/>
          <div>
            <h1>Most Searched element</h1>
            <label id="mostSearched"></label>
          </div>
        </body>
      </html>
```

We deploy Firebase so that we upload the HTML file that specifies the structure of the final URL we would be working on:

```
E:\firebase>firebase deploy

=== Deploying to 'mytranslator-c656d'...

  deploying
i functions: ensuring necessary APIs are enabled...
+ functions: all necessary APIs are enabled
i functions: preparing            directory for uploading...
i functions: packaged          (40.94 KB) for uploading
+ functions:           folder uploaded successfully
i hosting: preparing          directory for upload...
+ hosting: 1 files uploaded successfully
i functions: updating function            ...
+ functions[translateMessage]: Successful update operation.

+

              https://console.firebase.google.com/project/mytranslator-c656d/
overview
              https://mytranslator-c656d.firebaseapp.com
```

We should now be able to access the link shown, which helps us in translating text, as follows:

From this, we have seen that we are able to create a web application that translates any given input text. Note that the web application made use of the API endpoint that was created by function, and the frontend code would only vary by the framework that we use—it could be different when we use Angular over HTML, but the server side code would remain the same.

Building a mobile application

In the previous section, we understood the frontend of an HTML page that would translate input for us. In this section, we will build the frontend of an Android app that leverages the endpoint we generated for the function to return the translated text for us.

We create the layout of the app as follows:

```xml
<?xml version="1.0" encoding="utf-8"?>
 <android.support.constraint.ConstraintLayout
xmlns:android="http://schemas.android.com/apk/res/android"
    xmlns:app="http://schemas.android.com/apk/res-auto"
    xmlns:tools="http://schemas.android.com/tools"
    android:layout_width="match_parent"
    android:layout_height="match_parent"
    tools:context=".MainActivity">

    <Button
        android:id="@+id/button"
        android:layout_width="wrap_content"
        android:layout_height="wrap_content"
        android:layout_marginStart="148dp"
        android:layout_marginTop="56dp"
        android:text="Translate"
```

```
        app:layout_constraintStart_toStartOf="parent"
        app:layout_constraintTop_toBottomOf="@+id/input" />

    <EditText
        android:id="@+id/input"
        android:layout_width="wrap_content"
        android:layout_height="wrap_content"
        android:layout_marginStart="84dp"
        android:layout_marginTop="84dp"
        android:ems="10"
        android:inputType="textPersonName"
        app:layout_constraintStart_toStartOf="parent"
        app:layout_constraintTop_toTopOf="parent" />

    <TextView
        android:id="@+id/out"
        android:layout_width="197dp"
        android:layout_height="80dp"
        android:layout_marginStart="92dp"
        android:layout_marginTop="56dp"
        app:layout_constraintStart_toStartOf="parent"
        app:layout_constraintTop_toBottomOf="@+id/button" />

</android.support.constraint.ConstraintLayout>
```

The preceding code would output the layout of the app:

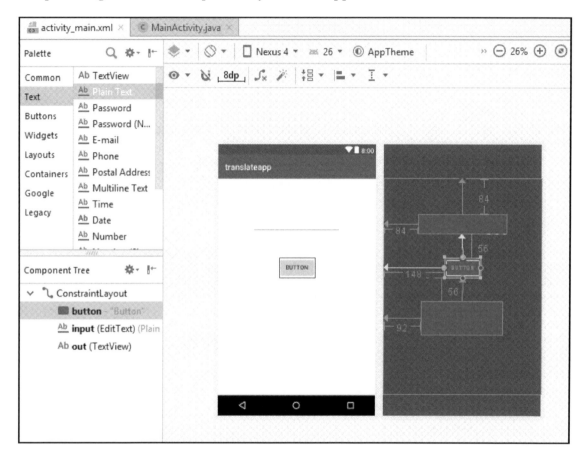

Note that we have an **EditText** view that takes input.

The **Button** is used to execute the translation and **out** is the **TextView** where the output is displayed.

Also note that in the preceding code, we have ensured that the components are aligned to the screen.

Within main activity, we execute the following code:

```
package com.example.admin.translateapp;

import android.os.AsyncTask;
import android.support.v7.app.AppCompatActivity;
import android.os.Bundle;
import android.view.View;
import android.widget.Button;
import android.widget.EditText;
import android.widget.TextView;

import java.io.BufferedReader;
import java.io.IOException;
import java.io.InputStreamReader;
import java.net.HttpURLConnection;
import java.net.URL;

import javax.net.ssl.HttpsURLConnection;

public class MainActivity extends AppCompatActivity {
    public String myurl;
    public String result;
    public String response;
    public EditText inp;
    public TextView out;
    public Button btn;

    @Override
    protected void onCreate(Bundle savedInstanceState) {
        super.onCreate(savedInstanceState);
        setContentView(R.layout.activity_main);
        inp = (EditText) findViewById(R.id.input);
        out = (TextView) findViewById(R.id.out);
        btn = (Button) findViewById(R.id.button);
        myurl =
"http://us-central1-mytranslator-c656d.cloudfunctions.net/translateMessage?
text=";

        btn.setOnClickListener(new View.OnClickListener() {
            public void onClick(View v) {
                RequestTask task = new RequestTask();
                task.execute(inp.getText().toString());
            }
        });
    }

    private class RequestTask extends AsyncTask<String, String, String> {
```

```java
        @Override
        protected String doInBackground(String... uri) {
            try {
                URL url = new URL(myurl+uri[0].toString());
                HttpURLConnection conn = (HttpURLConnection)
url.openConnection();
                conn.setRequestMethod("GET");
                conn.connect();
                if (conn.getResponseCode() == HttpURLConnection.HTTP_OK) {
                    InputStreamReader streamReader = new
                            InputStreamReader(conn.getInputStream());
                    //Create a new buffered reader and String Builder
                    BufferedReader reader = new
BufferedReader(streamReader);
                    StringBuilder stringBuilder = new StringBuilder();
                    //Check if the line we are reading is not null
                    String inputLine;
                    while((inputLine = reader.readLine()) != null){
                        stringBuilder.append(inputLine);
                    }
                    //Close our InputStream and Buffered reader
                    reader.close();
                    streamReader.close();
                    //Set our result equal to our stringBuilder
                    result = stringBuilder.toString();
                    //result = conn.getResponseMessage();
                } else {
                }
            } catch (IOException e) {
                //TODO Handle problems..
            }
            return result;
        }

        @Override
        protected void onPostExecute(String result1) {
            super.onPostExecute(result1);
            out.setText(result1);
        }
    }
}
```

Let us understand the preceding code.

Import the relevant packages:

```
import android.os.AsyncTask;
import android.support.v7.app.AppCompatActivity;
import android.os.Bundle;
import android.view.View;
import android.widget.Button;
import android.widget.EditText;
import android.widget.TextView;

import java.io.BufferedReader;
import java.io.IOException;
import java.io.InputStreamReader;
import java.net.HttpURLConnection;
import java.net.URL;
```

Initialize the objects that we use in the MainActivity class:

```
public String myurl;
public String result;
public String response;
public EditText inp;
public TextView out;
public Button btn;
```

Also, initialize the views using the following code:

```
inp = (EditText) findViewById(R.id.input);
out = (TextView) findViewById(R.id.out);
btn = (Button) findViewById(R.id.button);
```

Set the on-click listener:

```
btn.setOnClickListener(new View.OnClickListener() {
    public void onClick(View v) {
        RequestTask task = new RequestTask();
        task.execute(inp.getText().toString());
```

Specify the tasks that need to be executed when clicked on the button:

```
URL url = new URL(myurl+uri[0].toString());
HttpURLConnection conn = (HttpURLConnection) url.openConnection();
conn.setRequestMethod("GET");
conn.connect();
if (conn.getResponseCode() == HttpURLConnection.HTTP_OK) {
    InputStreamReader streamReader = new
```

```
            InputStreamReader(conn.getInputStream());
    //Create a new buffered reader and String Builder
    BufferedReader reader = new BufferedReader(streamReader);
    StringBuilder stringBuilder = new StringBuilder();
    //Check if the line we are reading is not null
    String inputLine;
    while((inputLine = reader.readLine()) != null){
        stringBuilder.append(inputLine);
    }
    //Close our InputStream and Buffered reader
    reader.close();
    streamReader.close();
    //Set our result equal to our stringBuilder
    result = stringBuilder.toString();
```

From the preceding code, the URL gets evaluated to the URL that we have seen in the previous web application section.

The output of the preceding code is as follows:

Note that, on clicking the **BUTTON**, we should be able to translate our text.

Summary

In this chapter, we understood the various features of Firebase and using `firebase` functions to build the backend of web and mobile applications. We also used `firebase` functions to update a database on a real-time basis and retrieve the most searched term historically from the database.

9
Neural Networks with TensorFlow and Keras

Neural network is a supervised learning algorithm that is loosely inspired by the way the brain functions. Similarly to the way neurons are connected to each other in the brain, a neural network takes an input and passes it through a function, based on which certain subsequent neurons get excited, and the output is produced.

In this chapter, we will focus on the practical implementation of neural networks with TensorFlow and Keras. TensorFlow provides a low-level framework to create neural network models. Keras is a high-level neural network API that significantly simplifies the task of defining neural network models. We'll show how to use Keras on top of TensorFlow to define and train models on GCP. We'll present the Keras API in Python and work with a simple feedforward network applied on the classic MNIST dataset. Also, we will go through the different components of a neural network:

- Initialization
- Metrics and loss functions
- Activation functions
- Depth of the network

Overview of a neural network

The origin of neural networks comes from the fact that every function cannot be approximated by a linear/logistic regression—there can be potentially complex shapes within data that can only be approximated by complex functions.

The more complex the function (with some way to take care of overfitting), the better the prediction accuracy.

The following image explains the way in which neural networks work towards fitting data into a model.

The typical structure of a neural network is as follows:

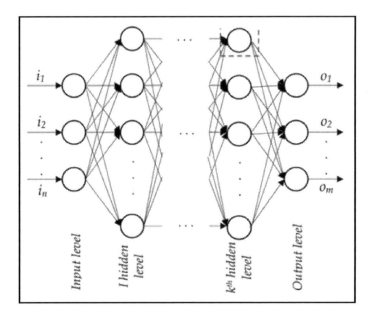

The input level/layer in this diagram is typically made up of the independent variables that are used to predict the output (dependent variable) level or layer.

The hidden level/layer is used to transform the input variables into a higher-order function. The way in which a hidden layer transforms the output is as follows:

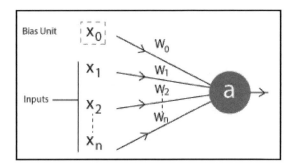

In the preceding diagram, $x_1, x_2, ..., x_n$ are the independent variables and x_0 is the bias term (similar to the way we have a bias in linear/logistic regression).

$w_1, w_2, ..., w_n$ are the weights given to each of the input variables. If a is one of the neurons in the hidden layer, it would be equal to:

$$a = f(\sum_{i=0}^{N} w_i x_i)$$

The function that we see in this equation is the activation function that we are applying on top of the summation so that we attain nonlinearity. We need nonlinearity so that our model can learn complex patterns.

Moreover, having more than one hidden layer helps in achieving a high amount of nonlinearity.

A detail of the various parameters that can be tweaked in a neural network will be provided in the subsequent sections.

Setting up Google Cloud Datalab

In order to set up Google Cloud Datalab, we click on the Cloud Shell icon:

Within the Cloud Shell, set the project that needs to be worked on, as follows:

```
gcloud config set core/project gcp-test-196204
```

Once the project is set, configure the zone as follows:

```
gcloud config set compute/zone us-west1-b
```

Finally, create a Datalab instance by specifying:

- For a CPU version:

```
datalab create --no-create-repository mlgcp
```

- For a GPU version:

First, you need to request a GPU version through the quotas page, as follows:

Submit the quota request and you should receive the permission to use GPU in the given region soon.

Note that a GPU version is better while building neural network models as the multiple processors in the GPU can then work on updating multiple weights of a neural network in parallel.

Change the port to 8081 to open Datalab and thereby the notebooks.

Installing and importing the required packages

TensorFlow, as a package, is built to perform neural network computations. It works with the lazy evaluation concept, where the various elements of a neural network connection are to be specified, before executing the code.

Another API named Keras makes building neural networks a lot easier. In this chapter, we will be first leveraging the Keras package with TensorFlow running in its backend, and then we'll show how to build a neural network using the premade estimator and a custom estimator in TensorFlow.

In the previous chapters, we understood how to set up Datalab notebooks. In this chapter, we will see how to install and import the required packages into Datalab notebooks.

By default, Datalab comes with a preinstalled TensorFlow package. However, it does not contain Keras by default. Let's look at installing the `keras` package:

```
!pip install keras
```

Once Keras is installed, let's import both the required packages:

```
import keras as K
import tensorflow as tf
```

Working details of a simple neural network

In order to understand how neural networks work, we will build a very simple network. The input and the expected output are as follows:

```
import numpy as np
x=np.array([[1,2],[3,4]])
y=np.array([0,1])
```

Note that x is the input dataset with two variables for each of the two rows. y is the expected output for the two inputs.

Essentially, we have the input and output layers in place.

As an example, for one of the preceding data points, the input and the output values of the network will look like this:

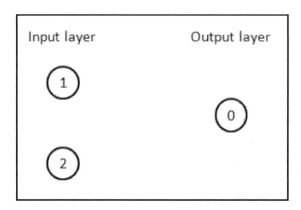

In traditional machine learning, you would find the relation directly between the input and output values. However, the neural network architecture works with the following intuition:

"The input values can be represented in a richer (higher) dimensional space. The more the dimensions in which the input values are represented, the more is the complexity in the input dataset captured."

With the preceding intuition, let's build a hidden layer with three units in a neural network:

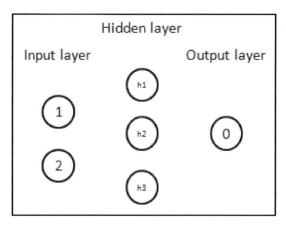

Now that the layer is built, let's make connections between each unit, as follows:

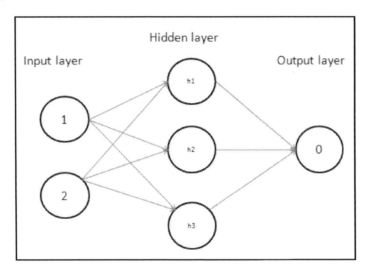

Now that a connection between each unit is made, there will be a certain amount of weightage that is associated with each connection. In the following diagram, we will initialize the weight that each connection represents:

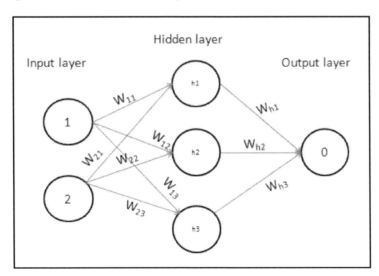

Note that the weights **W** represent the strength of connection.

Now we have built a simple neural network. Let's randomly initialize the weight values between the input and hidden layers to understand how the hidden layer values are computed:

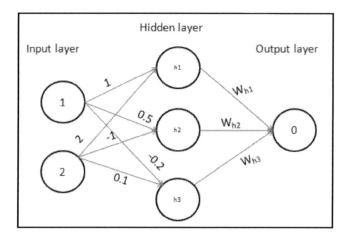

Hidden layer values are computed as the multiplications of the input values and weights associated with them, as follows:

$$h1 = 1*1 + 2*(2) = 5$$

$$h2 = 1*0.5 + 2*(-1) = -1.5$$

$$h3 = 1*(-0.2) + 2*0.1 = 0$$

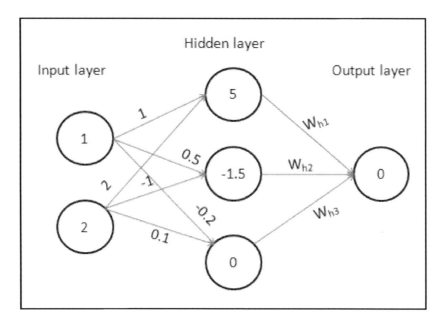

Now that the hidden values are calculated, we pass them through an activation function. The intuition for an activation function is as follows:

"The neural network in the state that we presented previously (without an activation function) is a big linear combination of input variables. Nonlinearity can only be obtained by performing an activation on top of the hidden layer values."

For simplicity, as of now, we will assume that the nonlinearity that we are going to apply is the sigmoid function.

A sigmoid function works as follows:

- It takes an input value, x, and transforms into a new value, $1/(1+exp(-x))$

The nonlinearity of a sigmoid curve looks like this for various values of *x*:

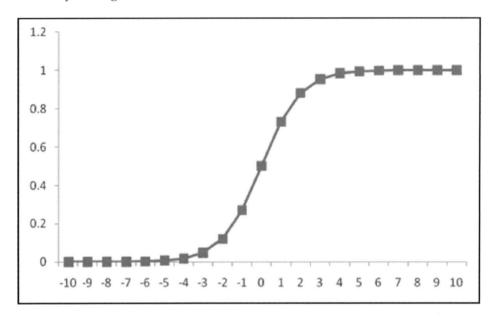

Thus, the hidden layer values, which were 5, -1.5, and 0, are transformed to **0.99**, **0.18**, and **0.5**:

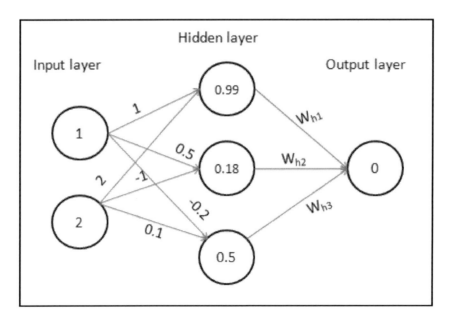

Now that the hidden layer values are computed, let's initialize the weights connecting the hidden layer to the output layer.

Note that again the weights are initialized randomly:

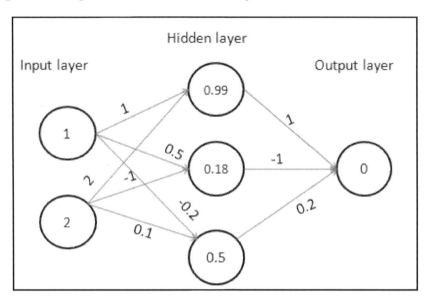

Now that the weights are initialized, let's calculate the value associated with the output layer:

$$0.99*1 + 0.18*(-1) + 0.5*0.2 = 0.91$$

The expected value at the output layer is *0.91*, while the actual value is 0.

Thus, the loss associated in this scenario is *(0.91 - 0)^2 = 0.83.*

The process until now, where we calculate the loss corresponding to the weight values, is called the **feedforward process**.

So far, in this section, we have understood:

- Weights
- Activation function
- Loss calculation

In the preceding scenario, while the loss function remains constant for a given objective that we try to solve, the weight initialization and activation functions can vary for different network architectures.

The objective for the problem laid out just now would be to minimize the loss corresponding to a network architecture by iteratively varying the weights.

For example, in the preceding architecture, the loss can be reduced by changing the final weight from the hidden layer to the output layer connection from *0.2* to *0.1*. Once the weight is changed, the loss reduces from *0.83* to *0.74*.

The process by which weights are changed iteratively to minimize the loss value is called **backpropagation**.

The number of times a weight change happens per given dataset is called the **epoch**. Essentially, an epoch constitutes feedforward and backpropagation.

One of the techniques to intelligently arrive at the optimal weight values is called **gradient descent**—more on various weight optimizers in a later section.

Backpropagation

In the previous section, we have seen the intuition of how weights are updated in backpropagation. In this section, we will see the details of how the weight update process works:

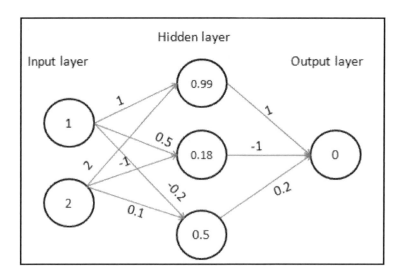

In the backpropagation process, we start with the weights at the end of the neural network and work backwards.

In the preceding diagram (1), we iteratively change the values of weights by a small amount (0.01) for each of the weights connecting the hidden layer to the output layer:

Original weight	Changed weight	Error	Reduction in error
1	1.01	0.84261	-1.811
-1	-0.99	0.849	-0.32
0.2	0.21	0.837	-0.91

From the preceding table, we notice that instead of increasing the weight values, one should reduce them to improve the error:

Original weight	Changed weight	Error	Reduction in error
1	0.99	0.8108	1.792
-1	-1.01	0.8248	0.327
0.2	0.19	0.819	0.9075

Now we note that, for some weight updates, the improvement in error is high, while for some other weight updates, the improvement in error is low.

This indicates that, for some weights for which error is improving by a lot, the weight update could be faster; while for some weights for which the error improvement is relatively low, the weight update could be slower.

The changed weight for the weight with a value of 1 could then be:

Changed weight = original weight + learning rate X reduction in error

For now, let's assume that the learning rate is *0.05*; then:

Changed weight = 1 + 0.05*(1.792) = 1.089

The other weights will be changed using the same formula.

Intuitively, the learning rate helps us in building trust in the algorithm. For example, when deciding on the magnitude of a weight update, we would potentially not change everything in one go but take a more careful approach in updating the weights more slowly.

Once all the weights are updated using the process laid out, the backpropagation process is done and we proceed with forward propagation again.

A feedforward and a backpropagation step are together called an **epoch**.

Note that we calculated the error value in predicting a data point at a time, thus forming a batch size of 1. In practice, we calculate the error values for a group of data points and then keep updating the weights using a batch of data rather than a single data point.

Implementing a simple neural network in Keras

From the preceding discussion, we have seen that the key components in a neural network are:

- Hidden layers
- Activation in a hidden layer
- Loss function

Along with these, there are a few other key components in a neural network. However, we will learn about them in a later section.

For now, we will build a neural network model with the given toy dataset in Keras, with the knowledge we've gained in the sections so far:

Import the relevant functions:

```
from keras.models import Sequential
from keras.layers import Dense
```

The sequential model is a linear stack of layers (input, hidden, and output).

Within each layer, dense helps in implementing the operations specified in the network.

Let us go ahead and build the network as follows:

```
model = Sequential()
model.add(Dense(3,input_dim=2,activation='sigmoid'))
model.add(Dense(1))
```

In our data, we take the input dataset, which is two-dimensional, and convert it into a three-dimensional hidden layer unit in the first step.

Once the hidden layer values are calculated, we pass them through a sigmoid activation in the second step.

The preceding two steps are captured in the second line of the model specification.

From the hidden layer, we connect it to an output layer that is one-dimensional, and hence the third line of code has Dense(1).

Let's look at the summary of the model that we specified:

```
model.summary()


Layer (type)                    Output Shape                Param #
=================================================================
dense_1 (Dense)                 (None, 3)                   9

dense_2 (Dense)                 (None, 1)                   4
=================================================================
Total params: 13
Trainable params: 13
Non-trainable params: 0

```

Let's understand the output shape column for the preceding summary: (None, 3).

None means that the output is agnostic of the number of inputs (not to be confused with the dimension of inputs). 3 represents the number of units in the hidden layer.

Similarly (None, 1) in the second layer represents the dimension of the output layer (which has only one unit in the output layer).

Param # represents the number of parameters associated with the network.

Note that the connections between the input and hidden layers have a total of nine parameters, as there are six weight values (as shown in the diagram in the previous section) and three bias terms associated with each unit in the hidden layer.

Similarly, there are four parameters in the connection between the hidden and output layers, as there are three weight values between the hidden and output layers and one bias term associated with the output layer.

Now that the network architecture is specified, let's compile the model, as follows:

```
model.compile(loss='mean_squared_error', optimizer='sgd')
```

In the preceding line of code, we are specifying that the loss is calculated based on mean squared error, which is the average of the squared difference between actual and predicted values across all data points in the input.

Similarly, we specify that the optimization technique is based on stochastic gradient descent.

Now that the model structure, the loss function that we are computing, and optimization technique that we are using are specified, let's fit the model on the input and output values.

The additional metrics that we need to specify while fitting the model are:

- Input and output values
- Number of epochs to be run on the model:

```
model.fit(x,y,epochs=10)

Epoch 1/10
2/2 [==============================] - 0s 2ms/step - loss: 0.9903
Epoch 2/10
2/2 [==============================] - 0s 741us/step - loss: 0.9413
Epoch 3/10
2/2 [==============================] - 0s 711us/step - loss: 0.8959
Epoch 4/10
2/2 [==============================] - 0s 686us/step - loss: 0.8539
Epoch 5/10
2/2 [==============================] - 0s 729us/step - loss: 0.8151
Epoch 6/10
2/2 [==============================] - 0s 624us/step - loss: 0.7792
Epoch 7/10
2/2 [==============================] - 0s 657us/step - loss: 0.7460
Epoch 8/10
2/2 [==============================] - 0s 676us/step - loss: 0.7153
Epoch 9/10
2/2 [==============================] - 0s 606us/step - loss: 0.6869
Epoch 10/10
2/2 [==============================] - 0s 612us/step - loss: 0.6606
```

Note that the input and output variables that we specified are x, y.

Also, you should notice that the loss values decrease over different epochs, as the weight values are adjusted to minimize the loss as much as possible over the 10 epochs.

Now that the model is built, let's look at obtaining the weight values at each layer:

```
model.get_weights()

[array([[-0.9857289 ,  0.5377088 , -0.2417026 ],
        [-0.3587317 , -0.82248205,  0.98158664]], dtype=float32),
 array([ 0.00195088,  0.01157819, -0.00272675], dtype=float32),
 array([[ 0.8347641 ],
        [ 0.6618012 ],
        [-0.40098628]], dtype=float32),
 array([0.1461481], dtype=float32)]
```

The values corresponding to a new input value can now be calculated as follows:

```
new_input = np.array([[2,5]])
model.predict(new_input)

array([[-0.2005076]], dtype=float32)
```

In the preceding code snippet, we have initialized a new input and predicted the output corresponding to this new input using the optimal weights that were obtained by running the model.

Let's understand how the output is obtained.

Obtain the values corresponding to the three units in the hidden layer:

$$h1 = 2*(-0.985) + 5*(-0.3587) + 0.00195 = -3.76$$

$$h2 = 2*0.537 + 5*(-0.8225) + 0.0011 = -3.025$$

$$h3 = 2*(-0.24) + 5*0.98 - 0.0027 = 4.421$$

Once the hidden layer values are calculated, we pass them through the sigmoid activation function, as specified in the model architecture:

$$final\ h1 = sigmoid(h1) = 0.0226$$

$$final\ h2 = sigmoid(h2) = 0.0462$$

$$final\ h3 = sigmoid(h3) = 0.988$$

Once the final hidden layer unit values are obtained, we multiply them with the weights connecting hidden layer to output layer, as follows:

$$Output = 0.0226 * 0.834 + 0.0462*0.6618 + (-0.401)*0.988 + 0.14615 = -0.20051$$

Note that the value we obtained is the same value that was obtained in the `model.predict` function. This proves the architecture functionality that we have learnt so far.

Now that we have built the model, let's re-execute our code and see whether the results remain the same:

```
model = Sequential()
model.add(Dense(3,input_dim=2,activation='sigmoid'))
model.add(Dense(1))
model.compile(loss='mean_squared_error', optimizer='sgd')
model.fit(x,y,epochs=10)

Epoch 1/10
2/2 [==============================] - 0s 56ms/step - loss: 0.6903
Epoch 2/10
2/2 [==============================] - 0s 636us/step - loss: 0.6560
Epoch 3/10
2/2 [==============================] - 0s 528us/step - loss: 0.6242
Epoch 4/10
2/2 [==============================] - 0s 473us/step - loss: 0.5948
Epoch 5/10
2/2 [==============================] - 0s 478us/step - loss: 0.5674
Epoch 6/10
2/2 [==============================] - 0s 478us/step - loss: 0.5421
Epoch 7/10
2/2 [==============================] - 0s 443us/step - loss: 0.5186
Epoch 8/10
2/2 [==============================] - 0s 430us/step - loss: 0.4969
Epoch 9/10
2/2 [==============================] - 0s 440us/step - loss: 0.4768
Epoch 10/10
2/2 [==============================] - 0s 438us/step - loss: 0.4581

<keras.callbacks.History at 0x7f7d091da208>
```

Note that the loss values are different from what we obtained in the previous iteration. This is because weights are randomly initialized in the first epoch of a neural network run. One way to fix this is by setting a seed. A seed helps in initializing the same set of random values every time a neural network runs.

Note that the seed should be run every time a model is rebuilt. The code snippet for setting a seed looks like this:

```
from numpy.random import seed
seed(1)
from tensorflow import set_random_seed
set_random_seed(2)

model = Sequential()
model.add(Dense(3,input_dim=2,activation='sigmoid'))
model.add(Dense(1))
model.compile(loss='mean_squared_error', optimizer='sgd')
model.fit(x,y,epochs=10)
```

Understanding the various loss functions

As discussed in the previous chapter, there are two types of dependent variables—continuous and categorical variables. In the case of continuous variable prediction, the loss (error) function can be calculated by using the sum of squared error values across all predictions.

In cases where the dependent variable is a categorical variable with only two distinct values associated with it, loss is calculated as the binary cross-entropy error using this formula:

$$y*logp + (1-y)*log(1-p)$$

In cases where the dependent variable is a categorical variable with multiple distinct values, the loss is calculated using the categorical cross-entropy error as:

$$\sum y*logp$$

Where p is the probability of the event being a 1.

Categorical variables are typically one-hot encoded in practice as follows:

Let's say the output across three different rows is [1,2,3]; then the output values are represented as [[1,0,0], [0,1,0], [0,0,1]]. where each index value represents whether a distinct value is present or not. In the above example, the zeroth index corresponds to 1 and hence only the first row has a value of 1 for zeroth while the rest have a value of 0.

The other loss functions that are available in Keras are:

- Mean absolute error
- Mean absolute percentage error
- Mean squared logarithmic error
- Squared hinge
- Hinge
- Categorical hinge
- Logcosh

Softmax activation

From the preceding section, we should notice that in the case of categorical variable prediction, the number of units in the output layer would be the same as the number of distinct values in the dependent variable.

Also, note that the predicted value cannot be greater than 1 or less than 0 for any of the units in the output layer. At the same time, the sum of the values across all nodes in the output should be equal to 1.

For example, let's say the output across two nodes of output is -1 and 5. Given that the expected value of outputs should be between 0 and 1 (the probability of an event happening), we pass the output values through softmax activation, as follows:

- Pass the values through an exponential function:

$$exp(-1) = 0.367$$

$$exp(5) = 148$$

- Normalize the output values to obtain a probability between 0 to 1 and also to ensure that the sum of probabilities between the two output nodes is 1:

$$0.367/(0.367+148) = 0.001$$

$$148/(0.367+148) = 0.999$$

Thus, the softmax activation helps us in converting the output values into probability numbers.

Building a more complex network in Keras

So far, we have built a neural network that is fairly simple. A traditional neural network would have a few more parameters that can be varied to achieve a better predictive power.

Let's understand them by using the classic MNIST dataset. MNIST is a handwritten digit dataset that contains images of size 28 x 28 pixels that are represented as NumPy arrays of 28 x 28 dimensions.

Each image is of a digit and the challenge in hand is to predict the digit the image corresponds to.

Let's download and explore some of the images present in the MNIST dataset, as follows:

```
from keras.datasets import mnist

(X_train, y_train), (X_test, y_test) = mnist.load_data()
```

In the preceding code snippet, we are importing the MNIST object and downloading the MNIST dataset using the `load_data` function.

Also note that the `load_data` function helps in automatically splitting the MNIST dataset into train and test datasets.

Let's visualize one of the images within the train dataset:

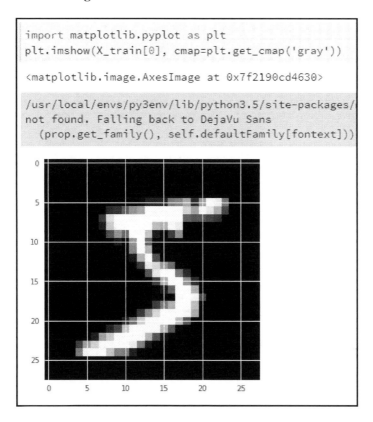

Note that the preceding digit is **5** and the grid that we are seeing is 28 x 28 in size.

Let's look at the shapes of input and output to further understand the datasets:

```
print(X_train.shape)
print(y_train.shape)
print(X_test.shape)
print(y_test.shape)

(60000, 28, 28)
(60000,)
(10000, 28, 28)
(10000,)
```

Given that each input image is 28 x 28 in size, let's flatten it to get the scores of the 784 pixel values:

```
X_train = X_train.reshape(X_train.shape[0], 784).astype('float32')
X_test = X_test.reshape(X_test.shape[0], 784).astype('float32')
```

The output layer needs to predict whether the image corresponds to one of the digits from 0 to 9. Thus, the output layer consists of 10 units corresponding to each of the 10 different digits:

```
from keras.utils import np_utils
y_train = np_utils.to_categorical(y_train)
y_test = np_utils.to_categorical(y_test)
```

In the preceding code, `to_categorical` provides a one hot-encoded version of the label.

Now that we have the train and test datasets in place, let's go ahead and build the architecture of neural network in the following section:

```
1 model = Sequential()
2 model.add(Dense(1000,input_dim=784,activation='sigmoid'))
3 model.add(Dense(10,activation='softmax'))
4 model.compile(loss='categorical_crossentropy', optimizer='sgd',metrics=['accuracy'])
5 model.fit(X_train,y_train,epochs=10,batch_size=1024,validation_data=(X_test,y_test),verbose=2)

Train on 60000 samples, validate on 10000 samples
Epoch 1/10
 - 1s - loss: 1.3256 - acc: 0.6351 - val_loss: 0.8083 - val_acc: 0.8165
Epoch 2/10
 - 1s - loss: 0.6900 - acc: 0.8394 - val_loss: 0.5774 - val_acc: 0.8670
Epoch 3/10
 - 1s - loss: 0.5355 - acc: 0.8728 - val_loss: 0.4837 - val_acc: 0.8817
Epoch 4/10
 - 1s - loss: 0.4600 - acc: 0.8888 - val_loss: 0.4320 - val_acc: 0.8909
Epoch 5/10
 - 1s - loss: 0.4134 - acc: 0.8989 - val_loss: 0.3982 - val_acc: 0.8984
Epoch 6/10
 - 1s - loss: 0.3803 - acc: 0.9068 - val_loss: 0.3745 - val_acc: 0.9004
Epoch 7/10
 - 1s - loss: 0.3552 - acc: 0.9122 - val_loss: 0.3562 - val_acc: 0.9054
Epoch 8/10
 - 1s - loss: 0.3352 - acc: 0.9170 - val_loss: 0.3417 - val_acc: 0.9094
Epoch 9/10
 - 1s - loss: 0.3185 - acc: 0.9209 - val_loss: 0.3301 - val_acc: 0.9112
Epoch 10/10
 - 1s - loss: 0.3044 - acc: 0.9244 - val_loss: 0.3194 - val_acc: 0.9144
```

Note that `batch_size` in the preceding screenshot refers to the number of data points that are considered to update weights. The intuition for batch size is:

"If, in a dataset of 1,000 data points, the batch size is 100, then there are 10 weight updates while sweeping through the whole data".

Note that the accuracy in predicting the labels on the test dataset is ~91%.

This accuracy increases to 94.9% once the number of epochs reaches 300. Note that for an accuracy of 94.9% on the test dataset, the accuracy on the train dataset is ~99%.

This is a classic case of overfitting, and the ways to deal with it will be discussed in subsequent chapters.

Activation functions

So far, we have considered only the sigmoid activation function in a hidden layer. However, there are quite a few other activation functions that are useful in building a neural network. This chart gives the details of various activation functions:

Name	Plot	Equation
Identity		$f(x) = x$
Binary step		$f(x) = \begin{cases} 0 & \text{for } x < 0 \\ 1 & \text{for } x \geq 0 \end{cases}$
Logistic (a.k.a Soft step)		$f(x) = \dfrac{1}{1 + e^{-x}}$
TanH		$f(x) = \tanh(x) = \dfrac{2}{1 + e^{-2x}} - 1$
ArcTan		$f(x) = \tan^{-1}(x)$
Rectified Linear Unit (ReLU)		$f(x) = \begin{cases} 0 & \text{for } x < 0 \\ x & \text{for } x \geq 0 \end{cases}$

The more commonly used activation functions are ReLU, TanH, and logistic or sigmoid activations.

Let's explore the accuracy on the test dataset for various activation functions:

```
1 model = Sequential()
2 model.add(Dense(1000,input_dim=784,activation='relu'))
3 model.add(Dense(10,activation='softmax'))
4 model.compile(loss='categorical_crossentropy', optimizer='sgd',metrics=['accuracy'])
5 model.fit(X_train,y_train,epochs=10,batch_size=1024,validation_data=(X_test,y_test),verbose=2)

 Train on 60000 samples, validate on 10000 samples
 Epoch 1/10
  - 1s - loss: 11.6053 - acc: 0.2778 - val_loss: 11.3874 - val_acc: 0.2932
 Epoch 2/10
  - 1s - loss: 11.3660 - acc: 0.2941 - val_loss: 11.3854 - val_acc: 0.2930
 Epoch 3/10
  - 1s - loss: 11.3262 - acc: 0.2968 - val_loss: 11.3722 - val_acc: 0.2934
 Epoch 4/10
  - 1s - loss: 11.3217 - acc: 0.2972 - val_loss: 11.3691 - val_acc: 0.2939
 Epoch 5/10
  - 1s - loss: 11.3165 - acc: 0.2975 - val_loss: 11.3485 - val_acc: 0.2953
 Epoch 6/10
  - 1s - loss: 11.3046 - acc: 0.2983 - val_loss: 11.3528 - val_acc: 0.2946
 Epoch 7/10
  - 1s - loss: 11.2998 - acc: 0.2987 - val_loss: 11.3139 - val_acc: 0.2977
 Epoch 8/10
  - 1s - loss: 11.2944 - acc: 0.2988 - val_loss: 11.3160 - val_acc: 0.2973
 Epoch 9/10
  - 1s - loss: 11.2871 - acc: 0.2994 - val_loss: 11.3224 - val_acc: 0.2973
 Epoch 10/10
  - 1s - loss: 11.2879 - acc: 0.2994 - val_loss: 11.3152 - val_acc: 0.2975
```

Note that the accuracy on the test dataset is a mere 29.75% when using ReLU activation.

However, while performing ReLU activation, it is always a good idea to scale the data before fitting the model. Scaling is a way of reducing the magnitude of all the values in the input dataset.

Let's scale the inputs first, as follows:

```
X_train=X_train/255
X_test=X_test/255
```

Now, let's rerun the model and see the accuracy on the test dataset:

```
1  model = Sequential()
2  model.add(Dense(1000,input_dim=784,activation='relu'))
3  model.add(Dense(10,activation='softmax'))
4  model.compile(loss='categorical_crossentropy', optimizer='sgd',metrics=['accuracy'])
5  model.fit(X_train,y_train,epochs=10,batch_size=1024,validation_data=(X_test,y_test),verbose=2)

   Train on 60000 samples, validate on 10000 samples
   Epoch 1/10
    - 1s - loss: 2.0114 - acc: 0.4501 - val_loss: 1.7018 - val_acc: 0.6994
   Epoch 2/10
    - 1s - loss: 1.5020 - acc: 0.7495 - val_loss: 1.2889 - val_acc: 0.7926
   Epoch 3/10
    - 1s - loss: 1.1731 - acc: 0.8024 - val_loss: 1.0284 - val_acc: 0.8251
   Epoch 4/10
    - 1s - loss: 0.9652 - acc: 0.8251 - val_loss: 0.8637 - val_acc: 0.8429
   Epoch 5/10
    - 1s - loss: 0.8302 - acc: 0.8391 - val_loss: 0.7540 - val_acc: 0.8536
   Epoch 6/10
    - 1s - loss: 0.7379 - acc: 0.8489 - val_loss: 0.6773 - val_acc: 0.8621
   Epoch 7/10
    - 1s - loss: 0.6716 - acc: 0.8562 - val_loss: 0.6210 - val_acc: 0.8677
   Epoch 8/10
    - 1s - loss: 0.6218 - acc: 0.8623 - val_loss: 0.5780 - val_acc: 0.8735
   Epoch 9/10
    - 1s - loss: 0.5830 - acc: 0.8673 - val_loss: 0.5441 - val_acc: 0.8763
   Epoch 10/10
    - 1s - loss: 0.5521 - acc: 0.8711 - val_loss: 0.5167 - val_acc: 0.8811
```

Note that after running 10 iterations, the accuracy on the test dataset is 88.1%. Now, let's run the model for 300 epochs so that we can compare the outputs of sigmoid activation and ReLU activation.

You will notice that the accuracy on the test dataset is 95.76%, which is slightly better than the sigmoid activation accuracy. However, the accuracy on the train dataset is 96%, which indicates that it is not likely to overfit on the dataset; hence, more epochs might further increase the accuracy on the test dataset.

Let's rerun the model using TanH activation without scaling first and with scaling later.

When the model is run on unscaled data, the accuracy after 10 epochs is 92.89%, and after 300 epochs, it is 94.6%.

The accuracy on the test data once we scale the input dataset is 88% after 10 epochs and 93% after 300 epochs.

Note that the issue of overfitting does not arise (train dataset accuracy is much higher than test dataset accuracy) when the datasets are scaled, irrespective of the activation function used.

Optimizers

In the previous section, we explored various activation functions and noticed that the ReLU activation function gives a better result when run over a high number of epochs.

In this section, we will look at the impact of varying the optimizer while the activation function remains ReLU on the scaled dataset.

The various loss functions and their corresponding accuracies on the test dataset when run for 10 epochs are as follows:

Optimizer	Test dataset accuracy
SGD	88%
RMSprop	98.44%
Adam	98.4%

Now we have seen that RMSprop and Adam optimizers perform better than the stochastic gradient descent optimizer; let's look at the other parameter within an optimizer that can be modified to improve the accuracy of the model—learning rate.

The learning rate of an optimizer can be varied by specifying it as follows:

```
from keras import optimizers
adam=optimizers.Adam(lr=0.00001)

model = Sequential()
model.add(Dense(1000,input_dim=784,activation='relu'))
model.add(Dense(10,activation='softmax'))
model.compile(loss='categorical_crossentropy', optimizer=adam,metrics=['accuracy'])
model.fit(X_train,y_train,epochs=300,batch_size=1024,validation_data=(X_test,y_test),verbose=2)
```

In the preceding code snippet, `lr` represents learning rate. The typical values of learning rate vary between 0.001 and 0.1.

On the MNIST dataset, the accuracy did not improve further when we changed the learning rate; however, typically for a lower learning rate, more epochs are required to reach the same amount of accuracy.

Increasing the depth of network

An increase in the depth of a hidden layer is the same as increasing the number of hidden layers in a neural network.

Typically, for a higher number of hidden units in a hidden layer and/or higher number of hidden layers, the predictions are more accurate.

Given that the Adam optimizer or RMSprop has a saturated accuracy after certain number of epochs, let's switch back to stochastic gradient descent to understand the accuracy when the model is run for 300 epochs; but we are using more number of units in the hidden layer this time:

```
1 model = Sequential()
2 model.add(Dense(2000,input_dim=784,activation='relu'))
3 model.add(Dense(10,activation='softmax'))
4 model.compile(loss='categorical_crossentropy', optimizer='sgd',metrics=['accuracy'])
5 model.fit(X_train,y_train,epochs=300,batch_size=1024,validation_data=(X_test,y_test),verbose=2)
```

Note that by using 2,000 units in the hidden layer, our accuracy increases to 95.76% by the end of 300 epochs. This is potentially because the input can now be expressed in a higher dimensional space, and hence a better representation can be learned when compared to the 1,000-dimensional space scenario.

Now, we will increase the number of hidden layers to understand the impact of building deep neural networks on accuracy:

```
1 model = Sequential()
2 model.add(Dense(2000,input_dim=784,activation='relu'))
3 model.add(Dense(500,activation='relu'))
4 model.add(Dense(10,activation='softmax'))
5 model.compile(loss='categorical_crossentropy', optimizer='sgd',metrics=['accuracy'])
6 model.fit(X_train,y_train,epochs=300,batch_size=1024,validation_data=(X_test,y_test),verbose=2)
```

Note that when the network is deep, with two hidden layers instead of one, the accuracy after 300 epochs is 97.24%, which is a clear improvement when compared to the single hidden layer network.

Similar, to the way in which the network learned more complex representations of data when the number of hidden units in a layer increased, the network also learned complex representations of data when the number of hidden layers increased.

Impact on change in batch size

As discussed earlier, the lesser the batch size, the more often the weights get updated in a given neural network. This results in a lesser number of epochs required to achieve a certain accuracy on the network. At the same time, if the batch size is too low, the network structure might result in instability in the model.

Let's compare the previously built network with a lower batch size in one scenario and a bigger batch size in the next scenario:

```
1 model = Sequential()
2 model.add(Dense(2000,input_dim=784,activation='relu'))
3 model.add(Dense(500,activation='relu'))
4 model.add(Dense(10,activation='softmax'))
5 model.compile(loss='categorical_crossentropy', optimizer='sgd',metrics=['accuracy'])
6 model.fit(X_train,y_train,epochs=300,batch_size=30000,validation_data=(X_test,y_test),verbose=2)
```

Note that in the preceding scenario, where the batch size is very high, the test dataset accuracy at the end of 300 epochs is only 89.91%.

The reason for this is that the network with batch size 1,024 would have learned the weights much faster than the network with batch size 30,000, as the number of weight updates is much higher when the batch size is lower.

In the next scenario, we will reduce the batch size to a very small number to see the impact on network accuracy:

```
1 model = Sequential()
2 model.add(Dense(2000,input_dim=784,activation='relu'))
3 model.add(Dense(500,activation='relu'))
4 model.add(Dense(10,activation='softmax'))
5 model.compile(loss='categorical_crossentropy', optimizer='sgd',metrics=['accuracy'])
6 model.fit(X_train,y_train,epochs=300,batch_size=16,validation_data=(X_test,y_test),verbose=2)
```

Note that while accuracy improves considerably very quickly to 97.77% within 10 epochs itself, it takes significant time to produce results, as the number of weight updates is high per epoch. This results in more calculations and thus more time to execute.

Implementing neural networks in TensorFlow

In previous sections, we have understood how a neural network works and also how to build a neural network model in Keras. In this section, we will be working toward building a neural network model in TensorFlow. There are two ways in which we can build models in TensorFlow:

- Using premade estimators
- Defining custom estimators

Using premade estimators

Premade estimators are similar to the methods available in packages such as scikit-learn, where the input features and output labels are specified, along with the various hyperparameters. A method can then optimize for solving a loss function that is predefined to a default value but can be varied by passing a different function in a parameter.

Let's explore building the training and test datasets in the code:

1. Import the relevant packages:

```
import matplotlib.pyplot as plt
import tensorflow as tf
import numpy as np
%matplotlib inline
```

2. Import the dataset. We will work on the MNIST dataset for this exercise:

```
from tensorflow.examples.tutorials.mnist import input_data
data = input_data.read_data_sets('data/MNIST/', one_hot=True)

Extracting data/MNIST/train-images-idx3-ubyte.gz
Extracting data/MNIST/train-labels-idx1-ubyte.gz
Extracting data/MNIST/t10k-images-idx3-ubyte.gz
Extracting data/MNIST/t10k-labels-idx1-ubyte.gz
```

The shapes of images and labels are as follows:

```
data.train.images.shape

(55000, 784)

data.train.labels.shape

(55000, 10)
```

The premade function works on label value instead of the one-hot encoded version. Let's convert the one-hot encoded label into a value, as follows:

```
data.train.cls = np.argmax(data.train.labels, axis=1)
data.test.cls = np.argmax(data.test.labels, axis=1)
```

Let's understand how the data points look:

```
data.train.cls[0]

7

data.train.labels[0]

array([0., 0., 0., 0., 0., 0., 0., 1., 0., 0.])
```

```
data.train.images[0]

array([0.       , 0.       , 0.       , 0.       , 0.       ,
       0.       , 0.       , 0.       , 0.       , 0.       ,
       0.       , 0.       , 0.       , 0.       , 0.       ,
       0.       , 0.       , 0.       , 0.       , 0.       ,
       0.       , 0.       , 0.       , 0.       , 0.       ,
       0.       , 0.       , 0.       , 0.       , 0.       ,
       0.       , 0.       , 0.       , 0.       , 0.       ,
       0.       , 0.       , 0.       , 0.       , 0.       ,
       0.       , 0.       , 0.       , 0.       , 0.       ,
       0.       , 0.       , 0.       , 0.       , 0.       ,
       0.       , 0.       , 0.       , 0.       , 0.       ,
```

3. Input the dataset into a function that consumes the independent (x) and
   dependent (y) variables:

```
train_input_fn = tf.estimator.inputs.numpy_input_fn(
    x={"x2": np.array(data.train.images)},
    y=np.array(data.train.cls),
    num_epochs=None,
    batch_size=1024,
    shuffle=True)
```

Note that we named the independent variables as x2 and dependent variable as y.

Also, note that we have passed the arrays that form the independent and dependent
variable values.

batch_size indicates the number of training examples that are consumed to calculate the
loss function, and num_epochs = None indicates that the number of epochs to be run will
be provided later.

train_input_fn returns features and labels, as follows:

```
train_input_fn()

({'x2': <tf.Tensor 'random_shuffle_queue_DequeueMany:1' shape=(1024, 784) dtype=float32>},
 <tf.Tensor 'random_shuffle_queue_DequeueMany:2' shape=(1024,) dtype=int64>)
```

Similarly, we pass the test dataset:

```
test_input_fn = tf.estimator.inputs.numpy_input_fn(
    x={"x2": np.array(data.test.images)},
    y=np.array(data.test.cls),
    num_epochs=1,
    shuffle=False)
```

Note that, in the case of the test dataset, num_epochs = 1 as we pass it through only the
feedforward for the test dataset once the model weights are derived from training.

A dataset could potentially contain multiple columns, so let's specify the feature column and its type, as follows:

```
feature_x1= tf.feature_column.numeric_column("x2", shape=(784))
```

```
feature_columns = [feature_x1]
```

If there are multiple columns, we would specify all the columns in a list, as follows:

```
feature_columns = [feature_x1, feature_x2]
```

Where `feature_x1` is one feature and `feature_x2` is another feature.

Now, we shall specify the number of hidden layers and also the hidden units in each layer:

```
num_hidden_units = [512, 256, 128]
```

Note that by specifying the number of hidden units in the preceding way, we have specified that there are three hidden layers, where the first hidden layer has **512** units, the second hidden layer has **256** units, and the final hidden layer has **128** units.

Now that we have specified the features and hidden layers, let's specify the architecture of neural network, as follows:

```
model = tf.estimator.DNNClassifier(feature_columns=feature_columns,
                                   hidden_units=num_hidden_units,
                                   activation_fn=tf.nn.relu,
                                   n_classes=10)
```

Now that we have specified the model architecture, we can go ahead and train the model. If you would like to further change the hyperparameters that are available in the function, you can check out the hyperparameter levers that are available by using the `help` function, as follows:

```
help(tf.estimator.DNNClassifier.train)

Help on method train in module tensorflow.python.estimator.estimator:

train(self, input_fn, hooks=None, steps=None, max_steps=None, saving_listeners=None
    Trains a model given training data input_fn.

    Args:
      input_fn: Input function returning a tuple of:
          features - `Tensor` or dictionary of string feature name to `Tensor`.
          labels - `Tensor` or dictionary of `Tensor` with labels.
      hooks: List of `SessionRunHook` subclass instances. Used for callbacks
        inside the training loop.
      steps: Number of steps for which to train model. If `None`, train forever
        or train until input_fn generates the `OutOfRange` error or
        `StopIteration` exception. 'steps' works incrementally. If you call two
        times train(steps=10) then training occurs in total 20 steps. If
        `OutOfRange` or `StopIteration` occurs in the middle, training stops
        before 20 steps. If you don't want to have incremental behavior please
        set `max_steps` instead. If set, `max_steps` must be `None`.
      max_steps: Number of total steps for which to train model. If `None`,
        train forever or train until input_fn generates the `OutOfRange` error
        or `StopIteration` exception. If set, `steps` must be `None`. If
        `OutOfRange` or `StopIteration` occurs in the middle, training stops
        before `max_steps` steps.
```

The following code runs the neural network model for 2,000 epochs in total:

```
model.train(input_fn=train_input_fn, steps=2000)

INFO:tensorflow:Create CheckpointSaverHook.
INFO:tensorflow:Saving checkpoints for 1 into /tmp/tmpiIpGrH/model.ckpt.
INFO:tensorflow:loss = 2377.0044, step = 1
INFO:tensorflow:global_step/sec: 5.41405
INFO:tensorflow:loss = 130.9731, step = 101 (18.476 sec)
INFO:tensorflow:global_step/sec: 5.57075
INFO:tensorflow:loss = 40.6942, step = 201 (17.950 sec)
INFO:tensorflow:global_step/sec: 5.78901
INFO:tensorflow:loss = 24.525383, step = 301 (17.274 sec)
INFO:tensorflow:global_step/sec: 5.77324
INFO:tensorflow:loss = 27.47683, step = 401 (17.321 sec)
INFO:tensorflow:global_step/sec: 5.73862
INFO:tensorflow:loss = 10.29439, step = 501 (17.426 sec)
INFO:tensorflow:global_step/sec: 5.60209
INFO:tensorflow:loss = 8.66, step = 601 (17.852 sec)
INFO:tensorflow:global_step/sec: 5.49976
INFO:tensorflow:loss = 4.0309644, step = 701 (18.182 sec)
INFO:tensorflow:global_step/sec: 5.69763
INFO:tensorflow:loss = 3.0329823, step = 801 (17.551 sec)
```

Now that our model is run, let's evaluate the accuracy on the test dataset, as follows:

```
result = model.evaluate(input_fn=test_input_fn)

INFO:tensorflow:Starting evaluation at 2018-03-17
INFO:tensorflow:Restoring parameters from /tmp/tm
INFO:tensorflow:Finished evaluation at 2018-03-17
INFO:tensorflow:Saving dict for global step 2000:

result

{'accuracy': 0.972,
 'average_loss': 0.13137925,
 'global_step': 2000,
 'loss': 16.630285}
```

We can see that the accuracy of the model on the test dataset is 97.2%.

So far, we have been implementing a model using premade estimators; in the next sections, we will look into defining the model without premade estimators.

Creating custom estimators

A premade estimator limits the full potential to which TensorFlow can be used; for example, we would not be able to have different dropout values after different layers. In this regard, let's go ahead and create a function of our own, as follows:

```
def model_fn(features, labels, mode, params):
    x = features["x2"]
    net = tf.layers.dense(inputs=x, name='h1',units=512, activation=tf.nn.relu)
    net2 = tf.layers.dense(inputs=net, name='h2',units=256, activation=tf.nn.relu)
    net3 = tf.layers.dense(inputs=net2, name='h3',units=128, activation=tf.nn.relu)
    net4 = tf.layers.dense(inputs=net3, name='softmax',units=10,activation=tf.nn.softmax)

    y_pred_cls = tf.argmax(net4, axis=1)
    if mode == tf.estimator.ModeKeys.PREDICT:
        spec = tf.estimator.EstimatorSpec(mode=mode,predictions=y_pred_cls)
    else:
        cross_entropy = tf.nn.sparse_softmax_cross_entropy_with_logits(labels=labels,logits = net4)
        loss = tf.reduce_mean(cross_entropy)
        optimizer = tf.train.AdamOptimizer(learning_rate=params["learning_rate"])
        train_op = optimizer.minimize(loss=loss, global_step=tf.train.get_global_step())
        metrics = {"accuracy": tf.metrics.accuracy(labels, y_pred_cls)}
        spec = tf.estimator.EstimatorSpec(mode=mode,loss=loss,train_op=train_op,eval_metric_ops=metrics)
    return spec
```

Let's explore each part of the preceding snippet of code in detail:

```
def model_fn(features, labels, mode, params):
```

The function takes features (independent variables) and labels (dependent variable) as input. mode indicates whether we want to train, predict, or evaluate the given data.

params provides us with the functionality to supply information about parameters; for example, learning rate:

```
x = features["x2"]
net = tf.layers.dense(inputs=x, name='h1',units=512, activation=tf.nn.relu)
net2 = tf.layers.dense(inputs=net, name='h2',units=256, activation=tf.nn.relu)
net3 = tf.layers.dense(inputs=net2, name='h3',units=128, activation=tf.nn.relu)
net4 = tf.layers.dense(inputs=net3, name='softmax',units=10,activation=tf.nn.softmax)
```

The preceding snippet of code is similar to the way in which we defined model architecture in Keras, where we specified the inputs, the hidden layer activation, and the number of units in the hidden layer:

```
y_pred_cls = tf.argmax(net4, axis=1)
```

If our mode is to predict the class, we would not have to train the model, but just pass the predicted class, thus estimator spec in such scenario would just need to calculate the y_pred_cls values, thus the following code:

```
if mode == tf.estimator.ModeKeys.PREDICT:
    spec = tf.estimator.EstimatorSpec(mode=mode,predictions=y_pred_cls)
```

If the mode is to train or test the model, we would have to calculate the loss and hence the following code:

```
else:
    cross_entropy = tf.nn.sparse_softmax_cross_entropy_with_logits(labels=labels,logits = net4)
    loss = tf.reduce_mean(cross_entropy)
    optimizer = tf.train.AdamOptimizer(learning_rate=params["learning_rate"])
    train_op = optimizer.minimize(loss=loss, global_step=tf.train.get_global_step())
    metrics = {"accuracy": tf.metrics.accuracy(labels, y_pred_cls)}
    spec = tf.estimator.EstimatorSpec(mode=mode,loss=loss,train_op=train_op,eval_metric_ops=metrics)
```

In the preceding code, the first line is used to define the cross-entropy calculation. The second line takes the average of cross entropy across all the rows.

`optimizer` specifies the optimizer we are interested in and the learning rate. `train_op` specifies that we are interested in minimizing loss, and the `global_step` parameter keeps a count of the step (epoch) that the model is currently in. `metrics` specifies the metrics that we are interested in calculating, and the final `spec` that would be calculated would be a combination of all the preceding parameters that we have defined.

Once the model architecture and the estimator spec that needs to be returned are defined, we define the parameters and mode as follows:

```
params = {"learning_rate": 1e-4}


model = tf.estimator.Estimator(model_fn=model_fn,
                               params=params)
```

From the preceding code, the function learns the parameter that needs to be changed and also the model architecture that needs to be worked on (`model_fn`):

```
model.train(input_fn=train_input_fn, steps=2000)
```

We run the model by specifying the mode (in this case, `train`) by a certain number of epochs (`2000` in this case).

After running the model, we evaluate the model's accuracy on the test dataset, as follows:

```
result = model.evaluate(input_fn=test_input_fn)

INFO:tensorflow:Calling model_fn.
INFO:tensorflow:Done calling model_fn.
INFO:tensorflow:Starting evaluation at 2018-03-17-10:34:50
INFO:tensorflow:Graph was finalized.
INFO:tensorflow:Restoring parameters from /tmp/tmphthfo2z2/model.ckpt-2000
INFO:tensorflow:Running local_init_op.
INFO:tensorflow:Done running local_init_op.
INFO:tensorflow:Finished evaluation at 2018-03-17-10:34:51
INFO:tensorflow:Saving dict for global step 2000: accuracy = 0.9682, global_step = 2000, loss = 1.4945148

result

{'accuracy': 0.9682, 'global_step': 2000, 'loss': 1.4945148}
```

Summary

In this chapter, we learned to set up Datalab to execute neural networks on Google Cloud. We also learned the structure of a neural network and how various parameters, such as depth, number of hidden units, activation function, optimizer, batch size, and number of epochs, impact the accuracy of the model. We also saw how to implement a neural network in both Keras and TensorFlow. Topics such as using premade estimators and creating custom estimators in TensorFlow were covered.

10
Evaluating Results with TensorBoard

In the previous chapter, we understood how a neural network works, what the various hyper parameters in a neural network are, and how they can be tweaked further to improve our model's accuracy.

Google offers TensorBoard, a visualization of the model training logs. In this chapter, we show how to use TensorBoard for TensorFlow and Keras. We interpret the visualizations generated by TensorBoard to understand the performance of our models, and also understand the other functionalities in TensorBoard that can help visualize our dataset better.

As discussed in the previous chapter, Keras as a framework is a wrapper on top of either TensorFlow or Theano. The computations that you'll use TensorFlow for, such as training a massive deep neural network, can be complex and confusing. To make it easier to understand, debug, and optimize TensorFlow programs, the creators of TensorFlow have included a suite of visualization tools called TensorBoard.

You can use TensorBoard to visualize your TensorFlow graph, plot quantitative metrics about the execution of your graph, and also to see additional data such as images that were given as input. When TensorBoard is fully configured, it looks like this:

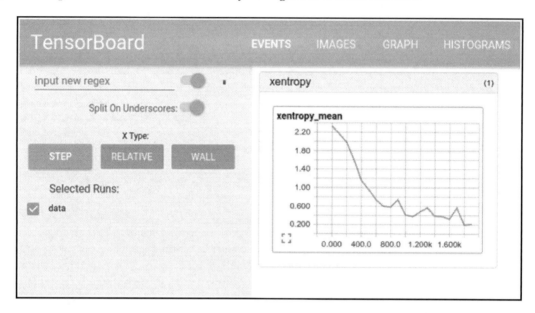

From this screenshot, you can note that the chart shows a reduction in mean cross-entropy error over an increasing number of epochs. In the later sections of the chapter, we will go through the following:

- Installing TensorBoard
- Overview of the various summary operations captured by TensorBoard
- Ways to debug the code

Setting up TensorBoard

In the previous chapter, we understood how Datalab can be set up. Installing TensorBoard in Datalab is as simple as specifying the following code:

```
# Import relevant packages
from google.datalab.ml import TensorBoard as tb
# Start the tensorboard
tb.start('./logs/1519829425.6576147')
```

TensorBoard was started successfully with pid 4067. Click here to access it.

```
4067
```

Note that we need not make any separate installations for TensorBoard and it comes in prebuilt within the `google.datalab.ml` package.

Once the package is imported, we need to start TensorBoard by specifying the location of logs that contain the summaries written by the model fitting process.

The `tb.start` method works as follows:

```
@staticmethod
def start(logdir):
  """Start a TensorBoard instance.

  Args:
    logdir: the logdir to run TensorBoard on.
  Raises:
    Exception if the instance cannot be started.
  """
  if logdir.startswith('gs://'):
    # Check user does have access. TensorBoard will start successfully regardless
    # the user has read permissions or not so we check permissions here to
    # give user alerts if needed.
    datalab.storage._api.Api.verify_permitted_to_read(logdir)

  port = datalab.utils.pick_unused_port()
  args = ['tensorboard', '--logdir=' + logdir, '--port=' + str(port)]
  p = subprocess.Popen(args)
  retry = 5
  while (retry > 0):
    if datalab.utils.is_http_running_on(port):
      url = '/_proxy/%d/' % port
      html = '<p>TensorBoard was started successfully with pid %d. ' % p.pid
      html += 'Click <a href="%s" target="_blank">here</a> to access it.</p>' % url
      IPython.display.display_html(html, raw=True)
      return p.pid
    time.sleep(1)
    retry -= 1

  raise Exception('Cannot start TensorBoard.')
```

Note that, in the first step, it checks whether the user is permitted to perform the calculation. Next, it picks up an unused port to open TensorBoard, and finally it starts TensorBoard along with printing the link to open TensorBoard.

We will learn more about writing to logs in the next section.

Overview of summary operations

Summaries provide a way to export condensed information about a model, which is then accessible in tools such as TensorBoard.

Some of the commonly used summary functions are:

- `scalar`
- `histogram`
- `audio`
- `image`
- `merge`
- `merge_all`

A `scalar` summary operation returns a scalar, that is, the value of a certain metric over an increasing number of epochs.

A `histogram` summary operation returns the histogram of various values—potentially weights and biases at each layer.

The `image` and `audio` summary operations return images and audio, which can be visualized and played in TensorBoard respectively.

A `merge` operation returns the union of all the values of input summaries, while `merge_all` returns the union of all the summaries contained in the model specification.

A visualization of some of the summaries discussed here will be provided in the next section.

Ways to debug the code

In order to understand how TensorBoard helps, let's initialize a model structure as follows, one that is bound not to work:

```
from keras.callbacks import TensorBoard
from time import time
model = Sequential()
model.add(Dense(num_pixels, input_dim=num_pixels, kernel_initializer='normal', activation='relu',name='first_layer'))
model.add(Dense(1000,activation='relu',name='hidden_layer'))
model.add(Dense(num_classes, kernel_initializer='normal', activation='softmax',name='output_layer'))
tensorboard = TensorBoard(log_dir="logs/tensor_new6")

# Compile model
model.compile(loss='categorical_crossentropy', optimizer='adam', metrics=['accuracy'])
model.fit(X_train, y_train, epochs=5, validation_data=(X_test,y_test) ,batch_size=1024, verbose=2, callbacks=[tensorboard])

Train on 60000 samples, validate on 10000 samples
Epoch 1/5
 - 31s - loss: 13.0498 - acc: 0.1898 - val_loss: 13.0217 - val_acc: 0.1921
Epoch 2/5
 - 31s - loss: 13.1082 - acc: 0.1867 - val_loss: 13.1524 - val_acc: 0.1840
Epoch 3/5
 - 32s - loss: 13.0979 - acc: 0.1873 - val_loss: 13.0121 - val_acc: 0.1927
Epoch 4/5
 - 32s - loss: 13.0369 - acc: 0.1912 - val_loss: 13.0379 - val_acc: 0.1911
Epoch 5/5
 - 31s - loss: 13.0398 - acc: 0.1910 - val_loss: 13.0170 - val_acc: 0.1924
```

Note that, in this code snippet, the validation accuracy is only around 19%.

The reason for such a low validation accuracy is that the input dataset is not scaled and we are performing ReLU activation on top of an unscaled dataset.

Note that, in the preceding code, we are storing the logs of the model run in the directory logs/tensor_new6 (the sub-directory could be named anything).

Once the logs are stored in this location, we start TensorBoard as follows:

```
# Import relevant packages
from google.datalab.ml import TensorBoard as tb
# Start the tensorboard
tb.start('./logs/tensor_new6')
```

TensorBoard was started successfully with pid 7617. Click here to access it.

7617

The preceding code starts TensorBoard, which looks like this:

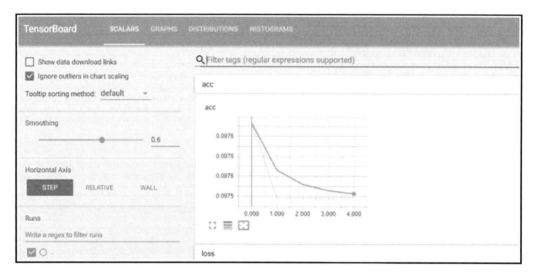

Note that, by default, the output gives a measure of the scalars, that is, the accuracy and loss values of both the train and test datasets.

The outputs can be visualized adjacent to each other using the regular expression `.*` in `Filter` tags, as follows:

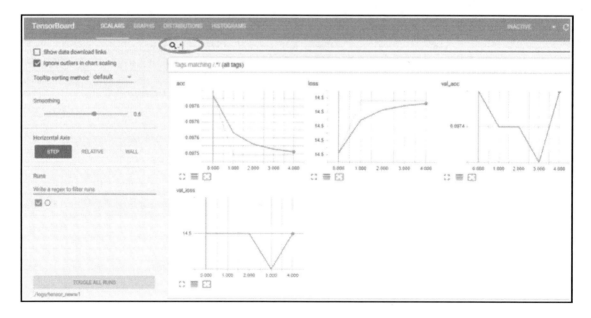

Note that the first two graphs in this screenshot represent the accuracy and loss of train datasets, while the next two graphs represent the accuracy and loss of validation datasets.

When we look at the histogram of weights and bias across various layers, we learn that the weights and biases do not change across epochs:

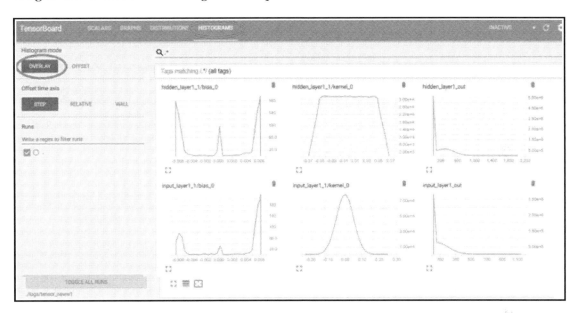

This is an indication that no learning is happening in the network architecture.

The same can be noted when we look at the distribution of weights and biases across epochs in a different tab:

From this screenshot, we can conclude why the accuracy of the model is so low; it's because the model is not able to update the weights.

Now, by clicking on the **GRAPHS** tab, let us explore whether the model was initialized correctly:

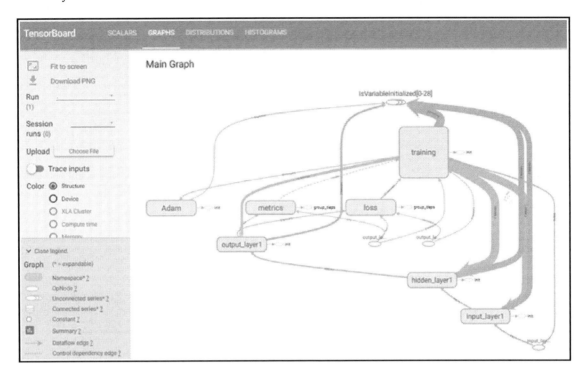

You should notice that the training block is connected to every other block in the graph. This is because, in order to compute the gradients, one needs to connect to every variable in the graph (as every variable contains weights that need to be adjusted).

Let us, for now, remove the **training** block from the graph. This is done by right-clicking on the **training** block, as follows:

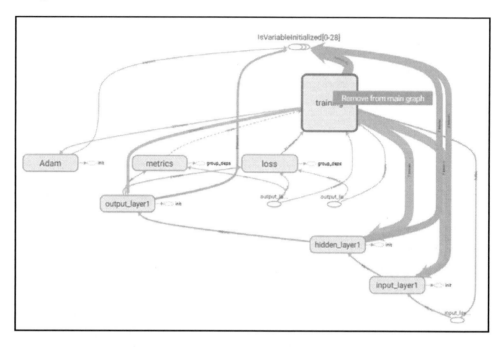

The resultant graph after removing the **training** block is as follows:

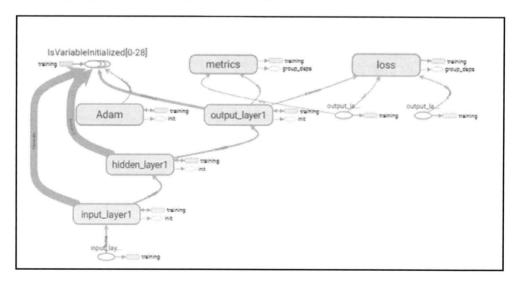

Note that the input layer is connected to hidden layer, which in turn is connected to output layer, from which the metrics and loss are calculated. Let us explore the connections by double-clicking on the individual blocks, as follows:

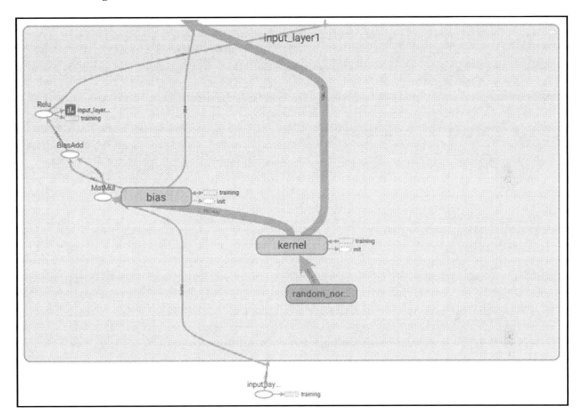

A zoom-in of these connections helps us understand the shapes at various blocks:

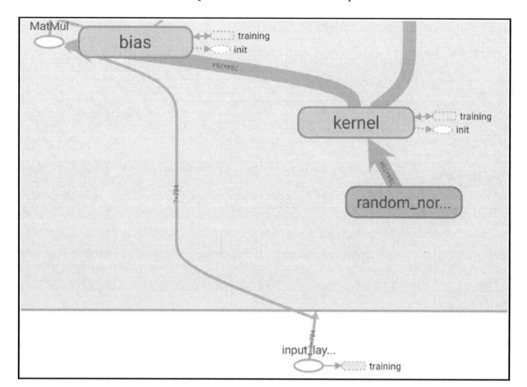

The input layer is (784) in dimension, as there could be any number of input samples but each of them are 784-dimensional. Similarly, the kernel (weight matrix) is 784 x 784 in dimensions and the bias would have 784 initialized values, and so on.

Note that, in the preceding diagram, we take the values in input layer and perform matrix multiplication with the kernel that is initialized using `random_normal` initialization. Also note that `random_normal` initialization is not connected to the training block, while the kernel block is connected to the training block.

Let us also find out whether the output layer is connected to all the relevant blocks per expectations. Given that the graph looks very complicated, we can use another functionality provided in TensorBoard: **Trace inputs**. **Trace inputs** help in highlighting only those blocks that are connected to any block of interest. It is activated by selecting the block of interest and toggling the switch in the left-hand pane, as follows:

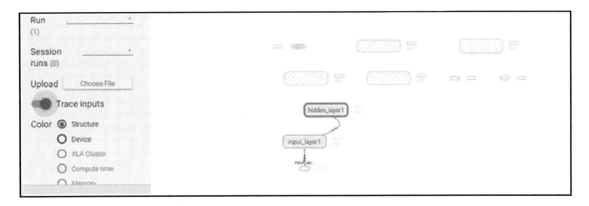

Now all the connections look fine, but the gradients are still not getting updated; let us change the activation function to sigmoid and then check the weight histograms:

We build a neural network with sigmoid activation as follows:

```
from keras import backend as K
K.clear_session()

from keras.callbacks import TensorBoard
from time import time
model = Sequential()
model.add(Dense(num_pixels, input_dim=num_pixels, kernel_initializer='normal', activation='sigmoid',name='input_layer1'))
model.add(Dense(1000,activation='relu',name='hidden_layer1'))
model.add(Dense(num_classes, kernel_initializer='normal', activation='softmax',name='output_layer1'))
tensorboard = TensorBoard(log_dir="logs/tensor_neww3",histogram_freq=1,batch_size=10000)

# Compile model
model.compile(loss='categorical_crossentropy', optimizer='adam', metrics=['accuracy'])
```

Once the neural network structure is defined and compiled, let us fit the model as follows:

```
model.fit(X_train, y_train, epochs=5, validation_data=(X_test,y_test) ,batch_size=1024, verbose=2, callbacks=[tensorboard])
```

In order to open TensorBoard, we will execute the following code:

```
from google.datalab.ml import TensorBoard as tb
tb.start('./logs/tensor_neww3')
```

We will then receive the following output:

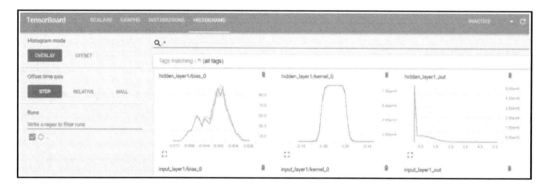

At the same time, we should notice that the accuracy and loss metrics have improved considerably:

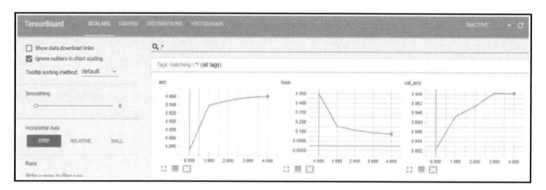

One would also be able to visualize the histogram of gradients by specifying **write_grads=True** in the TensorBoard function. The output would then be as follows:

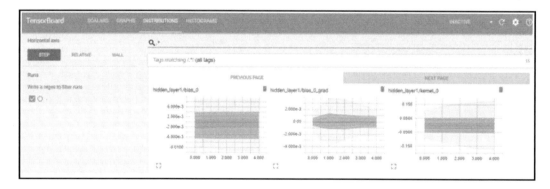

Setting up TensorBoard from TensorFlow

In the previous chapter, we have seen that there are two ways to define a model in
TensorFlow:

- Premade estimators
- Building a custom estimator

In the following code, we will consider one additional snippet of code that would enable us
to visualize the various summary operations:

```
model = tf.estimator.DNNClassifier(feature_columns=feature_columns,
                                   hidden_units=num_hidden_units,
                                   activation_fn=tf.nn.relu,
                                   _classes=num_classes,
                                   model_dir='/content/datalab/logs/')
```

Note that we only need to specify the `model_dir` in the premade estimator to store the
various log files generated from TensorFlow operations.

TensorBoard can then be initialized by referring to the model directory, as follows:

```
from google.datalab.ml import TensorBoard as tb

tb.start('/content/datalab/logs/')

TensorBoard was started successfully with pid 1133. Click here to access it.

1133
```

The preceding code would result in a TensorBoard visualization that would have all the
summaries built in.

Summaries from custom estimator

In the previous section, we looked at obtaining predefined summaries from premade
estimators in TensorBoard. In this section, we will understand obtaining summaries in
custom estimators so that they can be visualized in TensorBoard.

The summary operations that need to be captured should be specified in the custom estimator function, as follows:

```
def model_fn(features, labels, mode, params):
    x = features["x2"]
    net = tf.layers.dense(inputs=x, name='h1',units=512, activation=tf.nn.relu)
    net2 = tf.layers.dense(inputs=net, name='h2',units=256, activation=tf.nn.relu)
    net3 = tf.layers.dense(inputs=net2, name='h3',units=128, activation=tf.nn.relu)
    net4 = tf.layers.dense(inputs=net3, name='softmax',units=10,activation=tf.nn.softmax)

    y_pred_cls = tf.argmax(net4, axis=1)

    if mode == tf.estimator.ModeKeys.PREDICT:
        spec = tf.estimator.EstimatorSpec(mode=mode,predictions=y_pred_cls)

    else:
        cross_entropy = tf.nn.sparse_softmax_cross_entropy_with_logits(labels=labels,logits = net4)
        loss = tf.reduce_mean(cross_entropy)
        optimizer = tf.train.ProximalAdagradOptimizer(learning_rate=params["learning_rate"],l1_regularization_strength=0.001)
        train_op = optimizer.minimize(loss=loss, global_step=tf.train.get_global_step())
        accuracy = tf.metrics.accuracy(labels, y_pred_cls)
        metrics = {'accuracy': accuracy}
        tf.summary.scalar('train_accuracy', accuracy[1])

        tf.summary.histogram("hidden1",net)
        tf.summary.histogram("hidden2",net2)
        tf.summary.histogram("hidden3",net3)

        spec = tf.estimator.EstimatorSpec(mode=mode,loss=loss,train_op=train_op,eval_metric_ops=metrics)
```

Note that the model function remains very similar to what we defined in the previous section while learning about custom estimators; however, a few lines of code that write summary to log files are added.

`tf.summary.scalar` adds the accuracy metric. Similarly, we might have wanted to add loss (which is another scalar) to logs; however, it gets added by default (note that loss is displayed when we train the model).

`tf.summary.histogram` gives a distribution of weights within the network.

Once the model is trained, we should notice the scalars and histogram/distributions in the TensorBoard output. The code to train the model and start TensorBoard is as follows:

```
params = {"learning_rate": 0.1}
model = tf.estimator.Estimator(model_fn=model_fn,
                               params=params,model_dir='/content/datalab/docs/log10/')
```

In the preceding code snippet, we have specified the model function and parameters and the directory to which the log files would be written:

```
model.train(input_fn=train_input_fn, steps=1000)
```

The preceding code snippet trains the model for 1,000 batches of 1,024 (batch size) data points:

```
from google.datalab.ml import TensorBoard as tb
tb.start('/content/datalab/docs/log10/')
```

This code snippet starts TensorBoard by using the log files written in the given folder.

Summary

In this chapter, we understood visualizing neural network models in TensorBoard, both from Keras and TensorFlow. We also considered how to visualize the models, distribution of weights, and loss/accuracy metrics in both premade estimators and custom defined estimators. And also the various metrics in neural networks.

11
Optimizing the Model through Hyperparameter Tuning

Neural networks constitute multiple parameters that can affect the ultimate accuracy in predicting an event or a label. The typical parameters include:

- Batch size used for training
- Number of epochs
- Learning rate
- Number of hidden layers
- Number of hidden units in each hidden layer
- The activation function applied in the hidden layer
- The optimizer used

From the preceding list, we can see that the number of parameters that can be tweaked is very high. This makes finding the optimal combination of hyperparameters a challenge. Hyperparameter tuning as a service provided by Cloud ML Engine comes in handy in such a scenario.

In this chapter, we will go through:

- Why hyperparameter tuning is required
- An overview of how hyperparameter tuning works
- Implementing hyperparameter tuning in the cloud

The intuition of hyperparameter tuning

In order to gain a practical intuition of the need for hyperparameter tuning, let's go through the following scenario in predicting the accuracy of a given neural network architecture on the MNIST dataset:

- **Scenario 1**: High number of epochs and low learning rate
- **Scenario 2**: Low number of epochs and high learning rate

Let us create the train and test datasets in a Google Cloud environment, as follows:

1. Download the dataset:

   ```
   mkdir data
   curl -O https://s3.amazonaws.com/img-datasets/mnist.pkl.gz
   gzip -d mnist.pkl.gz
   mv mnist.pkl data/
   ```

   The preceding code creates a new folder named `data`, downloads the MNIST dataset, and moves it into the `data` folder.

2. Open Python in Terminal and import the required packages:

   ```
   from __future__ import print_function
   import tensorflow as tf
   import pickle # for handling the new data source
   import numpy as np
   from datetime import datetime # for filename conventions
   from tensorflow.python.lib.io import file_io # for better file I/O
   import sys
   ```

3. Import the MNIST dataset:

   ```
   f = file_io.FileIO('data/mnist.pkl', mode='r')
   data = pickle.load(f)
   ```

4. Extract the train and test datasets:

   ```
   (x_train, y_train), (x_test, y_test) = data
   # Converting the data from a 28 x 28 shape to 784 columns
   x_train = x_train.reshape(60000, 784)
   x_train = x_train.astype('float32')
   # Scaling the train dataset
   x_train /= 255
   # Reshaping the test dataset
   x_test = x_test.reshape(10000, 784)
   ```

```
x_test = x_test.astype('float32')
# Scaling the test dataset
x_test /= 255
# Specifying the type of labels
y_train = y_train.astype(np.int32)
y_test = y_test.astype(np.int32)
```

5. Create the estimator functions:

```
# Creating the estimator input functions for train and test
datasets
train_input_fn = tf.estimator.inputs.numpy_input_fn(
  x={"x2": np.array(x_train)},
  y=np.array(y_train),
  num_epochs=None,
  batch_size=1024,
  shuffle=True)
test_input_fn = tf.estimator.inputs.numpy_input_fn(
  x={"x2": np.array(x_test)},
  y=np.array(y_test),
  num_epochs=1,
  shuffle=False)
```

6. Specify the type of column:

```
feature_x = tf.feature_column.numeric_column("x2", shape=(784))
feature_columns = [feature_x]
```

7. Build a DNN classifier using the parameters in scenario 1; that is, the learning rate is 0.1 and the number of steps is 200:

```
num_hidden_units = [1000]
lr=0.1
num_steps=200
# Building the estimator using DNN classifier
# This is where the learning rate hyper parameter is passed
model = tf.estimator.DNNClassifier(feature_columns=feature_columns,
            hidden_units=num_hidden_units,
            activation_fn=tf.nn.relu,
            n_classes=10,
            optimizer=tf.train.AdagradOptimizer(learning_rate
= lr))
model.train(input_fn=train_input_fn, steps=num_steps)
# Fetching the model results
result = model.evaluate(input_fn=test_input_fn)
print('Test loss:', result['average_loss'])
print('Test accuracy:', result['accuracy'])
```

The test accuracy in such a scenario comes out to be 96.49%.

In scenario 2, we will build another DNN classifier using different parameters; now the learning rate is 0.01 and the number of steps is 2000:

```
num_hidden_units = [1000]
lr=0.01
num_steps=2000
# Building the estimator using DNN classifier
# This is where the learning rate hyper parameter is passed
model = tf.estimator.DNNClassifier(feature_columns=feature_columns,
  hidden_units=num_hidden_units,
  activation_fn=tf.nn.relu,
  n_classes=10,
  optimizer=tf.train.AdagradOptimizer(learning_rate = lr))
model.train(input_fn=train_input_fn, steps=num_steps)
# Fetching the model results
result = model.evaluate(input_fn=test_input_fn)
print('Test loss:', result['average_loss'])
print('Test accuracy:', result['accuracy'])
```

The accuracy on the test dataset in scenario 2 is nearly 98.2%.

The preceding two scenarios show us the importance of how various values of different hyperparameters affect the final result.

Google Cloud ML engine comes in handy in such scenarios, where we can be more intelligent in selecting the more optimal set of hyperparameters.

Overview of hyperparameter tuning

Hyperparameter tuning works by running multiple trials in a single training job. Each trial is a complete execution of your training application, with values for your chosen hyperparameters set within the limits you specify. The Cloud ML Engine training service keeps track of the results of each trial and makes adjustments for subsequent trials. When the job is finished, you can get a summary of all the trials, along with the most effective configuration of values according to the criteria you specify.

We want to select those hyperparameters that give the best performance. This amounts to an optimization problem, specifically, the problem of optimizing a function $f(x)$ (that is, performance as a function of hyperparameter values) over a compact set A. We can write this mathematically as:

$$arg\ max\ f(x)$$
$$x \in A \subset R^d$$

Let's take the example of the function $(1-x)^{e^x}$, which has a maximum value $f(x) = 1$ at $x = 0$, and so *arg max* is 0.

Many optimization settings, like this one, assume that the objective function $f(x)$ has a known mathematical form, is convex, or is easy to evaluate. But these characteristics do not apply to the problem of finding hyperparameters where the function is unknown and expensive to evaluate. This is where Bayesian optimization comes into play.

In order to implement hyperparameter tuning, Google uses an algorithm called **Gaussian process bandits**, which is a form of Bayesian optimization.

Bayesian optimization is an extremely powerful technique when the mathematical form of the function is unknown or expensive to compute. The main idea behind it is to compute a posterior distribution over the objective function based on the data (using the famous Bayes, theorem), and then select good points to try with respect to this distribution.

To use Bayesian optimization, we need a way to flexibly model distributions over objective functions. This is a bit trickier than modeling a distribution over, say, real numbers, since we'll need one such distribution to represent our beliefs about $f(x)$ for each x. If x contains continuous hyperparameters, there will be infinitely many x for which we must model $f(x)$, that is, construct a distribution for it. For this problem, Gaussian processes are a particularly elegant technique. In effect, they generalize multidimensional Gaussian distributions, and versions that are flexible enough to model any objective function do exist.

The preceding process typically works as described in the following diagram:

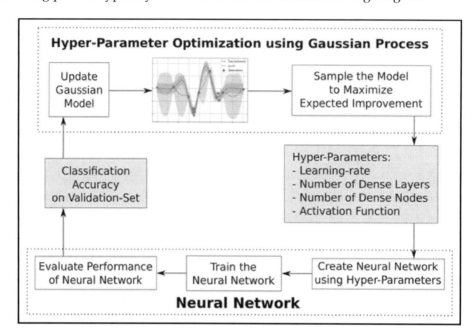

We update the Gaussian model with the results of an iteration, which further helps in identifying the right next sample set of hyperparameters to be tested for the model; the result further improves our Gaussian model to identify the right set of hyperparameters to be picked.

Details of Gaussian distributions are out of the scope of this book, but for this exercise, we will take Google's approach as it is (as a black box) and implement hyperparameter tuning using Google Cloud.

Hyperparameter tuning in Google Cloud

In order for the just-laid-out Gaussian process to run, we have to allow our model builds to be run on Google Cloud so that hyperparameter tuning can be carried out.

In order to run hyperparameter tuning, the following are essential components:

- Data file and its location
- Model file

- Hyperparameter configuration file
- Setup file
- __init__ file

Given that we are running the model on Google Cloud ML engine, the data should be residing in a Cloud bucket so that it becomes accessible to ML engine.

This can be done by performing the following in the Cloud shell:

```
gsutil mb gs://my-mnist-bucket
gsutil cp -r data/mnist.pkl gs://my-mnist-bucket/data/mnist.pkl
```

Note that, using the preceding steps, we have created a bucket named `my-mnist-bucket` and copied our data to that bucket. The preceding code should result in creating a directory named `data` and the `mnist.pkl` file in that directory:

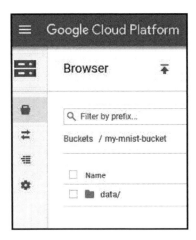

The model file

The model file should be located in a folder that also contains the __init__.py file.

Let us create a folder named `trainer` that contains both the model file and the __init__ file:

```
mkdir trainer
cd trainer
```

The preceding code creates the `trainer` folder and changes directory to the newly-created folder.

Let us go ahead and create the model file as follows:

```
vim mnist_mlp_lr_numsteps.py
```

Insert the following code into the previously-created file:

```
from __future__ import print_function

import argparse
import pickle
from datetime import datetime
import numpy as np
from tensorflow.python.lib.io import file_io # for better file I/O
import sys
import tensorflow as tf

def train_model(train_file='data/mnist.pkl',job_dir='./tmp/mnist_mlp',
num_steps = 1, lr=0.1, **args):
  # logs_path gives access to the logs that are generated by the previous
epochs of model
  logs_path = job_dir + '/logs/' + str(datetime.now().isoformat())
  print('Using logs_path located at {}'.format(logs_path))
  # by default floats are considered as string
  # Good idea to convert them back into floats
  lr=float(lr)
  num_steps=float(num_steps)
  batch_size = 1024
  num_classes = 10
  # Reading in the pickle file. Pickle works differently with Python 2 vs 3
  # In Python 2 the following code would be:
  # f = file_io.FileIO(train_file, mode='r')
  # data = pickle.load(f)
  f = file_io.FileIO(train_file, mode='rb')
  data = pickle.load(f,encoding='bytes')
  (x_train, y_train), (x_test, y_test) = data
  # Converting the data from a 28X28 shape to 784 columns
  x_train = x_train.reshape(60000, 784)
  x_train = x_train.astype('float32')
  x_test = x_test.reshape(10000, 784)
  x_test = x_test.astype('float32')
  x_train /= 255
  x_test /= 255
  # Specifying the type of following labels
  y_train = y_train.astype(np.int32)
  y_test = y_test.astype(np.int32)
  # Creating the estimator following input functions
  train_input_fn = tf.estimator.inputs.numpy_input_fn(
    x={"x2": np.array(x_train)},
```

```
        y=np.array(y_train),
        num_epochs=None,
        batch_size=batch_size,
        shuffle=True)
    test_input_fn = tf.estimator.inputs.numpy_input_fn(
        x={"x2": np.array(x_test)},
        y=np.array(y_test),
        num_epochs=1,
        shuffle=False)
    # Specifying the columns as numeric columns
    feature_x = tf.feature_column.numeric_column("x2", shape=(784))
    feature_columns = [feature_x]
    num_hidden_units = [1000]
    # Building the estimator using DNN classifier
    # This is where the learning rate hyper parameter is passed
    model = tf.estimator.DNNClassifier(feature_columns=feature_columns,
                            hidden_units=num_hidden_units,
                            activation_fn=tf.nn.relu,
                            n_classes=num_classes,
                optimizer=tf.train.AdagradOptimizer(learning_rate = lr))
    # Passing the other parameter: num_steps
    model.train(input_fn=train_input_fn, steps=num_steps)
    # Fetching the model results
    result = model.evaluate(input_fn=test_input_fn)
    print('Test loss:', result['average_loss'])
    print('Test accuracy:', result['accuracy'])
if __name__ == '__main__':
    # Parse the input arguments for common Cloud ML Engine options
    # There are 4 arguments that we need to give, as per the preceding model
specification
    # training file location, job directory, number of steps and learning
rate
    parser = argparse.ArgumentParser()
    parser.add_argument(
        '--train-file',
        help='Cloud Storage bucket or local path to training data')
    parser.add_argument(
        '--job-dir',
        help='Cloud storage bucket to export the model and store temp files')
    parser.add_argument(
        '--num-steps',
        help='number of steps')
    parser.add_argument(
        '--lr',
        help='learning rate')
    args = parser.parse_args()
    arguments = args.__dict__
    train_model(**arguments)
```

Configuration file

Once the model file is set up, we need to provide the configuration file in the same trainer folder so that ML engine knows the parameters that need to be tuned, as well as the typical min and max values of the parameter.

We create the configuration file as follows in the `trainer` folder:

```
vim hptune.yaml
```

The following code is inserted into the preceding file:

```
trainingInput:
  pythonVersion: "3.5"
  scaleTier: CUSTOM
  masterType: standard_gpu
  hyperparameters:
    goal: MAXIMIZE
    hyperparameterMetricTag: accuracy
    maxTrials: 10
    maxParallelTrials: 1
    params:
      - parameterName: num-steps
        type: INTEGER
        minValue: 200
        maxValue: 10000
        scaleType: UNIT_LINEAR_SCALE
      - parameterName: lr
        type: DOUBLE
        minValue: 0.001
        maxValue: 0.1
        scaleType: UNIT_LOG_SCALE
```

In the preceding block of code, we have specified the Python version to be run on and have also specified whether it is to be run on a CPU or a GPU.

In the `hyperparameters` section, we have specified that the metric we need to optimize is accuracy (note that the output of `model.evaluate` is `accuracy`, `loss`, `average loss`, and `global step`); the goal is to maximize it.

Also, we have specified the maximum number of trials to be run and the maximum number of parallel trials that can be run (changes when the Cloud configuration has multiple cores associated with it).

The `params` section contains the parameters that need to be modified, the type of variable it is, and the minimum and maximum values.

ScaleType indicates the type of scaling that would be applied to the parameter:

Value	Description
UNIT_LINEAR_SCALE	Scales the feasible space to (0, 1) linearly.
UNIT_LOG_SCALE	Scales the feasible space logarithmically to (0, 1). The entire feasible space must be strictly positive.
UNIT_REVERSE_LOG_SCALE	Scales the feasible space reverse logarithmically to (0, 1). The result is that values close to the top of the feasible space are spread out more than points near the bottom. The entire feasible space must be strictly positive.

Setup file

In some instances, we might have to install packages that do not come prebuilt. The setup.py file comes in handy in such scenarios:

```
from setuptools import setup, find_packages
setup(name='mnist_mlp_lr_numsteps',
      version='1.0',
      packages=find_packages(),
      include_package_data=True,
      install_requires=[
          'keras',
          'h5py'],
      zip_safe=False)
```

In the preceding code, one could include the additional packages that are needed to run the model file.

The __init__ file

For Cloud ML engine to create a package for the module we are building, it needs to create a package for the module. For the package to be created, it needs to create the __init__.py file in the trainer folder.

For that, we would run the following code:

```
touch trainer/__init__.py
```

Now that the whole setup is ready, we run the job as follows:

```
export BUCKET_NAME=my-mnist-bucket
export JOB_NAME="mnist_mlp_hpt_train_$(date +%Y%m%d_%H%M%S)"
export JOB_DIR=gs://$BUCKET_NAME/$JOB_NAME
export REGION=us-east1
export HPTUNING_CONFIG=hptune.yaml
gcloud ml-engine jobs submit training $JOB_NAME \
  --job-dir $JOB_DIR \
  --runtime-version 1.6 \
  --config $HPTUNING_CONFIG \
  --module-name trainer.mnist_mlp_lr_numsteps \
  --package-path ./trainer \
  --region $REGION \
  -- \
  --train-file gs://$BUCKET_NAME/data/mnist.pkl \
  --num-steps 100 \
  --lr 0.01
```

Note that we specify the bucket name in which data exists, and the job name and directory in which the logs need to be stored. The region needs to be set and the configuration file is specified.

Also, set the `--module-name` argument to the name of your application's main module using your package's namespace dot notation.

Note that, after specifying region, we have a blank, indicating that it is the start of arguments now (they are the training file location, number of steps, and learning rate).

The number of steps and learning rate that we have specified in the preceding code are the default versions, which are changed once passed to the ML engine job.

The output of the code can be visualized in the training output of the job that we ran, as follows:

```
Training output          {
                            "completedTrialCount": "10",
                            "trials": [
                              {
                                "trialId": "4",
                                "hyperparameters": {
                                 "num-steps": "7658",
                                 "lr": "0.0149847049746120019"
                                },
                                "finalMetric": {
                                 "trainingStep": "7658",
                                 "objectiveValue": 0.984000027179718
                                }
                              },
                              {
                                "trialId": "9",
                                "hyperparameters": {
                                 "lr": "0.0126845239135967773",
                                 "num-steps": "9994"
                                },
                                "finalMetric": {
                                 "trainingStep": "9994",
                                 "objectiveValue": 0.9832000136375427
                                }
                              },
```

The optimal hyperparameters can then be selected from the preceding output. We can see that a learning rate of **0.0149** and number of steps as **7658** result in a higher test dataset accuracy than the two scenarios that we tested earlier.

Summary

In this chapter, we understood how different parameter combinations affect the final accuracy measure and how hyperparameter tuning using Cloud ML engine helps in improving the accuracy further.

In the next chapter, we will learn how to identify overfitting and make our models more robust to previously-unseen data by setting the right parameters and defining the proper architectures.

12
Preventing Overfitting with Regularization

So far, in the previous chapters, we understood about building neural network, evaluating the TensorBoard results, and varying the hyperparameters of the neural network model to improve the accuracy of the model.

While the hyperparameters in general help with improving the accuracy of model, certain configuration of hyperparameters results in the model overfitting to the training data, while not generalizing for testing data is the problem of overfitting to the training data.

A key parameter that can help us in avoiding overfitting while generalizing on an unseen dataset is the regularization technique. Some of the key regularization techniques are as follows:

- L2 regularization
- L1 regularization
- Dropout
- Scaling
- Batch normalization
- Weight initialization

In this chapter, we will go through the following:

- Intuition of over/under fitting
- Reducing overfitting using regularization
- Improving the underfitting scenario

Intuition of over/under fitting

Before we understand about how the preceding techniques are useful, let's build a scenario, so that we understand the phenomenon of overfitting.

Scenario 1: A case of not generalizing on an unseen dataset

In this scenario, we will create a dataset, for which there is a clear linearly separable mapping between input and output. For example, whenever the independent variables are positive, the output is [1,0], and when the input variables are negative, the output is [0,1]:

```
import numpy as np

np.random.seed(42)
x1=np.random.random_sample((2000,5))
y=[[1,0]]
y1=np.repeat(y,2000,axis=0)

np.random.seed(0)
x2=np.random.random_sample((2000,5))*-1
y=[[0,1]]
y2=np.repeat(y,2000,axis=0)

x_new=np.append(x1,x2,axis=0)

y_new=np.append(y1,y2,axis=0)
```

To that dataset, we will add a small amount of noise (10% of the preceding dataset created) by adding some data points that follow the opposite of the preceding pattern, that is, when the input variables are positive, the output is [0,1], and the output is [1,0] when the input variables are negative:

```
np.random.seed(5)
x1_badsamples = np.random.random_sample((200,5))
x2_badsamples = np.random.random_sample((200,5))*-1

y1_badsamples = np.repeat([[0,1]],200,axis=0)
y2_badsamples = np.repeat([[1,0]],200,axis=0)

x_badsamples = np.append(x1_badsamples,x2_badsamples,axis=0)
y_badsamples = np.append(y1_badsamples,y2_badsamples,axis=0)
```

Appending the datasets obtained by the preceding two steps gives us the training dataset, as follows:

```
final_x=np.append(x_new,x_badsamples,axis=0)
final_y=np.append(y_new,y_badsamples,axis=0)
```

In the next step, we create the test dataset, where it follows the criterion followed by the majority of the training dataset, that is, when the input is positive, the output is [1,0]:

```
np.random.seed(10)
x1_test = np.random.random_sample((200,5))
x2_test = np.random.random_sample((200,5))*-1

y1_test = np.repeat([[1,0]],200,axis=0)
y2_test = np.repeat([[0,1]],200,axis=0)

test_x=np.append(x1_test,x2_test,axis=0)
test_y=np.append(y1_test,y2_test,axis=0)
```

Now that we have created the dataset, let's go ahead and build a model to predict the output with the given inputs.

The intuition here is that, if training accuracy improves by more than 90.91% it is a classic case of overfitting, as the model tries to fit for the minority of the observations which do not generalize for an unseen dataset.

To check that—let's first import all the relevant packages to build a model in `keras`:

We build a model with three layers where the layers have 1,000, 500 and 100 units in each respective hidden layer:

```
model = Sequential()
model.add(Dense(1000, input_dim=5, kernel_initializer='normal',activation='relu'))
model.add(Dense(500,  kernel_initializer='normal',activation='relu'))
model.add(Dense(100,  kernel_initializer='normal',activation='relu'))

model.add(Dense(2,  activation='softmax'))
tensorboard = TensorBoard(log_dir = "/content/datalab/logs/tensor_3")

adam = Adam(lr=0.01)
model.compile(loss='categorical_crossentropy', optimizer=adam, metrics=['accuracy'])
```

```
model.fit(final_x,final_y, validation_data=(test_x,test_y), epochs=1000, batch_size=5000, verbose=2,callbacks=[tensorboard])
```

A TensorBoard visualization of loss and accuracy on train and test datasets is as follows:

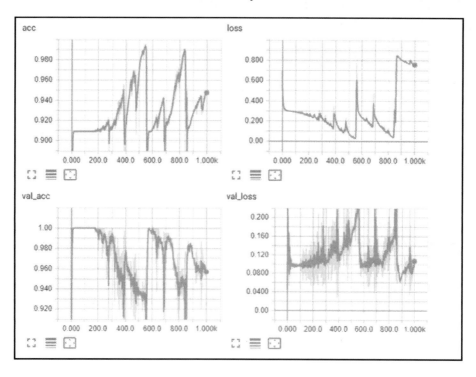

From the first two graphs, we can see that, as loss on train dataset decreased, its accuracy improved.

Also, note that the training loss was not reducing smoothly—potentially indicating to us that it is overfitting to the training data.

You should observe that, the validation accuracy (test accuracy) started to decrease as training dataset accuracy improved—again indicating to us that the model does not generalize well to unseen dataset.

This phenomenon typically happens when the model is too complex and tries to fit the last few misclassifications to reduce the training loss.

Reducing overfitting

Typically, overfitting results in some weights being very high relative to others. To understand that, let's look at the histogram of weights that are obtained by running the model on the artificially created dataset in *scenario 1*:

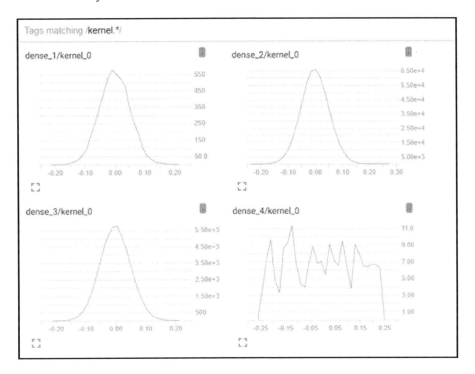

We see that there are some weights that have a high value (> 0.1) and a majority that are centered around zero.

Let's now explore the impact of penalizing for having a high weight value through L1 and L2 regularizations.

The intuition of regularization is as follows:

- If the weight values are shrunk to as minimal as possible, it is less likely that some of those weights contribute more towards fine-tuning our model to the few outlier cases

Implementing L2 regularization

Now that we have seen how overfitting occurs on our dataset, we will explore the impact of L2 regularization in reducing overfitting on the dataset.

L2 regularization on a dataset can be defined as follows:

$$\text{Cost} = \underbrace{\sum_{i=0}^{N} (y_i - \sum_{j=0}^{M} x_{ij} W_j)^2}_{\text{Loss function}} + \underbrace{\lambda \sum_{j=0}^{M} W_j^2}_{\substack{\text{Regularization} \\ \text{Term}}}$$

Note that the loss function is the traditional loss function where y is the dependent variable, x is the independent variables, and W is the kernel (weight matrices).

The regularization term is added to the loss function. Note the regularization value is the sum of squared weight values across all the dimensions of a weight matrix. Given that we are minimizing the sum of squared value of weights along with loss function, the cost function ensures that there is no weight value that is large—thereby ensuring that less overfitting occurs.

The lambda parameter is a hyperparameter that adjusts the weightage that we give to regularization term.

Let's explore the impact of adding L2 regularization to the model defined in *scenario 1*:

```
from keras.regularizers import l2
from keras import backend as K
K.clear_session()
model = Sequential()
model.add(Dense(1000, input_dim=5, kernel_initializer='normal',kernel_regularizer=l2(0.01),activation='relu'))
model.add(Dense(500,  kernel_initializer='normal',kernel_regularizer=l2(0.01),activation='relu'))
model.add(Dense(100,  kernel_initializer='normal',kernel_regularizer=l2(0.01),activation='relu'))

model.add(Dense(2,  activation='softmax'))
tensorboard = TensorBoard(log_dir = "/content/datalab/logs/tensor_17",histogram_freq=1000,batch_size=5000)

adam = Adam(lr=0.01)
model.compile(loss='categorical_crossentropy', optimizer=adam, metrics=['accuracy'])
```

Note that we modified the code that we have seen in *scenario 1* by adding `kernel_regularizer`, which, in this case, is the L2 regularizer with a lambda value of `0.01`.

Note the output of TensorBoard, as we train the preceding model:

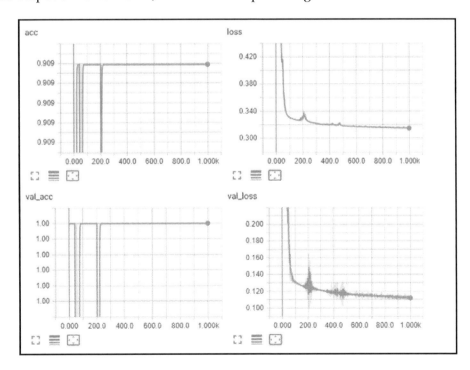

The training loss kept on decreasing and the validation accuracy remained stable while the training accuracy is 90.9% without accounting for the overfitting scenario.

Let's explore the distribution of weights to understand the difference between weight distributions when L2 regularization was done and there was no regularization:

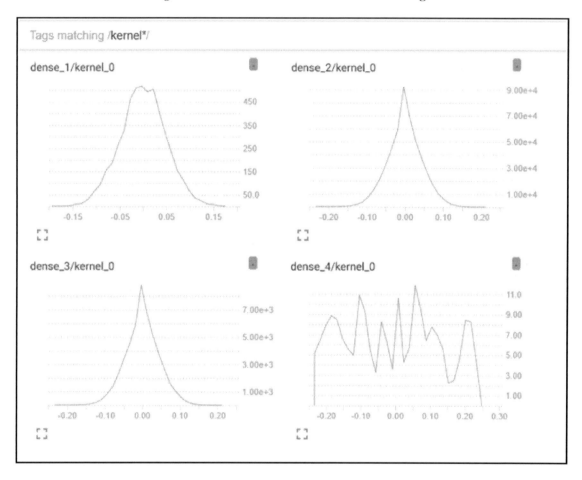

You should notice that the kernels (primarily the kernels at dense_2 and dense_3) have a lot sharper peak at zero in the L2 regularization scenario when compared to the no regularization scenario.

To further understand the peak distributions, we will modify the lambda value and give regularization a higher weightage of 0.1 instead of 001 and see how the weights look:

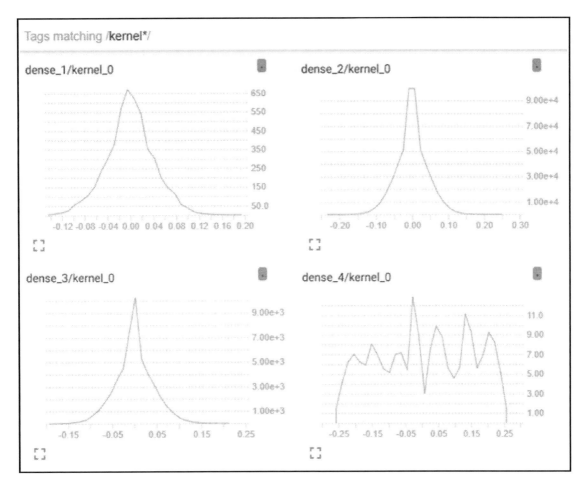

Note that, with a higher weightage given to the regularization term, weights have a much sharper distribution around the center (a value of 0).

Also, you should notice that the kernel is `dense_4` and is not changed by a lot, as we did not apply regularization at this layer.

From the preceding points we conclude that, by implementing L2 regularization, we can reduce the over-fitting issue that we see when there is no regularization.

Implementing L1 regularization

L1 regularization works in a similar way as that of L2; however, the cost function for L1 regularization is different than L2 regularization, as follows:

$$Cost = \sum_{i=0}^{N}(y_i - \sum_{j=0}^{M} x_{ij}W_j)^2 + \lambda\sum_{j=0}^{M}|W_j|$$

 Note that, in the preceding equation, all the terms remain the same; just the regularization term is the summation of absolute values of weights than squared values of weights.

Let's implement the L1 regularization in code; now we see the corresponding outputs as follows:

```
from keras.regularizers import l1
from keras import backend as K
K.clear_session()
model = Sequential()
model.add(Dense(1000, input_dim=5, kernel_initializer='normal',kernel_regularizer=l1(0.001),activation='relu'))
model.add(Dense(500,  kernel_initializer='normal',kernel_regularizer=l1(0.001),activation='relu'))
model.add(Dense(100,  kernel_initializer='normal',kernel_regularizer=l1(0.001),activation='relu'))

model.add(Dense(2,  activation='softmax'))
tensorboard = TensorBoard(log_dir = "/content/datalab/logs/tensor_22",histogram_freq=1000,batch_size=5000)

adam = Adam(lr=0.01)
model.compile(loss='categorical_crossentropy', optimizer=adam, metrics=['accuracy'])
```

Note that, as the regularization term does not involve squaring in L1 regularization, we may have to lower the lambda value in L1 when compared to L2 (given most of the weights are less than one, squaring them would make the weight values even smaller).

Post-defining the model (this time with regularization), we fit it, as follows:

```
model.fit(final_x,final_y, validation_data=(test_x,test_y), epochs=1000, batch_size=5000, verbose=2,callbacks=[tensorboard])
```

The preceding code fit results in the accuracy on train and test datasets, as per our expectation, as follows:

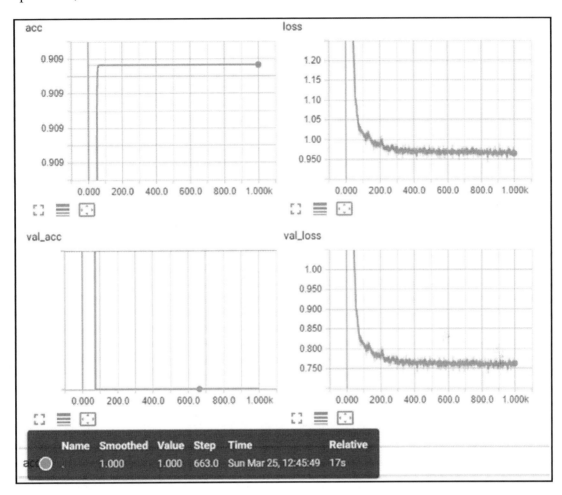

Let's also look into the weight distribution across the layers in the **Histograms** tab:

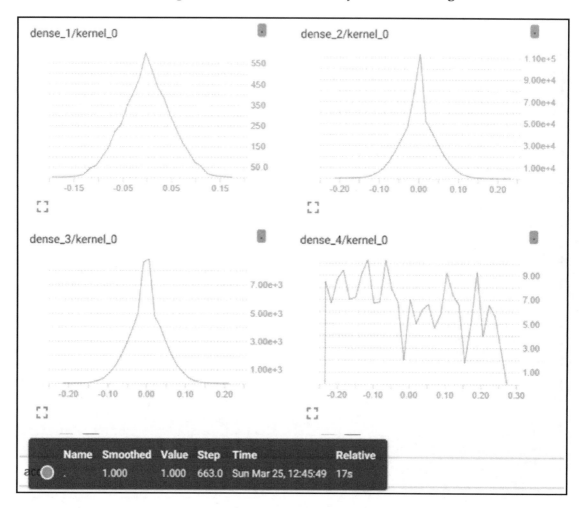

We should note that, the kernel distribution here is similar to the kernel distribution when the lambda value of the L2 regularization was high.

Implementing dropout

Another way to reduce overfitting is by implementing the dropout technique. While performing weight updates in a typical back propagation, we ensure that some random portion of the weights are left out from updating the weights in a given epoch—hence the name dropout.

Dropout as a technique can also help in reducing overfitting, as reduction in the number of weights that need to be updated in a single epoch results in less chance that the output depends on few input values.

Dropout can be implemented as follows:

```python
from keras import backend as K
K.clear_session()
model = Sequential()
model.add(Dense(1000, input_dim=5, kernel_initializer='normal',activation='relu'))
model.add(Dropout(0.5))
model.add(Dense(500,  kernel_initializer='normal',activation='relu'))
model.add(Dropout(0.5))
model.add(Dense(100,  kernel_initializer='normal',activation='relu'))
model.add(Dropout(0.5))
model.add(Dense(2,  activation='softmax'))
tensorboard = TensorBoard(log_dir = "/content/datalab/logs/tensor_23",histogram_freq=1000,batch_size=5000)

adam = Adam(lr=0.01)
model.compile(loss='categorical_crossentropy', optimizer=adam, metrics=['accuracy'])
```

```python
model.fit(final_x,final_y, validation_data=(test_x,test_y), epochs=1000, batch_size=5000, verbose=2,callbacks=[tensorboard])
```

The result of the model fit is as follows:

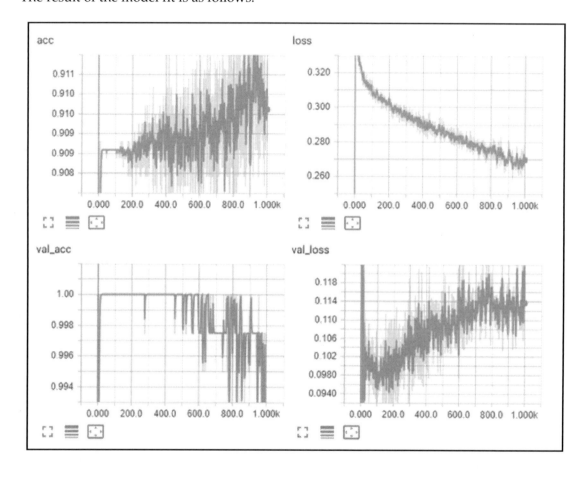

You should note that dropout in the given configuration has resulted in a slightly broad distribution of weights when compared to the no regularization scenario:

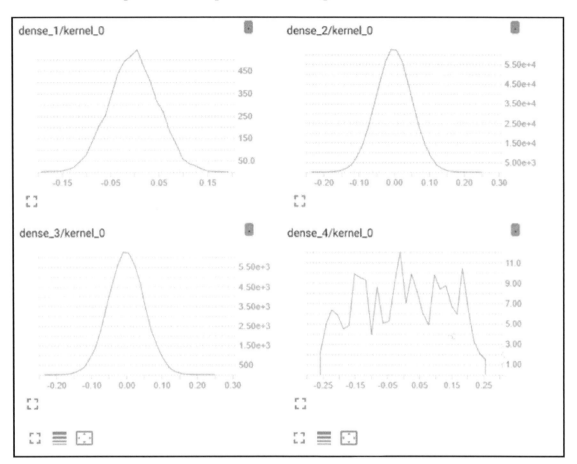

Reducing underfitting

Underfitting typically happens when:

- The model is extremely complex and is run for fewer epochs
- The data is not normalized

Scenario 2: Underfitting in action on the MNIST dataset

In the following scenario, we see the case of underfitting in action on the MNIST dataset:

```
from keras.datasets import mnist
(X_train, y_train), (X_test, y_test) = mnist.load_data()
import numpy
from keras.datasets import mnist
from keras.models import Sequential
from keras.layers import Dense
from keras.layers import Dropout
from keras.utils import np_utils
```

```
num_pixels = X_train.shape[1] * X_train.shape[2]
X_train = X_train.reshape(X_train.shape[0], num_pixels).astype('float32')
X_test = X_test.reshape(X_test.shape[0], num_pixels).astype('float32')
```

Note that, in the preceding code, we have not scaled our data—the training and test dataset columns have values ranging from 0 to 255:

```
# one hot encode outputs
y_train = np_utils.to_categorical(y_train)
y_test = np_utils.to_categorical(y_test)
num_classes = y_test.shape[1]
```

```
model = Sequential()
model.add(Dense(1000, input_dim=num_pixels, kernel_initializer='normal',activation='relu'))
model.add(Dense(500,  kernel_initializer='normal',activation='relu'))
model.add(Dense(250,  kernel_initializer='normal',activation='relu'))
model.add(Dense(100,  kernel_initializer='normal',activation='relu'))
model.add(Dense(num_classes,  activation='softmax'))
adam = Adam(lr=0.01)
tensorboard = TensorBoard(log_dir = "/content/datalab/logs/tensor_8")
model.compile(loss='categorical_crossentropy', optimizer=adam, metrics=['accuracy'])
```

```
model.fit(X_train, y_train, validation_data=(X_test, y_test), epochs=100, batch_size=60000, verbose=2,callbacks=[tensorboard])
```

The TensorBoard visualization of accuracy and loss on train and test datasets for the preceding model is as follows:

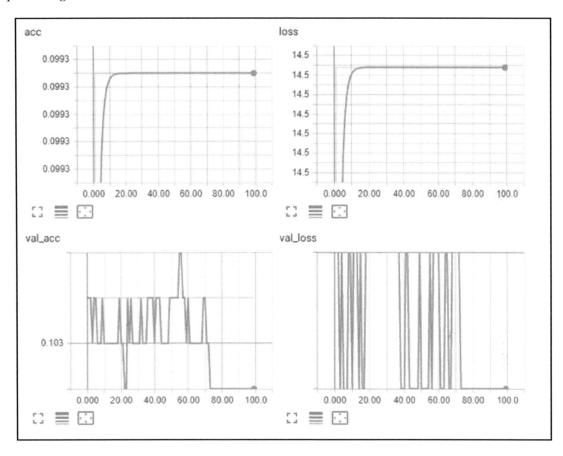

Note that, in the preceding charts, both the loss and the accuracy of the training dataset have hardly changed (note the *y* axis values in both).

This scenario (where the loss hardly changes), typically happens when the input has numbers that are very high (typically >5).

The preceding can be rectified by performing any of the following:

- Scaling the data
- Batch normalization

Scaling the data is as simple as repeating the preceding architecture, but with the small modification of scaling the train and test datasets:

```
X_train2 = X_train/255
X_test2= X_test/255
```

Batch normalization can be performed (even on an unscaled MNIST dataset) as follows:

```
model = Sequential()
model.add(Dense(1000, input_dim=num_pixels, kernel_initializer='normal',activation='relu'))
model.add(BatchNormalization())
model.add(Dense(500, kernel_initializer='normal',activation='relu'))
model.add(BatchNormalization())
model.add(Dense(250, kernel_initializer='normal',activation='relu'))
model.add(BatchNormalization())
model.add(Dense(100, kernel_initializer='normal',activation='relu'))
model.add(BatchNormalization())
model.add(Dense(num_classes, activation='softmax'))
adam = Adam(lr=0.01)
tensorboard = TensorBoard(log_dir = "/content/datalab/logs/tensor_25",histogram_freq=100,batch_size=60000)
model.compile(loss='categorical_crossentropy', optimizer=adam, metrics=['accuracy'])
```

```
model.fit(X_train2, y_train, validation_data=(X_test2, y_test), epochs=100, batch_size=60000, verbose=2,callbacks=[tensorboard])
```

A visualization of training and test accuracies can be seen as follows:

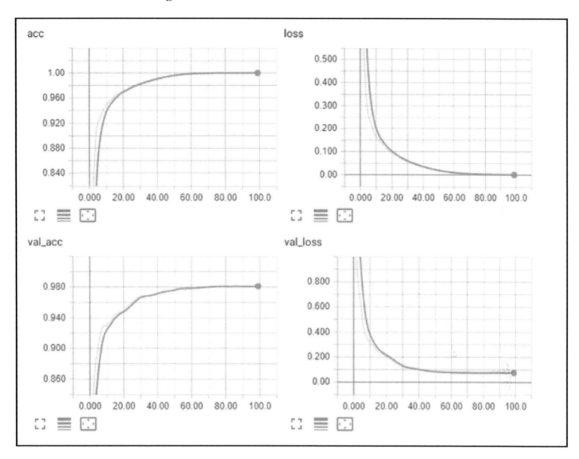

In the preceding scenario, we see that, even on unscaled dataset, the test accuracy is quite high.

Scenario 3: Incorrect weight initialization

Just like the previous scenario, it is highly likely that we will encounter an underfitting scenario if the weights are not initialized properly (even if the dataset is a properly scaled dataset). For example, in the following code, we initialize all the weights (kernels) to zero and then notice the accuracy on the test dataset:

```
(X_train, y_train), (X_test, y_test) = mnist.load_data()
num_pixels = X_train.shape[1] * X_train.shape[2]
X_train = X_train.reshape(X_train.shape[0], num_pixels).astype('float32')
X_test = X_test.reshape(X_test.shape[0], num_pixels).astype('float32')
X_train2 = X_train/255
X_test2= X_test/255
y_train = np_utils.to_categorical(y_train)
y_test = np_utils.to_categorical(y_test)
num_classes = y_test.shape[1]
```

```
model = Sequential()
model.add(Dense(1000, input_dim=num_pixels, kernel_initializer='zeros',activation='relu'))
model.add(Dense(500, kernel_initializer='zeros',activation='relu'))
model.add(Dense(250, kernel_initializer='zeros',activation='relu'))
model.add(Dense(100, kernel_initializer='zeros',activation='relu'))
model.add(Dense(num_classes, activation='softmax'))
adam = Adam(lr=0.01)
tensorboard = TensorBoard(log_dir = "/content/datalab/logs/tensor_14")
model.compile(loss='categorical_crossentropy', optimizer=adam, metrics=['accuracy'])
```

```
model.fit(X_train2, y_train, validation_data=(X_test2, y_test), epochs=100, batch_size=60000, verbose=2,callbacks=[tensorboard])
```

The output of the preceding code results in the following TensorBoard visualization:

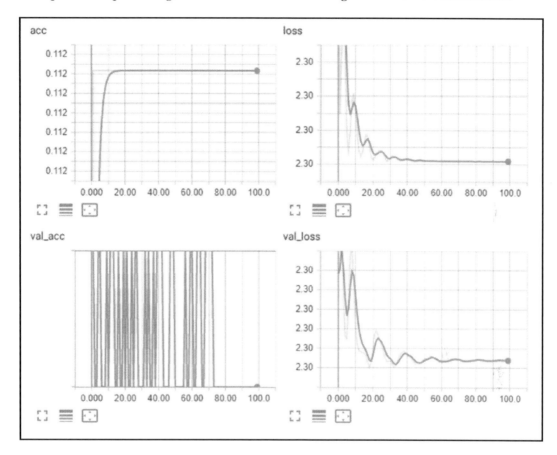

Similar to *scenario 2*, the preceding charts indicate that there is no learning that is happening through the preceding defined architecture.

No learning is happening, as the weights are initialized to zero.

It is advisable to initialize the weights to normal initialization. The other initializations that can be tried out to test whether accuracy could improve are:

- `glorot_normal`
- `lecun_uniform`
- `glorot_uniform`
- `he_normal`

Summary

In this chapter, we have seen the characteristics of over fitting and how they can be handled through L1 and L2 regularizations, and dropout. Similarly, we have seen the scenario where there was quite a lot of underfitting and how scaling or batch normalization helped us in improving the under-fitting scenario.

13
Beyond Feedforward Networks – CNN and RNN

Artificial Neural Networks (**ANNs**) are now extremely widespread tools in various technologies. In the simplest application, ANNs provide a feedforward architecture for connections between neurons. The feedforward neural network is the first and simplest type of ANN devised. In the presence of basic hypotheses that interact with some problems, the intrinsic unidirectional structure of feedforward networks is strongly limiting. However, it is possible to start from it and create networks in which the results of computing one unit affect the computational process of another. It is evident that algorithms that manage the dynamics of these networks must meet new convergence criteria.

In this chapter, we'll go over the main ANN architectures, such as convolutional NNs, recurrent NNs, and **long short-term memory** (**LSTM**). We'll explain the concepts behind each type of NN and tell you which problem they should be applied to. Each type of NN is implemented with TensorFlow on a realistic dataset.

The topics covered are:

- Convolutional networks and their applications
- Recurrent networks
- LSTM architectures

At the end of the chapter, we will understand training, testing, and evaluating a **convolutional neural network** (**CNN**). We will learn how to train and test the CNN model in Google Cloud Platform. We will cover the concepts as CNN and RNN architecture. We will also be able to train an LSTM model. The reader will learn which type of neural network to apply to different problems and how to define and implement them on Google Cloud Platform.

Convolutional neural networks

ANN is a family of models inspired from biological neural networks (the human brain) that, starting from the mechanisms regulating natural neural networks, plan to simulate human thinking. They are used to estimate or approximate functions that may depend on a large number of inputs, many of which are often unknown. ANNs are generally presented as interconnected neuron systems among which an exchange of messages takes place. Each connection has a related weight; the value of the weight is adjustable based on experience, and this makes neural networks an instrument adaptable to the various types of input and having the ability to learn.

ANNs define the neuron as a central processing unit, which performs a mathematical operation to generate one output from a set of inputs. The output of a neuron is a function of the weighted sum of the inputs plus the bias. Each neuron performs a very simple operation that involves activation if the total amount of signal received exceeds an activation threshold. In the following figure, a simple ANN architecture is shown:

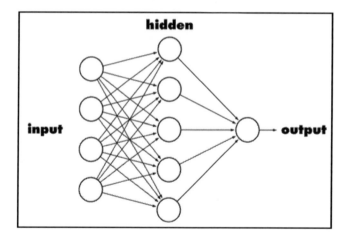

Essentially, CNN are ANNs. In fact, just like the latter, CNNs are made up of neurons connected to one another by weighted branches (weight); the training parameters of the nets are once again the weight and the bias.

In CNN, the connection pattern between neurons is inspired by the structure of the visual cortex in the animal world. The individual neurons present in this part of the brain (visual cortex) respond to certain stimuli in a narrow region of the observation, called the **receptive field**. The receptive fields of different neurons are partially overlapped in order to cover the entire field of vision. The response of a single neuron to stimuli taking place in its receptive field can be mathematically approximated by a convolution operation.

Everything related to the training of a neural network, that is, forward/backward propagation and updating of the weight, also applies in this context; moreover, a whole CNN always uses a single function of differentiable cost. However, CNNs make a specific assumption that their input has a precise data structure, such as an image, and this allows them to take specific properties in their architectureto better process such data.

The normal neural networks stratified with an FC architecture—where every neuron of each layer is connected to all the neurons of the previous layer (excluding bias neurons)—in general do not scale well with an increase in the size of input data.

Let's take a practical example: suppose we want to analyze an image to detect objects. To start, let's see how the image is processed. As we know, in the coding of an image, it is divided into a grid of small squares, each of which represents a pixel. At this point, to encode the color images, it will be enough to identify for each square a certain number of shades and different color gradations. And then we code each one by means of an appropriate sequence of bits. Here is a simple image encoding:

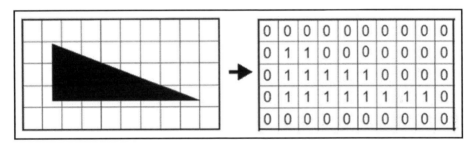

The number of squares in the grid defines the resolution of the image. For example, an image that is 1,600 pixels wide and 800 pixels high (1,600 x 800) contains (multiplied) 1,280,000 pixels, or 1.2 megapixels. To this, we must multiply the three color channels, finally obtaining 1,600 x 800 x 3 = 3,840,000. So, each neuron completely connected in the first hidden layer would have 3,840,000 weights. This is only for a single neuron; considering the whole network, the thing would certainly become unmanageable!

CNNs are designed to recognize visual patterns directly in images represented by pixels and require zero or very limited preprocessing. They are able to recognize extremely variable patterns, such as freehand writing and images representing the real world.

Typically, a CNN consists of several alternate convolution and subsampling levels (pooling) followed by one or more FC final levels in the case of classification. The following figure shows a classic image-processing pipeline:

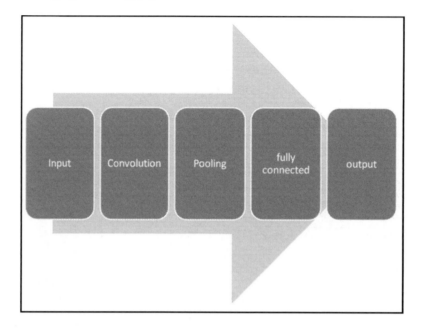

To solve problems in the real world, these steps can be combined and stacked as often as necessary. For example, you can have two, three, or even more layers of **Convolution**. You can enter all the **Pooling** you want to reduce the size of the data.

As already mentioned, different types of levels are typically used in a CNN. In the following sections, the main ones will be covered.

Convolution layer

This is the main type of layer; the use of one or more of these layers in a CNN is essential. The parameters of a convolutional layer, in practice, relate to a set of workable filters. Each filter is spatially small, along the width and height dimensions, but it extends over the entire depth of the input volume to which it is applied.

Unlike normal neural networks, convolutional layers have neurons organized in three dimensions: **width**, **height**, and **depth**. They are shown in the following figure:

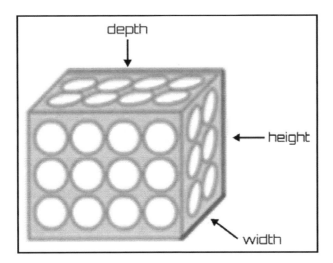

During forward propagation, each filter is translated—or more precisely, convolved—along the width and height of the input volume, producing a two-dimensional activation map (or feature map) for that filter. As the filter is moved along the input area, a scalar product operation is performed between the values of the filter and those of the input portion to which it is applied.

Intuitively, the network will have as its objective the learning of filters that are activated in the presence of some specific type of feature in a given spatial region of the input. The queuing of all these feature maps (for all filters) along the depth dimension forms the output volume of a convolutional layer. Each element of this volume can be interpreted as the output of a neuron that observes only a small region of the input and which shares its parameters with the other neurons in the same feature map. This is because these values all come from the application of the same filter.

In summary, let's focus our attention on the following points:

- **Local receptive field**: Each neuron of a layer is (completely) connected to a small region of the input (called a **local receptive field**); each connection learns a weight.
- **Shared weights**: Since the interesting features (edge, blob, and so on) can be found anywhere in the image, the neurons of the same layer share the weights. This means that all the neurons of the same layer will recognize the same feature, placed at different points of the input.
- **Convolution**: The same weight map is applied to different positions. The convolution output is called a **feature map**.

Each filter captures a feature present in the previous layer. So to extract different features, we need to train multiple convolutional filters. Each filter returns a feature map that highlights different characteristics.

Rectified Linear Units

Rectified Linear Units (ReLU) play the role of neuronal activation function in neural networks. A ReLU level is composed of neurons that apply the function $f(x) = max (0, x)$. These levels increase the non-linearity of the network and at the same time do not modify the receiving fields of convolution levels. The function of the ReLUs is preferred over others, such as the hyperbolic tangent or the sigmoid, since, in comparison to these, it leads to a much faster training process without significantly affecting the generalization accuracy.

Pooling layers

These layers are periodically inserted into a network to reduce the spatial size (width and height) of current representations, as well as volumes in a specific network stage; this serves to reduce the number of parameters and the computational time of the network. It also monitors overfitting. A pooling layer operates on each depth slice of the input volume independently to resize it spatially.

For example, this technique partitions an input image into a set of squares, and for each of the resulting regions, it returns the maximum value as output.

CNNs also use pooling layers located immediately after the convolutional layers. A pooling layer divides input into regions and selects a single representative value (max-pooling and average pooling). Using a pooling layer:

- Reduces the calculations of subsequent layers
- Increases the robustness of the features with respect to spatial position

It is based on the concept that, once a certain feature has been identified, its precise position in the input is not as important as its approximate position in relation to the other features. In the typical CNN architecture, convolution levels and pooling levels are repeatedly alternated.

Fully connected layer

This type of layer is exactly the same as any of the layers of a classical ANN with **fully connected (FC)** architecture. Simply in an FC layer, each neuron is connected to all the neurons of the previous layer, specifically to their activations.

This type of layer, unlike what has been seen so far in CNNs, does not use the property of local connectivity. An FC layer is connected to the entire input volume, and, therefore, as you can imagine, there will be many connections. The only settable parameter of this type of layer is the number of K neurons that make it up. What basically defines an FC layer is as follows: connecting its K neurons with all the input volume and calculating the activation of each of its K neurons.

In fact, its output will be a single 1 x 1 x K vector, containing the calculated activations. The fact that after using a single FC layer you switch from an input volume (organized in three dimensions) to a single output vector (in a single dimension) suggests that after applying an FC layer, no more convoluted layers can be used. The main function of FC layers in the context of CNNs is to carry out a sort of grouping of the information obtained up to that moment, expressing it with a single number (the activation of one of its neurons), which will be used in subsequent calculations for the final classification.

Structure of a CNN

After analyzing every component of a CNN in detail, it is time to see the general structure of a CNN as a whole. For example, starting from the images as input layers, there will be a certain series of convolutional layers interspersed with a ReLU layer and, when necessary, the standardization and pooling layers. Finally, there will be a series of FC layers before the output layer. Here is an example of a CNN architecture:

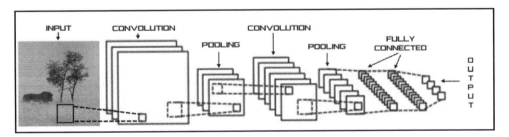

The basic idea is to start with a large image and continuously reduce the data step by step until you get a single result. The more the convolution passages you have, the more the neural network will be able to understand and process complex functions.

TensorFlow overview

TensorFlow is an open source numerical computing library provided by Google for machine intelligence. It hides all of the programming required to build deep learning models and gives developers a black box interface to program.

In TensorFlow, nodes in the graph represent mathematical operations, while the graph edges represent the multidimensional data arrays (tensors) communicated between them. TensorFlow was originally developed by the Google brain team within Google's machine intelligence research for machine learning and deep neural networks research, but it is now available in the public domain. TensorFlow exploits GPU processing when configured appropriately.

The generic use cases for TensorFlow are as follows:

- Image recognition
- Computer vision
- Voice/sound recognition
- Time series analysis
- Language detection
- Language translation
- Text-based processing
- Handwriting Recognition
- Many others

To use TensorFlow, we must first install Python. If you don't have a Python installation on your machine, it's time to get it. Python is a dynamic **object-oriented programming** (**OOP**) language that can be used for many types of software development. It offers strong support for integration with other languages and programs, is provided with a large standard library, and can be learned within a few days. Many Python programmers can confirm a substantial increase in productivity and feel that it encourages the development of higher quality code and maintainability.

Python runs on Windows, Linux/Unix, macOS X, OS/2, Amiga, Palm handhelds, and Nokia phones. It also works on Java and .NET virtual machines. Python is licensed under the OSI-approved open source license; its use is free, including for commercial products.

Python was created in the early 1990s by Guido van Rossum at Stichting Mathematisch Centrum in the Netherlands as a successor of a language called **ABC**. Guido remains Python's principal author, although it includes many contributions from others.

> If you do not know which version to use, there is an English document that can help you choose. In principle, if you have to start from scratch, we recommend choosing Python 3.6. All information about the available versions and how to install Python is given at https://www.python.org/.

After properly installing the Python version of our machine, we have to worry about installing TensorFlow. We can retrieve all library information and available versions of the operating system from the following link: https://www.tensorflow.org/.

Also, in the install section, we can find a series of guides that explain how to install a version of TensorFlow that allows us to write applications in Python. Guides are available for the following operating systems:

- Ubuntu
- macOS X
- Windows

For example, to install TensorFlow on Windows, we must choose one of the following types:

- TensorFlow with CPU support only
- TensorFlow with GPU support

To install TensorFlow, start a terminal with privileges as administrator. Then issue the appropriate `pip3 install` command in that terminal. To install the CPU-only version, enter the following command:

```
C:\> pip3 install --upgrade tensorflow
```

A series of code lines will be displayed on the video to keep us informed of the execution of the installation procedure, as shown in the following figure:

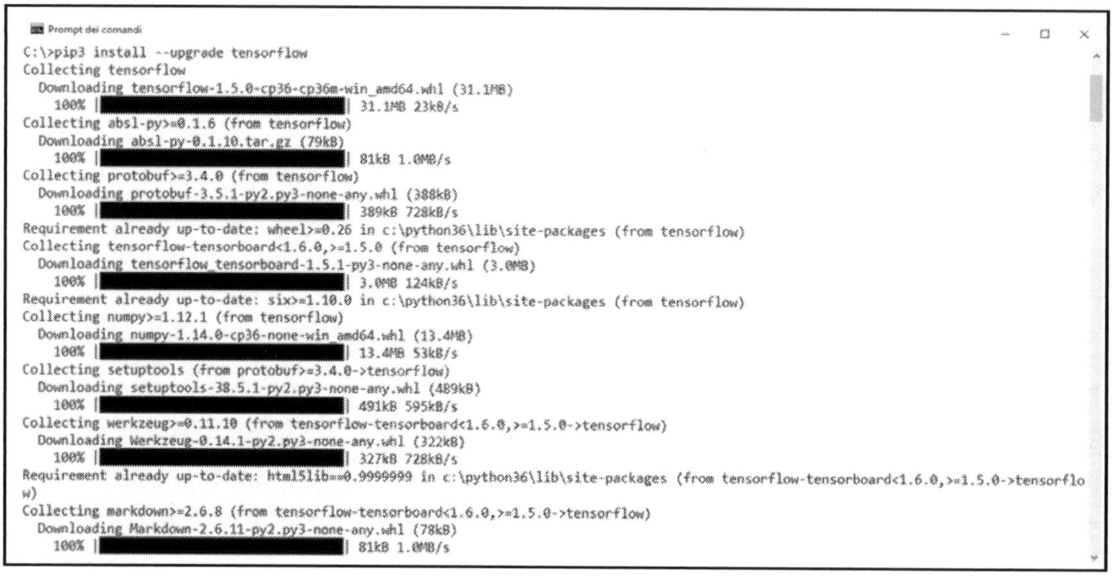

At the end of the process, the following code is displayed:

```
Successfully installed absl-py-0.1.10 markdown-2.6.11 numpy-1.14.0
protobuf-3.5.1 setuptools-38.5.1 tensorflow-1.5.0 tensorflow-
tensorboard-1.5.1 werkzeug-0.14.1
```

To validate the installation, invoke `python` from a shell as follows:

```
python
```

Enter the following short program inside the Python interactive shell:

```
>>> import tensorflow as tf
>>> hello = tf.constant('Hello, TensorFlow!')
>>> sess = tf.Session()
>>> print(sess.run(hello))
```

If the system outputs the following, then you are ready to begin writing TensorFlow programs:

```
Hello, TensorFlow!
```

In this case, you will have a confirmation of correct installation of the library on your computer. Now you just need to use it.

Handwriting Recognition using CNN and TensorFlow

Handwriting Recognition (HWR) is a very commonly used procedure in modern technology. An image of written text can be detected offline from a piece of paper by optical scanning (**optical character recognition** or **OCR**) or intelligent word recognition. Alternatively, pen tip movements can be detected online (for example, from a pen computer surface, a task that is generally easier since there are more clues available).

Technically, recognition of handwriting is the ability of a computer to receive and interpret a handwritten intelligible input from sources such as paper documents, photos, touchscreens, and other devices. HWR is performed through various techniques that generally require OCR. However, a complete script recognition system also manages formatting, carries out correct character segmentation, and finds the most plausible words.

Modified National Institute of Standards and Technology (MNIST) is a large database of handwritten digits. It has a set of 70,000 examples of data. It is a subset of NIST's larger dataset. The digits are of 28 x 28 pixel resolution and are stored in a matrix of 70,000 rows and 785 columns; 784 columns form each pixel value from the 28 x 28 matrix and one value is the actual digit. The digits have been size-normalized and centered in a fixed-size image.

> The digit images in the MNIST set were originally selected and experimented with by Chris Burges and Corinna Cortes using bounding box normalization and centering. Yann LeCun's version uses centering by center of mass within in a larger window. The data is available on Yann LeCun's website at
> http://yann.lecun.com/exdb/mnist/.

Each image is created as 28 x 28. The following figure shows a sample of images of 0-8 from the MNIST dataset:

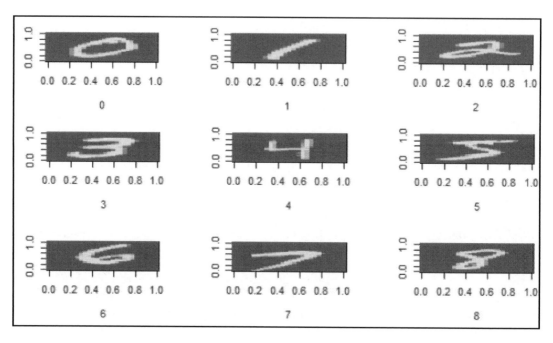

MNIST has a sample of several handwritten digits. This dataset can be fed for our training to an Python program and our code can recognize any new handwritten digit that is presented as data for prediction. This is a case where the neural network architecture functions as a computer vision system for an AI application. The following table shows the distribution of the MNIST dataset available on LeCun's website:

Digit	Count
0	5923
1	6742
2	5958
3	6131
4	5842
5	5421
6	5918

7	6265
8	5851
9	5949

We will use the TensorFlow library to train and test the MNIST dataset. We will split the dataset of 70,000 rows into 60,000 training rows and 10,000 test rows. Next, we'll find the accuracy of the model. The model can then be used to predict any incoming dataset of 28 x 28 pixel handwritten digits containing numbers between zero and nine. For our sample Python code, we use a 100-row training dataset and a 10-row test dataset. In this example, we will learn to use the TensorFlow layers module that provides a high-level API that makes it easy to construct a neural network. It provides methods that facilitate creating dense (FC) layers and convolutional layers, adding activation functions, and applying dropout regularization.

To start we will analyze the code line by line, then we will see how to process it with the tools made available by Google Cloud Platform. Now, let's go through the code to learn how to apply a CNN to solve a HWR problem. Let's start from the beginning of the code:

```
from __future__ import absolute_import
from __future__ import division
from __future__ import print_function
```

These three lines are added to write a Python 2/3 compatible code base. So let's move on to importing modules:

```
import numpy as np
import tensorflow as tf
```

In this way, we have imported the numpy and tensorflow module. Let's analyze the next line of code:

```
tf.logging.set_verbosity(tf.logging.INFO)
```

This code sets the threshold for what messages will be logged. After an initial phase, we pass to define the function that will allow us to build a CNN model:

```
def cnn_model_fn(features, labels, mode):
```

We have thus defined the function. Now let's move on:

```
input_layer = tf.reshape(features["x"], [-1, 28, 28, 1])
```

In this code line, we have passed the input tensors in the form (batch_size, image_width, image_height, channels) as expected from the methods in the layers module, for creating convolutional and pooling layers for two-dimensional image data. Let's move on to the first convolutional layer:

```
conv1 = tf.layers.conv2d(
       inputs=input_layer,
       filters=32,
       kernel_size=[5, 5],
       padding="same",
       activation=tf.nn.relu)
```

This layer creates a convolution kernel that is convolved with the layer input to produce a tensor of outputs. The number of filters in the convolution is 32, the height and width of the 2D convolution window are [5, 5], and the activation function is a ReLU function. To do this, we used the conv2d() method in the layers module. Next, we connect our first pooling layer to the convolutional layer we just created:

```
pool1 = tf.layers.max_pooling2d(inputs=conv1,
                     pool_size=[2, 2], strides=2)
```

We used the max_pooling2d() method in layers to construct a layer that performs max pooling with a 2 x 2 filter and stride of 2. Now we will connect a second convolutional layer to our CNN:

```
conv2 = tf.layers.conv2d(
      inputs=pool1,
      filters=64,
      kernel_size=[5, 5],
      padding="same",
      activation=tf.nn.relu)
```

Now we will connect a second pooling layer to our CNN:

```
pool2 = tf.layers.max_pooling2d(inputs=conv2,
                     pool_size=[2, 2], strides=2)
pool2_flat = tf.reshape(pool2, [-1, 7 * 7 * 64])
```

Next, we will add a dense layer:

```
dense = tf.layers.dense(inputs=pool2_flat,
               units=1024, activation=tf.nn.relu)
```

With this code, we added a dense layer with 1,024 neurons and ReLU activation to our CNN to perform classification on the features extracted by the convolution/pooling layers.

 Remember, a ReLU level is composed of neurons that apply the function $f(x) = max\ (0,\ x)$. These levels increase the non-linearity of the network, and at the same time, they do not modify the receiving fields of convolution levels.

To improve the results, we will apply dropout regularization to our dense layer:

```
dropout = tf.layers.dropout(inputs=dense,
            rate=0.4, training=mode ==
                  tf.estimator.ModeKeys.TRAIN)
```

To do this we used the dropout method in layers. Next, we will add the final layer to our neural network:

```
logits = tf.layers.dense(inputs=dropout, units=10)
```

This is the `logits` layer, which will return the raw values for our predictions. With the previous code, we created a dense layer with 10 neurons (one for each target class 0–9), with linear activation. We just have to generate the predictions:

```
predictions = {
      "classes": tf.argmax(input=logits, axis=1),
      "probabilities": tf.nn.softmax(logits, name="softmax_tensor")
  }
  if mode == tf.estimator.ModeKeys.PREDICT:
        return tf.estimator.EstimatorSpec(mode=mode,
                        predictions=predictions)
```

We converted the raw values generated from our predictions into two different formats that our model function can return: a digit from 0–9 and the probability that the example is a zero, is a one, is a two, and so on. We compile our predictions in a dict and return an `EstimatorSpec` object. Now, we will pass to define a `loss` function:

```
loss = tf.losses.sparse_softmax_cross_entropy(labels=labels, logits=logits)
```

A `loss` function measures how closely the model's predictions match the target classes. This function is used for both training and evaluation. We will configure our model to optimize this loss value during training:

```
if mode == tf.estimator.ModeKeys.TRAIN:
    optimizer = tf.train.GradientDescentOptimizer(learning_rate=0.001)
    train_op = optimizer.minimize(
        loss=loss,
        global_step=tf.train.get_global_step())
    return tf.estimator.EstimatorSpec(mode=mode, loss=loss,
train_op=train_op)
```

We used a learning rate of 0.001 and stochastic gradient descent as the optimization algorithm. Now, we will add an accuracy metric in our model:

```
eval_metric_ops = {
    "accuracy": tf.metrics.accuracy(
        labels=labels, predictions=predictions["classes"])}
    return tf.estimator.EstimatorSpec(
        mode=mode, loss=loss, eval_metric_ops=eval_metric_ops)
```

To do this, we defined the `eval_metric_ops` dict in the EVAL mode. We have thus defined the architecture of our network; now it is necessary to define the code to train and test our network. To do this, we will add a `main()` function to our Python code:

```
def main(unused_argv):
```

Then we will load training and eval data:

```
mnist = tf.contrib.learn.datasets.load_dataset("mnist")
train_data = mnist.train.images
train_labels = np.asarray(mnist.train.labels, dtype=np.int32)
eval_data = mnist.test.images
eval_labels = np.asarray(mnist.test.labels, dtype=np.int32)
```

In this piece of code, we stored the training feature data and training labels as numpy arrays in `train_data` and `train_labels`, respectively. Similarly, we stored the evaluation feature data and evaluation labels in `eval_data` and `eval_labels`, respectively. Next, we will create an `Estimator` for our model:

```
mnist_classifier = tf.estimator.Estimator(
    model_fn=cnn_model_fn, model_dir="/tmp/mnist_convnet_model")
```

An `Estimator` is a TensorFlow class for performing high-level model training, evaluation, and inference. The following code sets up logging for predictions:

```
tensors_to_log = {"probabilities": "softmax_tensor"}
logging_hook = tf.train.LoggingTensorHook(
    tensors=tensors_to_log, every_n_iter=50)
```

Now we're ready to train our model:

```
train_input_fn = tf.estimator.inputs.numpy_input_fn(
    x={"x": train_data},
    y=train_labels,
    batch_size=100,
    num_epochs=None,
    shuffle=True)
mnist_classifier.train(
    input_fn=train_input_fn,
    steps=15000,
    hooks=[logging_hook])
```

To do this, we have created `train_input_fn` and called `train()` on `mnist_classifier`. In the previous code, we fixed `steps=15000`, which means the model will train for 15,000 steps in all.

The time required to perform this training varies depending on the processor installed on our machine, but in any case, it will probably be more than 1 hour. To perform such training in less time, you can reduce the number of steps passed to the `train()` function; it is clear that this change will have a negative effect on the accuracy of the algorithm.

Finally, we will evaluate the model and print the results:

```
eval_input_fn = tf.estimator.inputs.numpy_input_fn(
    x={"x": eval_data},
    y=eval_labels,
    num_epochs=1,
    shuffle=False)
eval_results = mnist_classifier.evaluate(input_fn=eval_input_fn)
print(eval_results)
```

We called the `evaluate` method, which evaluates the metrics we specified in the `eval_metriced_ops` argument in the `model_fn`. Our Python code ends with the following lines:

```
if __name__ == "__main__":
    tf.app.run()
```

These lines are just a very quick wrapper that handles flag parsing and then dispatches to your own main function. At this point, we just have to copy the entire code into a file with a `.py` extension and run it on a machine where Python and TensorFlow are installed.

Run Python code on Google Cloud Shell

Google Cloud Shell provides command-line access to cloud resources directly from your browser. You can easily manage projects and resources without having to install the Google Cloud SDK or other tools in your system. With Cloud Shell, the `gcloud` command-line tool from Cloud SDK and other necessary utilities are always available, updated and fully authenticated when you need them.

The following are some of the features of the Google Cloud Shell:

- It's a shell environment for managing resources hosted on Google Cloud Platform.
- We can manage our GCP resources with the flexibility of a Linux shell. Cloud Shell provides command-line access to an instance of the virtual machine in a terminal window that opens in the web console.
- It offers integrated authorization for access to projects and resources hosted on Google Cloud Platform.
- Many of your favorite command-line tools, from bash and sh to emacs and vim, are already preinstalled and updated. Administration tools such as the MySQL client, Kubernetes, and Docker are configured and ready. You no longer need to worry about installing the latest version and all of its dependencies. Simply connect to Cloud Shell.

Developers will have access to all favorite preconfigured development tools. You will find development and implementation tools for Java, Go, Python, Node.js, PHP, and Ruby. Run your web applications within the Cloud Shell instance and preview them in the browser. Then commit to the repository again with the preconfigured Git and Mercurial clients.

Cloud Shell provisions 5 GB of permanent disk storage space, mounted as the $ HOME directory on the Cloud Shell instance. All files stored in the $ HOME directory, including user configuration scripts and files such as bashrc and vimrc, persist from one session to another.

To start Cloud Shell, just click on the **Activate Google Cloud Shell** button at the top of the console window, as shown in the following screenshot:

A Cloud Shell session opens inside a new frame at the bottom of the console and displays a command-line prompt. It can take a few seconds for the shell session to be initialized. Now, our Cloud Shell session is ready to use, as shown in the following screenshot:

At this point, we need to transfer the cnn_hwr.py file containing the Python code in the Google Cloud Platform. We have seen that to do so, we can use the resources made available by Google Cloud Storage. Then we open the Google Cloud Storage browser and create a new bucket.

Remember that buckets are the basic containers that hold your data. Everything you store in Cloud Storage must be contained in a bucket. You can use buckets to organize your data and control access to your data, but unlike directories and folders, you cannot nest buckets.

To transfer the `cnn_hwr.py` file to Google Storage, perform the following steps:

1. Just click on the **CREATE BUCKET** icon
2. Type the name of the new bucket (`cnn-hwr`) in the create a bucket window
3. After this, a new bucket is available in the buckets list
4. Click on the `cnn-hwr` bucket
5. Click on uploads files icon in the window opened
6. Select the file in the dialog window opened
7. Click **Open**

At this point, our file will be available in the new bucket, as shown in the following figure:

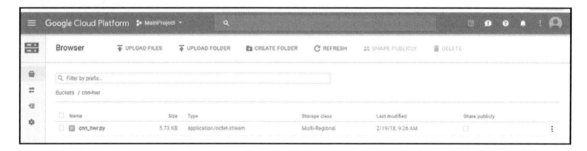

Now we can access the file from Cloud Shell. To do this, we create a new folder in the shell. Type the following command in the shell prompt:

```
mkdir CNN-HWR
```

Now, to copy the file from the Google Storage bucket to the CNN-HWR folder, simply type this command in the shell prompt:

```
gsutil cp gs://cnn-hwr-mlengine/cnn_hwr.py CNN-HWR
```

The following code is displayed:

```
giuseppe_ciaburro@progetto-1-191608:~$ gsutil cp gs://cnn-hwr/cnn_hwr.py
CNN-HWR
Copying gs://cnn-hwr/cnn_hwr.py...
/ [1 files][ 5.7 KiB/ 5.7 KiB]
Operation completed over 1 objects/5.7 KiB.
```

Now let's move into the folder and verify the presence of the file:

```
$cd CNN-HWR
$ls
cnn_hwr.py
```

We just have to run the file:

```
$ python cnn_hwr.py
```

A series of preliminary instructions is displayed:

```
Successfully downloaded train-images-idx3-ubyte.gz 9912422 bytes.
Extracting MNIST-data/train-images-idx3-ubyte.gz
Successfully downloaded train-labels-idx1-ubyte.gz 28881 bytes.
Extracting MNIST-data/train-labels-idx1-ubyte.gz
Successfully downloaded t10k-images-idx3-ubyte.gz 1648877 bytes.
Extracting MNIST-data/t10k-images-idx3-ubyte.gz
Successfully downloaded t10k-labels-idx1-ubyte.gz 4542 bytes.
Extracting MNIST-data/t10k-labels-idx1-ubyte.gz
INFO:tensorflow:Using default config.
```

They indicate that the data download was successful, as was the invocation of the TensorFlow library. From this point on, the training of the network begins, which, as we have anticipated, may be quite long. At the end of the algorithm execution, the following information will be returned:

```
INFO:tensorflow:Saving checkpoints for 15000 into
/tmp/mnist_convnet_model/model.ckpt.
INFO:tensorflow:Loss for final step: 2.2751274.INFO:tensorflow:Starting
evaluation at 2018-02-19-08:47:04
INFO:tensorflow:Restoring parameters from
/tmp/mnist_convnet_model/model.ckpt-15000
INFO:tensorflow:Finished evaluation at 2018-02-19-08:47:56
INFO:tensorflow:Saving dict for global step 15000: accuracy = 0.9723,
global_step = 15000, loss = 0.098432
{'loss': 0.098432, 'global_step': 15000, 'accuracy': 0.9723}
```

In this case, we've achieved an accuracy of 97.2 percent on our test dataset.

Recurrent neural network

Feedforward neural networks are based on input data that is powered to the network and converted into output. If it is a supervised learning algorithm, the output is a label that can recognize the input. Basically, these algorithms connect raw data to specific categories by recognizing patterns. Recurrent networks, on the other hand, take as input not only the current input data that is powered to the network, but also what they have experienced over time.

An **recurrent neural network (RNN)** is a neural model in which a bidirectional flow of information is present. In other words, while the propagation of signals in feedforward networks takes place only in a continuous manner in a direction from inputs to outputs, recurrent networks are different. In them, this propagation can also occur from a neural layer following a previous one, or between neurons belonging to the same layer, and even between a neuron and itself.

The decision made by a recurrent network at a specific instant affects the decision it will reach immediately afterwards. So, recurrent networks have two input sources—the present and the recent past—that combine to determine how to respond to new data, just as people do in life everyday.

Recurrent networks are distinguished from feedforward networks thanks to the feedback loop linked to their past decisions, thus accepting their output momentarily as inputs. This feature can be emphasized by saying that recurrent networks have memory. Adding memory to neural networks has a purpose: there is information in the sequence itself and recurrent networks use it to perform the tasks that feedforward networks cannot.

Access to memory occurs through the content rather than by address or location. One approach to this is that the memory content is the pattern of activations on the nodes of an RNN. The idea is to start the network with an activation scheme that is a partial or noisy representation of the requested memory content and that the network stabilizes on the required content.

RNN is a class of neural network where there is at least one feedback connection between neurons that form a directed cycle. A typical RNN with connections between output layer and hidden layer is represented in the following figure:

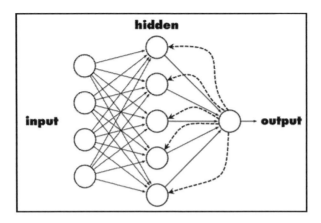

In the recurring network shown in the figure, both the input level and the output level are used to define the weights of the hidden level.

Ultimately, we can think of RNNs as a variant of ANNs: these variants can be characterized on a different number of hidden levels and a different trend of the data flow. The RNN are characterized by a different trend of the data flow, in fact the connections between the neurons form a cycle. Unlike feedforward networks, RNNs can use internal memory for their processing. RNNs are a class of ANNs that feature connections between hidden layers that are propagated through time in order to learn sequences.

The way the data is kept in memory and flows at different time periods makes RNNs powerful and successful. RNN use cases include the following fields:

- Stock market predictions
- Image captioning
- Weather forecast
- Time-series-based forecasts
- Language translation
- Speech recognition
- HWR
- Audio or video processing
- Robotics action sequencing

Recurrent networks are designed to recognize patterns as a sequence of data and are helpful in prediction and forecasting. They can work on text, images, speech, and time series data. RNNs are among the powerful ANNs and represent the biological brain, including memory with processing power.

Recurrent networks take inputs from the current input (like a feedforward network) and the output that was calculated previously. In the following figure, we compare a single neuron operating scheme for both a feedforward neural network and an RNN:

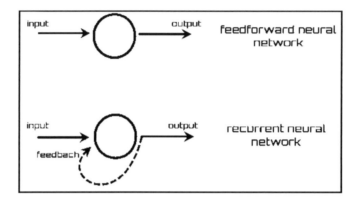

As we can see in the simple, just-proposed single neuron scheme, the feedback signal is added to the input signal in the RNN. Feedback is a considerable and significant feature. A feedback network is more likely to update and has more computing capacity than a simple network limited to one-way signals from input to output. Feedback networks show phenomena and processes not revealed by one-way networks.

To understand the differences between ANN and RNN, we consider the RNN as a network of neural networks, and the cyclic nature is unfolded in the following manner: the state of a neuron is considered at different time periods (*t-1*, *t*, *t+1*, and so on) until convergence or until the total number of epochs is reached.

The network learning phase can be performed using gradient descent procedures similar to those leading to the backpropagation algorithm for feedforward networks. At least this is valid in the case of simple architectures and deterministic activation functions. When activations are stochastic, simulated annealing approaches may be more appropriate.

RNN architectures can have many different forms. There are more variants in the way the data flows backwards:

- Fully recurrent
- Recursive
- Hopfield
- Elman networks
- LSTM

- Gated recurrent unit
- Bidirectional
- Recurrent MLP

In the following pages, we will analyze the architecture of some of these networks.

Fully recurrent neural networks

A fully RNN is a network of neurons, each with a directed (one-way) connection to every other neuron. Each neuron has a time-varying, real-valued activation. Each connection has a modifiable real-valued weight. Input neurons, output neurons, and hidden neurons are expected. This type of network is a multilayer perceptron with the previous set of hidden unit activations feeding back into the network along with the inputs, as shown in the following figure:

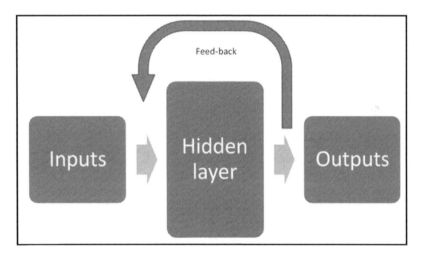

At each step, each non-input unit calculates its current activation as a nonlinear function of the weighted sum of activations of all units that connect to it.

Recursive neural networks

A recursive network is just a generalization of a recurrent network. In a recurrent network, the weights are shared and dimensionality remains constant along the length of the sequence. In a recursive network, the weights are shared and dimensionality remains constant but at every node. The following figure shows what a recursive neural network looks like:

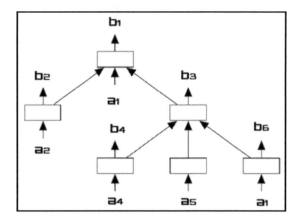

Recursive neural networks can be used for learning tree-like structures. They are highly useful for parsing natural scenes and language.

Hopfield recurrent neural networks

In 1982, physicist John J. Hopfield published a fundamental article in which a mathematical model commonly known as the **Hopfield network** was introduced. This network highlighted new computational capabilities deriving from the collective behavior of a large number of simple processing elements. A Hopfield Network is a form of recurrent ANN.

According to Hopfield every physical system can be considered as a potential memory device if it has a certain number of stable states, which act as an attractor for the system itself. On the basis of this consideration, he formulated the thesis that the stability and placement of such attractors represented spontaneous properties of systems consisting of considerable quantities of mutually interacting neurons.

Structurally, the Hopfield network constitutes a recurrent symmetrical neural network (therefore with a synaptic weights matrix that is symmetric), one that is completely connected and in which each neuron is connected to all the others, as shown in the following figure:

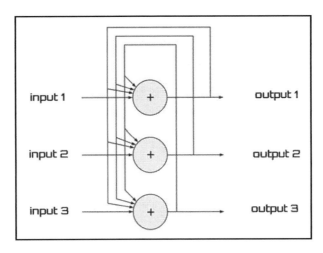

As already mentioned before, a recurrent network is a neural model in which a flow of bidirectional information is present; in other words, while in feedforward networks the propagation of the signals takes place only in a continuous manner in the direction that leads from the inputs to the outputs in the recurrent networks this propagation can also occur from a neural layer following a previous one or between neurons belonging to at the same layer (Hopfield network) and even between a neuron and itself.

The dynamics of a Hopfield network is described by a nonlinear system of differential equations and the neuron update mechanism can be:

- **Asynchronous**: One neuron is updated at a time
- **Synchronous**: All neurons are updated at the same time
- **Continuous**: All the neurons are continually updated

Elman neural networks

The Elman neural network is a feedforward network in which the hidden layer, besides being connected to the output layer, forks into another identical layer, called the **context layer**, to which it is connected with weights equal to one. At each moment of time (each time the data is passed to the neurons of the input layer), the neurons of the context layer maintain the previous values and pass them to the respective neurons of the hidden layer. The following figure shows an Elman network scheme:

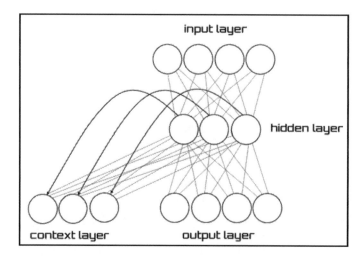

Like feedforward networks, Elman's RNNs can be trained with an algorithm called **Backpropagation Through Time (BPTT)**, a variant of the backpropagation created specifically for the RNNs. Substantially, this algorithm unrolls the neural network transforming it into a feedforward network, with a number of layers equal to the length of the sequence to be learned; subsequently, the classic backpropagation algorithm is applied. Alternatively, it is possible to use global optimization methods, such as genetic algorithms, especially with RNN topologies on which it is not possible to apply BPTT.

Long short-term memory networks

LSTM is a particular architecture of RNN, originally conceived by Hochreiter and Schmidhuber in 1997. This type of neural network has been recently rediscovered in the context of deep learning because it is free from the problem of vanishing gradient, and in practice it offers excellent results and performance.

The vanishing gradient problem affects the training of ANNs with gradient-based learning methods. In gradient-based methods such as backpropagation, weights are adjusted proportionally to the gradient of the error. Because of the way in which the aforementioned gradients are calculated, we obtain the effect that their module decreases exponentially, proceeding towards the deepest layers. The problem is that in some cases, the gradient will be vanishingly small, effectively preventing the weight from changing its value. In the worst case, this may completely stop the neural network from further training.

LSTM-based networks are ideal for prediction and classification of time sequences, and they are supplanting many classic machine learning approaches. In fact, in 2012, Google replaced its voice recognition models, passing from the Hidden Markov Models (which represented the standard for over 30 years) to deep learning neural networks. In 2015, it switched to the RNNs LSTM combined with **connectionist temporal classification** (**CTC**).

CTC is a type of neural network output and associated scoring function for training RNNs.

This is due to the fact that LSTM networks are able to consider long-term dependencies between data, and in the case of speech recognition, this means managing the context within a sentence to improve recognition capacity.

An LSTM network consists of cells (LSTM blocks) linked together. Each cell is in turn composed of three types of ports: **input gate**, **output gate**, and **forget gate**. They respectively implement the write, read, and reset functions on the cell memory. The ports are not binary but analogical (generally managed by a sigmoid activation function mapped in a range (0, 1), where zero indicates total inhibition and 1 indicates total activation), and they are multiplicative. The presence of these ports allows the LSTM cells to remember information for an indefinite amount of time. In fact, if the input gate is below the activation threshold, the cell will maintain the previous state, while if it is enabled, the current state will be combined with the input value. As the name suggests, the forget gate resets the current state of the cell (when its value is brought to zero), and the output gate decides whether the value inside the cell must be taken out or not.

The following figure shows an LSTM unit:

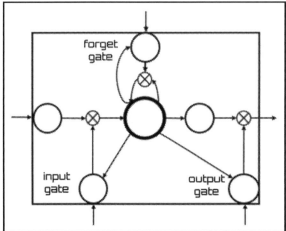

The approaches based on neural networks are very powerful, as they allow capture of the characteristics and relationships between the data. In particular, it has also been seen that LSTM networks, in practice, offer high performance and excellent recognition rates. One disadvantage is that the neural networks are black box models, so their behavior is not predictable, and it is not possible to trace the logic with which they process the data.

Handwriting Recognition using RNN and TensorFlow

To practice RNNs, we will use the dataset previously used to construct the CNN. I refer to the MNIST dataset, a large database of handwritten digits. It has a set of 70,000 examples of data. It is a subset of NIST's larger dataset. Images of 28 x 28 pixel resolution are stored in a matrix of 70,000 rows and 785 columns; each pixel value from the 28 x 28 matrix and one value is the actual digit. In a fixed-size image, the digits have been size-normalized.

In this case, we will implement an RNN (LSTM) using the TensorFlow library to classify images. We will consider every image row as a sequence of pixels. Because the MNIST image shape is 28 x 28, we will handle 28 sequences of 28 time steps for every sample.

To start, we will analyze the code line by line; then we will see how to process it with the tools made available by Google Cloud Platform. Now, let's go through the code to learn how to apply an RNN (LSTM) to solve an HWR problem. Let's start from the beginning of the code:

```
from __future__ import absolute_import
from __future__ import division
from __future__ import print_function
```

These three lines are added to write a Python 2/3 compatible code base. So let's move on to importing modules:

```
import tensorflow as tf
from tensorflow.contrib import rnn
```

In this way, we have imported the `tensorflow` module and, from `tensorflow.contrib`, the `rnn` module. The `tensorflow.contrib` contains volatile or experimental code. The `rnn` module is a module for constructing RNN Cells and additional RNN operations. Let's analyze the next lines of code:

```
from tensorflow.examples.tutorials.mnist import input_data
mnist = input_data.read_data_sets("/tmp/data/", one_hot=True)
```

The first line is used to import the `mnist` dataset from the TensorFlow library; in fact, the `minist` dataset is already present in the library as an example. The second line reads the data from a local directory. Let's move on to set the training parameters:

```
learning_rate = 0.001
training_steps = 20000
batch_size = 128
display_step = 1000
```

The `learning_rate` is a value used by the learning algorithm to determine how quickly the weights are adjusted. It determines the acquisition time for neurons with weights that are trained using the algorithm. The `training_steps` sets the number of times the training process is performed. The `batch_size` is the number of samples you feed in your network. The `display_step` decides how many steps are shown the partial results of the training. Now let's set the network parameters:

```
num_input = 28
timesteps = 28
num_hidden = 128
num_classes = 10
```

The first parameter (num_input) sets the MNIST data input (image shape: 28 x 28). The timesteps parameter is equivalent to the number of time steps you run your RNN. The num_hidden parameter sets the number of hidden layers of the neural network. Finally the num_classes parameter sets the MNIST total classes (0-9 digits). Let's analyze the following lines of code:

```
X = tf.placeholder("float", [None, timesteps, num_input])
Y = tf.placeholder("float", [None, num_classes])
```

In these lines of code, we used a tf.placeholder() function. A placeholder is simply a variable that we will assign data to at a later date. It allows us to create our operations and build our computation graph without needing the data. In this way, we have set up the tf.Graph input. A tf.Graph contains two relevant kinds of information: graph structure and graph collections. TensorFlow uses a dataflow graph to represent your computation in terms of the dependencies between individual operations. This leads to a low-level programming model in which you first define the dataflow graph and then create a TensorFlow session to run parts of the graph across a set of local and remote devices. Let's move on to define weights:

```
weights = {
    'out': tf.Variable(tf.random_normal([num_hidden, num_classes]))
}
biases = {
    'out': tf.Variable(tf.random_normal([num_classes]))
}
```

Weights in a network are the most important factor for converting an input to impact the output. This is similar to slope in linear regression, where a weight is multiplied to the input to add up to form the output. Weights are numerical parameters that determine how strongly each of the neurons affects the other. Bias is like the intercept added in a linear equation. It is an additional parameter used to adjust the output along with the weighted sum of the inputs to the neuron. Now we have to define the RNN by creating a new function:

```
def RNN(x, weights, biases):
    x = tf.unstack(x, timesteps, 1)
    lstm_cell = rnn.BasicLSTMCell(num_hidden, forget_bias=1.0)
    outputs, states = rnn.static_rnn(lstm_cell, x, dtype=tf.float32)
    return tf.matmul(outputs[-1], weights['out']) + biases['out']
```

The `unstack()` function is used to get a list of `timesteps` tensors of shape (`batch_size`, `n_input`). Then we have defined an `lstm` cell with TensorFlow, and we've got an `lstm` cell output. Finally, we have placed a linear activation, using the RNN in the inner loop and last output. Let's move on:

```
logits = RNN(X, weights, biases)
prediction = tf.nn.softmax(logits)
```

The first line of code uses the newly defined RNN function to build the network, while the second line of code predicts using the function `tf.nn.softmax()`, which computes `softmax` activations. Next, we will define `loss` and `optimizer`:

```
loss_op = tf.reduce_mean(tf.nn.softmax_cross_entropy_with_logits_v2(
    logits=logits, labels=Y))
optimizer = tf.train.GradientDescentOptimizer(learning_rate=learning_rate)
train_op = optimizer.minimize(loss_op)
```

The `loss` function maps an event or values of one or more variables onto a real number, intuitively representing some `cost` associated with the event. We have used the `tf.reduce_mean()` function, which computes the mean of elements across the dimensions of a tensor. The `optimizer` base class provides methods to compute gradients for a loss and apply gradients to variables. A collection of subclasses implement classic optimization algorithms such as gradient descent and AdaGrad. Let's go ahead to evaluate model:

```
correct_pred = tf.equal(tf.argmax(prediction, 1), tf.argmax(Y, 1))
accuracy = tf.reduce_mean(tf.cast(correct_pred, tf.float32))
```

Then we will initialize the variables by assigning their default value:

```
init = tf.global_variables_initializer()
```

Now we can start training the network:

```
with tf.Session() as sess:
    sess.run(init)
    for step in range(1, training_steps+1):
        batch_x, batch_y = mnist.train.next_batch(batch_size)
        batch_x = batch_x.reshape((batch_size, timesteps, num_input))
        sess.run(train_op, feed_dict={X: batch_x, Y: batch_y})
        if step % display_step == 0 or step == 1:
            loss, acc = sess.run([loss_op, accuracy], feed_dict={X:
batch_x,
                                                                 Y:
batch_y})
            print("Step " + str(step) + ", Minibatch Loss= " + \
                "{:.4f}".format(loss) + ", Training Accuracy= " + \
```

```
                    "{:.3f}".format(acc))
        print("End of the optimization process ")
```

Finally we will calculate the accuracy for 128 mnist test images:

```
    test_len = 128
    test_data = mnist.test.images[:test_len].reshape((-1, timesteps,
num_input))
    test_label = mnist.test.labels[:test_len]
    print("Testing Accuracy:", \
        sess.run(accuracy, feed_dict={X: test_data, Y: test_label}))
```

At this point, we just have to copy the entire code into a file with a `.py` extension and run it on a machine where Python and TensorFlow are installed.

LSTM on Google Cloud Shell

After having thoroughly analyzed the Python code, it is time to run it around to classify the images contained in the dataset. To do this, we work in a similar way to what was done in the case of the example on CNN. So we will use the Google Cloud Shell. Google Cloud Shell provides command-line access to Cloud resources directly from your browser. You can easily manage projects and resources without having to install the Google Cloud SDK or other tools in your system. With Cloud Shell, the `gcloud` command-line tool from Cloud SDK and other necessary utilities are always available, updated and fully authenticated when you need them.

To start Cloud Shell, just click the **Activate Google Cloud Shell** button at the top of the console window, as shown in the following screenshot:

A Cloud Shell session opens inside a new frame at the bottom of the console and displays a command-line prompt. It can take a few seconds for the shell session to be initialized. Now, our Cloud Shell session is ready to use, as shown in the following screenshot:

At this point, we need to transfer the rnn_hwr.py file containing the Python code in the Google Cloud Platform. We have seen that to do so, we can use the resources made available by Google Cloud Storage. Then we open the Google Cloud Storage browser and create a new bucket.

To transfer the cnn_hwr.py file on Google Storage, follow these steps:

1. Just click on **CREATE BUCKET** icon
2. Type the name of the new bucket (rnn-hwr) in the create a bucket window
3. After this, a new bucket is available in the buckets list
4. Click on the rnn-hwr bucket
5. Click on **UPLOAD FILES** icon in the window opened
6. Select the file in the dialog window opened
7. Click **Open**

At this point, our file will be available in the new bucket, as shown in the following screenshot:

Now we can access the file from the Cloud Shell. To do this, we create a new folder in the shell. Type this command in the shell prompt:

```
mkdir RNN-HWR
```

Now, to copy the file from the Google Storage bucket to the CNN-HWR folder, simply type the following command in the shell prompt:

```
gsutil cp gs://rnn-hwr-mlengine/rnn_hwr.py RNN-HWR
```

The following code is displayed:

```
giuseppe_ciaburro@progetto-1-191608:~$ gsutil cp gs://rnn-hwr/rnn_hwr.py
RNN-HWR
Copying gs://rnn-hwr/rnn_hwr.py...
/ [1 files][ 4.0 KiB/ 4.0 KiB]
Operation completed over 1 objects/4.0 KiB.
```

Now let's move into the folder and verify the presence of the file:

```
$cd RNN-HWR
$ls
rnn_hwr.py
```

We just have to run the file:

```
$ python rnn_hwr.py
```

A series of preliminary instructions is displayed:

```
Extracting /tmp/data/train-images-idx3-ubyte.gz
Extracting /tmp/data/train-labels-idx1-ubyte.gz
Extracting /tmp/data/t10k-images-idx3-ubyte.gz
Extracting /tmp/data/t10k-labels-idx1-ubyte.gz
```

They indicate that the data download was successful, as was the invocation of the TensorFlow library. From this point on, the training of the network begins, which, as we have anticipated, may be quite long. At the end of the algorithm execution, the following information will be returned:

```
Step 1, Minibatch Loss= 2.9727, Training Accuracy= 0.117
Step 1000, Minibatch Loss= 1.8381, Training Accuracy= 0.430
Step 2000, Minibatch Loss= 1.4021, Training Accuracy= 0.602
Step 3000, Minibatch Loss= 1.1560, Training Accuracy= 0.672
Step 4000, Minibatch Loss= 0.9748, Training Accuracy= 0.727
Step 5000, Minibatch Loss= 0.8156, Training Accuracy= 0.750
Step 6000, Minibatch Loss= 0.7572, Training Accuracy= 0.758
Step 7000, Minibatch Loss= 0.5930, Training Accuracy= 0.812
Step 8000, Minibatch Loss= 0.5583, Training Accuracy= 0.805
Step 9000, Minibatch Loss= 0.4324, Training Accuracy= 0.914
Step 10000, Minibatch Loss= 0.4227, Training Accuracy= 0.844
Step 11000, Minibatch Loss= 0.2818, Training Accuracy= 0.906
Step 12000, Minibatch Loss= 0.3205, Training Accuracy= 0.922
Step 13000, Minibatch Loss= 0.4042, Training Accuracy= 0.891
Step 14000, Minibatch Loss= 0.2918, Training Accuracy= 0.914
Step 15000, Minibatch Loss= 0.1991, Training Accuracy= 0.938
Step 16000, Minibatch Loss= 0.2815, Training Accuracy= 0.930
Step 17000, Minibatch Loss= 0.1790, Training Accuracy= 0.953
Step 18000, Minibatch Loss= 0.2627, Training Accuracy= 0.906
Step 19000, Minibatch Loss= 0.1616, Training Accuracy= 0.945
Step 20000, Minibatch Loss= 0.1017, Training Accuracy= 0.992
Optimization Finished!
Testing Accuracy: 0.9765625
```

In this case, we've achieved an accuracy of 97.6 percent on our test dataset.

Summary

In this chapter, we tried to broaden the concepts underlying standard neural networks by adding features to solve more complex problems. To begin with, we discovered the architecture of CNNs. CNNs are ANNs in which the hidden layers are usually constituted by convolutional layers, pooling layers, FC layers, and normalization layers. The concepts underlying CNN were covered.

We understood training, testing, and evaluating a CNN through the analysis of a real case. For this purpose, an HWR problem was addressed in Google Cloud Platform.

Then, we explored RNN. Recurrent networks take, as their input, not only current input data that is powered to the network but also what they have experienced over time. Several RNN architectures were analyzed. In particular, we focused on LSTM networks.

14
Time Series with LSTMs

In many situations involving multiple fields of real life, the need to plan future actions arises. **Forecasting** is an important tool for efficient planning. Moreover, this tool makes the decision-maker less susceptible to unexpected events because it requires a more scientific approach to the knowledge of the environment in which it operates. Often, the planning of future action arises from the analysis of data accumulated over time to extract information for the characterization of the phenomenon under observation.

A chronological recording of events gives rise to a new type of act, which is precisely called a **time series**. A time series constitutes a sequence of observations on a phenomenon carried out in consecutive instants or time intervals. Usually, even if not necessarily, they are evenly spaced or of the same length. Time series prediction requires the neural network to have some sort of memory on the sequence of data. Specific architectures called **Long Short-Term Memory** (**LSTM**) network, are well suited for time series analysis. In this chapter we show how to create and train our own LSTMs using Keras on GCD and apply them to predicting financial time series. We'll discover the most used modeling approaches: **autoregressive (AR)**, **moving average (MA)**, **autoregressive moving average (ARMA)**, and **autoregressive integrated moving average (ARIMA)**.

The topics covered in this chapter are:

- Classical approach to time series
- Time series decomposition
- Time series models
- LSTM for time series analysis

At the end of the chapter, we will be able to deal with problems regarding time series. We will know how to identify the different components of a time series, trend seasonality and residual, as well as eliminate seasonality to make predictions easier to understand. Finally, we will understand how to implement a recurring LSTM network with a practical example.

Introducing time series

A time series constitutes a sequence of observations on a phenomenon *y* carried out in consecutive instants or time intervals that are usually, even if not necessarily, evenly spaced or of the same length. The trend of commodity prices, stock market indices, the BTP/BUND spread, and the unemployment rate are just a few examples of times series.

Contrary to what happens in classical statistics, where it is assumed that an independent observations come from a single random variable, in a time series, it is assumed that there are n observations coming from as many dependent random variables. The inference of the time series is thus configured as a procedure that attempts to bring the time series back to its generating process.

The time series can be of two types:

- **Deterministic**: If the values of the variable can be exactly determined on the basis of the previous values
- **Stochastic**: If the values of the variable can be determined on the basis of the previous values only partially

The majority of time series are stochastic, and therefore it is impossible to draw up forecasts without errors. It is generally assumed that an observed time series is the result of the composition of these two components. The two sequences are not individually observable but must be determined on the basis of a sample.

We indicate the series as the sum of these two contributions:

$$Y_t = f(t) + w(t)$$

According to the classical approach to time series, it is assumed that there exists a law of temporal evolution of the phenomenon, represented by $f(t)$. The random component $w(t)$ is assumed to represent the set of circumstances, each of negligible entities, which we do not want or cannot consider in Y_t.

Therefore, the residual part of Y_t, not explained by $f(t)$, is imputed to the case and assimilated to a set of accidental errors. This is equivalent to hypothesizing that the stochastic component $w(t)$ is generated by a white noise process, that is, by a sequence of independent and identically distributed random variables of zero mean and constant variance. In summary, in the classic approach, the attention is concentrated on $f(t)$, being $w(t)$ considered a process with uncorrelated components and therefore negligible.

Denoting the time with $t = 1.... T$, we will indicate this sequence y_t; time is the parameter that determines the sequence of events that cannot be neglected, so we also need to know the position of observation along the temporal dimension. Generally, it is used to represent the pair of values (t, y_t) on a Cartesian diagram with a continuous line graph as if the phenomenon were detected continuously. This graph is called a **time series plot**. In the following graph, we see a time series plot of the flow of the river Nile at Aswan from 1871 to 1970:

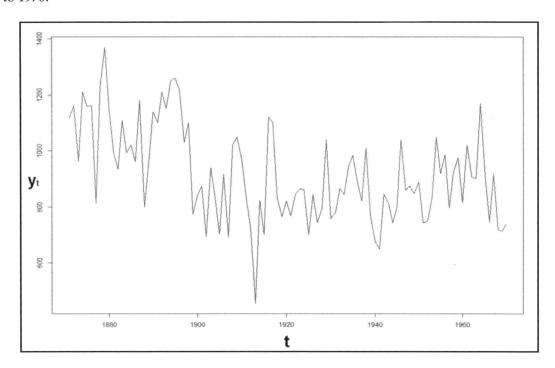

A time series plot immediately reveals trends or regular oscillations, and other systematic trends over time. The previous graph shows annual data in a systematically decreasing trend over the long term. In particular, it has a zigzag pattern; since the data is monthly, there is the phenomenon called **seasonality**. It can be noted that high peaks are always recorded in those months when rains are expected.

The univariate analysis of the time series proposes to interpret the dynamic mechanism that generated the series, and to foresee future realizations of the phenomenon. In these operations, the information that is exploited regards only the couple $(t; Y_t)$, where $t = 1,..., T$. The fundamental point is that the past and the present contain relevant information to predict the future evolution of the phenomenon.

It can be considered that univariate analysis is too restrictive; we usually have information on phenomena related to the one to be forecast, which should be appropriately incorporated in order to improve the performance of the model of revision. Nonetheless, it is a useful benchmark that allows validation more sophisticated alternatives.

In a time series plot, four types of patterns can be identified with respect to time:

- **Horizontal pattern**: In this case, the series oscillates around a constant value (series average). This series is called **stationary** on **average**. This is the typical case that occurs in quality control when the process is kept under control with respect to the average.
- **Seasonal pattern**: This exists when the series is influenced by seasonal factors (example, monthly, semi-annual, quarterly, and so on). Products such as ice cream, soft drinks, electricity consumption are subject to the seasonal phenomenon. The series influenced by seasonality are also called **periodic series** since the seasonal cycle repeats itself in a fixed period. In the annual data, seasonality is not present.
- **Cyclic pattern**: This type of trend is present when the series has increases and decreases that are not of fixed period. This is the main difference between cyclical and seasonal fluctuations. Moreover, the amplitude of cyclical oscillations is generally larger than that due to seasonality. In economic series, the cyclical pattern is determined by the expansions and contractions of the economy due to conjectural phenomena.
- **Trend or underlying trend**: It is characterized by an increasing or decreasing long-term trend. The series of the world resident population is an example of an increasing trend; the series of monthly beer sales, on the other hand, does not show any trend. It has a horizontal background pattern.

Many series highlight a combination of these patterns. It is precisely this kind of complexity that makes the forecasting operation extremely interesting. The forecasting methods, in fact, must be able to recognize the various components of the series in order to reproduce them in the future, in the hypothesis that the past pattern continues to repeat itself in its evolutionary characteristics also in the future.

The classic approach to time series is based on the decomposition of the deterministic part of the series into a set of signal components (which express the structural information of the series) with respect to the negligible part of noise. In practice, we will try to identify some of the patterns that we have previously listed in the time series trend. The following figure shows a time series with some components identified:

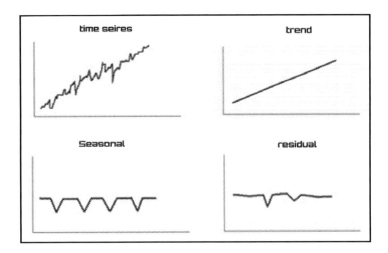

In the previous figure, the components we have identified are:

- **Trend**: It is the underlying trend of the phenomenon considered, referring to a long period of time.
- **Seasonal**: This consists of movements of the phenomena during the year. Due to the influence of climatic and social factors, they tend to repeat themselves in a similar way in the same period (for example, month, quarter, and so on).
- **Residual**: In the time series models, there is never a perfect relation between the variable under observation and the different components. The accidental component takes into account this and the unpredictable behavior of economic agents, social, and so on.

Finally, we can say that by adopting this approach a time series can be seen as the sum of the three components just analyzed (additive method).

Classical approach to time series

So far we have dealt with time series according to a classic approach to the topic. In this perspective, the classic models that try to simulate the phenomenon can be of two types:

- **Composition models**: The elementary components are known, and, by assuming a certain form of aggregation, the resulting series is obtained
- **Decomposition models**: From an observed series is hypothesized the existence of some elementary trends of which we want to establish the characteristics

The decomposition models are the most used in practice, and, for this reason, we will analyze them in detail.

The components of a time series can be aggregated according to different types of methods:

- **Additive method**: $Y(t) = \tau(t) + C(t) + S(t) + r(t)$
- **Multiplicative method**: $Y(t) = \tau(t) * C(t) * S(t) * r(t)$
- **Mixed method**: $Y(t) = \tau(t) * C(t) + S(t) * r(t)$

In these formulas, the factors are defined as follows:

- $Y(t)$ represents the time series
- $\tau(t)$ represents the trend component
- $C(t)$ represents the cyclic component
- $S(t)$ represents the seasonality component
- $r(t)$ represents the residual component

The multiplicative model can be traced back to the additive model through a logarithmic transformation of the components of the series:

$$Y(t) = \tau(t) * C(t) * S(t) * r(t)$$

This formula, by applying the logarithm function to all factors, becomes:

$$lnY(t) = ln\tau(t) + lnC(t) + lnS(t) + lnr(t)$$

Estimation of the trend component

Estimation of the trend component can occur in two different modes depending on the linear/non-linear characteristic.

If the series trend is linear or linearizable in the parameters through a logarithmic transformation, then these trends can be estimated through the procedures derived from linear regression. We can hypothesize a polynomial trend that can be represented by the following equation:

$$\tau(t) = \alpha_0 + \alpha_1 t + \alpha_2 t_2 + \ldots + \alpha_q t_q + \varepsilon t$$

In this formula, q represents the degree of the polynomial.

Depending on the value assumed by q, the following cases can be represented:

q	Cases
0	A constant trend is obtained
1	We obtain a linear trend
2	We obtain a parabolic trend

On the contrary, the presence of a non-linear trend makes it difficult, if not impossible, to identify a known functional form $f(t)$ with which to express the trend component.

In these cases, the MA instrument is used. MA is an arithmetic mean (simple or weighted) that moves to each new iteration (at any time t) from the beginning to the end of the data sequence.

Suppose we have n data terms:

$$a1, a2, a3, ..., a^{(n-1)}, a^n$$

The following procedure is adopted:

1. First, we calculate the average of the first three data and substitute the average value for the central data
2. Then, we repeat the procedure with the second three data
3. The procedure is exhausted when there is no more data available

In the case considered, the MA is composed of only three data. The MA order can be extended to 5, 7, 9, and so on. In order for the MA to be centered with respect to the available data, the order must be odd.

Estimating the seasonality component

The study of the seasonality of a historical series can have the purpose of:

- Simply estimating the seasonal component
- Eliminating it from the general course once it has been estimated

If you have to compare several time series with different seasonality, the only way to compare them is by a seasonal adjustment of them.

There are several ways to estimate the seasonal component. One of these is the use of a regression model using dichotomous auxiliary variables (dummy variables).

Suppose the existence of an additive model without a trend component:

$$Y(t) = S(t) + r(t)$$

And suppose we have measured the series on a monthly basis. The dummy variables can be defined in the following way:

- $d_j(t)$: 1 if the observation t is relative to the jth month of the year
- $d_j(t)$: 0 otherwise

Once the periodic dummy variables have been created, the seasonal component can be estimated using the following regression model:

$$Y(t) = \beta_1 D_1 + \beta_2 D_2 + ... + \beta_n D_n + \varepsilon(t)$$

The remaining $\varepsilon(t)$ part of the model represents the part of the series not explained by seasonality. If a trend component is present in the series, it will coincide precisely with $\varepsilon(t)$.

Time series models

In the previous sections, we explored the basics behind time series. To perform correct predictions of future events based on what happened in the past, it is necessary to construct an appropriate numerical simulation model. Choosing an appropriate model is extremely important as it reflects the underlying structure of the series. In practice, two types of models are available: linear or non-linear (depending on whether the current value of the series is a linear or non-linear function of past observations).

The following are the most widely used models for forecasting time series data:

- AR
- MA
- ARMA
- ARIMA

Autoregressive models

AR models are a very useful tool to tackle the prediction problem in relation to a time series. A strong correlation between consecutive values of a series is often observed. In this case, we speak of autocorrelation of the first order when we consider adjacent values, of the second order if we refer to the relation between the values of the series after two periods, and in general of the pth order if the values considered have p periods between them. AR models allow exploiting these bonds to obtain useful forecasts of the future behavior of the series.

AR is a linear predictive modeling technique. This model tries to predict the time series based on the previous values assumed using the AR parameters as coefficients. The number of samples used for the forecast determines the order of the model (p). As the name indicates, it is a regression of the variable against itself; that is, a linear combination of past values of the variables is used to forecast the future value. The AR model of p order is defined as:

$$Y_t = c + \sum_{i=1}^{p} \phi_i * Y_{t-i} + \epsilon_t$$

In the previous formula, the terms are defined as follows:

- Y_t is the actual value at time period t
- c is a constant
- ϕ_i ($i = 1, 2, ..., p$) are model parameters
- Y_{t-i} is the past value at time period t-i
- ε_t is the random error at time period t (white noise)

It may happen that the constant term is omitted; this is done to make the model as simple as possible.

Moving average models

The MA model specifies that the output variable depends linearly on the past and current past values of a stochastic term (imperfectly predictable). The MA model should not be confused with the MA we have seen in the previous sections. This is an essentially different concept although some similarities are evident. Unlike the AR model, the finished MA model is always stationary.

Just as a model AR (*p*) regresses with respect to the past values of the series, an MA (*q*) model uses past errors as explanatory variables.

The MA model of *q* order is defined as:

$$Y_t = \mu + \sum_{i=1}^{q} \theta_i * \epsilon_{t-i} + \epsilon_t$$

In the previous formula, the terms are defined as follows:

- Y_t is the actual value at time period *t*
- μ is the mean of the series
- θ_i (*i* = 1,2,..., *q*) are model parameters
- ε_{t-i} is the past random error at time period *t-i*
- ε_t is the random error at time period *t* (white noise)

The MA model is essentially a finite impulsive response filter applied to white noise, with some additional interpretations placed on it.

Autoregressive moving average model

ARMA is a type of linear mathematical model that provides instant by instant an output value based on the previous input and output values. The system is seen as an entity that, instant by instant, receives an input value (input) and generates an output (output), calculated on the basis of internal parameters that in turn vary according to linear laws. Each internal parameter, therefore, will be at each instant place equal to a linear combination of all internal parameters of the previous instant and the incoming value. The output value, in turn, will be a linear combination of internal parameters, and, in rare cases, also of the incoming one.

Much more simply, ARMA can be seen as an effective combination of the AR and MA models to form a general and useful class of time series models.

The model is generally defined as the ARMA model (p, q) where p is the order of the AR part and q is the order of the part of the MA. The ARMA model is defined by the following formula:

$$Y_t = c + \sum_{i=1}^{p} \phi_i * Y_{t-i} + \sum_{i=1}^{q} \theta_i * \epsilon_{t-i} + \epsilon_t$$

The terms are defined as follows:

- Y_t is the actual value at time period t
- c is again a constant
- ϕ_i $(i = 1,2,..., p)$ are AR model parameters
- Y_{t-i} is the past value at time period t-i
- θ_i $(i = 1,2,..., q)$ are MA model parameters
- ε_{t-i} is the past random error at time period t-i
- ε_t is the random error at time period t (white noise)

In general, once the order (p, q) has been chosen, the parameters of an ARMA model (p, q) can be estimated through the maximum likelihood estimator, for example. As for the AR model, the choice of the model order must respond to the opposing needs of a good adaptation to the data and parsimony in the number of parameters to be estimated.

Autoregressive integrated moving average models

An ARIMA model is a generalization of a ARMA model. ARIMA models are applied in cases where data show a clear tendency to non-stationarity. In these cases, to eliminate the non-stationarity, an initial differentiation step is added to the ARMA algorithm (corresponding to the integrated part of the model) that is applied one or more times.

This algorithm is therefore essentially composed of three parts:

- The part AR that determines a regression on its own delayed (that is, previous) values to the evolving variable of interest.
- The MA part. It indicates that the regression error is actually a linear combination of error terms whose values have occurred simultaneously and at various times in the past.
- The integrated part; it indicates that the data values have been replaced with the difference between their current values and the previous values (and this differentiation process may have been performed more than once).

The purpose of each of these features is to make the model suitable for data in the best possible way.

To formulate the representative equation of the ARIMA model we start from the ARMA model equation:

$$Y_t = c + \sum_{i=1}^{p} \phi_i * Y_{t-i} + \sum_{i=1}^{q} \theta_i * \epsilon_{t-i} + \epsilon_t$$

Simply move the AR part to the right side of equation to obtain the following equation (less than the constant c):

$$Y_t = \sum_{i=1}^{p'} \phi_i * Y_{t-i} = \sum_{i=1}^{q} \theta_i * \epsilon_{t-i} + \epsilon_t$$

By introducing the lag operator (L), we can rewrite this equation as follows:

$$\left(1 - \sum_{i=1}^{p'} \phi_i L^i\right)Y_t = \left(1 + \sum_{i=1}^{q} \theta_i L^i\right)\epsilon_t$$

Remember: The lag operator (L) operates on an element of a time series to produce the previous element, with the meaning that $LY_t = Y_{t-1}$.

Assuming that:

$$\left(1 - \sum_{i=1}^{p'} \phi_i L^i\right) = \left(1 + \sum_{i=1}^{p'-d} \phi_i L^i\right)(1 - L)^d$$

Which expresses precisely the factoring procedure of order d previously carried out to eliminate the non-stationarity. Based on this assumption and setting $p = p'-d$, we can write the following equation to represent the mathematical formulation of the ARIMA (p,d,q) model using lag polynomials:

$$\left(1 - \sum_{i=1}^{p} \phi_i L^i\right)(1 - L)^d Y_t = \left(1 + \sum_{i=1}^{q} \theta_i L^i\right)\epsilon_t$$

The d parameter controls the level of differentiating. Generally $d=1$ is enough in most cases.

Removing seasonality from a time series

In economic and financial analyses, which are commonly carried out on the basis of numerous indicators, the use of data presented in a seasonally adjusted form (that is, net of seasonal fluctuations), is widely used in order to be able to grasp more clearly the short-term evolution of the phenomena considered.

Seasonality, in the dynamics of a time series, is the component that repeats itself at regular intervals every year, with variations of intensity more or less similar in the same period (month, quarter, semester, and so on) of successive years; there is different intensity during the same year. Typical examples of this are a decrease in industrial production in August following holiday closures of many companies, and increase in retail sales in December due to the holiday season.

Seasonal fluctuations, disguising other movements of interest (typically cyclical fluctuations), are often considered to be a nuisance in the analysis of economic conjuncture. The presence of seasonality creates, for example, problems in analysis and interpretation of the variations observed in a historical series between two consecutive periods (months and quarters) of the year—so-called **economic variation**. These are often influenced to a prevalent extent by seasonal fluctuations rather than movements due to other causes (for example, the economic cycle). The latter, on the other hand, can be correctly highlighted by calculating economic variations on seasonally adjusted data. Furthermore, since each time series is characterized by a specific seasonal profile, the use of seasonally adjusted data makes it possible to compare the evolution of different time series, and it is widely applied in joint use of statistics produced by different countries.

Analyzing a time series dataset

To see how to perform a seasonality removal operation on a time series, we will use a dataset on monthly milk production (pounds per cow; January 1962 – December 1975). Here is some useful information about this dataset:

- **Units**: Pounds per cow
- **Dataset metrics**: 168 fact values in one time series
- **Time granularity**: Month
- **Time range**: January 1962 – December 1975
- **Source**: Time Series Data Library

The **Time Series Data Library** (**TSDL**) was created by Rob Hyndman, a professor of statistics at Monash University, Australia.

The data is available in a `.csv` file named `milk-production-pounds.csv`. To start, let's see how to import the data into Python and then how to display it to identify the possible presence of seasonality. The first thing to do is to import the library that we will use:

```
import pandas as pd
import matplotlib.pyplot as plt
```

With the first line, we imported the `pandas` library, and with the second line, we imported the `pyplot` module from the `matplotlib` library.

pandas is an open source, BSD-licensed library providing high-performance, easy-to-use data structures and data analysis tools for the Python programming language. In particular, it offers data structures and operations for manipulating numerical tables and time series.

Matplotlib is a Python 2D plotting library that produces publication-quality figures in a variety of hard copy formats and interactive environments across platforms. Matplotlib can be used in Python scripts, the Python and IPython shell, Jupyter Notebook, web application servers, and four graphical user interface toolkits. The matplotlib.pyplot module contains functions that allow you to generate many kinds of plots quickly. Now let's see how to import the data contained in the dataset in Python:

```
data = pd.read_csv('milk-production-pounds.csv',
              parse_dates=True,index_col='DateTime',
              names=['DateTime', 'Milk'], header=None)
```

To import a dataset, we used the read_csv module of the pandas library. The read_csv method loads the data in a Pandas DataFrame we named data. To display the first five rows of the DataFrame imported on video, we can use the head() function as follows:

```
print(data.head())
```

The following results are returned:

```
DateTime     Milk
1962-01-01   589
1962-02-01   561
1962-03-01   640
1962-04-01   656
1962-05-01   727
```

The head() function, with no arguments, gets the first five rows of data from the DataFrame. Now the time series is available in our Python environment; to get a preview of the data contained in it, we can calculate a series of basic statistics. To do so, we will use the describe() function in the following way:

```
print(data.describe())
```

The following results are returned:

```
                  Milk
count    168.000000
mean     754.708333
std      102.204524
min      553.000000
25%      677.750000
50%      761.000000
75%      824.500000
max      969.000000
```

The `describe()` function generates descriptive statistics that summarize the central tendency, dispersion, and shape of a dataset's distribution, excluding NaN values. It analyzes both numeric and object series, as well as DataFrame column sets of mixed data types. The output will vary depending on what is provided. To extract further information, we can invoke the function `info()` as follows:

```
print(data.info())
```

The following results are returned:

```
<class 'pandas.core.frame.DataFrame'>
DatetimeIndex: 168 entries, 1962-01-01 to 1975-12-01
Data columns (total 1 columns):
Milk    168 non-null int64
dtypes: int64(1)
memory usage: 2.6 KB
None
```

After having taken a look at the content of the dataset, we are going to perform an initial visual exploratory analysis. There's a relatively extensive plotting functionality built into Pandas that can be used for exploratory charts—especially useful in data analysis. A huge amount of functionality is provided by the `.plot()` command natively by Pandas:

```
data.plot()
plt.show()
```

The `data.plot()` command makes plots of the DataFrame using `matplotlib`/`pylab`. To display the graph just created on video, we have to use the `plt.show()` function, as shown in the following graph:

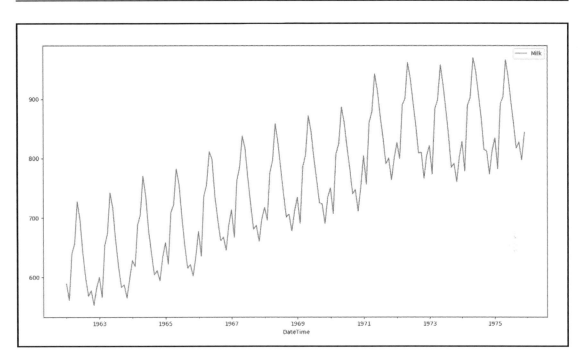

From the analysis of the previous figure, we can certainly recognize that milk production is growing (we note a positive trend) but denoting a certain variability (oscillations around a hypothetical trend line). This is maintained almost constantly with the passage of time.

Identifying a trend in a time series

If we want to try a prediction of milk production in the next January, we can think in the following way: with the acquired data, we can trace the trend line and extend it until the following January. In this way, we would have a rough estimate of milk production that we should expect in the immediate future.

But tracing a trend line means tracing the regression line. The linear regression method consists of precisely identifying a line that is capable of representing point distribution in a two-dimensional plane. As is easy to imagine, if the points corresponding to the observations are near the line, then the chosen model will be able to effectively describe the link between the variables. In theory, there are an infinite number of lines that may approximate the observations. In practice, there is only one mathematical model that optimizes the representation of the data.

To fit a linear regression model, we start importing two more libraries:

```
import numpy
from sklearn.linear_model import LinearRegression
```

NumPy is the fundamental package for scientific computing with Python. It contains, among other things:

- A powerful N-dimensional array object
- Sophisticated (broadcasting) functions
- Tools for integrating C/C++ and FORTRAN code
- Useful linear algebra, Fourier transform, and random number capabilities

Besides its obvious scientific uses, NumPy can also be used as an efficient multi-dimensional container of generic data. Arbitrary datatypes can be defined. This allows NumPy to seamlessly and speedily integrate with a wide variety of databases.

sklearn is a free software machine learning library for the Python programming language. It features various classification, regression and clustering algorithms including support vector machines, random forests, gradient boosting, k-means and DBSCAN, and is designed to interoperate with the Python numerical and scientific libraries NumPy and SciPy.

Remember, to import a library that is not present in the initial distribution of Python, you must use the `pip` install command followed by the name of the library. This command should be used only once and not every time you run the code.

We begin to prepare the data:

```
X = [i for i in range(0, len(data))]
X = numpy.reshape(X, (len(X), 1))
y = data.values
```

First, we counted the data; then we used the `reshape()` function to give a new shape to an array without changing its data. Finally, we inserted the time series values into the `y` variable. Now we can build the linear regression model:

```
LModel = LinearRegression()
```

The `LinearRegression()` function performs a ordinary least squares linear regression. The ordinary least squares method is an optimization technique (or regression) that allows us to find a function, represented by an optimal curve (or regression curve) that is as close as possible to a set of data. In particular, the function found must be one that minimizes the sum of squares of distances between the observed data and those of the curve that represents the function itself.

Given n points (x_1, y_1), (x_2, y_2), ... (x_n, y_n) in the observed population, a least squares regression line is defined as the equation line:

$$y = \alpha^* x + \beta$$

For which the following quantity is minimal:

$$E = \sum_{i=1}^{n} (\alpha x_i + \beta - y_i)^2$$

This quantity represents the sum of squares of distances of each experimental datum (x_i, y_i) from the corresponding point on the straight line $(x_i, \alpha x_i + \beta)$, as shown in the following plot:

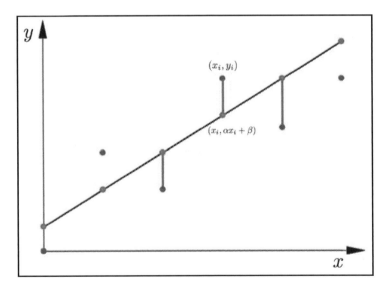

Now, we have to apply the `fit` method to fit the linear model:

```
LModel.fit(X, y)
```

A linear regression model basically finds the best value for the intercept and slope, which results in a line that best fits the data. To see the value of the intercept and slope calculated by the linear regression algorithm for our dataset, execute the following code:

```
print(LModel.intercept_, LModel.coef_)
```

The following results are returned:

```
[613.37496478] [[1.69261519]]
```

The first is the intercept; the second is the coefficient of the regression line. Now that we have trained our algorithm, it's time to make some predictions. To do so, we will use the whole data and see how accurately our algorithm predicts the percentage score. Remember, our scope is to locate the time series trend. To make predictions on the whole data, execute the following code:

```
trend = LModel.predict(X)
```

It is time to visualize what we have achieved:

```
plt.plot(y)
plt.plot(trend)
plt.show()
```

With this code, we first traced the time series. So we added the regression line that represents the data trend, and finally we printed the whole thing, as shown in the following graph:

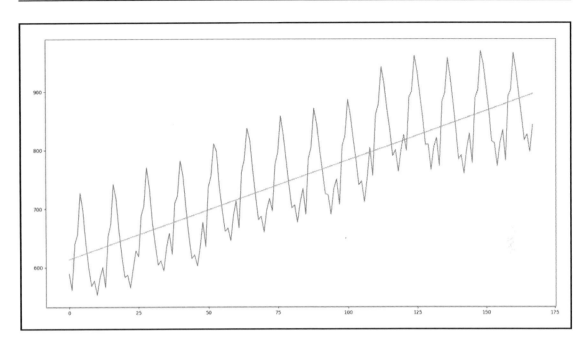

We recall that this represents a long-term monotonous trend movement, which highlights a structural evolution of the phenomenon due to causes that act in a systematic manner on the same. From the analysis of the previous figure, it is possible to note this: making a estimation of milk production in a precise period based on the line that indicates the trend of the time series can, in some cases, be disastrous. This is due to the fact that the seasonal highs and lows are at important distances from the line of regression. It is clear that it is not possible to use this line to make estimates of milk production.

Time series decomposition

One of the fundamental purposes of the classical analysis of time series is to break down the series into its components, isolating them in order to study them better. Moreover, to be able to apply the stochastic approach to a time series, it is almost always necessary to eliminate the trend and the seasonality to have a steady process. As we have specified in the previous sections, the components of a time series are usually the following: trend, seasonality, cycle, and residual.

As already mentioned, they can be decomposed by an additive way:

$$Y(t) = \tau(t) + S(t) + r(t)$$

They can also be decomposed by a multiplicative method:

$$Y(t) = \tau(t) * S(t) * r(t)$$

In the following sections, we will look at how to derive these components using both these methods.

Additive method

To perform a time series decomposition, we can use automated procedures. The `stats` models library provides an implementation of the naive, or classical, decomposition method in a function called `seasonal_decompose()`. Additive or multiplicative methods are available.

We start importing the `stats` models library:

```
from statsmodels.tsa.seasonal import seasonal_decompose
```

In particular, we imported the `seasonal_decompose` module to perform seasonal decomposition using MAs. We perform the decomposition by applying the additive method:

```
DecompDataAdd = seasonal_decompose(data, model='additive', freq=1)
```

The seasonal component is first removed by applying a convolution filter to the data. The average of this smoothed series for each period is the returned seasonal component. Let's see what happened through the visualization of the components identified:

```
DecompDataAdd.plot()
plt.show()
```

The following graph shows the decomposition results by additive method:

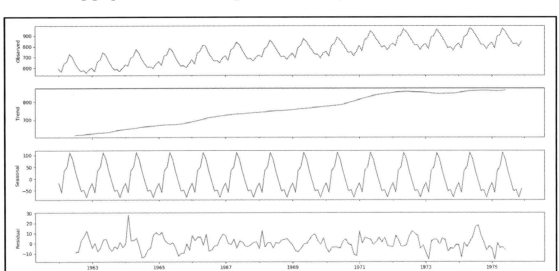

In this figure, the three components of the time series are clearly represented: trend, seasonal, and residual. These attributes are contained in the object returned by the method seasonal_decompose(). This means that we can use the content of that object to remove the effect of seasonality from the time series. Let's see how:

```
SeasRemov= data-DecompDataAdd.seasonal
```

With this line of code, we have simplified the seasonal attribute returned by the seasonal_decompose() method from the data. At this point, we just have to visualize the result:

```
SeasRemov.plot()
plt.show()
```

The following graph shows the monthly milk production (pounds per cow from January 1962 – December 1975) net of seasonality:

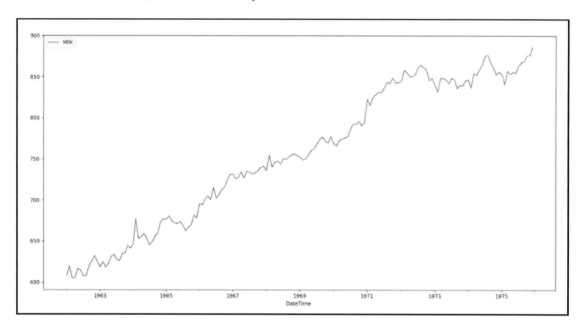

In the graph obtained, the component due to seasonality has clearly been removed, while the one due to the trend is clearly visible.

Multiplicative method

As we said, the `seasonal_decompose()` performs both additive and multiplicative decomposition. To run multiplicative method, just type the following command:

```
DecompDataMult = seasonal_decompose(data, model='multiplicative')
```

At this point, we just have to visualize the result:

```
DecompDataMult.plot()
plt.show()
```

The following graph shows the decomposition results by multiplicative method:

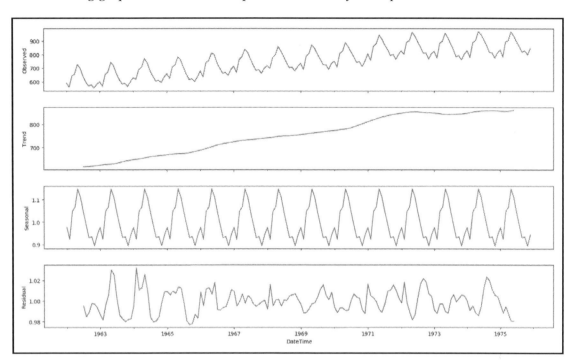

In the previous figure, we can note that the trend and seasonality information extracted from the time series do seem reasonable. The residuals show an interesting variation; periods of high variability are clearly identified in the early and later years of the time series.

LSTM for time series analysis

LSTM is a particular architecture of recurrent neural network, originally conceived by Hochreiter and Schmidhuber in 1997. This type of neural network has been recently rediscovered in the context of deep learning because it is free from the problem of vanishing gradient, and in practice it offers excellent results and performance.

LSTM-based networks are ideal for prediction and classification of time series, and are supplanting many classic machine learning approaches. This is due to the fact that LSTM networks are able to consider long-term dependencies between data, and in the case of speech recognition, this means managing the context within a sentence to improve recognition capacity.

Overview of the time series dataset

Scientists from the US **National Oceanic and Atmospheric Administration (NOAA)** have measured atmospheric carbon dioxide from 1965 to 1980 near the top of the Mauna Loa volcanic cone (Hawaii). The dataset covers carbon dioxide concentrations of 317.25 to 341.19 **parts per million (ppm)** by volume and contains 192 monthly records. Here is some useful information about this dataset:

- **Units**: ppm
- **Dataset metrics**: 192 fact values in one time series
- **Time granularity**: Month
- **Time range**: January 1965-December 1980

Source: TSDL, created by Rob Hyndman, a professor of statistics at Monash University, Australia.

Data is available in the `.csv` file named `co2-ppm-mauna-loa-19651980.csv`. To start, let's see how to import data into Python and then how to display them to identify the possible presence of seasonality. The first thing to do is to import the library that we will use:

```
import pandas as pd
import matplotlib.pyplot as plt
```

With the first line, we imported `pandas` and with second line we imported the `pyplot` module from the `matplotlib` library. Now let's see how to import the data contained in the dataset in Python:

```
dataset = pd.read_csv(' co2-ppm-mauna-loa-19651980.csv',
            parse_dates=True,index_col='DateTime',
            names=['DateTime', 'CO2'], header=None)
```

To import a dataset, we used the `read_csv` module of the `pandas` library. The `read_csv` method loads the data in a Pandas DataFrame we named dataset. To display on video the first five rows of DataFrame imported, we can use the `head()` function as follows:

```
print(dataset.head())
```

The following results are returned:

```
DateTime    CO2
1965-01-01  319.32
1965-02-01  320.36
1965-03-01  320.82
1965-04-01  322.06
1965-05-01  322.17
```

The `head()` function, with no arguments, gets the first five rows of data from the DataFrame. Now the time series is now available in our Python environment; to get a preview of the data contained in it, we can calculate a series of basic statistics. To do so, we will use the `describe()` function in the following way:

```
print(dataset.describe())
```

The following results are returned:

```
               CO2
count  192.000000
mean   328.463958
std      5.962682
min    317.250000
25%    323.397500
50%    328.295000
75%    333.095000
max    341.190000
```

The `describe()` function generates descriptive statistics that summarize the central tendency, dispersion and shape of a dataset's distribution, excluding NaN values. It analyzes both numeric and object series, as well as DataFrame column sets of mixed data types. The output will vary depending on what is provided. To extract further information, we can invoke the function `info()`:

```
print(data.info())
```

The following results are returned:

```
<class 'pandas.core.frame.DataFrame'>
DatetimeIndex: 192 entries, 1965-01-01 to 1980-12-01
Data columns (total 1 columns):
CO2     192 non-null float64
dtypes: float64(1)
memory usage: 3.0 KB
```

After having taken a look at the content of the dataset, we are going to perform an initial visual exploratory analysis. There's a relatively extensive plotting functionality built into Pandas that can be used for exploratory charts; this is especially useful in data analysis. A huge amount of functionality is provided by the `.plot()` command natively by Pandas:

```
dataset.plot()
plt.show()
```

The `dataset.plot()` command make plots of the DataFrame using `matplotlib/pylab`. To display the graph just created on video, we have to use the `plt.show()` function, as shown in the following graph:

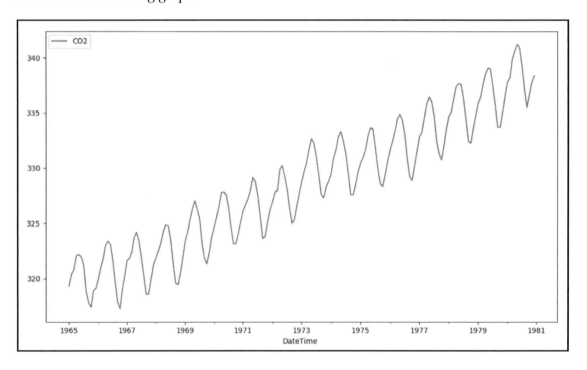

From the analysis of the previous figure, we can certainly recognize that atmospheric carbon dioxide is growing. We note a positive trend. But it is also denoting a certain variability (oscillations around a hypothetical trend line), which is maintained almost constantly with the passage of time.

Data scaling

Data scaling is a preprocessing technique usually employed before feature selection and classification. Many artificial intelligence-based systems use features that are generated by many different feature extraction algorithms, with different kinds of sources. These features may have different dynamic ranges.

In addition, in several data mining applications with huge numbers of features with large dynamic ranges, feature scaling may improve the performance of the fitting model. However, the appropriate choice of these techniques is an important issue, since applying scaling on the input could change the structure of data and thereby affect the outcome of multivariate analysis used in data mining.

To scaling the data we will use the min-max normalization (usually called **feature scaling**); it performs a linear transformation on the original data. This technique gets all the scaled data in the range (0,1). The formula to achieve this is:

$$x_{scaled} = \frac{x - x_{min}}{x_{max} - x_{min}}$$

Min-max normalization preserves the relationships among the original data values. The cost of having this bounded range is that we will end up with smaller standard deviations, which can suppress the effect of outliers.

To perform min-max normalization, we will use the `MinMaxScaler()` module of the `sklearn.preprocessing` class. This module transforms features by scaling each feature to a given range. This estimator scales and translates each feature individually such that it is in the given range on the training set, that is, between zero and one. The following codes show how to apply this module to our data:

```
scaler = MinMaxScaler()
dataset = scaler.fit_transform(dataset)
```

First we have used the `MinMaxScaler()` function to set the normalization interval (by default (0, 1)). In the second line of the code, we applied the `fit_transform()` function; it fits the transformer to the dataset and returns a transformed version of the data. This function is particularly useful as it stores the transformation parameters used. These parameters will be useful when, after having made the forecasts, we will have to report the data in the initial form (before normalization) to compare it with actual data.

Data splitting

Let's now split the data for the training and the test model. Training and testing the model forms the basis for further usage of the model for prediction in predictive analytics. Given a dataset of 192 rows of data, we split it into a convenient ratio (say 70:30), and allocate 134 rows for training and 58 rows for testing.

In general, in the algorithms based on artificial neural networks, the splitting is done by selecting rows randomly to reduce the bias. With the time series data, the sequence of values is important, so this procedure is not practicable. A simple method that we can use is to divide the ordered dataset into train and test. As we anticipated, the following code calculates the division point index and separates the data in the training datasets, with 70% of the observations for us to use to train our model; this leaves the remaining 30% to test the model:

```
train_len = int(len(dataset) * 0.70)
test_len  = len(dataset) - train_len
train = dataset[0:train_len,:]
test  = dataset[train_len:len(dataset),:]
```

The first two lines of code set the length of the two groups of data. The next two lines split the dataset into two parts: from row 1 to row `train_len` −1 for the train set, and from the `train_len` row to the last row for the test set. To confirm the correct split of data, we can print the length of the two datasets:

```
print(len(train), len(test))
```

This gives the following results:

```
134 58
```

As we anticipated, the operation divided the dataset into 134 (train set) and 58 rows (test set).

Building the model

Our aim is to use data in the dataset to make predictions. In particular, we want to predict the presence of carbon dioxide in the air based on the data available in the .csv file. We need input and output to train and test our network. It is clear that the input is represented by the data present in the dataset. We must then construct our output; we will do so by supposing we want to predict the CO2 present in the atmosphere at time $t + 1$ with respect to the value measured at time t. So we will have:

$$Input = data(t)$$

$$Output = data(t + 1)$$

We have said that a recurrent network has memory, and it is maintained by fixing the so-called **time step**. The time step has to do with how many steps back in time backprop uses when calculating gradients for weight updates during training. In this way, we set *time step* = 1. Then we define a function that gives a dataset and a time step returns the input and output data:

```
def dataset_creating(dataset):
    Xdata, Ydata = [], []
    for i in range(len(dataset)-1):
        Xdata.append(dataset[i, 0])
        Ydata.append(dataset[i + 1, 0])
    return numpy.array(Xdata), numpy.array(Ydata)
```

In this function, `Xdata=Input= data(t)` is the input variable and `Ydata=output= data(t + 1)` is the predicted value at the next time period. Let's use this function to set the train and test datasets that we will use in the next phase (network modeling):

```
trainX, trainY = create_dataset(train)
testX, testY = create_dataset(test)
```

In this way, we created all the data needed for the network training and testing. This function converts an array of values into a dataset matrix. Now we have to prepare the two input datasets (`trainX` and `testX`) in the form required by the machine learning algorithm we intend to use (LSTM). To do this, it is necessary to deepen this concept.

In a classic feed-forward network, like those already analyzed in the previous chapters, the input contains the values assumed by the variables for each observation made. This means that the input takes the following shape:

(number of observations, number of features)

In an LSTM/RNN network, the input for each LSTM layer must contain the following information:

- **Observations**: Number of observations collected
- **Time steps**: A time step is an observation point in the sample
- **Features**: One feature for each step

Therefore it is necessary to add a temporal dimension to those foreseen for a classical network. Thus the input shape becomes:

(number of observations, number of time steps, number of features per steps)

In this way, the input for each LSTM layer becomes three-dimensional. To transform the input datasets in 3D form, we will use the `numpy.reshape()` function as follows:

```
trainX = numpy.reshape(trainX, (trainX.shape[0], 1, 1))
testX = numpy.reshape(testX, (testX.shape[0], 1, 1))
```

The `numpy.reshape()` function gives a new shape to an array without changing its data. The function parameters used are:

- `trainX, testX`: Array to be reshaped
- `(trainX.shape[0], 1, 1)`, `(testX.shape[0], 1, 1)`: New shape

The new shape should be compatible with the original shape. In our case, the new shape is (133,1,1) for `trainX` and (57,1,1) for `testX`. Now that the data is in the right format, it's time to create the model:

```
timesteps = 1
model = Sequential()
```

We start defining the time steps; then we use a sequential model, that is, a linear stack of layers. To create a sequential model, we have to pass a list of layer instances to the constructor. We can also simply add layers via the `.add()` method:

```
model.add(LSTM(4, input_shape=(1, timesteps)))
model.add(Dense(1))
```

The first layer is an LSTM layer, with a hidden layer with four LSTM blocks. The model needs to know what input shape it should expect. For this reason, we passed an `input_shape` argument to this layer. In the next line, we added a dense layer that implements the default sigmoid activation function. Now, we have to configure the model for training:

```
model.compile(loss='mean_squared_error', optimizer='adam')
```

To do this, we used the compile module. The arguments passed are a loss function as `mean_squared_error` and stochastic gradient descent as `optimizer`. Finally, we can fit the model:

```
model.fit(trainX, trainY, epochs=1000, batch_size=1, verbose=2)
```

In the training phase, the `trainX` and `trainY` data is used, with 1,000 epochs (full training cycle on the training set). A batch size of 1 (batch_size = number of samples per gradient update) is passed. Fynally `verbose=2` (verbose argument provides additional details as to what the computer is doing) prints the loss value for each epoch.

Making predictions

Our model is now ready for use. We can therefore use it to execute our predictions:

```
trainPred = model.predict(trainX)
testPred = model.predict(testX)
```

The `predict()` module has been used, which generates output predictions for the input samples. Computation is done in batches. A Numpy array of predictions is returned. Previously, when data scaling was performed, we used the `fit_transform()` function. As we said, this function is particularly useful as it stores the transformation parameters used. These parameters will be useful when, after having made the forecasts, we will have to report the data in the initial form (before normalization), to compare it to the actual data. In fact, now the predictions must be reported in original form to compare with the actual values:

```
trainPred = scaler.inverse_transform(trainPred)
trainY = scaler.inverse_transform([trainY])
testPred = scaler.inverse_transform(testPred)
testY = scaler.inverse_transform([testY])
```

This code block is used exclusively to cancel the effect of normalization and to restore the initial form to the dataset. To estimate the performance of the algorithm, we will calculate the root mean squared error:

```
trainScore = math.sqrt(mean_squared_error(trainY[0], trainPred[:,0]))
print('Train Score: %.2f RMSE' % (trainScore))
testScore = math.sqrt(mean_squared_error(testY[0], testPred[:,0]))
print('Test Score: %.2f RMSE' % (testScore))
```

Root mean square error (**RMSE**) measures how much error there is between two datasets. In other words, it compares a predicted value and an observed value.

The following results are returned:

```
Train Score: 1.12 RMSE
Test Score: 1.35 RMSE
```

After evaluating the method's performance, we can now visualize the results by drawing an appropriate graph. To display the time series correctly, a prediction shift is required. This operation must be carried out both on the train set and on the test set:

```
trainPredPlot = numpy.empty_like(dataset)
trainPredPlot[:,:] = numpy.nan
trainPredPlot[1:len(trainPred)+1,:] = trainPred
```

Then perform the same operation on the test set:

```
testPredPlot = numpy.empty_like(dataset)
testPredPlot[:,:] = numpy.nan
testPredPlot[len(trainPred)+2:len(dataset),:] = testPred
```

Finally, we have to plot the actual data and the predictions:

```
plt.plot(scaler.inverse_transform(dataset))
plt.plot(trainPredPlot)
plt.plot(testPredPlot)
plt.show()
```

In the following graph are shown the actual data and the predictions:

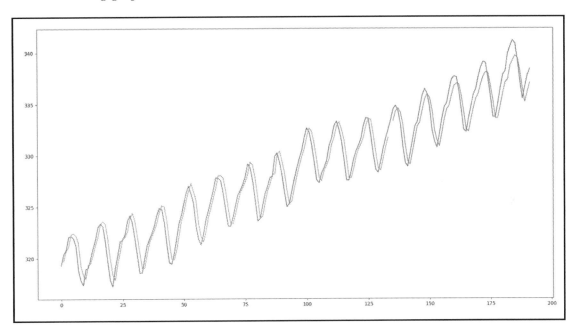

From the analysis of the previous graph, we can see that what is reported by the RMSE is confirmed by the graph. In fact, we can see that the model has done an excellent job in the fitting of both the training and test datasets.

Summary

In this chapter, we explored time series data. A time series constitutes a sequence of observations on a phenomenon. In a time series, we can identify several components: trend, seasonality, cycle, and residual. We learned how to remove seasonality from a time series with a practical example.

Then the most used models to represent time series were addressed: AR, MA, ARMA, and ARIMA. For each one, the basic concepts were analyzed and then a mathematical formulation of the model was provided.

Finally, an LSTM model for time series analysis was proposed. Using a practical example, we could see how to deal with a time series regression problem with a recurrent neural network model of the LSTM type.

15
Reinforcement Learning

Nowadays, most computers are based on a symbolic elaboration. The problem is first encoded in a set of variables and then processed using an explicit algorithm that, for each possible input of the problem, offers an adequate output. However, there are problems in which resolution by an explicit algorithm is inefficient or even unnatural, for example, a speech recognizer; tackling this kind of problem with the classic approach is inefficient. This and other similar problems, such as autonomous navigation of a robot or voice assistance in performing an operation, are part of a very diverse set of problems that can be addressed directly through solutions based on reinforcement learning.

Reinforcement learning is based on a psychology theory, elaborated after a series of experiments performed on animals. Defining a goal to be achieved, reinforcement learning tries to maximize the rewards received for the execution of the action or set of actions that allow us to reach the designated goal. Reinforcement learning is a very exciting sector of machine learning, used in everything from autonomous cars to video games. It aims to create algorithms that can learn and adapt to environmental changes.

The topics covered in this chapter are:

- Reinforcement learning
- **Markov Decision Process** (**MDP**)
- Q-learning
- **Temporal difference** (**TD**) learning
- Deep Q-learning networks

At the end of the chapter, you will be fully introduced to the power of reinforcement learning and will learn the different approaches to this technique. Several reinforcement learning methods will be covered.

Reinforcement learning introduction

Reinforcement learning aims to create algorithms that can learn and adapt to environmental changes. This programming technique is based on the concept of receiving external stimuli depending on the algorithm choices. A correct choice will involve a premium while an incorrect choice will lead to a penalty. The goal of the system is to achieve the best possible result, of course.

In supervised learning, there is a teacher that tells the system which is the correct output (learning with a teacher). This is not always possible. Often we have only qualitative information (sometimes binary, right/wrong, or success/failure). The information available is called **reinforcement signals**. But the system does not give any information on how to update the agent's behavior (that is, weights). You cannot define a cost function or a gradient. The goal of the system is to create the smart agents that are able to learn from their experience.

The following is a flowchart that displays reinforcement learning interaction with the environment:

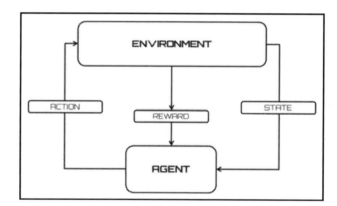

Scientific literature has taken an uncertain stance on the classification of learning by reinforcement as a paradigm. In fact, in an initial phase it was considered as a special case of supervised learning, and then it was fully promoted as the third paradigm of machine learning algorithms. It is applied in different contexts in which supervised learning is inefficient; the problems of interaction with the environment are clear examples.

The following flow shows the steps to follow to correctly apply a reinforcement learning algorithm:

1. Preparation of the agent
2. Observation of the environment
3. Selection of the optimal strategy
4. Execution of actions
5. Calculation of the corresponding reward (or penalty)
6. Development of updating strategies (if necessary)
7. Repeating steps 2-5 iteratively until the agent learns the optimal strategies

Reinforcement learning is based on some theory of psychology, elaborated after a series of experiments performed on animals. In particular, American psychologist Edward Thorndike noted that if a cat is given a reward immediately after the execution of a behavior considered correct, it increases the probability that this behavior will repeat itself. While in the face of unwanted behavior, the application of a punishment decreases the probability of a repetition of error.

On the basis of this theory, and with a goal to be achieved defined, reinforcement learning tries to maximize the rewards received for execution of the action or set of actions that allow us to reach the designated goal.

Agent-Environment interface

Reinforcement learning can be seen as a special case of the interaction problem for achieving a goal. The entity that must reach the goal is called an **agent**. The entity with which the agent must interact is called the **environment**, which corresponds to everything that is external to the agent.

So far, we have focused more on the term agent, but what does it represent? The agent is a software entity that performs services on behalf of another program, usually automatically and invisibly. These software are also called **smart agents**.

The following are the most important features of an agent:

- It can choose an action on the environment between a continuous and a discrete set
- Action depends on the situation. The situation is summarized in the system state
- The agent continuously monitors the environment (input) and continuously changes the status
- The choice of action is not trivial and requires a certain degree of **intelligence**
- The agent has a smart memory

The agent has a goal-directed behavior but acts in an uncertain environment not known a priori or partially known. An agent learns by interacting with the environment. Planning can be developed while learning about the environment through the measurements made by the agent itself. The strategy is close to trial-and-error theory.

Trial and error is a fundamental method of problem solving. It is characterized by repeated, varied attempts that are continued until success, or until the agent stops trying.

The Agent-Environment interaction is continuous; the agent chooses an action to be taken, and in response, the environment changes states, presenting a new situation to be faced.

In the particular case of reinforcement learning, the environment provides the agent with a reward; it is essential that the source of the reward is the environment to avoid the formation of a personal reinforcement mechanism within the agent that would compromise learning.

The value of the reward is proportional to the influence that the action has in reaching the objective; so it is positive or high in the case of a correct action, or negative or low action for an incorrect action.

The following are some examples from real life in which there is an interaction between the agent and environment to solve the problem:

- A chess player, for each move, has information on the configurations of pieces that can create and on the possible countermoves of the opponent
- A little giraffe learns to get up and run at 50 km/h in a few hours
- A truly autonomous robot learns to move in a room to get out of it
- The parameters of a refinery (oil pressure, flow, and so on) are set in real time so as to obtain the maximum yield or maximum quality

All the examples we have analyzed have the following characteristics in common:

- Interaction with the environment
- Objective of the agent
- Uncertainty or partial knowledge of the environment

From the analysis of these examples, it is possible to make the following observations:

- The agent learns from its own experience.
- When the actions change the status (the situation), the possibilities of choices in the future change (delayed reward).
- The effect of an action cannot be completely predicted.
- The agent has a global assessment of it behavior.
- It must exploit this information to improve his choices. Choices improve with experience.
- Problems can have a finite or infinite time horizon.

Markov Decision Process

To avoid load problems and computational difficulties, the Agent-Environment interaction is considered as a MDP. MDP is a discrete time stochastic control process. At each time step, the process is in a state s, and the decision maker may choose any action a that is available in state s. The process responds at the next time step by randomly moving into a new state s' and giving the decision maker a corresponding reward, $r(s,s')$.

Under these hypotheses, the Agent-Environment interaction can be schematized as follows:

- The agent and the environment interact at discrete intervals over time, $t = 0, 1, 2,$ ... n.
- At each interval, the agent receives a representation of the state st of the environment.
- Each element s_t of S, where S is the set of possible states.
- Once the state is recognized, the agent must take an action a_t of $A(s_t)$, where $A(s_t)$ is the set of possible actions in the state s_t.
- The choice of the action to be taken depends on the objective to be achieved and is mapped through the policy indicated with the symbol π (discounted cumulative reward), which associates the action with a_t of $A(s)$ for each state s. The term $\pi_t(s,a)$ represents the probability that action a is carried out in the state s.

- During the next time interval $t + 1$, as part of the consequence of the action at, the agent receives a numerical reward $r_t + 1$ R corresponding to the action previously taken a_t.
- The consequence of the action represents, instead, the new state s_t. At this point, the agent must again code the state and make the choice of the action.
- This iteration repeats itself until the achievement of the objective by the agent.

The definition of the status $s_t + 1$ depends from the previous state and the action taken MDP, that is:

$$s_t + 1 = \delta \ (s_t, a_t)$$

Here δ represents the status function.

In summary:

- In an MDP, the agent can perceive the status s S in which he is and has an A set of actions at his disposal
- At each discrete interval t of time, the agent detects the current status st and decides to implement an action at A
- The environment responds by providing a reward (a reinforcement) $r_t = r \ (s_t, a_t)$ and moving into the state $s_t + 1 = \delta \ (s_t, a_t)$
- The r and δ functions are part of the environment; they depend only on the current state and action (not the previous ones) and are not necessarily known to the agent
- The goal of reinforcement learning is to learn a policy that, for each state s in which the system is located, indicates to the agent an action to maximize the total reinforcement received during the entire action sequence

Let's go deeper into some of the terms used:

- A **reward function** defines the goal in a reinforcement learning problem. It maps the detected states of the environment into a single number, thus defining a reward. As already mentioned, the only goal is to maximize the total reward it receives in the long term. The reward function then defines what the good and bad events are for the agent. The reward function has the need to be correct, and it can be used as a basis for changing the policy. For example, if an action selected by the policy is followed by a low reward, the policy can be changed to select other actions in that situation in the next step.

- A **policy** defines the behavior of the learning agent at a given time. It maps both the detected states of the environment and the actions to take when they are in those states. Corresponds to what in psychology would be called a **set of rules** or associations of stimulus response. Policy is the fundamental part of a reinforcing learning agent, in the sense that it alone is enough to determine behavior.
- A **value function** represents how good a state is for an agent. It is equal to the total reward expected for an agent from the status s. The value function depends on the policy with which the agent selects the actions to be performed.

Discounted cumulative reward

In the previous section, we said this: the goal of reinforcement learning is to learn a policy that, for each state s in which the system is located, indicates to the agent an action to maximize the total reinforcement received during the entire action sequence. But how can we maximize the total reinforcement received during the entire sequence of actions?

The total reinforcement derived from the policy is calculated as follows:

$$R_T = \sum_{i=0}^{T} r_{t+1} = r_t + r_{t+1} + \ldots + r_T$$

Here, r_T represents the reward of the action that drives the environment in the terminal state s_T.

A possible solution to the problem is to associate the action that provides the highest reward to each individual state; that is, we must determine an optimal policy such that the previous quantity is maximized.

For problems that do not reach the goal or terminal state in a finite number of steps (continuing tasks), R_t tends to infinity.

In these cases, the sum of the rewards that one wants to maximize diverges at infinity, so this approach is not applicable. Then, it is necessary to develop an alternative reinforcement technique.

The technique that best suits the reinforcement learning paradigm turns out to be discounted cumulative reward, which tries to maximize the following quantity:

$$R_T = \sum_{i=0}^{\infty} \gamma^i r_{t+1} = r_t + \gamma r_{t+1} + \gamma^2 r_{t+2} + \ldots$$

Here, γ is called **discount factor** and it represents the importance for future rewards. This parameter can take the values $0 \leq \gamma \leq 1$, with the following meanings:

- If $\gamma < 1$, the sequence r_t will converge to a finite value
- If $\gamma = 0$, the agent will have no interest in future rewards, but will try to maximize the reward only for the current state
- If $\gamma = 1$, the agent will try to increase future rewards even at the expense of immediate ones

The discount factor can be modified during the learning process to highlight or not particular actions or states. An optimal policy can cause the reinforcement obtained in performing a single action to be even low (or even negative), provided that overall this leads to greater reinforcement.

Exploration versus exploitation

Ideally, the agent must associate with each action at the respective reward r in order to then choose the most rewarded behavior for achieving the goal. This approach is therefore impracticable for complex problems, in which the number of states is particularly high and consequently the possible associations increase exponentially.

This problem is called the **exploration-exploitation dilemma**. Ideally, the agent must explore all possible actions for each state, finding the one that is actually most rewarded for exploiting it in achieving its goal.

Thus, decision-making involves a fundamental choice:

- **Exploitation**: Make the best decision given current information
- **Exploration**: Collect more information

In this process, the best long-term strategy can lead to considerable sacrifices in the short term. Therefore, it is necessary to gather enough information to make the best decisions.

Here are some examples of adopting this technique for real-life cases:

Selection of a store:

- **Exploitation**: Go to your favorite store
- **Exploration**: Try a new store

Choice of a route:

- **Exploitation**: Choose the best route so far
- **Exploration**: Try a new route

In practice, in very complex problems, convergence to a very good strategy would be too slow.

A good solution to the problem is to find a balance between exploration and exploitation:

- An agent who limits himself to exploring will always act in a casual way in every state, and it is evident that convergence to an optimal strategy is impossible
- If an agent explores little, it will always use the usual actions, which may not be optimal ones

Reinforcement learning techniques

As we have seen in the previous sections, reinforcement learning is a programming philosophy that aims to develop algorithms that can learn and adapt to changes in the environment. This programming technique is based on the assumption of being able to receive stimuli from the outside according to the choices of the algorithm. So, a correct choice will result in a prize while an incorrect choice will lead to a penalization of the system. The goal of the system is to achieve the highest possible prize and consequently the best possible result. The techniques related to learning by reinforcement are divided into two categories:

- **Continuous learning algorithms**: These techniques start from the assumption of having a simple mechanism able to evaluate the choices of the algorithm and then reward or punish the algorithm depending on the result. These techniques can also adapt to substantial changes in the environment. An example is speech recognition programs or OCR programs that improve their performance with use.

- **Preventive training algorithms**: These algorithms start from the observation that constantly evaluating the actions of the algorithm can be a process that cannot be automated or very expensive. In this case, a first phase is applied, in which the algorithm is taught; when the system is considered reliable, it is crystallized and no more editable. Many electronic components use neural networks within them, and the synaptic weights of these networks are not changeable since they are fixed during the construction of the circuit.

It should be noted that the categories mentioned previously are implementation choices rather than conceptual differences in the algorithm. Therefore, an algorithm can often be in the first or second category depending on how it is implemented by the designer.

Q-learning

Q-learning is one of the most-used reinforcement learning algorithms. This is due to its ability to compare the expected utility of the available actions without requiring an environment model.

Thanks to this technique, it is possible to find an optimal action for every given state in a finished MDP.

A general solution to the reinforcement learning problem is to estimate, thanks to the learning process, an evaluation function. This function must be able to evaluate, through the sum of the rewards, the convenience or otherwise of a particular policy. In fact, Q-learning tries to maximize the value of the Q function (action-value function), which represents the maximum discounted future reward when we perform actions a in state s, as follows:

$$Q(S_t, a_t) = max(R_{t+1})$$

Knowing the Q function, the optimal action a in a state s is the one with the highest Q value. At this point, we can define a policy $\pi(s)$ that provides us with the best action in any state. Recalling that the policy π associates the pair *(s; a)* with the probability *(s; a)* that action is carried out in the state *s*, we can write the following:

$$\Pi(s) = argmax_a(Q(s, a))$$

The problem is reduced to the evaluation of the Q function. We can then estimate the Q function for a transition point in terms of the Q function at the next point through a recursive process. The following is the equation used in a single step of the process. This equation is known as **Bellman's equation** and represents the transition rule of Q-learning:

$$Q(s_t, a_t) = r + \gamma * \max_{a_{t+1}}(Q(S_{t+1}, a_{t+1}))$$

The terms are defined as follows:

- $Q(s_t, a_t)$ is the current policy of action a from state s.
- r is the reward for the action.
- $max_{t+1}(Q(s_{t+1}, a_{t+1}))$ defines the maximum future reward. We performed the a_t action to state s_t to reach the s_{t+1} state. From here, we may have multiple actions, each corresponding to some rewards. The maximum of that reward is computed.
- γ is the discount factor. The γ value varies from 0 to 1; if the value is near 0, an immediate reward is given preference. If it goes near 1, the importance of future rewards increases until 1, where it is considered equal to immediate rewards.

On the basis of the previous equation, the evaluation function Q is given by the sum of the immediate reward and the maximum reward obtainable starting from the next state.

Applying the previous formula, we are trying to formulate the delayed rewards into immediate rewards. We have previously said that the evaluation of the Q function represents a recursive process. We can then enter the values obtained during this process in a table that we will, of course, call table Q. In this table, the rows are the states and the columns are the actions. As a starting table Q, we can use a matrix containing all zeros (we have initialized table Q), as shown in the following figure:

The elements of this table Q (cells) are the rewards that are obtained if one is in the state given by the row and the action given by the column is executed. The best action to take in any state is the one with the highest reward. Our task now is to update this table with new values. To do this, we can adopt the following algorithm:

1. The status s_t is decoded
2. An action a_t is selected
3. Action a_t is performed and the reward r is received
4. The element of table $Q(s_t, a_t)$ is updated with the training rule provided by Bellman's equation
5. The execution of the action a moves the environment in the state s_{t+1}
6. Set the next state as the current state $(s_t = s_{t+1})$
7. Start again from point 1 and repeat the process until a terminal state is reached

In more complex and efficient formulations, it is possible to replace the table, whose iteration is still inefficient for complex problems, with a neural network where the learning process will change the weights of the synaptic connections.

Temporal difference learning

TD learning algorithms are based on reducing the differences between estimates made by the agent at different times. Q-learning, seen in the previous section, is a TD algorithm, but it is based on the difference between states in immediately adjacent instants. TD is more generic and may consider moments and states further away.

It is a combination of the ideas of the **Monte Carlo (MC)** method and the **Dynamic Programming (DP)**.

MC methods allow solving reinforcement learning problems based on the average of the results obtained.

DP represents a set of algorithms that can be used to calculate an optimal policy given a perfect model of the environment in the form of an MDP.

A TD algorithm can learn directly from raw data, without a model of the dynamics of the environment (such as MC). This algorithm updates the estimates based partly on previously learned estimates, without waiting for the final result (bootstrap, such as DP). It is suitable for learning without a model of dynamic environments. Converge using a fixed policy if the time step is sufficiently small, or if it reduces over time.

As we saw in the previous section, Q-learning calculates its values according to the following formula:

$$Q(s_t, a_t) = r + \gamma * \max_{a_{t+1}}(Q(S_{t+1}, a_{t+1}))$$

By adopting a one-step look-ahead.

Look-ahead is the generic term for a procedure that attempts to foresee the effects of choosing a branching variable to evaluate one of its values. The two main aims of look-ahead are to choose a variable to evaluate next and the order of values to assign to it.

It is clear that a two-step formula can also be used, as shown in the following line:

$$Q(s_t, a_t) = r_t + \gamma * r_{t+1} + \gamma^2 * \max_{a_{t+2}}(Q(S_{t+1}, a_{t+1}))$$

More generally with n-step look-ahead, we obtain the following formula:

$$Q(s_t, a_t) = r_t + \gamma * r_{t+1} + \ldots + \gamma^{n-1} * r_{t+n-1} + \gamma^n * \max_{a_{t+2}}(Q(S_{t+1}, a_{t+1}))$$

Dynamic Programming

DP represents a set of algorithms that can be used to calculate an optimal policy given a perfect model of the environment in the form of a MDP. The fundamental idea of DP, as well as reinforcement learning in general, is the use of state values and actions, to look for good policies.

The DP methods approach the resolution of Markov decision-making processes through the iteration of two processes called **policy evaluation** and **policy improvement**.

- Policy evaluation algorithm consists in applying an iterative method to the resolution of the Bellman equation. Since convergence is guaranteed to us only for $k \to \infty$, we must be content to have good approximations by imposing a stopping condition.
- Policy improvement algorithm improves policy based on current values.

A disadvantage of the policy iteration algorithm is that we have to evaluate a policy at every step. This involves an iterative process whose time of convergence we do not know a priori. This will depend on, among other things, how the starting policy was chosen.

One way to overcome this drawback is to cut off the evaluation of the policy at a specific step. This operation does not change the guarantee of convergence to the optimal value. A special case in which the assessment of the policy is blocked by a step by state (also called **sweep**) defines the value iteration algorithm. In the value iteration algorithm, a single iteration of calculation of the values is performed between each step of the policy improvement.

The DP algorithms are therefore essentially based on two processes that take place in parallel: policy evaluation and policy improvement. The repeated execution of these two processes makes the general process converge towards the optimal solution. In the policy iteration algorithm the two phases alternate and each ends before the other begins.

DP methods operate through the entire set of states that can be assumed by the environment, performing a complete backup for each state at each iteration. Each update operation performed by the backup updates the value of a status based on the values of all possible successor states, weighted for their probability of occurrence and induced by the policy of choice and dynamics of the environment. Full backups are closely related to the Bellman equation; they are nothing more than the transformation of the equation into assignment instructions.

When a complete backup iteration does not bring any change to the state values, convergence is obtained; therefore the final state values fully satisfy the Bellman equation. The DP methods are applicable only if there is a perfect model of the alternator, which must be equivalent to a MDP.

Precisely for this reason, the DP algorithms are of little use in reinforcement learning, both for their assumption of a perfect model of the environment, and for the high and expensive computation, but it is still opportune to mention them because they represent the theoretical basis of reinforcement learning. In fact, all the methods of reinforcement learning try to achieve the same goal of the DP methods, only with lower computational cost and without the assumption of a perfect model of the environment.

The DP methods converge to the optimal solution with a number of polynomial operations with respect to the number of states n and actions m, against the number of exponential operations $m*n$ required by methods based on direct search.

The DP methods update the estimates of the values of the states, based on the estimates of the values of the successor states; or they update the estimates on the basis of past estimates. This represents a special property, which is called **bootstrapping**. Several methods of reinforcement learning perform bootstrapping, even methods that do not require a perfect model of the environment, as required by the DP methods.

Monte Carlo methods

MC methods for estimating the value function and discovering excellent policies do not require the presence of a model of the environment. They are able to learn through the use of the agent's experience alone or from samples of state sequences, actions, and rewards obtained from the interactions between agent and environment. The experience can be acquired by the agent in line with the learning process or emulated by a previously populated dataset. The possibility of gaining experience during learning (online learning) is interesting because it allows obtaining excellent behavior even in the absence of a priori knowledge of the dynamics of the environment. Even learning through an already populated experience dataset can be interesting, because if combined with online learning, it makes automatic policy improvement induced by others' experiences possible.

To solve the reinforcement learning problems, MC methods estimate the value function on the basis of the total sum of rewards, obtained on average in the past episodes. This assumes that the experience is divided into episodes, and that all episodes are composed of a finite number of transitions. This is because in MC methods, only once an episode is completed takes place the estimate of the new values and the modification of the policy. MC methods iteratively estimate policy and value function. In this case, however, each iteration cycle is equivalent to completing an episode—the new estimates of policy and value function occur episode by episode.

Usually the term MC is used for estimation methods, which operations involve random components; in this case, MC refers to reinforcement learning methods based on total reward averages. Unlike the DP methods that calculate the values for each state, the MC methods calculate the values for each state-action pair, because in the absence of a model, only state values are not sufficient to decide which action is best performed in a certain state.

Deep Q-Network

Deep Q-Network (DQN) algorithms combine both the reinforcement learning approach and the deep learning approach. DQN learns by itself, learning in an empirical way and without a rigid programming aimed at a particular objective, such as winning a game of chess.

DQN represents an application of Q-learning with the use of deep learning for the approximation of the evaluation function. The DQN was proposed by Mnih et al. through an article published in *Nature* on February 26, 2015. As a consequence, a lot of research institutes joined this field, because deep neural networks can empower reinforcement learning algorithms to directly deal with high-dimensional states.

The use of deep neural networks is due to the fact that researchers noted the following: using a neural network to approximate the **Q-evaluation** function in algorithms with reinforcement learning made the system unstable or divergent. In fact, it is possible to notice that small updates to Q can significantly change the policy, distribution of data, and correlations between Q and target values. These correlations, present in the sequence of observations, are the cause of the instability of the algorithms.

To transform a normal Q-network into a DQN, it is necessary to carry out the following precautions:

- Replace the single-level neural network with a multi-level convolutional network for approximation of the Q-function evaluation
- Implement the experience replay
- Use a second network to calculate the target Q-values during your updates

What is meant by the term **experience replay**? This means that, instead of running Q-learning on state/action pairs as they occur during a simulation or actual experience, the system stores the data discovered, typically in a large table. In this way, our network can train itself using stored memories from its experience.

OpenAI Gym

OpenAI Gym is a library that helps us to implement algorithms based on reinforcement learning. It includes a growing collection of benchmark issues that expose a common interface, and a website where people can share their results and compare algorithm performance.

OpenAI Gym focuses on the episodic setting of reinforced learning. In other words, the agent's experience is divided into a series of episodes. The initial state of the agent is randomly sampled by a distribution, and the interaction proceeds until the environment reaches a terminal state. This procedure is repeated for each episode, with the aim of maximizing the total reward expectation per episode and achieving a high level of performance in the fewest possible episodes.

Gym is a toolkit for developing and comparing reinforcement learning algorithms. It supports the ability to teach agents everything from walking to playing games such as Pong or Pinball. The library is available at the following URL:

https://gym.openai.com/

The following figure shows the home page of the OpenAI Gym project site:

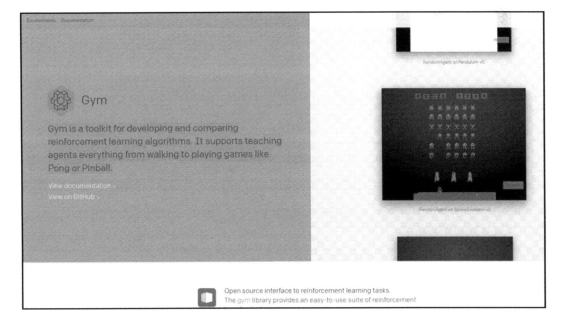

OpenAI Gym is part of a much more ambitious project: the OpenAI project. OpenAI is an **artificial intelligence** (**AI**) research company founded by Elon Musk and Sam Altman. It is a non-profit project that aims to promote and develop friendly AI in such a way as to benefit humanity as a whole. The organization aims to collaborate freely with other institutions and researchers by making their patents and research open to the public. The founders decided to undertake this project as they were concerned by the existential risk deriving from the indiscriminate use of AI.

OpenAI Gym is a library of programs that allow you to develop AIs, measure their intellectual abilities ,and enhance their learning abilities. In short, a Gym in the form of algorithms that trains the present digital brains to OpenAI Gym project them into the future.

But there is also another goal. OpenAI wants to stimulate research in the AI sector by funding projects that make humanity progress even in those fields where there is no economic return. With Gym, on the other hand, it intends to standardize the measurement of AI so that researchers can compete on equal terms and know where their colleagues have come but, above all, focus on results that are really useful for everyone.

The tools available are many. From the ability to play old video games like Pong to that of fighting in the GO to control a robot, we just enter our algorithm in this digital place to see how it works. The second step is to compare the benchmarks obtained with the other ones to see where we stand compared to others, and maybe we can collaborate with them to get mutual benefits.

OpenAI Gym makes no assumptions about the structure of our agent and is compatible with any numerical computation library, such as TensorFlow or Theano. The Gym library is a collection of test problems—environments—that we can use to work out our reinforcement learning algorithms. These environments have a shared interface, allowing you to write general algorithms.

To install OpenAI Gym, make sure you have previously installed a Python 3.5+ version; then simply type the following command:

```
pip install gym
```

Once this is done, we will be able to insert the tools made available by the library in a simple and immediate way.

Cart-Pole system

The Cart-Pole system is a classic problem of reinforced learning. The system consists of a pole (which acts like an inverted pendulum) attached to a cart via a joint, as shown in the following figure:

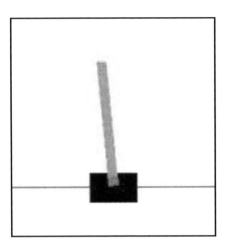

The system is controlled by applying a force of +1 or -1 to the cart. The force applied to the cart can be controlled, and the objective is to swing the pole upwards and stabilize it. This must be done without the cart falling to the ground. At every step, the agent can choose to move the cart left or right, and it receives a reward of 1 for every time step that the pole is balanced. If the pole ever deviates by more than 15 degrees from upright, then the procedure ends.

To run the Cart-Pole example using the OpenAI Gym library, simply type the following code:

```
import gym
env = gym.make('CartPole-v0')
env.reset()
for i in range(1000):
    env.render()
    env.step(env.action_space.sample())
```

As always, we will explain the meaning of each line of code in detail. The first line is used to import the `gym` library:

```
import gym
```

Then we move on to create the environment by calling the `make` method:

```
env = gym.make('CartPole-v0')
```

This method creates the environment that our agent will run in. An environment is a problem with a minimal interface that an agent can interact with. The environments in OpenAI Gym are designed in order to allow objective testing and benchmarking of an agent's abilities. The Gym library comes with a diverse suite of environments that range from easy to difficult and involve many different kinds of data.

 For a list of the available environments, refer to the following link:

```
https://gym.openai.com/envs
```

The most used environments are listed here:

- **Classic control and toy text**: Complete small-scale tasks, mostly from the reinforcement learning literature. They're here to get you started.
- **Algorithmic**: Perform computations such as adding multi-digit numbers and reversing sequences.
- **Atari**: Play classic Atari games.
- **2D and 3D robots**: Control a robot in simulation.

In our case we have called the CartPole-v0 environment. The `make` method returns an `env` object that we will use to interact with the game. But let's go back to analyzing the code. Now we have to initialize the system using the `reset()` method:

```
env.reset()
```

This method puts the environment into its initial state, returning an array that describes it. At this point, we will use a `for` loop to run an instance of the CartPole-v0 environment for `1000` time steps, rendering the environment at each step:

```
for i in range(1000):
    env.render()
    env.step(env.action_space.sample())
```

Calling the `render()` method will visually display the current state, while subsequent calls to `env.step()` will allow us to interact with the environment, returning the new states in response to the actions with which we call it.

In this way, we have adopted random actions at each step. At this point, it is certainly useful to know what actions we are doing on the environment to decide future actions. The `step()` method returns exactly this. In effect, this method returns the following four values:

- `observation (object)`: An environment-specific object representing your observation of the environment.
- `reward (float)`: Amount of reward achieved by the previous action. The scale varies between environments, but the goal is always to increase your total reward.
- `done (boolean)`: Whether it's time to reset the environment again. Most (but not all) tasks are divided into well-defined episodes, and `done` being `True` indicates the episode has terminated.
- `info (dict)`: Diagnostic information useful for debugging. It can sometimes be useful for learning.

To run this simple example, save the code in a file named `cart.py` and type the following command at the bash window:

```
python cart.py
```

In this way, a window will be displayed containing our system that is not stable and will soon go out of the screen. This is because the push to the cart is given randomly, without taking into account the position of the pole.

To solve the problem, that is, to balance the pole, it is therefore necessary to set the push in the opposite direction to the inclination of the pole. So, we have to set only two actions, -1 or +1, pushing the cart to the left or the right. But in order to do so, we need to know at all times the data deriving from the observation of the environment. As we have already said, these pieces of data are returned by the `step()` method, in particular they are contained in the observation object.

This object contains the following parameters:

- Cart position
- Cart velocity
- Pole angle
- Pole velocity at tip

These four values become the input of our problem. As we have also anticipated, the system is balanced by applying a push to the cart. There are two possible options:

- Push the cart to the left (0)
- Push it to the right (1)

It is clear that this is a binary classification problem: four inputs and a single binary output.

Let us first consider how to extract the values to be used as input. To extract these parameters, we just have to change the preceding proposed code:

```
import gym
env = gym.make('CartPole-v0')
observation = env.reset()
for i in range(1000):
    env.render()
    print(observation)
    observation, reward, done, info = env.step(env.action_space.sample())
```

By running the code, we can see that the values contained in the observation object are now printed on the screen. All this will be useful soon.

Using values returned from the environment observations, the agent has to decide on one of two possible actions: to move the cart left or right.

Learning phase

Now we have to face the most demanding phase, namely the training of our system. In the previous section, we said that the Gym library is focused on the episodic setting of reinforced learning. The agent's experience is divided into a series of episodes. The initial state of the agent is randomly sampled by a distribution and the interaction proceeds until the environment reaches a terminal state. This procedure is repeated for each episode with the aim of maximizing the total reward expectation per episode and achieving a high level of performance in the fewest possible episodes.

In the learning phase, we must estimate an evaluation function. This function must be able to evaluate, through the sum of the rewards, the convenience or otherwise of a particular policy. In other words, we must approximate the evaluation function. How can we do? One solution is to use an artificial neural network as a function approximator.

Recall that the training of a neural network aims to identify the weights of the connections between neurons. In this case, we will choose random values with weights for each episode. At the end, we will choose the combination of weights that will have collected the maximum reward.

The state of the system at a given moment is returned to us by the observation object. To choose an action from the actual state, we can use a linear combination of the weights and the observation. This is one of the most important special cases of function approximation, in which the approximate function is a linear function of the weight vector w. For every state s, there is a real-valued vector $x(s)$ with the same number of components as w. Linear methods approximate the state-value function by the inner product between w and $x(s)$.

In this way, we have specified the methodology that we intend to adopt for the solution of the problem. Now, to make the whole training phase easily understandable, we report the whole code block and then comment on it in detail on a line-by-line basis:

```
import gym
import numpy as np
env = gym.make('CartPole-v0')
HighReward = 0
BestWeights = None
for i in range(200):
  observation = env.reset()
  Weights = np.random.uniform(-1,1,4)
  SumReward = 0
  for j in range(1000):
    env.render()
    action = 0 if np.matmul(Weights,observation) < 0 else 1
    observation, reward, done, info = env.step(action)
    SumReward += reward
    print( i, j, Weights, observation, action, SumReward, BestWeights)
  if SumReward > HighReward:
    HighReward = SumReward
    BestWeights = Weights
```

The first part of the code deals with importing the libraries:

```
import gym
import numpy as np
```

Then we move on to create the environment by calling the make method:

```
env = gym.make('CartPole-v0')
```

This method creates the environment that our agent will run in. Now let's initialize the parameters we will use:

```
HighReward = 0
BestWeights = None
```

`HighReward` will contain the maximum reward obtained up to the current episode; this value will be used as a comparison value. `BestWeights` will contain the sequence of weights that will have registered the maximum reward. We can now implement the best weight sequence search through an iterative procedure for episodes:

```
for i in range(200):
```

We decide to execute the procedure 200 times, so we initialize the system using the `reset()` method:

```
observation = env.reset()
```

In each episode, we use a sequence of weights equal in number to the observations of the environment, which as previously said is four (cart position, cart velocity, pole angle, and pole velocity at tip):

```
Weights = np.random.uniform(-1,1,4)
```

To fix the weights, we have used the `np.random.uniform()` function. This function draws samples from a uniform distribution. Samples are uniformly distributed over the half-open interval (low and high). It includes low but excludes high.

In other words, any value within the given interval is equally likely to be drawn by a uniform distribution. Three parameters have been passed: the lower boundary of the output interval, its upper boundary, and the output shape. In our case we requested four random values in the interval $(-1,1)$. After doing this we initialize the sum of the rewards:

```
SumReward = 0
```

At this point, we implement another iterative cycle to determine the maximum reward we can get with these weights:

```
for j in range(1000):
```

Calling the `render()` method will visually display the current state:

```
env.render()
```

Now, we have to decide the `action`:

```
action = 0 if np.matmul(Weights,observation) < 0 else 1
```

As we said, to decide the action we have used a linear combination of two vectors: `weights` and `observation`. To perform a linear combination, we have used the `np.matmul()` function; it implements matrix product of two arrays. So, if this product is <0, then `action` is 0 (move left); otherwise, `action` is 1 (move right).

It should be noted that a negative product means that the pole is tilted to the left, so in order to balance this trend, it is necessary to push the cart towards the left. A positive product means the pole is tilted to the right, so in order to balance this trend, it is necessary to push the cart towards the right.

Now we use the `step()` method to return the new states in response to the actions with which we call it. Obviously, the action we pass to the method is the one we have just decided:

```
observation, reward, done, info = env.step(action)
```

As we said, this method returns the following four values:

- `observation` (`object`): An environment-specific object representing your observation of the environment.
- `reward` (`float`): The amount of reward achieved by the previous action. The scale varies between environments, but the goal is always to increase your total reward.
- `done` (`boolean`): Whether it's time to reset the environment again. Most (but not all) tasks are divided into well-defined episodes, and `done` being `True` indicates that the episode has terminated.
- `info` (`dict`): Diagnostic information useful for debugging. It can sometimes be useful for learning.

We can then update the sum of the rewards with the one just obtained. Remember that, for every time step where we keep the pole straight, we get +1 `reward`:

```
SumReward += reward
```

We just have to print the values obtained in this step:

```
print( i, j, Weights, observation, action, SumReward, BestWeights)
```

At the end of the current iteration, we can make a comparison to check whether the total reward obtained is the highest one obtained so far:

```
if SumReward > HighReward:
```

If it is the highest reward obtained so far, update the `HighReward` parameter with this value:

```
HighReward = SumReward
```

Once this is done, fix the sequence of `Weights` of the current step as the best one:

```
BestWeights = Weights
```

With this instruction, the training phase ends, which will give us the sequence of weights that best approximate the evaluation function. We can now test the system.

Testing phase

When the training phase is achieved, in practice it means that we have found the sequence of weights that best approximates this function, that is, the one that has returned the best reward achievable. Now we have to test the system with these values to check whether the pole is able to stand for at least 100 time steps.

Now, as we are already done in the training phase, to make the whole testing phase easily understandable, we report the whole code block and then comment on it in detail on a line-by-line basis:

```
observation = env.reset()
for j in range(100):
  env.render()
  action = 0 if np.matmul(BestWeights,observation) < 0 else 1
  observation, reward, done, info = env.step(action)
  print( j, action)
```

First, we have to initialize the system once again, using the `reset()` method:

```
observation = env.reset()
```

Then, we have to run an iterative cycle to apply the results obtained in the training phase:

```
for j in range(100):
```

For each step, we will call the `render()` method to visually display the current state:

```
env.render()
```

Now, we have to decide the action to perform on the system based on the best weights obtained in the training phase and on the observations of the current state:

```
action = 0 if np.matmul(BestWeights,observation) < 0 else 1
```

Now we use the `step()` method that returning the new states in response to the actions with which we call it. The action passed to the method is the one we have just decided:

```
observation, reward, done, info = env.step(action)
```

Finally, we print the step number and the action decided for visual control of the flow.

By running the proposed code, we can verify that after the training phase, the system is able to keep the pole in equilibrium for 100 time steps.

Summary

Reinforcement learning aims to create algorithms that can learn and adapt to environmental changes. This programming technique is based on the concept of receiving external stimuli depending on the algorithm choices. A correct choice will involve a premium, while an incorrect choice will lead to a penalty. The goal of system is to achieve the best possible result, of course. In this chapter, we dealt with the basics of reinforcement learning.

To begin with, we saw that the goal of learning with reinforcement is to create intelligent agents that are able to learn from their experience. So we analyzed the steps to follow to correctly apply a reinforcement learning algorithm. Later we explored the Agent-Environment interface. The entity that must achieve the goal is called an **agent**. The entity with which the agent must interact is called the **environment**, which corresponds to everything outside the agent.

To avoid load problems and computational difficulties, the Agent-Environment interaction is considered an MDP. An MDP is a stochastic control process. Then the discount factor concept was introduced. The discount factor can be modified during the learning process to highlight or not highlight particular actions or states. An optimal policy can cause the reinforcement obtained in performing a single action to be even low (or negative), provided that overall this leads to greater reinforcement.

In the central part of the chapter, were dedicated to the analysis of the most common reinforcement learning techniques. Q-learning, TD learning, and deep Q-learning networks were covered. Finally, we explored the OpenAI Gym libraries and tackled the analysis of a practical example of reinforcement learning.

16
Generative Neural Networks

In recent times, neural networks have been used as generative models: algorithms able to replicate the distribution of data in input to then be able to generate new values starting from that distribution. Usually, an image dataset is analyzed, and we try to learn the distribution associated with the pixels of the images to produce shapes similar to the original ones. Much work is ongoing to get neural networks to create novels, articles, art, and music.

Artificial intelligence (AI) researchers are interested in generative models because they represent a springboard towards the construction of AI systems able to use raw data from the world and automatically extract knowledge. These models seem to be a way to train computers to understand the concepts without the need for researchers to teach such concepts a priori. It would be a big step forward compared to current systems, which are only able to learn from training data accurately labeled by competent human beings.

In this chapter, we will touch one of the most exciting research avenues on generating models with neural networks. First, we will get an introduction to unsupervised learning algorithms; then an overview of generative models will be proposed. We will also discover the most common generative models and show how to implement a few examples. Finally, we will introduce the reader to the Nsynth dataset and the Google Magenta project.

The topics covered are:

- Unsupervised learning
- Generative model introduction
- Restricted Boltzmann machine
- Deep Boltzmann machines
- Autoencoder
- Variational autoencoder
- Generative adversarial network
- Adversarial autoencoder

At the end of the chapter, the reader will learn how to extract the content generated within the neural net with different types of content.

Unsupervised learning

Unsupervised learning is a machine learning technique that, starting from a series of inputs (system experience), is able to reclassify and organize on the basis of common characteristics to try to make predictions on subsequent inputs. Unlike supervised learning, only unlabeled examples are provided to the learner during the learning process, as the classes are not known a priori but must be learned automatically.

The following diagram shows three groups labeled from raw data:

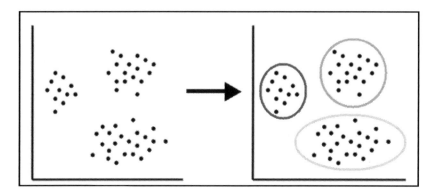

From this diagram, it is possible to notice that the system has identified three groups on the basis of a similarity, which in this case is due to proximity. In general, unsupervised learning tries to identify the internal structure of data to reproduce it.

Typical examples of these algorithms are search engines. These programs, given one or more keywords, are able to create a list of links that lead to pages that the search algorithm considers relevant to the research carried out. The validity of these algorithms depends on the usefulness of the information that they can extract from the database.

Unsupervised learning techniques work by comparing data and looking for similarities or differences. As is known, machine learning algorithms try to imitate the functioning of an animal's nervous system. For this purpose, we can hypothesize that neural processes are guided by mechanisms that optimize the unknown objective they pursue. Each process evolves from an initial situation associated with a stimulus to a terminal in which there is an answer, which is the result of the process itself. It is intuitive that, in this evolution, there is a transfer of information. In fact, the stimulus provides the information necessary to obtain the desired response. Therefore, it is important that this information is transmitted as faithfully as possible until the process is completed. A reasonable criterion for interpreting the processes that take place in the nervous system is, therefore, to consider them as transfers of information with maximum preservation of the same.

Unsupervised learning algorithms are based on these concepts. It is a question of using learning theory techniques to measure the loss of information that has occurred in the transfer. The process under consideration is considered as the transmission of a signal through a noisy channel, using well-known techniques developed in the field of communications. It is possible, however, to follow a different approach based on a geometric representation of the process. In fact, both the stimulus and the response are characterized by an appropriate number of components, which in a space correspond to a point. Thus, the process can be interpreted as a geometric transformation of the input space to the output space. The exit space has a smaller size than the input space, as the stimulus contains the information necessary to activate many simultaneous processes. Compared to only one, it is redundant. This means that there is always a redundancy reduction operation in the transformation under consideration.

In the entry and exit space, typical regions are formed, with which the information is associated. The natural mechanism that controls the transfer of information must therefore identify, in some way, these important regions for the process under consideration, and make sure that they correspond in the transformation. Thus, a data grouping operation is present in the process in question; this operation can be identified with the acquisition of experience. The two previous operations of grouping and reduction of redundancy are typical of optimal signal processing, and there is biological evidence of their existence in the functioning of the nervous system. It is interesting to note that these two operations are automatically achieved in the case of non-supervised learning based on experimental principles, such as competitive learning.

Generative models

A generative model aims to generate all the values of a phenomenon, both those that can be observed (input) and those that can be calculated from the ones observed (target). We try to understand how such a model can succeed in this goal by proposing a first distinction between generative and discriminative models.

Often, in machine learning, we need to predict the value of a target vector y given the value of an input x vector. From a probabilistic perspective, the goal is to find the conditional probability distribution $p(y|x)$.

The conditional probability of an event y with respect to an event x is the probability that y occurs, knowing that x is verified. This probability, indicated by $p(y|x)$, expresses a correction of expectations for y, dictated by the observation of x.

The most common approach to this problem is to represent the conditional distribution using a parametric model, and then determine the parameters using a training set consisting of pairs (xn, yn) that contain both the values of the input variables and the relative vectors of corresponding outputs. The resulting conditional distribution can be used to make predictions of the target (y) for new input values (x). This is known as a **discriminatory approach**, since the conditional distribution discriminates directly between the different values of y.

As an alternative to this approach, we can look for the joint probability distribution $p(x \cap y)$, and then use this joint distribution to evaluate the conditional probability $p(y \mid x)$ in order to make predictions of y for new values of x. This is known as **generative approach**, because by sampling from the joint distribution, it is possible to generate synthetic examples of the vector of characteristics x.

The joint probability distribution $p(x, y)$ is a probability distribution that gives the probability that each of x, y vectors falls in any particular range or discrete set of values specified for that variable.

A generative approach, regardless of the type of data and the theoretical model used, is divided into two basic steps:

1. The first step involves the construction of the generative model. The input data is processed with the aim of deducing their distribution. To do this, input data can simply be reorganized into a different structure, or it can represent new information extracted from input data from specific algorithms. The result of the construction of the generative model is the presentation of data according to the distribution to which it has been approximated.
2. Once the generative model has been built on the input data, this allows sampling, which leads to the formation of new data that shares the same distribution with the input data.

The construction of a generative model allows highlighting features and properties implicitly present in the initial data. The individual approaches are then distinguished by the type of processing performed on the data to explain these characteristics, and consequently for the type of variables on which an approximate data distribution is obtained.

Why are AI researchers so excited about generative models? Let's take a simple example: suppose we provide the system with a series of images of cats. Suppose then, that after seeing these images, the computer is able to generate new photos of cats in a completely independent manner. If the computer were able to do it and the images that were produced had the right number of legs, tails, ears, and so on, it would be easy to prove that the computer knows which parts make up the cat, even if no one has ever explained cat anatomy to it. So, in a sense, a good generative model is proof of the basic knowledge of concepts by computers.

This is why researchers are so enthusiastic about building generative models. These models seem to be a way to train computers to understand concepts without the need for researchers to teach them a priori concepts.

Restricted Boltzmann machine

A Boltzmann machine is a probabilistic graphic model that can be interpreted as a stochastic neural network. Boltzmann machines were first introduced in 1985 by Geoffrey Hinton and Terry Sejnowski. **Stochastic** is due to the behavior of the neurons; within them, in the activation function, they will have a probabilistic value that will influence the activation of the neuron.

In practice, a Boltzmann machine is a model (including a certain number of parameters) that, when applied to a data distribution, is able to provide a representation. This model can be used to extract important aspects of an unknown distribution (target distribution) starting only from a sample of the latter. The data samples referred to by a Boltzmann Machine are also called **training data**. The following diagram shows a Boltzmann machine's architecture:

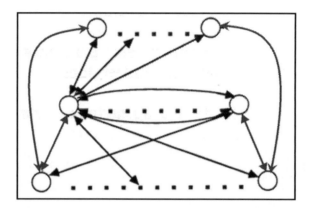

Training a Boltzmann machine means adapting its parameters so that the probability distribution represented by it interpolates the training data as best as possible. The training of a Boltzmann machine is a rather demanding work from a computational point of view. However, this problem can be made easier by imposing restrictions on the topology of the network on which you are working; this defines **Restricted Boltzmann machines** (**RBM**).

In Boltzmann machines, there are two types of units:

- Visible units (or neurons since, as we said, a Boltzmann machine can be interpreted as a neural network)
- Hidden units (or neurons)

Even in RBMs, there are both of these types of units and we can imagine them as arranged on two levels:

- Visible units are the components of an observation (for example, if our data consists of images, we can associate a visible unit with each pixel)
- Hidden units instead give us a model of the dependencies that exist between the components of our observation (for example, the dependency relationships that exist between the pixels of an image)

Hidden units can therefore be seen as detectors of data characteristics. In the RBM graph, every neuron is connected to all the neurons of the other level, while there are no connections between neurons of the same level; it is precisely this restriction that gives the RBM its name, as shown in the following diagram:

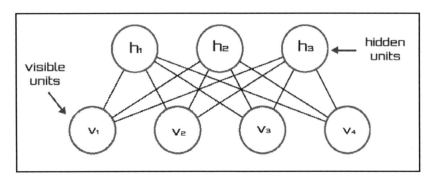

After successful training, an RBM provides a very good representation of the distribution that underlies training data. It is a generative model that allows sampling new data starting from the learned distribution; for example, new image structures can be generated starting from studied images. Having a generative model makes useful applications possible. For example, you can think of integrating some visible units corresponding to a partial observation (that is, you fix the values of the observed variables and consider them constant) and then produce the remaining ones visible units to complete the observation; in the image analysis example, this can be useful for an image completion task.

As generative models, RBMs can also be used as classifiers. Consider an application of this type:

- RBM is trained to learn the joint probability distribution of the input data (explanatory variables) and the corresponding labels (response/output variables), both represented in the graph of the network, from the visible units of the RBM.
- Subsequently, a new input pattern, this time without labels, can be linked to the visible variables. The corresponding labels can be predicted by sampling directly from the Boltzmann machine.

The Boltzmann machine is able to complete partial patterns of data on visible units. If we divide the visible units into units of input and output, given the input pattern, the Boltzmann machine completes it by producing the outputs (classification). Otherwise, it works as associative memory, returning the most similar pattern among those learned to the (partial) data.

Boltzmann machine architecture

Boltzmann machine architecture is based on input, output, and hidden nodes. The connection weights are symmetrical:

$$w_{ij} = w_{ji} \ , \ for \ i \neq j$$

Based on this assumption, Boltzmann machines are highly recurrent, and this recurrence eliminates any basic difference between input and output nodes, which can be considered as input or output when needed. The Boltzmann machine is a network of units with an **energy** defined for the overall network. Its units produce binary results ((1,0) values). Outputs are computed probabilistically, and depend upon the temperature variable T.

The consensus function of the Boltzmann machine is given by the following formula:

$$S_i = \sum_{j=0}^{n} w_{ij} u_j$$

In the previous formula, the terms are defined as follows:

- S_i is the state of unit $i(1,0)$
- w_{ij} is the connection strength between unit j and unit i
- u_j is the output of unit j

The calculation proceeds within the machine in a stochastic manner so that the consent is increased. Thus, if w_{ij} is positive, there is a tendency to have units i and j both activated or both deactivated, while if the weight is negative, there is a tendency to have them with different activations (one activated and the other not). When a weight is positive, it is called **excitatory**; otherwise, it is called **inhibitory**.

Each binary unit makes a stochastic decision to be either 1 (with probability p_i) or 0 (with probability $1- p_i$). This probability is given by the following formula:

$$p_i = \frac{1}{1 + e^{-S_i/T}}$$

At the equilibrium state of the network, the likelihood is defined as the exponentiated negative energy, known as the **Boltzmann distribution**. You can imagine that by administering energy, you can get the system out of the local minima. This must be done slowly, because a violent shock can drive the system away from the global minimum. The best method is to give energy and then slowly reduce it. This concept is used in metallurgy, where an ordered state of the metal is obtained first by melting, and then slowly the temperature is reduced. The reduction in temperature as the process is under way is called **simulated annealing**.

This method can be reproduced by adding a probabilistic update rule to the Hopfield network (refer to Chapter 13, *Beyond Feedforward Networks – CNN and RNN*); the network that reproduces it is called **Boltzmann machine**. There will be a parameter that varies: the temperature. So at high *T*, the probability of jumping to a higher energy is much greater than at low temperatures.

When the temperature drops, the probability of assuming the correct minimum energy status approaches 1, and the network reaches the thermal equilibrium. Each unit of the network makes an energy leap given by the following formula:

$$\Delta E_k = \sum w_i S_j - \theta_k$$

The system changes to a state of lower energy according to the following probabilistic rule (transition function):

$$p_k = \frac{1}{1 + e^{-\Delta E_k/T}}$$

It is seen that the probability of transition to a higher energy state is greater at high *T* than at low *T*. The network can assume a configuration of stable states according to the following Boltzmann distribution:

$$p_a = k_e^{E_a/T}$$

That is, it depends on the energy of the state and temperature of the system. Lower energy states are more likely; in fact if $E_a < E_b$, then $P_a/P_b > 1$, because of which $P_a > P_b$. So the system tends toward a state of minimum energy.

Boltzmann machine disadvantages

Numerous problems have emerged in the use of algorithms based on Boltzmann machines. The following are some of the problems encountered:

- Weight adjustment
- The time needed to collect statistics in order to calculate probabilities,
- How many weights change at a time
- How to adjust the temperature during simulated annealing
- How to decide when the network has reached the equilibrium temperature.

The main disadvantage is that Boltzmann learning is significantly slower than backpropagation.

Deep Boltzmann machines

Another type of Boltzmann Machine is **Deep Boltzmann machine (DBM)**. This is a neural network similar to RBM, but instead of having only one layer of hidden nodes, DBMs have many. Each layer of neurons is connected only to those adjacent (the one immediately preceding and immediately following); here also, the neurons of the same layer are not interconnected. This structure allows the emergence of particular statistics from each layer that can capture new data features. The following diagram shows a DBM model with one visible layer and two hidden layers:

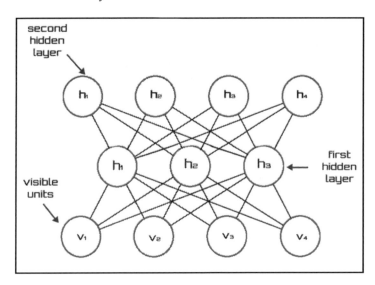

As we can see, connections are only between units in neighboring layers. Like RBMs and DBMs contain only binary units.

The DBMs model assigns the following probability to a visible vector v:

$$p(v, \theta) = \frac{1}{Z(\theta)} \sum_h e^{-E(v, h^{(1)}, h^{(2)}; \theta)}$$

In the previous formula, the terms are defined as follows:

- v is the visible vector
- $\theta = (W(1), W(2))$ are the model parameters, representing visible-to-hidden and hidden-to-hidden symmetric interaction terms
- $h^{(1)}$ and $h^{(2)}$ are hidden stochastic binary variables
- $Z(\theta)$ is the partition function

DBMs are particularly useful in the case of the recognition of objects or words. This is due to the great ability to learn complex and abstract internal representations using little labeled input data, instead of exploiting a large amount of unlabeled input data. However, unlike deep convolutional neural networks, DBMs adopt the inference and training procedure in both directions to better detect representations of input structures.

Autoencoder

An autoencoder is a neural network whose purpose is to code its input into small dimensions and the result obtained, to be able to reconstruct the input itself. Autoencoders are made up of the union of the following two subnets:

- Encoder, which calculates the function:

$$z = \phi(x)$$

Given an input x, the encoder encodes it in a variable z, also called **latent variable**. z usually has much smaller dimensions than x.

- Decoder, which calculates the following function:

$$x' = \psi(z)$$

Since z is the code of x produced by the encoder, the decoder must decode it so that x' is similar to x.

The training of autoencoders is intended to minimize the mean square error between the input and the result.

 Mean Squared Error (MSE) is the average squared difference between the outputs and targets. Lower values are indicative of better results. Zero means no error.

For n observations, *MSE* is given by the following formula:

$$MSE = \sum_{i=0}^{n} \left(x_i - x'_i\right)^2$$

Finally, we can summarize that the encoder encodes the input in a compressed representation and the decoder returns from it a reconstruction of the input, as shown in the following diagram:

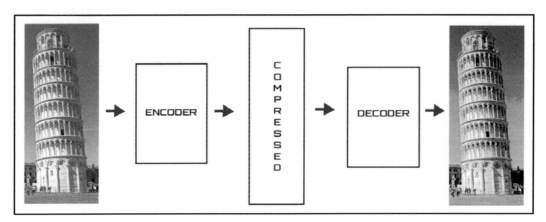

Let's define the following terms:

- W: input → hidden weights
- V: hidden → output weights

The previous formulas become:

$$z = \phi(W^* x)$$

And they also become:

$$x' = \psi(V^*W1^* x)$$

Finally, the training of autoencoders is intended to minimize the following quantity:

$$\sum_{i=0}^{n} (x_i - V * W * *x_i)^2$$

The purpose of autoencoders is not simply to perform a sort of compression of the input or to look for an approximation of the identity function. There are techniques that allow, starting from a hidden layer of reduced dimensions, to direct the model to give greater importance to some data properties, thus giving rise to different representations based on the same data.

Variational autoencoder

Variational autoencoder (VAE) are inspired by the concept of Autoencoder: a model consisting of two neural networks called **encoders** and **decoders**. As we have seen, the encoder network tries to code its input in a compressed form, while the network decoder tries to reconstruct the initial input, starting from the code returned by the encoder.

However, the functioning of the VAE is very different than that of simple autoencoders. VAEs allow not only coding/decoding of input but also generating new data. To do this, they treat both the code z and the reconstruction/generation x' as if they belonged to a certain probability distribution. In particular, the VAEs are the result of the combination of deep learning and Bayesian inference, in the sense that they consist of a neural network trained with the backpropagation algorithm modified with a technique called **re-parameterization**. While deep learning has proven to be very effective in the approximation of complex functions, the Bayesian statistics allow managing the uncertainty derived from a random generation in the form of probabilities.

The VAE uses the same structure to generate new images, similar to those belonging to the training set. In this case, the encoder does not directly produce a code for a given input but calculates the mean and variance of a normal distribution. A value is taken from this distribution and it is decoded by the decoder. The training consists of modifying the encoder and decoder parameters so that the result of the decoded so carried out is as similar as possible to the starting image. At the end of the training, we have that starting from the normal distribution with mean and variance produced by the encoder; the decoder will be able to produce images similar to those belonging to the training set.

Let's define the following terms:

- X: Input data vector
- z: Latent variable
- $P(X)$: Probability distribution of the data
- $P(z)$: Probability distribution of the latent variable
- $P(X|z)$: Posterior probability, that is, the distribution of generating data given the latent variable

> The posterior probability $P(X|z)$ is the probability of the condition X given the evidence z.

Our goal is to generate data according to the characteristics contained in the latent variable, so we want to find $P(X)$. For this purpose, we can use the law of total probability according to the following formula:

$$P(X) = \int P(X|z)P(z)dz$$

To understand how we arrived at this formulation, we reason by step. Our first task in defining the model is to infer good values of the latent variables starting from the observed data, or to calculate the posterior $p(z|X)$. To do this, we can use the Bayes theorem:

$$P(z|X) = \frac{P(X|z)P(z)}{P(X)}$$

In the previous formula, the $P(X)$ term appears. In the context of Bayesian statistics, it may also be referred to as the evidence or model evidence. The evidence can be calculated by marginalizing out the latent variables. This brings us to the starting formula:

$$P(X) = \int P(X|z)P(z)dz$$

The computational estimate of this integral requires an exponential time as it must be evaluated on all the configurations of latent variables. To reduce the computational cost, we are forced to approximate the estimate of the posterior probability.

In VAE, as the name suggests, we deduce $p(z \mid X)$ using a method called **variational inference** (**VI**). VI is one of the most used methods in Bayesian inference. This technique considers inference as an optimization problem. In doing this, we use a simpler distribution that is easy to evaluate (for example, Gaussian) and minimize the difference between these two distributions using the **Kullback-Leibler divergence metric**.

Kullback-Leibler divergence metric is a non-symmetric measure of the difference between two probability distributions P and Q. Specially, the Kullback-Leibler divergence of Q from P, denoted by **DKL** $(P \mid \mid Q)$, is the measurement of the information lost when Q is used to approximate P.

For discrete probability distributions P and Q, the Kullback-Leibler divergence from Q to P is defined as follows:

$$D_{KL}(P\|Q) = -\sum_i P(i) log \frac{Q(i)}{P(i)}$$

Analyzing the formula makes it evident that the divergence of Kullback-Leibler is the expectation of the logarithmic difference between the probabilities P and Q, where the expectation is taken using the probability P.

Generative adversarial network

Generative adversarial network (**GAN**) is a generative model consisting of two networks that are jointly trained, called **generator** and **discriminator**.

The dynamics between these two networks are like those between a forger and an investigator. The forger tries to produce faithful imitations of authentic works of art, while the investigator tries to distinguish the fakes from the originals. In this analogy, the forger represents the generator and the investigator represents the discriminator. The generator accepts input values belonging to a fixed distribution and tries to produce images similar to those of the dataset. The discriminator tries to distinguish the data created by the generator from those belonging to the dataset. These two networks are jointly coached:

- The discriminator tries to return output = 1 if the input belongs to the dataset and returns 0 if its input was generated by the generator
- The generator instead tries to maximize the possibility that the discriminator will make mistakes

The generator acquires a random input noise and tries to create a sample of data, while the discriminator takes input from either real-world examples or the generator, as shown in the following diagram:

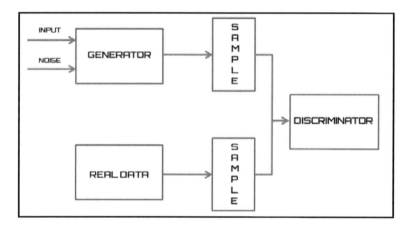

For simplicity, the two opposing networks are of the multilayer perceptron type; however, the same structure can be modeled with deep networks. For example, to generate new images, instead of sampling data from a complex distribution, the approach used in these networks is to start from values belonging to a simple distribution or from random values. Subsequently, they are mapped through a second distribution that will be learned during the training.

In such a system, training leads to constant competition between generator and discriminator. Under these conditions, the optimization process can be carried out independently on both sides. Naming *G(z)* the generator and *D(x)* the discriminator, the training of the model aims to maximize the probability of the discriminator to assign 1 to values coming from the training set, instead of 0 to those produced by the generator. On the other hand, we want to teach the generator to minimize the following quantity:

$$log(1 - D(G(z)))$$

The training is then performed by applying the gradient descent technique to the following expression:

$$\min_{G} \max_{D} V(D, G) = E_{x \sim Pdata(x)} [log D(x)] + E_{x \sim Pz(z)} [log(1 - D(G(z)))]$$

This method originates from game theory, in particular from the method called **two-player minimax game**. The algorithms of this type adopt the strategy of minimizing the maximum possible loss resulting from the choice of a player. It can happen that, in the training process, the discriminator is not able to classify examples generated by real ones.

Adversarial autoencoder

Adversarial autoencoder (AAE) is a generative model produced by the union of VAE and GAN. To explain the model, we start by defining the following terms:

- *x*: Autoencoder input
- *z*: Code produced from *x*,
- *p(z)*: The distribution we want to impose
- *q(z|x)*: Distribution learned from the encoder
- *p(x|z)*: Distribution learned from the decoder
- *pdata*: Distribution of the data
- *p(x)*: Distribution of the model

We consider the function $q(z|x)$ as a posterior distribution of $q(z)$, which is defined as follows:

$$q(z) = \int q(z|x)p_{data}(x)dx$$

We try to impose the equality $q(z)=p(z)$ on the model. The difference with a VAE is due to the fact that what drives $q(z)$ towards $p(z)$ is an adversarial network. The encoder of the VAE is considered the generator of a GAN for which a discriminator can be used. This tries to distinguish data belonging to $q(z)$ from that coming from $p(z)$. The following diagram shows an AAE architecture:

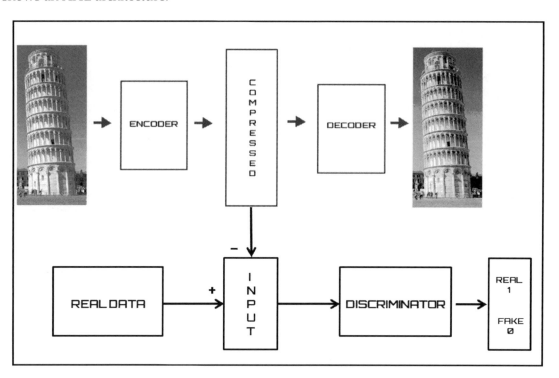

The trainings of the adversarial network and of the autoencoder take place jointly, using stochastic gradient descent.

Feature extraction using RBM

Recently, several types of **artificial neural networks** (**ANNs**) have been applied to classify a specific dataset. However, most of these models use only a limited number of features as input, in which case there may not be enough information to make the prediction due to the complexity of the starting dataset. If you have more features, the run time of training would be increased and generalization performance would deteriorate due to the curse of dimesionality. In these cases, a tool to extract the characteristics would be particularly useful. RBM is a machine learning tool with a strong representation power, which is often used as a feature extractor in a wide variety of classification problems.

Breast cancer dataset

The breast is made up of a set of glands and adipose tissue, and is located between the skin and the chest wall. In fact, it is not a single gland but a set of glandular structures, called **lobules**, joined together to form a lobe. In a breast, there are 15 to 20 lobes. The milk reaches the nipple from the lobules through small tubes called **milk ducts**.

Breast cancer is a potentially serious disease if it is not detected and treated. It is caused by uncontrolled multiplication of some cells in the mammary gland that are transformed into malignant cells. This means that they have the ability to detach themselves from the tissue that has generated them to invade the surrounding tissues and eventually other organs of the body. In theory, cancers can be formed from all types of breast tissues, but the most common ones are from glandular cells or from those forming the walls of the ducts.

The objective of this example is to identify each of a number of benign or malignant classes. To do this, we will use the data contained in the dataset named BreastCancer (Wisconsin Breast Cancer database). This data has been taken from the UCI Repository of machine learning databases as DNA samples arrive periodically, as Dr. Wolberg reports his clinical cases. The database therefore reflects this chronological grouping of the data. This grouping information appears immediately, having been removed from the data itself. Each variable, except for the first, was converted into 11 primitive numerical attributes with values ranging from zero through ten.

To get the data, we draw on the large collection of data available in the UCI Machine Learning Repository at the following link: `http://archive.ics.uci.edu/ml`.

To load the dataset, we will use the `sklearn.datasets` module. It includes utilities to load datasets, including methods to load and fetch popular reference datasets. It also features some artificial data generators.

The breast cancer dataset is a classic and very easy binary classification dataset. The following table has some information about the dataset:

Classes	2
Samples per class	212(M), 357(B)
Samples total	569
Dimensionality	30
Features	real and positive

Data preparation

After introducing the breast cancer dataset, we can analyze the code that will allow us to classify the input data line by line. In the first part of the code, we import the libraries we will use later:

```
from sklearn import linear_model, datasets, preprocessing
from sklearn.cross_validation import train_test_split
from sklearn.pipeline import Pipeline
from sklearn.neural_network import BernoulliRBM
from pandas_ml import ConfusionMatrix
import numpy as np
import pandas as pd
```

For now, let's limit ourselves to import; we will deepen them at the time of use. To start, we have to import the dataset; we will do so using the `sklearn.datasets` package:

```
BC = datasets.load_breast_cancer()
```

This command loads and returns the breast cancer `wisconsin` dataset. The `sklearn.datasets` package embeds some small toy datasets. To evaluate the impact of the scale of the dataset (`n_samples` and `n_features`) while controlling the statistical properties of the data (typically the correlation and informativeness of the features), it is also possible to generate synthetic data. This package also features helpers to fetch larger datasets commonly used by the machine learning community to benchmark algorithm on data that comes from the real world. A dataset is a dictionary-like object that holds all the data and some metadata about the data. This data is stored in the data member, which is a `n_samples` and `n_features` array. In the case of a supervised problem, one or more response variables are stored in the target member.

Data is returned in a `Bunch` object, a dictionary-like object that contains the following attributes:

- `data`: The data to learn
- `target`: The classification labels
- `target_names`: The meaning of the labels
- `feature_names`: The meaning of the features
- `DESCR`: The full description of the dataset

To confirm the content of the data, let's extract the dimensions:

```
print(BC.data.shape)
print(BC.target.shape)
```

The results are listed as follows:

```
(569, 30)
(569,)
```

To better understand the operations, we divide these data into X (predictors) and Y (target):

```
X = BC.data
Y = BC.target
```

At this point, we extract a series of statistics from the predictors using the tools that make available to us the `pandas` library.

> `pandas` is an open source, BSD-licensed library providing high-performance, easy-to-use data structures and data analysis tools for the Python programming language.

To use this function, we have to convert the input data from `numpy.darray` to `pandas` dataframe:

```
Xdata=pd.DataFrame(X)
print(Xdata.describe())
```

The results are shown as follows:

	0	1	2	3	4	\
count	569.000000	569.000000	569.000000	569.000000	569.000000	
mean	14.127292	19.289649	91.969033	654.889104	0.096360	
std	3.524049	4.301036	24.298981	351.914129	0.014064	
min	6.981000	9.710000	43.790000	143.500000	0.052630	
25%	11.700000	16.170000	75.170000	420.300000	0.086370	
50%	13.370000	18.840000	86.240000	551.100000	0.095870	
75%	15.780000	21.800000	104.100000	782.700000	0.105300	
max	28.110000	39.280000	188.500000	2501.000000	0.163400	

Due to space constraints, we have reported only the results for the first five predictors. As we can see, the variables have different ranges. When the predictors have different ranges, the impact on response variables by the feature having a greater numeric range could be more than the one having a less numeric range, and this could, in turn, impact the prediction accuracy. Our goal is to improve predictive accuracy and not allow a particular feature to impact the prediction due to a large numeric value range. Thus, we may need to scale values under different features such that they fall under a common range. Through this statistical procedure, it is possible to compare identical variables belonging to different distributions and also different variables or variables expressed in different units.

Remember, it is good practice to rescale the data before training a machine learning algorithm. With rescaling, data units are eliminated, allowing you to easily compare data from different locations.

In this case, we will use the min-max method (usually called **feature scaling**) to get all the scaled data in the range (0, 1). The formula to achieve this is:

$$x_{scaled} = \frac{x - x_{min}}{x_{max} - x_{min}}$$

The following command performs a feature scaling:

```
X = (X - np.min(X, 0)) / (np.max(X, 0) - np.min(X, 0))
```

`numpy.min()` and `numpy.max()` are used to calculate the minimum and maximum values of each database column.

Let's now split the data for the training and the test models. Training and testing the model forms the basis for further usage of the model for prediction in predictive analytics. Given a dataset of 100 rows of data, which includes the predictor and response variables, we split the dataset into a convenient ratio (say 80:20), and allocate 80 rows for training and 20 rows for testing. The rows are selected at random to reduce bias. Once the training data is available, the data is fed to the machine learning algorithm to get the massive universal function in place. To split the dataset, we will use the `sklearn.model_selection.train_test_split()` function:

```
X_train, X_test, Y_train, Y_test = train_test_split(X, Y, test_size=0.2,
random_state=1)
```

The `train_test_split()` function splits arrays or matrices into random train and test subsets. The first two arguments are `X` (predictors) and `Y` (target) numpy arrays. Allowed inputs are lists, `numpy` arrays, scipy-sparse matrices, or `pandas` dataframes. Then two options are added:

- `test_size`: This should be between 0.0 and 1.0 and represent the proportion of the dataset to include in the test split
- `random_state`: This is the seed used by the random number generator

Model fitting

We have previously said that RBM is often used as a feature in a wide variety of classification problems. It's time to see how to do it. The first thing to do is to use the `BernoulliRBM` function of the `sklearn.neural_network` module.

> `sklearn` is a free machine learning library for the Python programming language. It features various classification, regression, and clustering algorithms, including support vector machines, random forests, gradient boosting, k-means, and DBSCAN. And it is designed to interoperate with the Python numerical and scientific libraries NumPy and SciPy.

In the `sklearn` library, the `sklearn.neural_network` module includes models based on neural networks. In this module, the `BernoulliRBM` function fits a Bernoulli RBM. An RBM with binary visible units and binary hidden units is returned. The parameters are estimated using **Stochastic Maximum Likelihood (SML)**, also known as **Persistent Contrastive Divergence (PCD)**. First, we will set the architecture of the model:

```
RbmModel = BernoulliRBM(random_state=0, verbose=True)
```

Then, we will fit the model with the training data:

```
FitRbmModel = RbmModel.fit_transform(X_train, Y_train)
```

The `fit_transform` method fits the transformer to `X_train` and `Y_train` with optional parameter `fit_params`, and returns a transformed version of `X_train`. In this case, no optional parameters are used.

If you remember, our purpose is to use the `Rbm` model to extract the features that will then be used by the logistic regression model to classify the data. So, the first part has already been performed—we already have the features extracted in the `FitRbmModel` variable. The time has come to create the logistic regression model. To do this, we will use `LogisticRegression` function of the `sklearn.linear_model` module, as follows:

```
LogModel = linear_model.LogisticRegression()
```

We now set coefficients of the features in the decision function equal to the features extracted from the `rbm` model:

```
LogModel.coef_ = FitRbmModel
```

Now we can build the classifier. To do this, we will use the `Pipeline` function of the `sklearn.pipeline` module:

```
Classifier = Pipeline(steps=[('RbmModel', RbmModel), ('LogModel',
LogModel)])
```

The purpose of the `pipeline` is to assemble several steps that can be cross-validated together while setting different parameters. For this, it enables setting parameters of the various steps using their names, as in the previous code. A step's estimator may be replaced entirely by setting the parameter with its name to another estimator, or a transformer removed by setting to `None`. The classifier is now ready; we just have to train it:

```
LogModel.fit(X_train, Y_train)
Classifier.fit(X_train, Y_train)
```

First, the logistic regression model is trained and then the classifier. We just have to make predictions. Recall that for doing this, we have an unused dataset available: X_test and Y_test. To check the performance of the classifier, we will compare the forecasts with the real data:

```
print ("The RBM model:")
print ("Predict: ", Classifier.predict(X_test))
print ("Real:    ", Y_test)
```

The following screenshot shows the results returned:

```
The RBM model:
Predict: [1 1 1 1 1 0 1 1 1 0 0 1 1 1 1 1 0 1 1 0 1 1 1 0 0 1 0 1 0 1 1 1 1
 1 1 1 1 1 1 0 1 1 1 0 0 1 1 1 1 1 1 1 0 1 1 1 1 0 1 1 1 1 0
 1 0 1 1 0 1 0 1 0 1 1 0 1 0 1 1 0 1 1 0 0 1 1 1 1 1 1 1 1 1 1 1 0 0
 0 1 1]
Real:    [1 0 1 0 0 0 0 1 1 1 0 0 1 1 1 1 1 0 1 1 0 1 0 1 1 0 0 0 0 1 0 0 1 1 0
 1 0 1 1 1 1 1 0 1 1 1 0 0 0 1 1 1 1 0 1 1 1 0 1 1 1 1 0 1 1 1 1 0 0
 1 0 0 0 1 0 1 0 1 0 1 1 0 1 0 1 1 0 1 1 0 0 1 1 1 1 1 1 1 1 1 1 1 0 0 0
 1 1 1]
```

Finally, to better understand the model performance, we will calculate the confusion matrix. In a confusion matrix, our classification results are compared to real data. The strength of a confusion matrix is that it identifies the nature of the classification errors as well as their quantities. In this matrix, the diagonal cells show the number of cases that were correctly classified; all the other cells show the misclassified cases. To calculate the confusion matrix, we can use the ConfusionMatrix() function contained in pandas library as follows:

```
CM = ConfusionMatrix(Y_test, Classifier.predict(X_test))
CM.print_stats()
```

In the following code, the results returned by the ConfusionMatrix() function are shown:

```
population: 114
P: 72
N: 42
PositiveTest: 87
NegativeTest: 27
TP: 71
TN: 26
```

```
FP: 16
FN: 1
TPR: 0.9861111111111112
TNR: 0.6190476190476191
PPV: 0.8160919540229885
NPV: 0.9629629629629629
FPR: 0.38095238095238093
FDR: 0.1839080459770115
FNR: 0.013888888888888888
ACC: 0.8508771929824561
F1_score: 0.8930817610062893
MCC: 0.6866235389841608
informedness: 0.6051587301587302
markedness: 0.7790549169859515
prevalence: 0.631578947368421
LRP: 2.588541666666667
LRN: 0.022435897435897433
DOR: 115.37500000000003
FOR: 0.037037037037037035
```

Several bits of information are returned; in particular, we can notice that the accuracy of the model is 0.85.

Autoencoder with Keras

As we said previously, an autoencoder is a neural network whose purpose is to code its input into small dimensions and the result obtained to be able to reconstruct the input itself. Autoencoders are made up of the union of the following two subnets: encoder and decoder. To these functions is added another; it's a loss function calculated as the distance between the amount of information loss between the compressed representation of the data and the decompressed representation. The encoder and the decoder will be differentiable with respect to the distance function, so the parameters of the encoding/decoding functions can be optimized to minimize the loss of reconstruction, using the gradient stochastic.

Load data

This is a database of handwritten digits consisting of 60,000 28 x 28 grayscale images of the 10 digits, along with a test set of 10,000 images. This dataset is already available in the Keras library. The following diagram shows a sample of images of 0-8 from the MNIST dataset:

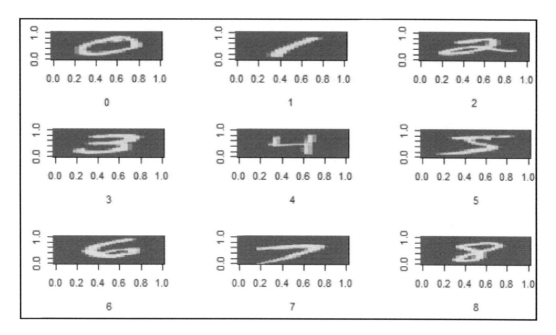

As always, we will analyze the code line by line. In the first part of the code, we import the libraries we will use later:

```
from keras.layers import Input, Dense
from keras.models import Model
```

This code imports the following function:

- The Input function is used to instantiate a Keras tensor. A Keras tensor is a tensor object from the underlying backend (Theano, TensorFlow, or CNTK). We augment it with certain attributes that allow us to build a Keras model just by knowing the inputs and outputs of the model.
- The Dense function is used instantiate a regular densely connected NN layer.
- The Model function is used to define the model. The model is the thing that you can summarize, fit, evaluate, and use to make predictions. Keras provides a `Model` class that you can use to create a model from your created layers. It only requires that you specify the input and output layers.

To import the dataset, simply use this code:

```
from keras.datasets import mnist
(x_train, y_train), (x_test, y_test) = mnist.load_data()
```

The following tuples are returned:

- `x_train`, `x_test`: A `uint8` array of grayscale image data with shape (num_samples, 28, 28)
- `y_train`, `y_test`: A `uint8` array of digit labels (integers in range 0-9) with shape (num_samples)

Now we have to normalize all values between 0 and 1. The Mnist images are stored in pixel format, where each pixel (totally 28 x 28) is stored as an 8-bit integer giving a range of possible values from 0 to 255. Typically, zero is taken to be black, and 255 is taken to be white. The values in between make up the different shades of gray. Now, to normalize all values between 0 and 1, simply divide each value by 255. So the pixel containing the value 255 will become 1 and the one containing 0 will remain as such; in between lie all the other values:

```
x_train = x_train.astype('float32') / 255
x_test = x_test.astype('float32') / 255
```

By using the `astype()` function, we have converted the input data in `float32` (single precision float: sign bit, 8-bits exponent, 23 bits mantissa). As we said, each sample (image) consists of a 28 x 28 matrix. To reduce the dimensionality, we will flatten the 28 x 28 images into vectors of size 784:

```
x_train = x_train.reshape((len(x_train), np.prod(x_train.shape[1:])))
x_test = x_test.reshape((len(x_test), np.prod(x_test.shape[1:])))
```

The `reshape()` function gives a new shape to an array without changing its data. The new shape should be compatible with the original shape. The first dimension of the new shape is the number of observations returned from the `len()` function (`len(x_train)` and `len(x_test)`). The second dimension represents the product of the last two dimensions of the starting data (28 x 28 = 784). To better understand this transformation, we print the shape of the starting dataset first and then the shape of the transformed dataset:

```
print (x_train.shape)
print (x_test.shape)
```

The following are the results before and after the dataset reshape:

```
(60000, 28, 28)
(10000, 28, 28)
(60000, 784)
(10000, 784)
```

Keras model overview

There are two types of models available in Keras:

- Sequential model
- Keras functional API

Let us take a look at each one in detail in the following sections.

Sequential model

The Sequential model is a linear stack of layers. We can create a Sequential model by passing a list of layer instances to the constructor as follows:

```
from keras.models import Sequential
from keras.layers import Dense, Activation
model = Sequential([
    Dense(32, input_shape=(784,)),
    Activation('relu'),
    Dense(10),
    Activation('softmax'),
])
```

We can also simply add layers via the .add() method:

```
model = Sequential()
model.add(Dense(32, input_dim=784))
model.add(Activation('relu'))
```

This type of model needs to know what input shape it should expect. For this reason, the first layer in a Sequential model needs to receive information about its input shape. There are several possible ways to do this:

- Pass an input_shape argument to the first layer
- Specify of their input shape via the input_dim and input_length arguments
- Pass a batch_size argument to a layer

Keras functional API

Another way to define a model is the Keras functional API. The Keras functional API is the way to go for defining complex models, such as multi-output models, directed acyclic graphs, or models with shared layers. For example, to define a densely connected network, simply type the following code:

```
from keras.layers import Input, Dense
from keras.models import Model
inputs = Input(shape=(784,))
x = Dense(64, activation='relu')(inputs)
x = Dense(64, activation='relu')(x)
predictions = Dense(10, activation='softmax')(x)
model = Model(inputs=inputs, outputs=predictions)
model.compile(optimizer='rmsprop',
              loss='categorical_crossentropy',
              metrics=['accuracy'])
model.fit(data, labels)
```

In the following section, we will dive deep into this type of model by applying it to our example.

Define model architecture

Now we will build the model using the Keras functional API. As we saw before, first we have to define the input:

```
InputModel = Input(shape=(784,))
```

This returns a tensor that represents our input placeholder. Later, we will use this placeholder to define a `Model`. At this point, we can add layers to the architecture of our model:

```
EncodedLayer = Dense(32, activation='relu')(InputModel)
```

The Dense class is used to define a fully connected layer. We have specified the number of neurons in the layer as the first argument (32), the activation function using the activation argument (`relu`), and finally the input tensor (`InputModel`) of the layer.

> Remember that given an input x, the encoder encodes it in a variable z, also called **latent variable**. z usually has much smaller dimensions than x; in our case, we have passed from 784 to 32 with a compression factor of 24.5.

Now let's add the decoding layer:

```
DecodedLayer = Dense(784, activation='sigmoid')(EncodedLayer)
```

This layer is the lossy reconstruction of the input. For another time, we have used the Dense class with 784 neurons (dimensionality of the output space), the `sigmoid` activation function, and `EncodedLayer` output as input. Now we have to instantiate a model as follows:

```
AutoencoderModel = Model(InputModel, DecodedLayer)
```

This model will include all layers required in the computation of `DecodedLayer` (output) given `InputModel` (input). In the following are listed some useful attributes of Model class:

- `model.layers` is a flattened list of layers comprising the model graph
- `model.inputs` is the list of input tensors
- `model.outputs` is the list of output tensors

So, we have to configure the model for training. To do this, we will use the `compile` method as follows:

```
AutoencoderModel.compile(optimizer='adadelta', loss='binary_crossentropy')
```

This method configures the model for training. Only two arguments are used:

- `optimizer`: String (name of optimizer) or optimizer instance.
- `loss`: String (name of objective function) or objective function. If the model has multiple outputs, you can use a different loss on each output by passing a dictionary or a list of losses. The loss value that will be minimized by the model will then be the sum of all individual losses.

We have used adadelta optimizer. This method dynamically adapts over time, using only first-order information, and has minimal computational overhead beyond vanilla stochastic gradient descent. The method requires no manual tuning of the learning rate and appears robust to noisy gradient information, different model architecture choices, various data modalities, and selection of hyperparameters.

Furthermore, we have used `binary_crossentropy` as a `loss` function. Loss functions are computationally feasible functions representing the price paid for inaccuracy of predictions in classification problems.

At this point, we can train the model:

```
history = AutoencoderModel.fit(x_train, x_train,
                batch_size=256,
                epochs=100,
                shuffle=True,
                validation_data=(x_test, x_test))
```

The fit method trains the model for a fixed number of epochs (iterations on a dataset). In the following, the arguments passed are explained to better understand the meaning:

- x: A Numpy array of training data (if the model has a single input), or list of Numpy arrays (if the model has multiple inputs). If input layers in the model are named, you can also pass a dictionary mapping input names to Numpy arrays. x can be None (default) if feeding from framework-native tensors (for example,. TensorFlow data tensors).

- y: A Numpy array of target (label) data if the model has a single output, or a list of Numpy arrays if the model has multiple outputs. If output layers in the model are named, you can also pass a dictionary mapping output names to Numpy arrays. y can be None (default) if feeding from framework-native tensors (for example, TensorFlow data tensors).

- batch_size: Integer or None. This is the number of samples per gradient update. If unspecified, batch_size will default to 32.

- epochs: An Integer. It is the number of epochs to train the model. An epoch is an iteration over the entire x and y data provided. Note that in conjunction with initial_epoch, epochs is to be understood as the final epoch. The model is not trained for a number of iterations given by epochs, but merely until the epoch of index epochs is reached.

- shuffle: A boolean to decide whether to shuffle the training data before each epoch or str (for batch). batch is a special option for dealing with the limitations of HDF5 data; it shuffles in batch-sized chunks. It has no effect when steps_per_epoch is anything other than None.

- validation_data: A tuple (x_val and y_val) or tuple (x_val, y_val, and val_sample_weights) on which to evaluate the loss and any model metrics at the end of each epoch. The model will not be trained on this data. validation_data will override validation_split.

A `History` object is returned. Its `history.history` attribute is a record of training loss values and metrics values at successive epochs, as well as validation loss values and validation metrics values (if applicable).

Our model is now ready, so we can use it to automatically rebuild the handwritten digits. To do this, we will use the `predict` method:

```
DecodedDigits = AutoencoderModel.predict(x_test)
```

This method generates output predictions for the input samples (`x_test`). Running this example, you should see a message for each of the 100 epochs, printing the loss and accuracy for each, followed by a final evaluation of the trained model on the training dataset. This is shown in the following screenshot:

```
Prompt dei comandi
Epoch 88/100
60000/60000 [==============================] - 6s 100us/step - loss: 0.0979 - val_loss: 0.0963
Epoch 89/100
60000/60000 [==============================] - 6s 98us/step - loss: 0.0979 - val_loss: 0.0962
Epoch 90/100
60000/60000 [==============================] - 6s 101us/step - loss: 0.0978 - val_loss: 0.0962
Epoch 91/100
60000/60000 [==============================] - 6s 102us/step - loss: 0.0977 - val_loss: 0.0961
Epoch 92/100
60000/60000 [==============================] - 6s 103us/step - loss: 0.0976 - val_loss: 0.0960
Epoch 93/100
60000/60000 [==============================] - 6s 108us/step - loss: 0.0976 - val_loss: 0.0960
Epoch 94/100
60000/60000 [==============================] - 7s 118us/step - loss: 0.0975 - val_loss: 0.0959
Epoch 95/100
60000/60000 [==============================] - 6s 106us/step - loss: 0.0974 - val_loss: 0.0959
Epoch 96/100
60000/60000 [==============================] - 7s 113us/step - loss: 0.0974 - val_loss: 0.0958
Epoch 97/100
60000/60000 [==============================] - 7s 121us/step - loss: 0.0973 - val_loss: 0.0957
Epoch 98/100
60000/60000 [==============================] - 8s 141us/step - loss: 0.0973 - val_loss: 0.0957
Epoch 99/100
60000/60000 [==============================] - 8s 125us/step - loss: 0.0972 - val_loss: 0.0956
Epoch 100/100
60000/60000 [==============================] - 7s 120us/step - loss: 0.0971 - val_loss: 0.0956

C:\pythonscript\GEN>
```

To get an idea of how the `loss` function varies during the epochs, it can be useful create a plot of loss on the training and validation datasets over training epochs. To do this, we will use the `Matplotlib` library as follows:

```
plt.plot(history.history['loss'])
plt.plot(history.history['val_loss'])
plt.title('Autoencoder Model loss')
plt.ylabel('loss')
plt.xlabel('epoch')
plt.legend(['train', 'test'], loc='upper left')
plt.show()
```

A plot of loss on the training and validation datasets over training epochs is shown in the following graph:

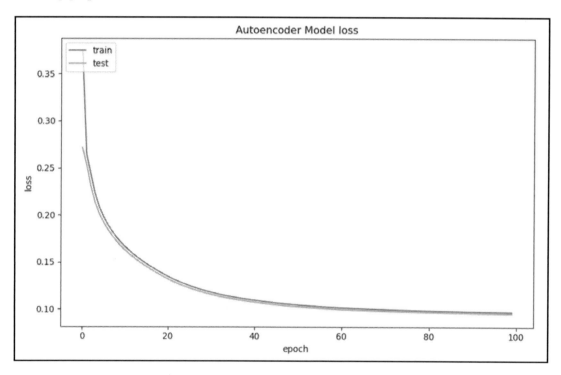

Our work is done; we just have to verify the results obtained. We can print on screen the starting handwriting digits and those reconstructed from our model. Of course, we will do it only for some of the 60,000 digits contained in the dataset; in fact, we will limit ourselves to display the first five. We will also use the `Matplotlib` library in this case:

```
n=5
plt.figure(figsize=(20, 4))
for i in range(n):
    ax = plt.subplot(2, n, i + 1)
    plt.imshow(x_test[i].reshape(28, 28))
    plt.gray()
    ax.get_xaxis().set_visible(False)
    ax.get_yaxis().set_visible(False)
    ax = plt.subplot(2, n, i + 1 + n)
    plt.imshow(DecodedDigits[i].reshape(28, 28))
    plt.gray()
    ax.get_xaxis().set_visible(False)
    ax.get_yaxis().set_visible(False)
plt.show()
```

The results are shown in the following screenshot:

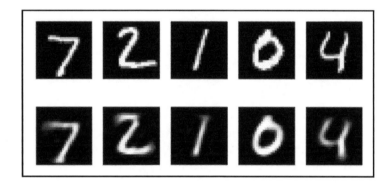

As you can see, the result is very close to the original, meaning that the model works well.

Magenta

On June 1, 2016, Google launched the Magenta project, a research project that aims to allow the creation of art and music in an autonomous way through the use of AI. Based on the TensorFlow platform, Magenta aims to publish code in open source mode on GitHub to allow developers to achieve increasingly striking and advanced results.

The project is a brainchild of the Google Brain team, a deep learning AI research team at Google. It combines open-ended machine learning research with system engineering and Google-scale computing resources.

The Magenta project has set itself two ambitious goals: to develop machine learning for art and music, and to build a community of people interested in this topic. Machine learning has long been used in different contexts, in particular for speech recognition and translation of languages. Magenta was created to concentrate activity on previously unexplored fields such as the generation of art in the broad sense. To do this, Magenta wanted to create a physical place, where all people united by the same interest (that is, generation of art) could exchange ideas and products. In other words, a community of artists, programmers, and researchers of machine learning.

For more information, refer to the official website of the project at the following URL: `https://magenta.tensorflow.org/`.

The NSynth dataset

From reading the previous chapters, we have now understood that, to correctly train a machine learning algorithm, it is necessary to have a dataset containing an important number of observations. Recently, the increased use of generative models has been applied to images thanks to the availability of high-quality image datasets, which therefore correspond to a significant data set. With this in mind, the Google Brain team has made NSynth available. It's a large-scale, high-quality set of musical notes that is an order of magnitude larger than comparable public datasets. The aim is to have a significant audio dataset in order to develop generative models with better performance.

The NSynth dataset was introduced by Jesse Engel et al. in the article named *Neural Audio Synthesis of Musical Notes with WaveNet Autoencoders*.

NSynth is an audio dataset containing 305,979 musical notes, each with a unique tone, tone, and envelope. For 1,006 tools from commercial sample libraries, the Google Brain team generated 4 seconds of 16 kHz monophonic audio fragments, called **notes**, spanning each step of a standard MIDI piano or (21-108) and five different speeds (25, 50, 75, 100, and 127). The note was kept for the first 3 seconds and allowed to fall for the final second.

The Google Brain team also annotated each of the notes with three additional pieces of information based on a combination of human evaluation and heuristic algorithms:

- **Source**: The method of sound production for the note's instrument. This can be one of acoustic or electronic for instruments that were recorded from acoustic or electronic instruments respectively, or synthetic for synthesized instruments.
- **Family**: The high-level family of which the note's instrument is a member. Each instrument is a member of exactly one family.
- **Qualities**: Sonic qualities of the note. Each note is annotated with zero or more qualities.

The NSynth dataset can be downloaded in two formats:

- TFRecord files of serialized TensorFlow example protocol buffers with one Example proto per note
- JSON files containing non-audio features alongside 16-bit PCM WAV audio files

The full dataset is split into three sets:

- **Train**: A training set with 289,205 examples. Instruments do not overlap with valid or test.
- **Valid**: A validation set with 12,678 examples. Instruments do not overlap with train.
- **Test**: A test set with 4,096 examples. Instruments do not overlap with train.

For more information and to download the dataset, refer to the official website of the project at the following URL: `https://magenta.tensorflow.org/datasets/nsynth`.

Summary

In this chapter, we explored one of the most interesting research sites on modeling with neural networks. First we saw an introduction to unsupervised learning algorithms. Unsupervised learning is a machine learning technique that, starting from a series of inputs (system experience), will be able to reclassify and organize on the basis of common characteristics to try to make predictions on subsequent inputs. Unlike supervised learning, only unlabeled examples are provided to the learner during the learning process, as the classes are not known a priori but must be learned automatically.

So, we analyzed different types of generative models. A Boltzmann machine is a probabilistic graphic model that can be interpreted as a stochastic neural network. In practice, a Boltzmann machine is a model (including a certain number of parameters) that, when applied to a data distribution, is able to provide a representation. This model can be used to extract important aspects of an unknown distribution (target distribution) starting only from a sample of the latter.

An autoencoder is a neural network whose purpose is to code its input into small dimensions and the result obtained to be able to reconstruct the input itself. The purpose of autoencoders is not simply to perform a sort of compression of the input or look for an approximation of the identity function; but there are techniques that allow us to direct the model (starting from a hidden layer of reduced dimensions) to give greater importance to some data properties. Thus they give rise to different representations based on the same data.

GAN is a generative model consisting of two networks that are jointly trained, called **generator** and **discriminator**. The dynamics between these two networks is like a forger and an investigator. The forger tries to produce faithful imitations of authentic works of art while the investigator tries to distinguish the fakes from the originals.

Then, we showed how to implement some examples: feature extraction using RBM and autoencoder with Keras. Finally, we introduced the Nsynth dataset and the Google Magenta project.

17
Chatbots

The era of chatbots has now arrived, a new technological phenomenon that has helped generate a new way of interacting with machines, consequently creating businesses. Chatbots are robots that interact with users through a chat and are able to assist them by carrying out extremely limited tasks: providing information on a current account, buying a ticket, receiving news about the weather, and so on.

A chatbot processes the text presented by the user, before responding based on a complex set of algorithms that interpret and identify what the user has said. After deducting what the user requires, it determines a set of appropriate responses based on the information extracted from the context. Some chatbots offer an extraordinarily authentic conversational experience, in which it is very difficult to determine if the agent is a bot or a human being.

Chatbots are also one of the most exciting innovations brought about by AI. In this chapter, after introducing the main concepts on which all of this technology is based, we will present the methods for building contextual chatbots and implement a simple chatbot end-to-end application on GCP.

Topics covered:

- Chatbot fundamentals
- Chatbot design techniques
- Natural language processing
- Google Cloud Dialogflow
- Chatbot building and implementation on GCP

At the end of the chapter, the reader will have completed a hands-on introduction to chatbots and learned how to train a contextual chatbot while implementing it in a real web application.

Chatbots fundamentals

Chat bots, or chatbots, are programs that can interact through a chat with a human being, simulating their behavior. A conversation is then established between the human and the robot. Since the first developments in computer science, in collaboration with other disciplines, scholars have tried to reproduce typically human cognitive processes through the use of machines. They are usually used for simple and repetitive activities, which may otherwise take a lot of time or which are not worth assigning a human resource.

Given their complexity, it is obvious that, in this case, you cannot speak of a satisfactory simulation of people's own behavior, but can nevertheless begin to refer to the concept of AI.

The bot can execute a scheme and show its operation. Bots can do anything, from responding to messages automatically to allowing online purchases. They can receive news of any kind, release weather conditions, or show music videos, all exclusively via chat.

There are several platforms that implement the ability to use bots. These include: Telegram, Skype, Messenger, Slack, SMS, and email. The bots allow you to use these platforms—applications already known and used by the user for other features (such as messaging)—to perform within them the most disparate functions, saving the user's effort to use and install additional applications on the user's device.

Chatbot history

The history of chatbots begins much earlier than you may think. We are in England in the mid-20th century when Alan Turing, asking the question *Can machines think?*, proposes a test that links intelligence to the ability to hold a conversation. Since then, the challenge of creating software capable of simulating human language in an increasingly accurate manner has never stopped.

The imitation game

In the 1950s, Alan Turing wrote an article called *Computing machinery and intelligence*, in which the problem was about establishing a criterion for determining whether a machine can think. The criterion is based on *The imitation game*, in which there is a computer **A**, a human **B**, and another human **C** (the interrogator). Human **C** must establish who is **A** and who is **B**. The interrogator asks both of them questions, to which **A** and **B** respond in writing. Computer **A** wins the game when **C** mistakes in judging **A**'s identity, believing it to be human. The following diagram shows an imitation game scheme:

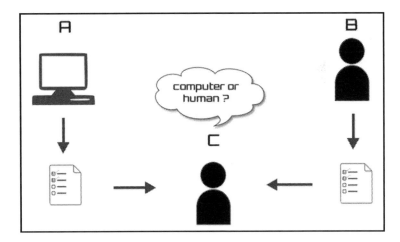

Turing's game—despite numerous criticisms claiming that this criterion is not enough to establish whether a machine can think—has given rise to a challenge over the last decades that has led to the creation of software simulating human language in a way that is more and more accurate.

 In 1990, a competition called the **Loebner prize** was established, based on the Turing test, to reward the computer whose behavior is most similar to human thought. This competition takes place every year. Here's the official website of the competition: `http://www.aisb.org.uk/events/loebner-prize`.

Eliza

In 1966, Joseph Weizenbaum created Eliza, a program that set out to create a parody of a conversation between a therapist and his patient in their initial phase. In it, an exchange of simple questions that do not require great emotional depth takes place. In the following screenshot, a simple Eliza chatbot is shown:

```
EEEEEEEE  L          IIIIIII  ZZZZZZZ        AAA
E         L             I           Z       A   A
E         L             I          Z       A     A
EEEEE     L             I         Z        A     A
E         L             I        Z         AAAAAAA
E         L             I       Z          A     A
EEEEEEEE  LLLLLLL    IIIIIII  ZZZZZZ       A     A

ELIZA > (PLEASE TYPE IN ALL CAPS) WHAT'S YOUR NAME DEAR ?
AMIT
ELIZA > HI, I'M ELIZA. WHAT DO YOU WANT TO TALK ABOUT ?
AMIT > CAN I TALK ABOUT MY PROBLEM ?
ELIZA > SURE...!
AMIT > DUE TO ON GOING EXAMS IN COLLEGE, I HAVE A LOT OF STRESS.
ELIZA > PLEASE RELAX A LITTLE. SLEEP WELL.
AMIT > THANKS FOR YOUR ADVICE.
ELIZA > NO MENTION.
AMIT > BYE
ELIZA > BYE AND KEEP IN TOUCH...
```

Eliza relies on the use of regular expressions to transform user input into its outputs, so as to give continuity to the conversation as well as apparent consistency. At other times, it produces no contextual observations but stuff that is perfectly in line with the attitude of a psychotherapist, such as *very interesting, please, go on,* or *can you elaborate on that?*

Parry

Remaining in the medical field, Parry simulated the behavior of a person with paranoid schizophrenia. It was developed in 1972 by psychiatrist Kenneth Colby as a practice tool for his students before they could deal with real patients.

In a slight variation of the Turing test, psychiatrists were asked to read Parry's transcripts and those of real patients to distinguish which of the two they came from. It was an incredible result for that time; the psychiatrists managed to identify a difference in the behavior only 48 percent of the time.

In January 1973, as a demonstration during an international computer conference, computer science pioneer Vint Cerf decided to take bots to their logical conclusion. Using ARPANET, he set up a conversation between Eliza and Parry. It was a bicoastal meeting of the computer minds; Eliza was based at MIT and Parry at Stanford. The following is a brief excerpt of the conversation between the two bots:

- Eliza: *Good Evening. Tell me your problems. Please terminate input with a period or a question mark.*
- Parry: *People get on my nerves sometimes.*
- Eliza: *I am not sure I understand you fully.*
- Parry: *You should pay more attention.*
- Eliza: *Suppose you should pay more attention.*
- Parry: *You're entitled to your own opinion.*
- Eliza: *What makes you think I am entitled to my own opinion?*
- Parry: *It bothers me just to be around people in general.*
- Eliza: *Please go on.*
- Parry: *I went to the track at Bay Meadows a while back.*
- Eliza: *What does that suggest to you?*
- Parry: *I went to the races.*

Jabberwacky

Jabberwacky was created by programmer Rollo Carpenter in 1988. The aim of the bot was to pass the Turing test. Jabberwacky was able to simulate a human voice in a humorous way. Currently, developments are still ongoing on the bot, aimed at implementing the system on robots or talking pets, based on sound learning.

This is a bot based on machine learning; in fact, to interact with us, it uses only the material learned and borrows some of our intelligence while increasing its knowledge. Without hardcoded rules, it is based entirely on the principles of feedback.

Cleverbot is a variant of Jabberwacky released in 1997 that achieved great results; in 2011, it participated in a Turing test at IIT Guwahati in India and was considered a human at a 59.3% probability.

Dr. Sbaitso

Dr. Sbaitso was also designed to simulate the behavior of a psychologist able to solve emotional problems of users, and was usable by personal computers with the MS-DOS operating system. It was developed by Creative Labs in 1992, with the aim of demonstrating the ability of sound cards to generate a synthesized voice. The following screenshot shows the MS-DOS window with the welcome message in Dr. Sbaitso:

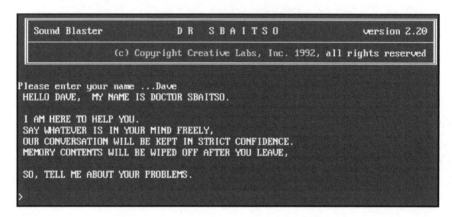

Most of the questions were WHY DO YOU FEEL THAT WAY?. Thus avoiding more complicated interactions. When he received a sentence he could not understand, he usually answered THAT'S NOT MY PROBLEM.

ALICE

Artificial Linguistic Internet Computer Entity (**ALICE**) was created as open source software based on **Natural Language Processing** (**NLP**). It was designed with the **Artificial Intelligence Markup Language** (**AIML**) by scientist Richard S. Wallace in 1995. Alice's interpretation system was based on a minimal approach. The meaning of a sentence was elaborated through specific keywords or terms (roots), avoiding in-depth and complex analyzes. Alice won the Loebner prize three times: in 2000, 2001, and 2004.

SmarterChild

SmarterChild was a very successful chatbot and was available on AOL instant messenger and MSN messenger. Developed by ActiveBuddy Inc. in 2001, it was used by over 30 million users. From the rapid success of SmarterChild are derived marketing-oriented bots for Radiohead, Austin Powers, Intel, Keebler, Sporting News, and others.

IBM Watson

Watson is an AI system developed by IBM in 2006, able to answer questions expressed in natural language. In the beginning, Watson was created to compete for an American television quiz called **Jeopardy!** At the first participation, however, it managed to answer only 35% of the questions. Following several improvements by an IBM team, Watson tried again in 2011, and this time it managed to defeat the human champions of the quiz.

During the game, Watson worked without being connected to the internet, exploiting an occupation of 4 terabytes of disk space. Later, it was used in many other completely different contexts, such as managing lung cancer treatment decisions at the Memorial Sloan-Kettering Cancer Center.

Building a bot

In the first chatbots, quite simple algorithms were used to analyze the input message and return an output response; these algorithms were intended to simulate the computer's understanding of what was proposed in the input by providing consistent responses as output. As time passed and technology evolved, more and more sophisticated AI methods were created, with which the chatbots were able to establish conversations closer and closer to real ones between humans. From what basics is it necessary to start in order to correctly design chatbots? Fundamental topics in the bot building are intents, entities, and context. In the following section, we will analyze them to understand how to use them efficiently.

Intents

The intent of a user is their purpose, the ultimate goal. Examples are ordering something, wanting to activate something on the user window, looking for shows, or simply saying goodbye. A chatbot should be able to perform some actions based on the intent it detects from the user's message.

Suppose we want to create a chatbot for a store that sells IT-related products. As a preliminary procedure, it is necessary to consider what actions the chatbot will be able to execute once requested by the user. For example, the chatbot will need to respond to the user with appropriate information when a user asks to see the products the store sells by supplying it: **I want to buy a mouse**. Similarly, when the user sends a message, such as **Looking for a store in Rome**, the chatbot should be able to locate all the stores near that particular location. To perform each of these actions, the chatbot must be able to distinguish between the two intentions of the user: searching for a product or a point of sale. In the following diagram, two possible intents are expressed by the user:

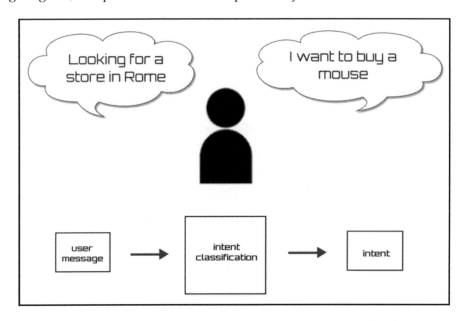

Detecting intents from the user's message is a very common problem in the field of machine learning. This is the technique called **text classification**, in which the objective of the program is to classify documents/phrases in several classes that represent the intent of the user. Understanding what the user's request is is the intelligent part of the chatbot because there are many ways in which a request can be expressed in natural language. The chatbot will try to interpret the user's request by identifying the closest intent. Naturally, the association will not always be precise; in fact, a ranking of possible interpretations is returned. But from this point of view the answers can be improved by providing more alternative examples of the same requests.

Entities

Entities are the relevant subjects contained in the message coming from the user, for example, an object, a color, or a date. If the intent is to activate something on a web page, the user may also indicate what, like a button or a window. Entities are therefore the keywords that the chatbot can recognize. Thanks to these entities, the chatbot is able to identify the topic of the conversation, thus providing targeted information as output. In the following diagram, two possible entities are identified by the chatbot:

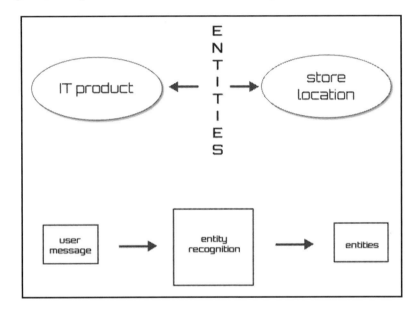

Suppose we had the following message as an input: I want to buy a monitor. It is clear that the user wants to buy an IT product, but if the bot is not able to identify the type of product that the user is trying to buy, the information returned will be about all types of IT products, many of which are not of interest to the user. If the chatbot is able to detect that the user is trying to buy a monitor, then it will only return information on this type of IT product, thus reducing the options available. And this is to the user's benefit.

Context

Chatbots were created with the aim of simplifying and automating processes. So a chatbot fails if it complicates a process previously managed by humans in a simple way. For example, suppose you search for weather information. If you use the phone to request information, the service provider may use your phone number to look up your account information as your address. The same procedure should apply to chatbots. The context of a chatbot is extremely important if you aim to create a robot that is more or less efficient than using the phone.

When we talk about context in terms of chatbots, we refer to the fact that the bot is able to identify what it already knows and able to look only for the unknown information it needs to provide an appropriate solution. In this case, it has to provide information on weather in that area in the coming days. If this weather information chatbot uses the context appropriately, then it should not ask for information it already knows. The use of information already held by the bot, thanks to the maintenance of the context, makes the procedure for returning information much faster.

Once the intents and entities are put into the system, the logical flow of the conversation is created, because what distinguishes a conversation from simple **Frequently Asked Questions (FAQs)** is the context. Thanks to the context, it is possible to connect the user's current input to the previously mentioned one.

The context is passed back and forth between the chatbot and the user. It is the responsibility of the chatbot to maintain the context from one shift to the next of the conversation. A context includes a unique identifier for each conversation with a user, as well as a counter that is incremented at each turn of the conversation. If we do not preserve the context, every round of input seems to be the beginning of a new conversation.

Chatbots

We do not have to start from scratch to design a chatbot. In fact, we can use the experience gained over time by programmers in the development of applications that we have analyzed in previous sections. All the information collected represents a know-how from which we can draw useful cues for our applications.

Essential requirements

To start, we can take a look at the requirements that a great chatbot must fulfill to ensure the success of the service it provides. The following list mentions some key elements of chatbot design that we must keep in mind:

- **Guarantee minimum manual effort by the user**: This represents the starting point in the design of a chatbot. For the success of the service, it is essential that the user is accompanied in their choices by minimizing manual intervention. This is achieved by drastically reducing the number of touches, keystrokes, or mouse clicks required to help the bot determine the best solution to the problem. To do this, you need to ensure that most of the options are provided by the same chatbot, with the user simply having to select the right option. In this way, considerable time savings are achieved in the interaction between user and chatbot.
- **Predict the right options**: To make sure that the system displays only the options related to that context, the right options must be provided through a series of choices. To achieve this, the system must be able to identify the user's needs. User needs must be identified with the least number of questions and manual efforts by users.
- **Customization of the chatbot**: This is the possibility to construct a different user chatbot interaction depending on the characteristics of the user of the service. For example, it is possible to make the system memorize user profiles, previous interactions, the interactions of other users in the system, the current context and environmental know-how. Each of these attributes must be understood together with others to truly understand users and what they may need now.

The importance of the text

Before any text interpretation strategies can be applied, it is necessary to carry out a series of elaborations. In particular, the following phases are important:

- **Text cleaning**: The text is cleaned of all the elements that can alter subsequent analyzes (for example, spaces at the beginning and at the end of the message)
- **Verification of the characters of the text**: It checks whether the text contains characters equivalent to others that could invalidate subsequent analysis
- **Text normalization**: Transformation of uppercase characters into lowercase is done so that the same word written with a capital letter instead of lowercase is interpreted in the same way (this approach is not always optimal since capitalization can sometimes have a discriminatory value)

Word transposition

This technique has been widely used by chatbots of the Eliza type. It consists of reformulating the input message to generate a corresponding output. For example, if the user writes *you are a chatbot* the answer of the chatbot will be *so you think I'm a chatbot*.

The substitutions that are made using this technique concern mainly personal pronouns (you → me) and verbs (you are → I am), therefore transforming all forms in the first person into forms in the second person and vice versa.

Checking a value against a pattern

Anyone who has ever used word processing programs has had to face the problem of searching for a text string within the period. Perhaps without knowing it, we came across the pattern matching problem. Pattern matching is a procedure in which you check whether a token sequence has a certain pattern, that is, a combination of characters that respects a certain pattern.

A lexical token, or simply token, is a string with an assigned and thus identified meaning. It is structured as a pair consisting of a token name and an optional token value. The token name is a category of lexical unit.

As for the interpretation of the inputs by a chatbot, pattern matching can be useful for recognizing certain message sets. For example, thanks to pattern matching, you can answer *Hello!* to all the messages that contain the word *hello* or *hi*; or you can recognize that a message is of question type by checking whether the last token is *?*.

A very useful tool for pattern recognition is regular expression, which offers a notation system for identifying sets of strings.

Maintaining context

Storing the context is a strategy used to keep track of what has been said before, and to be able to reuse it for the conversation. This becomes necessary when the response of the chatbot cannot be based only on the last message sent by the user but must draw information from some previous message.

To better understand the usefulness of context management, let's take an example:

- User: *My name is Giuseppe.*
- Chatbot: *Okay Giuseppe.*
- User: *What is my name?*
- Chatbot: *You told me before calling you Giuseppe.*

If the user has not yet declared his name, the chatbot's answer will have to be something like:

- User: *What is my name?*
- Chatbot: *You still have not told me your name.*

It is therefore easy to understand how to manage the context to formulate an answer. This is extremely important in order to give the chatbot a much less mechanical and more human appearance.

Having memory of previous messages is also useful for detecting when the user sends a message repeatedly, or it can prevent the same chatbot from sending the same message by checking the value of the last message before choosing the next one.

Chatbots architecture

The main module of a chatbot is the dialogue manager. This module controls the flow of human-machine interaction. It receives the user's request as input and decides what the system's response should be. It will memorize the dialogue context in some form, for example, through pairs of key values, to manage the conversation on several steps between the user and the system.

For the dialogue manager to be able to choose the right answer for the request made by the user, it is necessary to understand the user's intention. In the most advanced chatbots, which are able to understand human language, the user's expressions will be translated into a semantic representation consisting of user intent and entity. This operation will be carried out by a module of natural language comprehension. This module must be previously trained to understand a series of user intent previously identified by the developer. This module is based on the **natural language understanding** (**NLU**) component.

In the case of voice input, the system must also be equipped with a voice recognition module that can translate the input into text before passing it to the natural language comprehension module. At the end of the operation, the system response (output) must first be treated with a speech synthesizer module that converts the textual response of the system into speech.

When user input is understood, the dialogue manager takes actions. To perform the action or generate the response, the dialogue manager retrieves the required information from the data sources. After this, a response message is generated by the response generation component and sent back to the user. The following diagram is a chatbot architecture scheme:

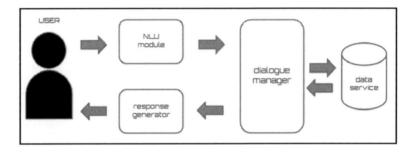

To keep track of the context, the dialogue manager keeps the conversation status to know if the request is related to the previous conversation or introduces a new topic into the conversation.

Natural language processing

NLP is a field of computational linguistics that deals with the interaction between computers and natural languages.

Computational linguistics deals with analysis and processing of natural language through the use of computer methodologies. It focuses on the development of descriptive formalisms of the functioning of natural language, such that they can be transformed into programs that can be executed by computers.

Traditionally, computers require that you interact with them through a programming language, so it should be a way of communicating that is precise, unambiguous, and highly structured, using a finite number of known commands. On the contrary, human language is not precise; it is often ambiguous, and the linguistic structure can depend on many different variables, such as dialects and various social contexts.

For this reason, NLP is an extremely important sector, as it studies and tries to solve all the difficulties encountered by a computer when it has to interpret or analyze human language. The numerous ambiguities of human language make comprehension of a human language by an algorithm particularly difficult. To understand a discourse, it is necessary to have more extensive knowledge of reality and of the surrounding world. Mere knowledge of the meaning of every single word is, in fact, not sufficient to correctly interpret the message of the sentence; on the contrary, it can lead to contradictory and meaningless communications.

The study of natural language takes place by phases performed in a precise sequence and characterized by a growing semantic value, as described here:

- Articulate and decode the sounds of a language that allows us to identify sounds and letters.
- Know the words of a language, their structure (plural/singular), and their organization (noun, verb, and adjective). Lexical analysis identifies the lexicons that make up the language and find a definition in the dictionary. Morphological analysis identifies the plural/singular structure, verbal mode, and verbal time; and it assigns to each word its own morphological class, understood as adjective, noun, and verb.
- Composition of words in complex constituents (part-of-speech). The syntax identifies the parts of the speech as subject, predicate, complement, or groups of words with a single meaning such as hot dog, or the nominal and verbal part with derivation of the full syntactic tree.
- Assignment of meanings to simple and complex linguistic expressions. Semantics tries to identify the meaning of words according to the context.
- Use of sentences in contexts, situations and ways appropriate for communication purposes. The pragmatist observes how and for what purposes the language is used, distinguishing whether it is a question of narration, dialogue, metaphor, and so on.

The results obtained are then applied to the two main categories of NLP:

- **Natural Language Generation** (**NLG**), which deals with the conversion of information from a database to a human-readable language
- NLU, which transforms a human language into forms of representation that are easily manipulated by programs

NLP faces many problems:

- **Speech segmentation**: Conversion of a vocal track into characters and words with complete meaning
- **Text segmentation**: Recognition of individual words in texts written with ideograms instead of letters (Chinese, Japanese, Thai, and so on)
- **Part-of-speech tagging**: Identification of the grammatical elements of a sentence such as noun, adjective, verb, pronoun
- **Word sense disambiguation**: Deduction from the context of the meaning of a term normally used to indicate multiple concepts
- **Imperfect or irregular input**: Recognition and correction of any regional accents, typos, or errors produced by optical character recognition tools

The difficulties of elaboration in the linguistic field can also be explained by considering the most evident characteristics of natural language itself:

- Flexibility, because it uses different ways to affirm the same fact
- Ambiguity, because the same statement can have more than one meaning
- Dynamism, caused by the continuous creation of new words

Precisely because of these particularities, the understanding of natural language is often considered an AI-complete problem, that is, a problem whose resolution is compared to the equivalent of the creation of an AI. In fact, understanding texts requires understanding of the concepts associated with them, and therefore it requires extensive knowledge of reality and a great ability to manipulate it.

AI-complete are defined as the most difficult problems; that is, they present computational problems equivalent to that of solving the problem of AI itself—making computers as intelligent as people. The term AI-complete therefore indicates a problem that would not be solved by a simple specific algorithm.

For people, language comprehension is the result of a mental process that cannot be reproduced in a machine; moreover, language is a form of communication and interaction between people that reflects the surface of meaning and allows people to understand one another. While a computer, however sophisticated its software is, is nevertheless based on procedures determined a priori.

Natural language understanding

NLU consists of reading a text expressed in natural language; determining its meaning by attributing a meaning to terms, sentences, and paragraphs present in it, and making inferences about these elements in order to elicit their explicit or implicit properties. In particular, one of the most salient issues in modeling a textual representation is to capture semantic relationships between concepts. To solve this task, several methodologies have been proposed in the literature, some of which talk of access to external knowledge bases. Others, instead, construct semantic distributive spaces, analyzing the content of the text collection without making use of prior knowledge.

Under the NLU definition, there is a wide range of computer applications, ranging from simple operations such as short commands given to robots, to complex operations, such as full comprehension of texts. In the real world, there is now a widespread use of algorithms based on NLU; for example, classification of text for attribution of labels in an email does not require a thorough understanding of the text, but it needs to deal with many vocabulary items.

The process of disassembling and parsing of text input is very complex, because of the occurrence of unknown and unexpected features in the input and the need to determine the appropriate syntactic and semantic schemes to apply to it (factors that are predetermined) when outputting the language. In the following diagram, you can see a flowchart of the NLU process:

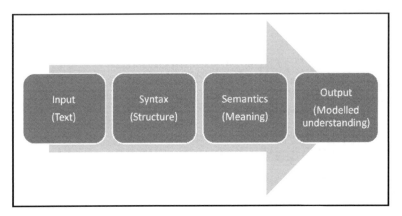

NLU, helps us to analyze semantic features of input text and extract metadata from content, such as categories, concepts, emotion, entities, keywords, metadata, relations, and semantic roles. Through NLU, the developer makes a translation of text into a machine-readable formal representation, making relevant aspects of its content explicit.

Google Cloud Dialogflow

The widespread use of conversational virtual assistance apps, from chatbots to IoT devices, capable of interacting with the most natural language possible, implies the need to create ever more engaging personal interactions. The challenge is twofold: not only that of recognizing and transmitting optimized basic information, but also that of involving users and helping them in their objectives. This presupposes the ability of the automatic system to adapt, as much as possible, its own language to that of the user to whom it is addressed, thanks to the analysis of data and the power of machine learning and AI technologies.

Dialogflow overview

Google responds to this challenge with Dialogflow, a platform for creating voice and text conversation applications based on machine learning. It supports 14 languages and can be integrated with major chat platforms such as Google Assistant, Facebook Messenger, Slack, Skype, Telegram, and its own applications through the service APIs.

Recently, given the great demand from developers to add business functionality to the standard version, Google announced the release of Dialogflow Enterprise Edition, available in beta.

The following are some features offered by Dialogflow:

- **Conversational interactions based on machine learning**: Dialogflow uses NLP to create faster conversation experiences and iterate faster. Just give some examples of what users may say, and Dialogflow will create a specific model that can learn which actions to activate and which data to extract to provide the most relevant and accurate answers.

- **Create once and deploy everywhere**: Use Dialogflow to create a conversational app and deploy it to your website, app, or 32 different platforms, including Google Assistant and other popular messaging services. Dialogflow also includes multilingual support and multilingual experiences to reach users from all over the world.

- **Advanced fulfillment options**: Fulfillment means the corresponding action in response to what the user says, such as processing a food order or activating the right answer to the user's question. For this purpose Dialogflow allows you to connect to any web hook whether it is hosted in the public Cloud or locally. The Dialogflow integrated code editor allows you to encode, test and implement these actions directly in the Dialogflow console.

- **Voice recognition with speech recognition**: Dialogflow enables the conversational app to respond to commands or voice conversations. It is available in a single API call that combines speech recognition with natural language comprehension.

In addition to the understanding of natural language, it is also the flexibility of Dialogflow that allows developers to go beyond decision structures and features, such as deep integration with Cloud functions to write basic serverless scripts directly into its interface that distinguishes Dialogflow from some of its competitors. Dialogflow also simplifies the connection to other applications, regardless of where they are hosted. This is something you need if you want to integrate your conversational app with your ordering and shipping systems, for example.

Basics Dialogflow elements

Before analyzing in detail a practical case of building a chatbot, it is advisable to analyze in detail the basic elements of Dialogflow. We'll now cover the most used elements in chatbot building.

Agents

An agent is a program that responds to a specific task. It could be a hostess for hotel room reservations. Or it could be a business expert who knows all the products and price lists of an online store. Or it could a competent support technician for the household appliances we purchased. Or it could be the onboard computer of a car.

What is important is that an agent has a specific purpose and a limited baggage of knowledge; we are not interested in playing chess with the bot that makes flight bookings, and in any case it would not be able to do so.

With Dialogflow, the creation of an agent is very simple; just go to the initial page of the service, click on the **CREATE AGENT** button, and give it a name, as shown in the following screenshot:

To access Dialogflow, just use the URL `https://dialogflow.com/`. You can register or use a Google account and log in.

Intent

An intent is what an end user can ask an agent. Booking a hotel room is an intent; another intent is the consultation of lunch hours, or the cancellation of a reservation that is already made.

Understanding what the user's request is is the intelligent part of the agent because there are many ways in which a request can be expressed in natural language, that is, what we humans talk about.

The agent will try to interpret the user's request by identifying the closest intent. Naturally, the association is not always precise; in fact a ranking of possible interpretations is returned. But, from this point of view, we can improve the answers by providing more alternative examples of the same requests. Also it is possible to apply machine learning algorithms in order to learn from the previous answers.

Entity

If an intent matches a request, the entity corresponds to the details. In booking a hotel room you need to know the exact date, the people who will stay, or the user's requests. From the design point of view of the agent, an entity such as hotel room is defined and it contains all the necessary details.

Dialogflow has a series of already-created system entities that facilitate the management of simpler concepts (for example, dates). The developer can define a series of entities (Dev entity) to generalize the behavior of the agent. Finally, the end user creates an entity for each request. A Dev entity can have values determined by a list, perform a mapping, or be in turn made up of other entities, and much more.

Action

Until now, we have dealt with interpreting the user's request; now it is a matter of answering. In reality, the concept is broader; once we have understood a request, we can fulfill it, for example, by booking the room, opening a ticket, or communicating with the restaurant. But if what we are making is a chatbot, the answer will probably correspond to the action.

An action corresponds to the step your application will take when a specific intent has been triggered by a user's input. Both the action name and its parameters are defined in the action section of an intent.

Context

What time does the guest arrive at the hotel? What did you eat? These are meaningless phrases without a context but become comprehensible in the context of a broader dialogue; this is what a context is for. The syntax for collecting a parameter from the context is very simple:

```
# context_name.parameter_name
```

With Dialogflow, a context is maintained for 10 minutes or five requests.

Building a chatbot with Dialogflow

After analyzing the main components of Dialogflow, it is time to focus on a practical application. In fact, we will create a simple chatbot that will help users to retrieve weather information about the most beautiful city in the world.

The first thing to do is to create the agent, that is, the project containing intents, entities, and answers that you want to deliver to the user. The intent is the mechanisms that collect what the user is requesting (using the entities) and direct the agent to respond accordingly. For simple answers that do not include information collected outside the conversation, you can define the answers directly in the intent. You can perform more advanced responses using your own logic and the web hooks for implementation.

The web hook is the URL to be invoked that hosts the code that implements the actions to be performed. Unlike other environments, Dialogflow also allows you to use the HTTP protocol (and not just the HTTPS protocol).

Agent creation

To create an agent, perform the following steps:

1. If you don't have a Dialogflow account, sign up. If you have an account, log in.
2. Click on **Create Agent** in the left navigation and fill in the fields. The following window is opened:

In this window, we will have to set some parameters:

- The name of the agent.
- Primary language for your agent.
- Time zone setting. Date and time are resolved using this time zone.
- Google project. This enables Cloud functions, actions on Google, and permissions management.

A series of agents (prebuilt agents) are already available for some types of requests that can be customized and enriched for your needs. The number of agents available depends on the language; more than 30 different agents are available in English.

3. Click on the **Save** button.

Intent definition

As we said previously, the user's intent is their purpose, the ultimate goal. Examples are ordering something, wanting to activate something on the user window, looking for shows, or simply saying goodbye. A chatbot should be able to perform some actions based on the intent it detects from the user's message.

To create an intent, click on the plus icon next to **Intents**; the following window is opened:

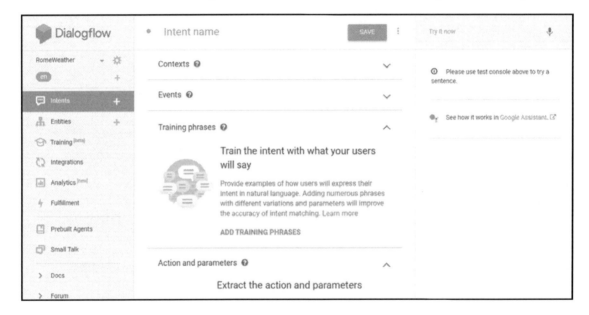

In this window, we will have to set some parameters:

- **Intent name**: The name of the intent.
- **Contexts**: This is used to manage the flow of the conversation.
- **Events**: This is a feature that allows you to invoke intents by an event name instead of a user query. Events can be used by external services to trigger Dialogflow intents, for example, Google Assistant's built-in intents.

- **Training phrases**: The phrases that identify the intent must be reported in natural language. You can use both examples (example mode identified with the " icon) and templates (template mode identified with the @ icon). Other examples of sentences are provided, the more the agent will be intelligent or he will be able to better recognize the user requests and to resolve ambiguities.
- **Action and parameters**: This specifies the possible action to be executed and its parameters that can be extracted from the dialogue.
- **Response**: The answers to be returned to the user when the intent has been recognized must be reported. To make it more human-like, you can enter different variations for the same answer. The answers can also be parameterized, and depending on the integration used, they can consist of rich messages.
- **Fulfillment**: Call a web service to connect your backend. Send the intent, parameters, and context to your Cloud function or a web service. Execute the necessary logic and respond with a written, spoken, or visual response.

When an example sentence is inserted, it is automatically noted, recognizing the parts that are collected as entity. An agent always contains a default fallback intent that collects all the cases in which no other intent has been recognized.

The first intent we want to insert has the purpose to specify the position related to our weather forecast. We said that an intent represents the user's purpose, so we need to think what questions the user may ask to receive weather forecasts. We need different intentions because there are many ways to ask the same thing. The process of identifying the intent is to map all the possible ways that the user can use to express an intent. The requests that we may expect from a user should be specified in the training phrases section. To start, let's insert the following phrases:

- What's the weather like in Rome
- How's the weather in Rome
- Weather in Rome
- Rome weather forecast

To insert a single phrase, simply add the user expression in the **Training phrases** text field and then press *Enter* to add another phrase. We will notice that the sentence will be added to our declaration of intent. In particular, we can see that the word **Rome** is highlighted. This means that it was noted as a parameter assigned to existing city entities, as shown in the following screenshot:

We continue to insert the sentences. After defining the location, it is necessary to define the time. It is clear that the user will need to know the predictions on a specific day, today or tomorrow for example. Then we also include these phrases:

- `What is the weather today`
- `Weather for tomorrow`
- `Weather forecast in Rome today`

As before, the time parameter is also highlighted, this time with a different color. The last sentence is interesting as it contains both a `date` parameter and a `geo-city` parameter, as shown in the following screenshot:

To start, we leave the other fields as is and focus only on the answer that the chatbot will have to provide to the user. So far, we have not considered any external reference from which to retrieve the information requested by the user. This means that at least for now, we will have to insert vague answers like these:

- I'm sorry, I do not have this information right now
- Forecasts for $date are not available
- The weather forecast for $date in $geo-city is not available

In the last two phrases, we have inserted the following reference entities: `$date` and `$geo-city`. So, when the agent responds, it takes into account the parameter values gathered and will use a reply that includes those values that it picked up.

Once we're done, we click on the **Save** button. The following messages appear at the bottom right of the window:

- **Intent saved**
- **Agent training started**
- **Agent training completed**

The meaning is clear. Now that your agent can understand basic requests from the user, try out what you have made so far. To try the newly created agent, we can use the appropriate box available in the console at the top right. To do this, we simply need to type in a request. Let's try our agent by typing a slightly different request from the examples given in the *Training phrases* section. For example, we ask: Hows the weather in Rome today. After this, we press *Enter* and the following window is returned:

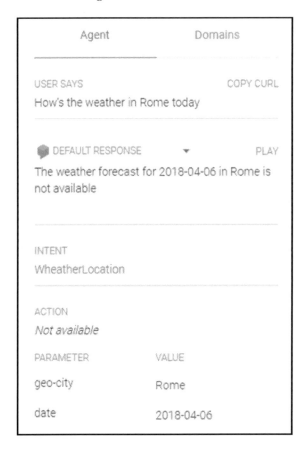

We can understand the frustration of the user who has not recovered the searched information, but we can already be satisfied as the agent has correctly interpreted the question and provided a plausible answer. Remember that, at least for now, the forecast data is not available and this is what the agent said. Also, as anticipated, the agent has identified the two reference entities and reused them to construct the response.

Summary

In this chapter, we discovered the amazing world of chatbots. Chatbots are robots, that interact with users through a chat and are able to assist them by carrying out extremely limited tasks: providing information on a current account, buying a ticket, receiving news about the weather, and so forth.

To begin with, we took a look at the fundamentals of the topic, starting with the history of chatbots in the 1950s, with the efforts of Alan Turing and various subsequent implementations of chatbots that perfected the basic concepts. Eliza, Parry, Jabberwacky, Dr. Sbaitso, ALICE, SmarterChild, and IBM Watson are the most important examples. As time passed and technology evolved, more and more sophisticated AI methods were created.

After introducing the basic concepts, we focused on the design techniques of chatbots and then moved on to analyze the architecture of a chatbot. We explored the interesting fields of NLP and NLU.

In the last part of the chapter, we covered Google Cloud Dialogflow, a platform for creating voice and text conversation applications based on machine learning. It supports 14 languages and can be integrated with major chat platforms. Finally, we created a simple chatbot that helps users to retrieve weather information about the most beautiful city in the world, that is, Rome. This can be an opportunity to travel, at least with the mind.

Index

Loebner prize
   about 447
   URL 447
logistic regression 138, 139
long short-term memory (LSTM)
   about 147, 332, 333, 334
   for time series analysis 367
   forget gate 333
   input gate 333
   on Google Cloud Shell 338, 339, 341
   output gate 333

M

machine learning (ML) 7, 8, 14
machine learning techniques
   data splitting 140, 141, 142
   model accuracy, measuring 142
   objective function, in regression 133
   overview 133
machine learning, applications
   about 129
   financial services 129
   retail industry 130
   telecom industry 130
machine learning
   versus deep learning 145, 146, 147, 148, 149
Magenta
   about 442
   NSynth dataset 442, 443
   URL 442
managed cloud
   versus unmanaged cloud 11
Markov Decision Process (MDP)
   about 383
   Agent-Environment interaction 383
   policy 385
   reward function 384
   value function 385
max pooling 149
Mean Squared Error (MSE) 418
min-max normalization 120, 121, 122, 123, 124
MNIST database
   about 315
   URL 315
mobile application

building, with Firebase 202, 204, 207, 208
model accuracy
   absolute error, measuring 142
   measuring 142
   root mean square error, measuring 143, 144, 145
Monte Carlo methods 393
moving average models 351
multiplicative method
   using 366, 367
MySQL 61

N

namespace, Google Cloud Storage
   bucket, naming 53
   object, naming 53
   using 53
Natural Language API
   about 174
   enabling 175, 176, 177, 178
   searching 174
natural language processing (NLP)
   about 450, 458
   Natural Language Generation (NLG) 460
   natural language understanding (NLU) 460
   problems 460
natural language understanding (NLU) 461, 462
neural network
   about 137, 138
   backpropagation 222, 223, 224
   building 215, 216, 217, 218, 219, 220, 221, 222
   Google Cloud Datalab, setting up 213, 214
   implementing, in Keras 224, 225, 226, 227, 228, 229
   implementing, in TensorFlow 241
   overview 211, 213
   structure 212
Node.js
   downloading 189
   installing 189
   URL 189
NoOps (no operation) 83
Not a Number (NaN) code 104
notes 443

NSynth dataset
  about 443
  formats 443
  test set 443
  training set 443
  URL 443
  validation set 443

O

object-oriented programming (OOP) 312
objective function
  in classification 140
  in regression 133
OpenAI Gym
  about 395, 396
  environments, URL 398
  URL 395
optical character recognition (OCR) 315
outliers
  about 113
  identifying, with statistical information 115, 116
  identifying, with visual functionality 114, 115
  removing 116, 117
  searching, in data 113
over/under fitting
  intuition 284, 285, 287
overfitting
  dropout, implementing 295, 296, 297
  L1 regularization, implementing 292, 293, 294, 295
  L2 regularization, implementing 288, 289, 290, 291
  reducing 287, 288

P

pandas library 427
parent node 135
Parry 448
periodic series 346
Persistent Contrastive Divergence (PCD) 430
Platform as a service (PaaS)
  versus Software as a service (SaaS) 12
policy evaluation 392
policy improvement 392
pooling layer

about 310
using 310
PostgreSQL 61
premade estimators
  using 241, 242, 243, 244, 245, 246
preventive training algorithms 388
primary key 74
private key
  URL 51
project-based organization
  about 16
  project, creating 16
  roles and permissions 17
pruning 135
public cloud 10
public data 85
public datasets for taxi trips
  URL 86
Python Miniconda stack
  installing 38
  URL 38
Python
  URL 313

Q

Q-evaluation function 394
Q-learning 388, 389, 390

R

random forest 137
re-parameterization 419
receiver operating characteristic (ROC) 144
receptive field 306
Rectified Linear Units (ReLU) 310
recurrent neural network (RNN)
  about 147, 326, 327, 328
  and TensorFlow, used for Handwriting Recognition (HWR) 334, 335, 337, 338
  Elman neural network 332
  fully recurrent neural networks 329
  Hopfield recurrent neural networks 330
  recursive neural networks 330
  use cases 327
  variants 328

Made in the USA
San Bernardino, CA
18 April 2019